one-coat painting

Dutch Boy

WALL REFRIGERATOR-FREEZER

No special wiring necessary! This ~~G~~eral Electric Dryer is completely autom~~atic~~ on either 115-volt or 230-volt circuit. T~~~~ slightly longer on 115-volt.

No more tedious hand sprinkl~~ing~~ Whenever you're ready to iron, put in ~~the~~ Automatic Sprinkler . . . add clothes t~~o be~~ dampened and turn the dial to SPRINK~~LE~~

Clothes smell fresh as all outdoors ~~be~~cause this Air Freshener releases a g~~ood~~ fragrance into the air stream. Adjustabl~~e to~~ select any amount of fragrance you wan~~t~~

Fast, perfect drying . . . indoors . . . can be yours any time at all with this new, high-speed General Electric Dryer. A family wash can actually dry in about a half hour. Most synthetics take less than 8 minutes. Your clothes will smell fresh . . . feel soft . . . and be so wrinkle-free you'll actually save hours of ironing time every week! See it at your General Electric dealer's soon. General Electric Company, Appliance Park, Louisville 1, Ky.

system . . . snug house!

Homes

HOUSES FOR A NEW WORLD

BARBARA MILLER LANE

HOUSES FOR A NEW WORLD

BUILDERS AND BUYERS IN AMERICAN SUBURBS, 1945–1965

Princeton University Press
Princeton and Oxford

Copyright © 2015 by Princeton University Press
Published by Princeton University Press,
41 William Street, Princeton, New Jersey 08540
In the United Kingdom: Princeton University Press,
6 Oxford Street, Woodstock, Oxfordshire OX20 1TW
press.princeton.edu

Front jacket photograph: Visitors to model houses, Lakewood,
CA, 1950. City of Lakewood.
Back jacket photograph: Modern view of cul-de-sac,
Weathersfield. Photo by Amanda Robbins-Butcher.
Page ii: Levittown, PA, aerial view of street layout ca. 1953.
Mercer Museum Library, Bucks County Historical Society.
Page xii: Jean Valjean Vandruff, Cinderella Homes sales
brochure, 1955–57, five models.

Library of Congress Cataloging-in-Publication Data
Lane, Barbara Miller.
Houses for a new world : builders and buyers in American
suburbs, 1945–1965 / Barbara Miller Lane.
pages cm
Includes bibliographical references and index.
ISBN 978-0-691-16761-9 (hardback : alk. paper) 1. Suburban
homes—United States—History—20th century. 2. Architecture
and society—United States—History—20th century. I. Title.
NA7571.L37 2015
728'.37097309'04—dc23
2015004110

British Library Cataloging-in-Publication Data is available

Designed and composed by Yve Ludwig in Benton Modern
and Futura
Printed on acid-free paper
Printed in China
10 9 8 7 6 5 4 3 2 1

CONTENTS

A PERSONAL NOTE

The motives for writing a book like this have much to do with personal experiences, and these in turn may lead to particular emphases and biases. In my case, four different types of experience led to the formulation of my project and to the emphases of my research and interpretation.

I grew up as the only child of a rural social worker in upstate New York. My mother's work focused on the rural poor; I often accompanied her on her visits to clients. While she talked to the parents, I would play with the children. As a result, I received very clear impressions of rural houses and rural lifestyles, especially those of the poor. So I have always been interested in houses and the lives led within them. In later life, my work as an architectural historian focused in part on house design and especially on public housing in Germany and the Scandinavian countries.

During most of my adult life, I have lived in houses designed by my husband, an architect and builder. So in addition to my work as an architectural historian, I have gained a firsthand understanding of good house design.

Retiring in 1999 at the end of a long career at Bryn Mawr College, I continued to teach a single course on the theme of "Housing and Dwelling." The main paper assignment for students was to investigate and write about their grandparents' houses.

Without thinking it through very fully, I had expected these homes to resemble my own grandparents' house—a freestanding large house in a village, strongly "Victorian" in design. Instead, to my surprise, many of the grandparents had lived in suburban tract houses—ranch houses or splits. From these papers, I learned to respect and analyze a type of house that I had earlier ignored and that I had privately believed to be rather ugly.

During the same period of teaching "Housing and Dwelling," our son, his wife, and their young son moved into a split-level house in Arlington Heights, Illinois—a "Stoltzner-built" house that makes frequent appearances in the Stoltzner Builders section of chapter 4. Soon, a daughter joined their family. In the course of many visits to enjoy my new grandchildren, I learned to admire and fully appreciate their house too.

ACKNOWLEDGMENTS

I began the research for this book more than eight years ago, with the generous help of an Emeritus Fellowship from the Andrew W. Mellon Foundation. A later research fellowship from the Mellon Foundation, and grants from the Bryn Mawr College Provost and the Elisha Bolton Fund of the "Cities" Department continued to support the work. The Furthermore Foundation has recently helped to defray the costs of preparation of the manuscript and illustrations for publication. I am very grateful to these foundations and funding organizations.

Over this long period of time, many, many people and institutions have made important contributions to the work. My wonderful research assistants Helen Vong, Tienfong Ho, Amy Haavik-MacKinnon, Amanda Robbins-Butcher, Amy Tindell, Maude Baggetto, Katherine Rochester, and Carrie Robbins have combed newspapers and local archives in pursuit of information. Carrie Robbins has worked on the book in one capacity or another for more than six years; I owe her some of the most hard-to-find illustrations, and the factual foundations for many aspects of my thought. And I owe much of the richness of the illustration program to the talent of Nathanael Roesch in creating and re-creating handsome and legible images.

Distant friends and friends of friends have often pitched in: my special thanks to Ken Liss, Marissa Vigneault, Dave Colamaria, Mark Bourne, John Fierst, Zachary Silvia, Alexander Brey, and Granger Riach. Staff at Bryn Mawr College are immensely kind and helpful to retired researchers; I am especially grateful to Pamela Cohen and Margaret Kelly in the Cities Office; Del Ramers and Nancy Halli in Visual Resources; Iliana Chaleva and Judith Barr in the Interlibrary Loan Department; and Jeremy Blatchley and Camilla MacKay in Carpenter Library. The students in my course on "Housing and Dwelling" contributed to the gestation of the book.

Colleagues and friends from Bryn Mawr College and elsewhere have read parts of the book and offered trenchant criticisms. My thanks for this especially to Gary W. McDonogh and Jeff Cohen, and to the anonymous readers for Princeton University Press. Erika Esau, Elliott Shore, and Richard Voith have commented on the argument and helped me to develop it. Kathleen Kelly Broomer, a preservation historian in the Boston area, was a magnificent guide to the housing developments of Martin Cerel and Campanelli Brothers. Greg Hise, Becky Nicolaides, Dana Cuff, James T. Keane, and William Deverell eased my way in learning about Southern California's landscape and architecture. San Marino's Huntington Library contains a wealth of material for the researcher; I particularly thank Jenny Watts, curator of photographs, for introducing me to the Maynard Parker collection. When I was just beginning the project, Sam Bass Warner and Ken Jackson gave me excellent advice on how to do research on builders.

I was delighted at the powerful enthusiasm for my work among local historians and history buffs, and within local government offices. Local librarians and historians in Dallas, Texas (Carol Roark and Bryan McKinney), Arlington Heights, Illinois (Mickey Horndasch), Schaumburg, Illinois (Jane Rozek), and Natick, Massachusetts (James Morley), were enormously helpful in lending me sales brochures and newspaper clippings, and in introducing me to other local historians. Henry A. L. Brown and Diane Brannon in Governor Francis Farms, Rhode Island, provided much information, and helped me negotiate government records in Warwick, Rhode Island. Lee Gershenfeld of the Marple Township Zoning Office lent me vital drawings and diagrams, and offered a wealth of information about the work of Frank Facciolo and Ralph Bodek. Greg Feroli, of the Brockton City Engineering Department, found the copies that his office had kept of Saivetz/Campanelli site and plot plans, and copied them for me, thus overcoming some of the disadvantages for the researcher of the Campanelli office fire of 1977. Martha Roberts and Beverly Keagle, successive presidents of the Rolling Meadows Historical Association, provided endless local information. Don Waldie's help with records and photographs in Lakewood, California, was unparalleled.

The testimonies of original owners in several of the developments enrich chapter 5 and are documented in appendix 3. My conversations with these individuals contributed extensively to my thinking. They remain anonymous, in order to protect their privacy.

I have learned a huge amount from interviews and correspondence with the principal players in my stories of builders, and from their families. I was fortunate to converse with Nicholas Campanelli (one of the original four brothers) before he died. His son Jon and Salvatore DeMarco's son Robert P. DeMarco have answered my questions over a number of years. Ronald Campanelli, son of Michael, has also been helpful. Ronald Cerel, son of Martin Cerel, explained a good deal to me about his father's office (where Ronald himself worked). Cynthia Cerel Sandler and her son Bradford Sandler (Martin's grandson) also helped with the Cerel history. Jack Conway, prominent Massachusetts realtor, gave me my initial contact with the Campanellis, and also told me a lot about advertising techniques in the fifties. Bradford Saivetz, the Campanellis' engineer ("the fifth brother"), and I have talked and written back and forth for at least six years; I have learned from him not only about the Campanellis, but also about more general issues in building, planning, and civil engineering in the fifties.

In the Philadelphia area, I was able to interview Joe and Carl Bodek, Ralph Bodek's sons, and Evelyn Bodek Rosen, his daughter. Claude De Botton, Bodek's associate for some years, revealed new dimensions of Bodek's work. David Damon, of Damon Engineering, copied plot plans and specifications for me, for both Rose Tree Woods and Lawrence Park, and shared many reminiscences. From the far-flung Stoltzner family, Roberta Stoltzner Burckle, Jim Stoltzner, John Stoltzner, and Tara Stoltzner Blum were unfailingly helpful. Jean Vandruff has been a frequent correspondent. Heidi Cortese has kept a large number of documents related to her father's (Ross Cortese's) life and work, and has kindly had them copied for me. Peter Choate and his daughter Courtney Moritz told me about the relationships of his father, Chris Choate, with Cliff May and Ross Cortese. Welton Macdonald Becket gave me new insights into the work of his father Welton Becket.

In this research and writing, my family played a vital part. My daughter Ellie and her husband Richard Webber offered hospitality and encouragement at their home in the Boston area while I worked on the Campanellis. My son Steve Lane and his wife K. Signe Hansen looked after me in Arlington Heights while I was working on the Stoltzners; they also took pictures and discovered neighborhood stories. Signe compiled the index. My husband Jonathan Lane asked the right questions, provided insights from his own work, and made certain that I got it done.

This is their book too.

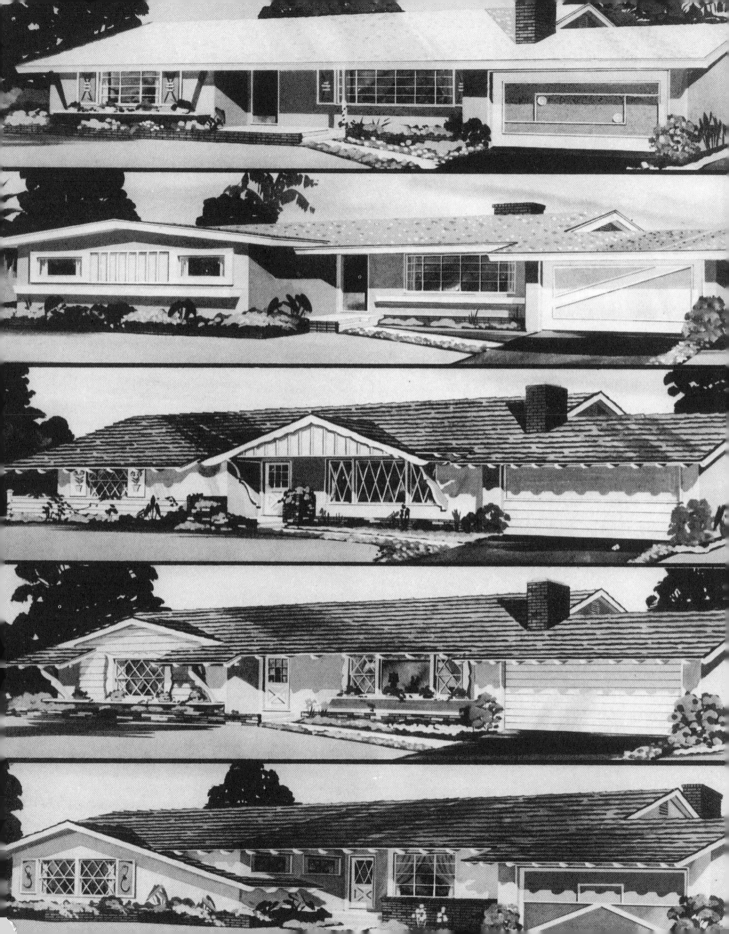

HOUSES FOR A NEW WORLD

PROLOGUE

The following passages are distilled from interviews with original buyers of builders' houses and combined as a single voice.[1] The buyers, as they speak here, are reporting their thoughts about their houses soon after they first moved in:

> The house was new, our family had never had a new house before. And it was new to us: we had come a distance to live there, and left our earlier families and neighborhoods behind. It was all new: bright new paint and floors, a shiny kitchen and bathroom with new kinds of machines and fixtures, lots of light inside with big windows looking out front and back, a bedroom for each kid or pair of kids, easy to move around in. A garage, for the new family car. It seemed new in another way too: it seemed right for a whole new time.
>
> Outside, there were front and back yards where the kids could run free. Of course you had to get to know the neighbors from scratch, because everyone was from somewhere else. But that didn't take long, and the place was paradise for kids. It was paradise for us, too: owning our own house and yard for the first time. The house was about 1,000 square feet, a lot roomier than the place we'd been living before, and roomier than the places we grew up in too. Or at least it was less crowded. There were hardly any stairs to climb; everything was neat and tidy and within reach. It was really "modern" in every way: up-to-date, sleek-looking, efficient, light and airy, but cozy at the same time. It seemed bigger, too, because of the yards. Maybe thirty feet in the front and fifty in the back: you could sit out both places, grow some vegetables and flowers in back, have a place, sometimes, to hang clothes. And the front yards seemed even bigger than they were, because the streets were so wide and quiet: the kids could play there. There was a park; soon there would be a new school and a shopping center.
>
> Sometimes the neighbors would come over for a barbecue in the backyard; sometimes there would be block parties on the street and in the front yards. The neighbors were pretty interesting: many of them weren't very much like us. They had different religions, different kinds of jobs, different upbringing, sometimes they came from far away places. But they were about the same age, they had about the same number of kids, and they wanted to make a decent life in the new place, for themselves and the kids, like us. It was quite an adventure.

At the beginning, it was exciting seeing the new house being built: the whole family went over every weekend to watch. (The kids would play around on the building sites. They liked doing that later, too.) Afterward, we just kept on fixing it up. It was home for us. It was a big investment, of course, even with the FHA mortgage. But with luck, and hard work, it seemed like we could manage it. And then it would last—it would be a place for the kids to come back to.

CHAPTER 1

New Houses
and New Communities

The recollections excerpted in the prologue describe the dominant "American Dream" of the 1940s and 1950s: homeownership for (practically) everyone who wanted it.[1] Ownership of a new, well-functioning little house and yard, and the opportunity to found a new way of life in a new place. These recollections come from people who bought houses during the first postwar years—that is, 1945 to 1960 or 1965. When prospective owners made their choices about where and how to live during these fifteen to twenty years, they selected among radically new dwelling designs. American house types, house plans, and housing environments were utterly transformed in this period. The transformation was achieved by "merchant builders," a new type of builder/developer. The builders of this era responded to the desires and preferences of the buyers, at the same time as they, the builders, helped to shape those preferences. In thousands of new suburban communities, a builder erected a few model houses, usually split-levels or ranches, and a family selected the one that suited its members. The new suburbs of these years were formed by the multiplication of these actions and choices.

This book examines these builders and buyers: the new house types they built during the first two decades after World War II, and the new communities that the houses formed. More than thirteen million of these predominantly ranch and split-level houses were constructed after the war, on large "tracts" or subdivisions outside the old city centers and older suburban rings of settlement.[2] By 1970, more than 20 percent of the entire population of the United States lived in tract houses, which occupied at least three million acres of newly developed land. A great many of us still live in these places.

I focus on twelve tract house developments in a range of sizes, built by nine builder-developers in four metropolitan areas: Los Angeles, Philadelphia, Boston, and Chicago.[3] I chose these builders and developments to illustrate the varieties of builders' careers and enterprises, their varied design procedures, and the different ways the development and planning process took place in larger and smaller tracts, and in different regions of the country. Although regionalism played a part in the design of the earliest builders' houses and communities of the postwar period, I also show that later houses and subdivisions offered a mix of regional aspects and wider influences. With the exception of Panorama City in Los Angeles, built by Fritz Burns, these tract house developments are discoveries of my own: scholars have not yet written about them, nor have their builders been studied. Yet several of these twelve settlements are huge (each more than a thousand dwellings), and their builders were among the most innovative of their time.

From among the original buyers of houses within the twelve developments, I have been able to contact and interview twelve families; this has provided me with many insights into the lives, motives, and attitudes of the first generation of buyers.

The new dwellings and their new communities provided housing for vast numbers of young couples and their young children, together with a host of others: people who were moving away from older crowded neighborhoods or who were leaving the farm for a new kind of urban life. These were veterans and their families, people who had worked in war industries, and many, many others whose older ties to place and group had been loosened in wartime while their aspirations (and prosperity) had increased. These new buyers were responding to the severe housing shortage created by depression and war, and their needs for housing were greatly increased by their new and growing families. (The birthrate skyrocketed from the 1940s to the mid-1960s.)[4] Long lines of new buyers converged on model houses: contemporary observers spoke of buildings "selling like hotcakes" (fig. 1).[5]

Making possible the new houses and their new communities were four major events: the rapid spread of automobile ownership among American families after the war; the rise of a new highway system; the institution of low-interest long-term government loans, especially for veterans; and a new prosperity for lower-income people. The Interstate Highway System that was signed into law under President Eisenhower in 1956 and intended at least partly as a defense measure during the Cold War was based on a national system going back to the 1920s.[6] This system

entered into a period of rapid growth during and immediately after the war: new state highways were built during this period, and many metropolitan areas were soon encircled, or partially encircled, by "ring roads" that allowed automobiles to bypass direct routes through the city. At more or less the same time, vast systems of "freeways" (limited access expressways) connected cities with their hinterlands and with the new Interstate system. The "journey to work" changed profoundly: with an automobile, one could commute to work, relatively inexpensively, over great distances, especially during the early years of the highway system, when the roads were new and the traffic light. During the same period, the Federal Housing Administration (FHA) and the Veterans' Administration sponsored mortgages at rates that enabled millions of nuclear families to afford their own homes for the first time. Without new roads and cheap money, America's postwar

1. Visitors to model houses, Lakewood, CA, 1950. City of Lakewood.

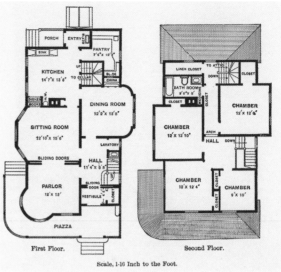

First Floor. Second Floor.

Scale, 1-16 Inch to the Foot.

2. The George and J. P. Kingston House, Worcester, MA, ca. 1897, exterior. *Modern American Dwellings*, 49–51.

3. Kingston House, Worcester, MA, ca. 1897, *Modern American Dwellings*, plan.

suburbanization would never have happened. And behind these events, a subtler shift was occurring: prosperity for the working classes, already high during the intense productivity of wartime, continued to increase for many years after World War II. Prosperity, new roads, cheap money, and the availability of inexpensive single-family dwellings made possible the creation of a new suburban society, transforming the American built environment. But history is made by individuals, and so it was the decisions and choices of builders and buyers that so dramatically transformed the character of American houses and streets.

The new house designs, in addition to being smaller than the ideal houses of the American past, were different in elevation, profile, plan, and interior furnishing. An ideal middle-class house of fifty years earlier rose two or three stories high (figs. 2, 3, Kingston House). It sat on a deep lawn; one approached the house on a walkway to a generous porch. The porch provided an additional reception space before one entered the house.[7] Inside were an entrance foyer, a hall, and a number of separate and formal rooms: parlor, sitting room (sometimes called the "second parlor"), dining room, and kitchen on the ground floor, with four to six bedrooms on the upper floors, and a single bathroom on the second floor. There was no garage. With the first floor raised above ground level, the house did not encourage in any obvious way a relationship between interior and exterior. The house was separated from its neighbors by a fence or hedge. The overall visual impression given by such a building was of a vertical-oriented mass, freestanding, self-contained, and neither strongly related to its surrounding environment nor welcoming to passersby. Its interior plan, sometimes described as a "polite plan," was geared to formal reception and entertaining, with the more private

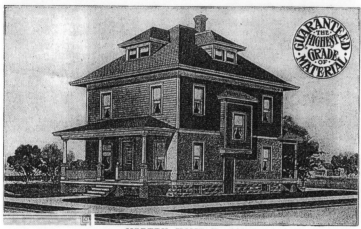

MODERN HOME No. 111

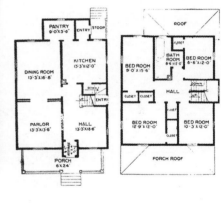

areas restricted to upper floors.[8] Its most public room, the parlor, was often lavishly decorated (fig. 4). These features appeared in the dwellings of relatively affluent buyers, as in figures 2 to 4, but also throughout the economic spectrum, as in Sears's "Modern Home No. 111" of 1908 (fig. 5).

The typical tract house or development house of the 1940s and 1950s, in contrast, was much smaller. It was one or one and a half stories high, and followed the contours of the land on which it was built. It sat back from the street, but not as far back as many earlier houses of towns and suburbs. The entrance was not greatly emphasized, but the garage was prominent, and appeared, from the street, to offer the main access to the house (figs. 6, 7). Entry was directly into

4. Victorian Parlor, ca. 1891. English Heritage, National Monuments Record.

5. Sears Roebuck House, "The Chelsea," 1908, exterior and plan. *Sears Roebuck Modern Homes,* 30.

6. Campanelli Brothers, ranch house, Brockton, MA, ca. 1960, exterior. Photo by the author.

7. Ralph Bodek, split-level house, Philadelphia area, exterior, ca. 1956. Bodek, *How and Why.*

the "living room," the eating area was not fully separate (in fact it was often part of the kitchen), kitchens were large and open to other living areas (figs. 8, 11). The kitchen, no longer the domain of a household servant, formed a significant part of the living space of the house.[9] Bedrooms were separate only in the sense that they were located away from the living room (figs. 8, 9). A large "picture window" gave the living room a powerful connection to the street, and windows or sliding doors in the rear gave easy visual access to a deep interior back yard. Light flooded the interiors through these large windows. Interior finishes were sleek and shiny; furniture was sparse (sometimes built-in) and "modern-looking," appliances lavish for the time (figs. 10, 11, 12). With their bare surfaces, relative absence of historical references, and open and functional planning, the new houses corresponded in almost every way to what we now think of as "modern" (or "modernist") architecture. Gone were all the formal elements of late nineteenth- and early twentieth-century domestic planning: the porch, the formal entry, the formal reception rooms. Gone was the air of self-sufficiency that is expressed in the exterior in figure 2. The new houses faced the street instead of turning away from it, and they were visually related to one another as a result of their siting. It is clear from plans and exterior views alone that these were houses for a new time and for a different lifestyle.

For an observer standing on the sidewalk, looking up and down the street, the houses, front yards, sidewalks, and, frequently, grass strips created a striking new pattern (fig. 13). The houses were close together: sometimes no more than twenty-five feet separated them. From some angles the houses looked almost connected. No fences or hedges divided the front yards,[10] and these contained little landscaping: usually low bushes around the base of the house, occasionally a tree next to the driveway. Front lawns, in the past visually an entryway to the house—a carpet flanking the walk leading to the entry—now appeared

8. Campanelli Brothers, "The Crest," Brockton, MA, 1957, plan. Restored by Nathanael Roesch from a newspaper advertisement of October 1958.

9. Ralph Bodek, split-level house, Lawrence Park, PA, ca. 1955, plan. Nathanael Roesch from a detailed plan in the Marple Township Zoning Office.

almost continuous along the street, a parallel verge along streets and sidewalks, with a cross-pattern created by driveways rather than front walks. Grass strips between the sidewalk and the curb formed a further complementary pattern, punctuated by trees.[11] The large front windows invited the gaze of passersby. The streets themselves were relatively wide, compared to the local streets of earlier suburbs and small towns. Thus one's overall impression is of an exceptionally wide public way, composed of streets, grass strips, sidewalks, and lawns (fig. 14). At the same time, the low profiles of the houses create a sense of openness, of wide-open spaces. The whole ensemble gives an impression of order combined with greenery; it possesses both "rural" and "urban" qualities.

10. "Danish modern" furniture, Lakewood, CA, ca. 1950. City of Lakewood.

11. The "Moscow Kitchen," US Model House Exhibition, Moscow, 1959. National Archives.

12. H. F. Fischbach bathroom, Harold Schwartz designer, 1954. Gottscho-Schleisner Collection, Library of Congress.

Back yards complemented the front by offering another continuous swath of greenery: there were few fences or hedges in the rear yards in the early years. Here the property was deeper—perhaps sixty feet—so there was room for planting trees and for some elaboration of recreation areas: a patio and sometimes a pool, or children's toys and play equipment. Many householders hung their laundry out to dry here as well, before the automatic dryer became a staple of household equipment. Vegetable and flower gardens (large and small) were also located at the rear. In having a relatively private recreation area in the rear, the tract houses of the first postwar decades were not very different from the suburban houses of the twenties, but the earlier suburban houses nearly always fenced the yard. The rear facades of the new houses were different from the front—they were much less elaborated. Back yards were above all the domain of small children and barbecues; their much-advertised "patios" were often merely small concrete slabs outside the back door (figs. 15, 16, 161).[12]

The distance of the houses from the street varied greatly from place to place and from region to region (they were much shallower in Los Angeles, much deeper in Massachusetts), but these distances were uniform within each community. Together with the consistent orientation of the new houses—facing the street—uniform setbacks heightened the sense of horizontality along streets

13. Lakewood, CA, modern street view. Photo by the author.

and sidewalks. Of course the siting of the houses, together with their similarities of design, led to a somewhat repetitious appearance, prompting the scorn of contemporary hostile critics. Yet a curving street reduces this impression; many builders said that this motivated their street planning. Builders also worked against the appearance of uniformity by reversing plans from side to side and by varying exterior materials and colors. Sometimes, too, they alternated larger and smaller models, and interspersed ranches and splits. Buyers also chose to vary their houses by materials, colors, and additions, although they proved very reluctant to alter roofs and street facades.

The origins of street and lot layout were complex. They were the work of builders and their engineers, but they were also strongly affected by local traditions and regulations. Local zoning ordinances based on local traditions lie behind the wide streets, grass strips with trees, and uniform setbacks that created the new kinds of spaces characteristic of the new developments. These ordinances functioned sometimes at the county level (as in Los Angeles County, Orange County, and Chicago's Cook County), and sometimes at the most local level (as in Natick, MA, or Broomall, PA). Builders and their engineers negotiated lot sizes with local zoning boards, and sometimes they resisted local requirements about the provision of public space. But they had to bow to local ordinances on setbacks, sidewalks, street width, curbs, paving, sewers, street lighting, and road construction, and the builder was normally responsible for providing these kinds of infrastructure. On the other hand, street patterns, the overall layout of a subdivision or group of subdivisions, and the positioning of the houses (within the limits of setback ordinances) came from the builder and engineer. These features too, though, were sometimes the subject of negotiation, especially when the local officials accepted the suggestions of the FHA about neighborhood and subdivision planning. Builders (and their engineers) succeeded rather often in negotiating changes in land use policy, at several levels of government.

In many cases, a new tract house development was advertised, and perceived, as the core of a "new city." The overall arrangement of streets in some of the larger developments conformed to new or quite recent neighborhood planning practices, popularized by the FHA. Even when this was not the case, streets were often curvilinear, differentiating the subdivision from surrounding grids. The resulting street views are different from those to be found in small towns, earlier suburbs, or prewar American cities. In plan and form, in relationship to one another and to the street and the larger community, the new houses marked a revolutionary break from the past.

Plans of the new subdivisions varied according to the ideas of the builders and their engineers, but the size of the subdivision itself was also critical. Such giant developments as the Levittowns, Lakewood, California, and Park Forest, Illinois, could be conceived as whole cities in themselves. Because many readers are familiar with Lakewood and the Levittowns, and because many contemporaries were impressed by Park Forest, I make comparisons between the builders I focus on, and the houses and plans of these three large places. Among the communities discussed in the following chapters, Panorama City, Rossmoor, Lawrence Park, Rolling Meadows, Elk Grove Village, and Weathersfield at

15. Torrance, CA, children with pool in backyard of ranch house, 1955. Mrs. FC.

16. Five-year-old boy dressed for Easter, Campanelli ranch house, Natick, 1957. Mr. LT.

17. Fritz Burns, Westchester area, Los Angeles, ca. 1948, modern street view. Photo by Jonathan Lane.

Schaumburg were large enough to be based on overall plans; these plans incorporated common open spaces, and sites for schools. In addition, the engineers who designed these new developments strongly preferred curvilinear street patterns (figs. 17, 136, 137, and others). Together with the engineers, the builders also planned for, or hoped for, the construction of a nearby shopping center, and most also believed that new communities required a new industrial base. But the builders of this era seldom controlled enough land or financial resources actually to include new industry in their planned communities.

The larger among the new tract house communities (twelve hundred to four thousand houses) were built on land acquired from large farms or estates; each was surrounded by countryside at the start. The original inhabitants perceived themselves as residing within a "greenbelt," a planning idea that had been dear to the hearts of American (and European) garden city theorists. Yet there were no real, legally protected greenbelts; just the rather rural-appearing surroundings. As the building boom moved on, as the demand for new housing continued, each of these "new towns" was soon surrounded by smaller developments built by other builders. In some cases, in Los Angeles, Chicago, and Orange County, the smaller builders laid down new grid plans, following the pattern of the older urban core: plans that rarely meshed with those of the communities they surrounded. Outside Boston and Philadelphia, smaller builders developed their own curvilinear patterns, which of course did not "fit" those of the larger communities, and did not create a sense of continuity either. Quite soon, as the older lacunae were filled, each of these metropolitan centers was surrounded by areas that looked featureless to outsiders: this was the much-castigated "sprawl."

Despite the absence of real greenbelts, and despite variations in plan and size, there existed a surprising sense of common identity among the inhabitants of each new development. In the larger settlements, a sense of identity was conferred by shared schools and parks, by a common experience of street pattern and street life, by a shared history, and by shared homeowners' associations. Yet even the smaller developments display a sense of identity. Sometimes this sense came (and still comes) simply from the name of the development, which the residents remember and emphasize: "Westfield-at-Natick" is still the well-remembered name of one small community outside Boston. Sometimes a sense of identity came from the "brand name" of the houses ("Cinderella Homes" in Anaheim), sometimes from the reputation of the builders themselves ("Stoltzner-built" in Arlington Heights outside Chicago, "the Campi" on a website for Boston-area fans of Campanelli ranches). And the shared "look" of the houses themselves conferred a sense of identity: this may help to explain why, despite changing times and skyrocketing prices, additions and modifications to most of these houses have occurred at the rear, thus preserving the appearance of the street facades.

The Evolution of Ranch and Split-Level Houses

The houses built by tract developers can be described as having five different types, the first three rapidly outdistanced by the last two. The Levitt "Cape," or Cape Cod cottage, of 1947 (fig. 18) was a simple, tiny, box-like affair, with 750 square feet of living space,[13] on a 6,000-square-foot lot (0.14 acres). Two bedrooms, a living room, and a kitchen occupied the ground floor space; above was a partial attic that owners could remodel into an extra room or two, it was said. As in all the early postwar Levitt houses, the kitchen was located at the front, an innovation in house planning, but not one that most builders adopted. Built primarily for rental units, the Levitt Cape bore a strong resemblance to the schematic drawings of the "minimum house" published in the FHA handbooks from 1936 onward (see fig. 41).

The Levitts quickly turned to a different and more sophisticated house design, a modified Cape that they called a "ranch" (1949–50). The house again had the kitchen at the front, but so was the living room; in effect, the plan was that of their earlier Cape, rotated ninety degrees. This was the first house built

in Levittown, New York, that was built for sale (rather than for rent); Bill Levitt designed it himself, he said, by having the workmen construct a model, then tearing it down and starting over, a process that took several tries.[14] The Levitt "ranch" was somewhat larger than the Cape, and the upper level was a little roomier, easier to expand (figs. 19, 20). The house was extremely popular, and frequently imitated (actually often replicated by imitators) in the early 1950s, especially by builders in the Northeast, who usually added a garage. The early Levitt house types were built on concrete slabs with radiant heating, as were their imitations.

The houses built at Lakewood in Los Angeles in huge numbers between 1950 and 1953 form another type, common in the West in the first years of the fifties. The Lakewood houses were part of one of the largest postwar housing developments: builders S. Mark Taper, Ben Weingart, and Louis Boyar constructed 17,500 houses on more than 3,000 acres between 1950 and 1953. The two-bedroom, 800-square-foot model sold for $7,575 to $8,225 in 1950 ($68,538–74,419 in 2010 dollars).[15] The houses were modeled on those built on smaller parcels in the late forties by Taper and Boyar.[16] There were many plan variations among the models: most of the earliest houses at Lakewood had a detached garage at the rear; later, an attached garage was added (figs. 21, 22). Exteriors were finished in stucco.

Soon, however, these early house types were virtually supplanted by two others, the mature "ranch house" and the "split-level" house. The typical ranch of the 1950s had one story. It was long and spread out and thus required a wider lot

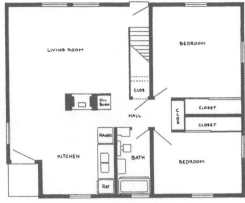

(sixty to seventy feet) than had been common in the 1940s and earlier. Its roof was sometimes flat, but more commonly it had a gently sloping gable or hip shape. The ranch house appeared in many variations, from rather rustic-looking versions on the West Coast, to a brick "bungalow look" in the Midwest, to a version in the East that hinted at colonial traditions. Nearly always it faced the street, with the living room at the front and a view from the living room toward the street through some version of a picture window (fig. 23). With the growing practice of attaching a garage, the overall profile of many ranch houses changed from simple and rather slab-like in the early fifties to an L-shaped plan in the later 1950s, the ell accommodating the garage. Or alternatively the attached garage prolonged the street front of the building, leading to a strongly horizontal emphasis. (By the end of the fifties, most garages were large enough for two cars.)

The ranch house type had a long evolution within American housing history, and in the fifties it came to be overwhelmingly preferred among builders and new homebuyers. I will trace something of its history in the section on Fritz Burns in chapter 2. The split-level was rather different. It normally had three

19. Levitt Brothers, "Ranch House" model, Levittown, NY, 1949, exterior. Nassau County Department of Parks, Recreation & Museums.

20. Levitt Brothers, "Ranch House," Levittown, NY, 1949, plan. Nathanael Roesch, from Kelly, *Expanding the American Dream.*

21. Lakewood, CA, early house, ca. 1950, modern view, exterior. Photo by the author.

22. Lakewood, CA, builder's sales brochure, model 30, plan, ca. 1950. City of Lakewood.

levels: a basement level on a slab, containing the garage, a utility enclosure, and sometimes a small "den"; then, half a level up, the living room and kitchen; then, another half level up, the bedrooms and bath (usually over the garage) (fig. 24). This arrangement allowed a smaller footprint than that of the ranch, perhaps 50 percent smaller for a house of comparable square footage (figs. 8, 9). The smaller footprint meant that much narrower lots could be employed, often fifty feet. The split-level was originally developed for hilly ground, where the first-level garage could be cut into the hill while the main level did not rise very far above the street. But as the type spread and became more popular, builders erected split-levels on flat ground as well, heaping up earth to help provide the "cut" for the garage and basement level. Or when the site sloped steeply away from the street, what was visible from the front looked like a one-story ranch; two half levels down in the rear were the garage at the bottom and the bedrooms at midlevel (see fig. 112).

Like the ranch, the split faced the street, with a view through a large picture window. Being smaller in footprint, and needing more internal space for stairs, it usually contained smaller rooms. Entry was directly into the living room; stairs then acted partially as hallways, leading directly to bedrooms and bath above and garage and utilities below. In all its versions, the split-level seemed more closed off from the outdoors than the ranch (where one could often see through the house to the backyard from the living room), more focused on its interior spaces (despite the fact that advertisements and salesmen touted it as providing "indoor-outdoor living"), which were spatially somewhat more dynamic because of their vertical organization. Like the ranch, the split appeared in several variations, sometimes looking a bit like a "colonial" two-story, sometimes somewhat like the modern "A-line" house with an asymmetrical roof, and sometimes (in Chicago) somewhat reminiscent of the midwestern masonry bungalow (figs. 25, 26).[17] Although in the early to mid-fifties split-levels were usually exceptionally small, with growing popularity they swelled in size, and their lots

24. Diagram of typical split-level house. Nathanael Roesch.

25. Ralph Bodek, split-level house, Lawrence Park, PA, ca. 1960, exterior, modern view. Photo by the author.

26. Stoltzner Builders, front-to-back split-level, Greenview subdivision, Arlington Heights, IL, modern view. Photo by the author.

27. Devon, PA, larger split-level house, ca. 1960, modern view. Photo by the author.

expanded (fig. 27). They were also usually somewhat more expensive than comparable ranch houses, because of the higher construction costs for the builder.[18] But in some areas during the early fifties, such as parts of New Jersey, lower-cost splits were more available than comparable ranches.[19] Yet, over time, on the national stage, they did not approach the ranch in popularity.

Ranches and splits shared many common features. Coming up the walk from the driveway and entering directly into the living room, one often saw almost immediately a large mirror, either built-in, on the coat closets, or hung by the buyers on the main wall facing the front windows (fig. 28). (Further mirrors would appear on the doors of the bedroom closets and in the bathroom, as in figure 12 above. The builders provided these mirrors.) To the rear of the living room was either an open L containing a dining area, or just the kitchen itself. There might be an opening in the wall from the dinette or the living room to the kitchen (a "pass-though" that could also be closed in some cases); there might be additional folding doors to close off kitchen odors; or the kitchen might be quite open to other rooms. Off to the side (in the ranch) or up the stairs (in the split-level) were the two or three small bedrooms, with high windows for privacy. In the split-level, there was sometimes a "den" or small "recreation room" at the bottom of the stairs, together with heating equipment. In the ranch, an additional den or small "family room" appeared in the mid-fifties; increasingly it was added on to the kitchen.[20] Most houses contained a fireplace, in the living room, or—later—in the "family room."

Also inside the "typical" house, there were further surprises for anyone accustomed to interiors from earlier decades. In addition to the mirrors mentioned above, it is notable that the walls were painted rather than wallpapered: usually white or a pale color (fig. 28).[21] Ceilings were relatively low. There were no chandeliers: ceiling fixtures were flush to the ceiling or built into it. Large windows in the living room were framed with floor-to-ceiling draperies (present earlier in houses for the well-to-do but now, in the fifties, almost universal in new houses). Furniture might be in some sort of neocolonial mode, but much more often it was spare and light-looking, in a style that came to be known as "Danish modern" (fig. 10). The bedrooms were smaller than in earlier suburban houses: twelve by fourteen feet for the parents, eight by eleven or ten by thirteen for the children (fig. 8). A queen-size bed fit in the master bedroom, but the children's rooms were outfitted with bunk beds (fig. 29). Unlike the smaller houses of the twenties, closets were large and generous: deep enough for standard size hangers, they often contained built-in shelving as well (fig. 30).

The bathroom was shiny with high-gloss surfaces and mirrors, and the kitchen a showpiece of modern equipment (figs. 11, 12, 31). In these utilitarian

28. Campanelli Brothers, ranch house, 1954, interior view of living room at Christmas, 1956. Mr. LT.

29. Children's bunk beds, ca. 1948. Koues, *Encyclopedia of Decorating*, 1948.

30. Model house, Lakewood, CA, ca. 1950, interior of bedroom with closet. City of Lakewood.

31. Kitchen interior, Pittsburgh Plate Glass Company, house 4 (architects Landefeld & Hatch), World's Fair 1939–40, Flushing Meadows, NY, Gottscho-Schleisner Collection, Library of Congress.

spaces, builders added new amenities with each passing year. By 1960, one might find an "electric built-in wall oven, counter-top range, dishwasher, wall-hung refrigerator, waste disposer, automatic washer,"[22] in addition to a double sink and wall-mounted cabinets. And there might be a riot of color in the kitchen: appliances in turquoise, pink, or yellow. (Some builders employed "color psychologists" to advise them as to the most cheerful combination of colors.)[23] A good-size window was usually placed above the sink.

The element of choice for new buyers was always stressed in advertisements and sales brochures; Campanelli Brothers in Natick, Massachusetts, offered sample books of carpet, wall coverings, styles of appliances, and fabrics for upholstery and draperies.[24] From the late forties on, it was normal for builders to partner with local furniture houses and kitchen supply wholesalers who would furnish and equip the model houses on display. If buyers wished, they could purchase a completely furnished model house. They could also choose the exterior color for their house, or they could repaint it themselves soon after they moved in. It is important to remember, when we look at the largely black-and-white photographs of these houses, that they were colorful, giving their surrounding communities a lot of variation.

The new houses within the new communities employed new modes of construction. They were not prefabricated, although many people at the time expected them to be, and they were not "mass-produced," a term that is often used, rather inaccurately, to describe them. In fact, they were built using time-honored American construction techniques: they were "stick-built"—framed with wooden studs—and usually erected a few at a time (fig. 32).[25] But they were built in larger groups than before, using new machines, new techniques, and new materials. Builders used new earth-moving equipment to clear sizeable plots of land at once, and new kinds of excavating machines to lay down a number of concrete foundations at once. Framing was completed for a group of houses, before they were sheathed in plywood or other new materials and finished as a group. Standardized lumber sizes and new tools emancipated builders to a certain extent from lumber suppliers, who had previously often acted as builders themselves.[26] The larger builders set up lumber-cutting operations on site, the

32. View of construction, Levittown, PA, ca. 1952. Temple University Libraries, Philadelphia.

SCENIC WINDOW STYLE 2

SCENIC WINDOW STYLE 8

SCENIC WINDOW STYLE 10

33. Sketch for advertisement of Aladdin picture windows in Aladdin Catalog of 1954. Clarke Historical Library, Central Michigan University.

smaller builders entered into new arrangements with local lumber suppliers. Other new tools (the Skilsaw, the nail gun, paint sprayers) allowed fast production, and required less skill in execution. New finishing materials (siding of wood substitutes, brick or masonry veneer, sprayed-on stucco-like material, roofing mass-produced in sheets, drywall instead of plaster on the interiors), new kinds of insulation, new kinds of floor covering, all produced new economies and promoted speed of construction. These procedures required numbers of new kinds of laborers, less skilled than construction workers had been in the past and usually nonunion. All these techniques permitted, but did not require, large-scale production. Many builders entered into relatively long-term contracts with appliance manufacturers, kitchen suppliers, furniture businesses, and suppliers of building materials. The revolution in domestic construction was a mixture of some mass production methods, together with relatively small-scale enterprise and on-site innovation.

In all these houses the picture window was ubiquitous. All builders used them, all buyers insisted on them. John Keats's 1956 book *The Crack in the Picture Window* assumed that the picture window could serve as a symbol for the entire enterprise of tract house building.[27] This window was not the great expanse of plate glass that the glass companies always recommended in their postwar advertising. Instead, the earliest postwar picture windows were large, multipaned affairs, often floor-to-ceiling, composed of twelve to eighteen panels separated by the narrow wooden strips called muntins. These windows appeared sometimes at the corner of the facade, but over time they came to be located more toward the center. Slowly, over the course of the 1940s and early 1950s, other forms of central window displaced these complicated-looking affairs with fewer panes, as we see in the typical patterns of "scenic windows" offered by Aladdin Ready Cut Homes in 1954 (fig. 33). Of the three forms offered by Aladdin, it was the tripartite style, with one large, clear pane in the middle and two flanking panels with glass and muntins that was most widespread.

Advertisements published by glass manufacturers in the forties and fifties usually showed the window looking out to a natural landscape, but this was not the view seen by the occupants of tract houses. The obvious function of the picture window in typical housing developments of the period was *seeing out*. What one saw was the other tract houses across the street, the street itself, with passing vehicles, and sidewalks with pedestrians, either passing by or approaching one's own house. And one also saw the children at play (fig. 34) who crowded the streets and sidewalks of these places. Thus, the picture window had some of the function of permitting "eyes on the street," in Jane Jacobs's later phrase about safe urban neighborhoods. It also had some of the function of the front porch, which it partially replaced, a place, as Sue Bridwell Beckham writes, of "liminal space," a space where public and private functions of the household

intersected.[28] Needless to say, the window was not a door, as the Fuller Brush Man and the lady of the house discover in the Leonard Dove *New Yorker* cartoon of 1948 (fig. 35). But it was a place where one could see the approach of the brush salesman, the paper boy, the delivery person, and get up to receive them.

So the picture window was a place for looking out: at children at play, at approaching visitors, at the activities of the neighbors, and at people and vehicles passing by. These functions were well understood by the occupants, and desired by them.[29] But what about looking in? In contemporary advertisements and illustrations, the new floor-to-ceiling draperies, which could shelter the inside from onlookers, are seldom closed. In fact, it was common to leave the draperies open even in the evening, a practice that continues (fig. 36).[30] Part of the function of the picture window was therefore to display what was inside, to the outside.[31]

Picture windows appeared in the houses of all ethnic groups, all religious affiliations, and all income levels; they were as common in upscale Rossmoor as in working-class Lawrence Park. Scholarly research on the history of window treatments is scarce, but anthropologists have argued that bourgeois householders in the seventeenth-century Netherlands insisted on uncurtained windows, as showcases for their lifestyle.[32] Some writers about postwar suburbs even go so far as to suggest that there was a Puritan-like urge to conformity in the new postwar settlements; everyone monitored everyone else to ensure that their lifestyles were similar. There is no way to be very sure about this now, since scarcely any sound sociological or anthropological studies were done at the time, but if we think about the kinds of choices new householders could make—in size, color, interior decoration, appliances, and the like—and about the individualistic ways in which they remodeled their houses, the conformity argument seems overdone. Instead, I think the picture window allowed the house, the front yard, the sidewalk, and the street to be perceived as extensions of one another, so that the quasi-public spaces of the house formed a partial continuum with the more

34. View from window showing child on bicycle, Torrance, CA, 1956. Mrs. FC.

35. Leonard Dove, cartoon: brush salesman approaches picture window 1948. *New Yorker* Collection.

36. Stoltzner Builders, Greenview subdivision, front-to-back split-level: looking in at night, modern view. Photo by the author.

37. Torrance, Los Angeles, CA, family in front yard, 1960. Mrs. FC.

public spaces of the surrounding community. Given the strong sense of community identity in these early postwar housing developments, this is the most plausible explanation.

There was also a sense in which picture windows, together with the mirrors inside, were about *seeing*: seeing in *and* seeing out *and* seeing around inside. This was a generation for whom seeing offered new kinds of experience: they not only saw in and out through large glass areas, but also saw the world through movie screens, television screens, and the large windshields of their large automobiles.[33] And they looked through the lenses of cameras at every opportunity—no family was without its "Brownie" camera or its equivalent, and a great many owned the eight-millimeter home movie camera as well.[34] These photographic records, of the house (and the remodeling of the house), the yard, the neighborhood, the barbecues, the block parties, the trips to vacation sites with neighbors, filled photo albums and video collections everywhere.

By far the most frequent image of the new houses taken by their new owners was a family photograph in front of the house. Such pictures showed the proud family, in front of the new house soon after moving in (usually only one parent with two or three children—the other parent was holding the camera) (fig. 37). These were essentially views of the proprietors, carefully kept in albums for the use of future generations. Sometimes they marked, in the history of the family, the first moment of home ownership. Ownership itself—ownership of property— was on display in the picture made by the picture window.

Generations of Critics and Scholars

Astonishingly, there are modern studies of only a dozen or so of the new tract-based communities and their houses, and of only a handful of their builders. The classic general work by Kenneth Jackson, *The Crabgrass Frontier*, remains, after more than twenty-five years, the most widely used and authoritative introduction to the subject. But Jackson does not discuss house types or specific suburbs (except for Levittown, Long Island) at any length. Recently, interest in tract housing has revived somewhat, but scholarship has been delayed and distorted by decades of neglect and dislike.

Tract house development in the postwar period attracted harsh criticism over a long period of time: from social commentators and critics, and from many historians. These dwellings have had such a bad reputation among both popular writers and scholars for so long (ever since John Keats's *The Crack in the Picture Window* of 1956 and Richard and Katherine Gordon's *The Split-Level Trap* of 1961) that few writers have taken a careful and objective look at them. Beginning in the 1950s, social critics described American tract developments as the homes of white middle-class status-seekers (the "organization man" in the "gray flannel suit"), oppressed and neurotic women, adulterous marriages, delinquent children, declining community bonds, and uniformly bad taste: "little boxes . . . made of ticky-tacky," in Malvina Reynolds's famous song.[35] The builders of tract house developments were rapacious entrepreneurs, in the business of wringing the last penny out of substandard construction, so the argument went. The inhabitants, it was said, moved on to better housing as fast as they possibly could. The tract developments lacked any sense of community, and bled into one another in a visually and socially indistinguishable mass: in a new and repellent mass society. These condemnations were truly extraordinary in their number and extent.[36]

These generalizations were largely false. Socially, the tracts varied a great deal according to the income level of the new inhabitants, but they did not conform to the stereotypes of social science or popular critiques. The majority were occupied originally by people of relatively low incomes, not by upwardly mobile, status-seeking "organization men." Women were not isolated within them, consigned by lack of transportation and lack of work to being dependent "home-makers": indeed they usually worked, and, when spouses carpooled or used the train, the wives had the use of the family car. Builders sometimes amassed great new fortunes during the building boom, but most of them were conscientious about quality, and had, in fact, rather high ideals about their work. Neighborhood consciousness was high and constructive. The first inhabitants tended to be young couples with young children, but (among those I interviewed) they also tended to stay; not seldom, their children and grandchildren now live in these developments. All but the smallest tracts contained some provision for schools, parks, and shopping. And even the smallest developed a sense of identity and neighborhood cohesion.[37]

More recently, a number of persuasive historians of urbanization have built on these social critiques to make ecological judgments, deploring the impact of suburban expansion on the environment, and on the character of American urbanism overall. The proliferation of single-family houses in the American landscape has led, it is argued, to wasteful use of land and resources.[38] While such condemnations of "sprawl" raise important points, they ignore the obvious fact that Americans have always preferred to live in single-family houses. With very few exceptions, American urban growth has been driven by the proliferation of stand-alone dwellings. The notion that the first generation of builders after the war should have imagined a different solution to the postwar housing crisis and to the construction of mass housing, or that the American government would have supported it, ignores the realities of centuries of American urbanism. Yet such arguments, like those of the earlier social critics, have distracted us from looking at postwar tract housing in its own terms.

During the past fifteen to twenty years, critics of tract housing have focused on issues of discrimination and segregation. As many have rightly said, the new communities were inaccessible to "people of color" during the 1950s. This was of course at least partly a result of the mandates involved in FHA financing, buttressed by traditional social mores, and it began to change in the 1960s. Another obvious aspect of social life is overlooked by these writers: the new inhabitants were *new*: they came from all over the country, from different places and backgrounds—often they were second-generation immigrants whose families had been segregated within urban settings. So there was a very significant melting-pot experience in the new postwar communities. Italians, Jews, Catholics, Irish, Polish, and others who had been segregated in American cities and excluded from earlier American suburbs now mingled together freely, forming new kinds of communities that they valued intensely. I think that this experience may have helped Americans to become more accepting of diversity, even where color lines were initially maintained. In fact, suburbs became integrated more quickly than cities: by the 1970s, barriers were broken down nearly everywhere. As historian Becky Nicolaides recently described Lakewood, California, "within twenty years, history flipped. Like many sitcom suburbs, lily-white Lakewood became a town of whites, Latinos, Asians, and blacks. Sitcom suburbia . . . had become the staging ground of neighborhood diversity."[39]

Meanwhile, for many of the same reasons that social critics found suburbs undesirable, architectural historians ignored the development of tract housing: to them these houses did not seem to be "architecture." Traditionally, architectural historians have preferred to deal with the creative work of a well-known and influential individual architect, and with the single architectural work or monument. The lack of identifiable architects and of observable major monuments has made the tract developments uninteresting to most architectural historians, as has the "low-brow" taste supposedly represented in such buildings. Very recently, though, postwar tract houses have begun to appear in general studies of modern American house design like those of Sandy Isenstadt and John Archer.[40] But Isenstadt and Archer do not examine any specific housing developments in detail. The same is true of Witold Rybczynski's popular books on American ideas of home and on the practices of American developers.[41]

Builders too have begun to fare a little better recently. Elaborating on some of Kenneth Jackson's remarks, a few writers have attempted to discuss the business methods of the larger builders: Fritz Burns, the Levitts, Frank Sharp in Houston, David Bohannon in the San Francisco Bay area, are always included, while some also mention the work of Joseph Eichler in Northern California.[42] Greg Hise, Dana Cuff, and James Keane have examined the extraordinary housing production of Fritz Burns in Los Angeles. Hise and Cuff have carried this work further, to discuss tract housing as an integral aspect of urbanization in the modern period. In general, writing about the history of tract house development in California has been more comprehensive and sophisticated than building histories dealing with other parts of the country.[43]

Yet, with the exception of the Levitts, none of these builders was especially large for his era: thousands of other builders constructed developments on a similar sale (one to three thousand homes each). In terms of size, even the Levitts and Weingart, Taper and Boyar at Lakewood, were dwarfed by such building giants of

38. Levittown, PA, aerial view of street layout ca. 1953. Mercer Museum Library, Bucks County Historical Society.

the later fifties as Centex Corporation and Kaufman and Broad.[44] A few writers have begun to provide more information about the Levittowns and about Lakewood. The Levittowns of New York and Pennsylvania, developed and designed by the Levitt family (Abraham and his sons William and Alfred) from 1946 onward, have long been the best known of postwar developments. The Levitts, experienced builders before the war, emerged from wartime with new ambitions to build mass housing. Their first effort, "Island Trees" in Hempstead, Long Island, grew rather haphazardly over a period of five years to number 17,500 dwelling units by 1951. The enormous demand startled the builders; when they acquired new large tracts near the Fairless steel works of Bucks County, Pennsylvania, in 1951, they created a sophisticated overall plan for the new community (fig. 38). Over a period of seven years, the Levitts built 17,311 houses in Levittown, Pennsylvania.

With the work of Barbara Kelly, Dianne Harris, and Richard Longstreth, we are finally beginning to understand the history of these Levittowns.[45]

Lakewood was almost as well known on the West Coast as the Levittowns were in the East. Begun in 1949 on 2,300 acres (with another 3,375 acres added in 1950) just to the southeast of the Los Angeles city limits, Lakewood was developed by a corporation headed by businessmen: builder Louis Boyar (Aetna Construction), banker Ben Weingart, and builder and insurance executive S. Mark Taper (Biltmore Homes), working with planner J. R. Newville of the Engineering Service Corporation. The huge overall plan was laid out on a grid (as was most of Los Angeles and Orange County), and was sometimes photographed by contemporaries as an example of how *not* to plan (fig. 39). Construction proceeded with extraordinary rapidity: 17,500 houses were constructed within the first three years, and by 1957 the population exceeded 70,000, "twice the size of Levittown, NY."[46] Whether or not the Newville plan was intended to embrace an

39. "Finished Housing," Lakewood, CA, aerial view by William A. Garnett, 1950.

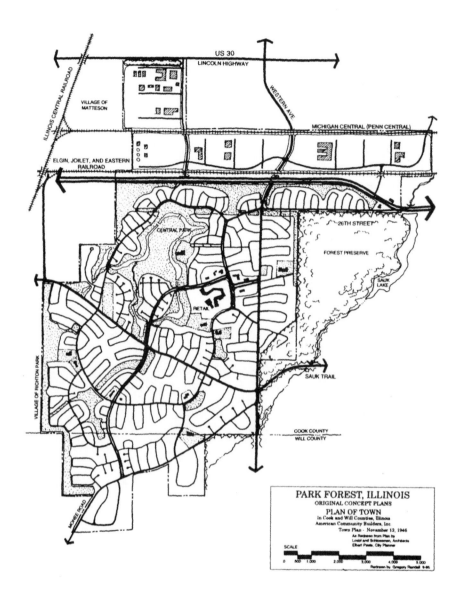

Within the map:

US 30
LINCOLN HIGHWAY

MICHIGAN CENTRAL (PENN CENTRAL)

WESTERN AVE

VILLAGE OF MATTESON

ILLINOIS CENTRAL RAILROAD

ELGIN, JOILET, AND EASTERN RAILROAD

CENTRAL PARK

26TH STREET

FOREST PRESERVE

SAUK LAKE

RETAIL

VILLAGE OF RICHTON PARK

SAUK TRAIL

COOK COUNTY
WILL COUNTY

MONEE ROAD

PARK FOREST, ILLINOIS
ORIGINAL CONCEPT PLANS
PLAN OF TOWN
In Cook and Will Counties, Illinois
American Community Builders, Inc.
Town Plan · November 12, 1946
As Redrawn from Plan by
Loebl and Schlossman, Architects
Elbert Peets, City Planner

SCALE
0   500 1,000   2,000   3,000   4,000   5,000
Redrawn by Gregory Randall 9-96

40. Park Forest, IL, Elbert Peets Plan, 1946. From Randall, *America's Original GI Town*.

entire new community is unclear today, but the place grew so fast that Lakewood was able to incorporate as a city in 1954.[47] Thus, in the years after incorporation, Lakewood city governments themselves decided the choice and location of public facilities. Don Waldie's books about Lakewood, part personal experiences and insights, part poetry, and full of important historical information, have provided an intimate window on the history of the largest of all postwar housing developments.[48]

The third of the best-known early new communities, Park Forest, Illinois, in its time came to be the subject of much discussion among social scientists.[49]

Now, it is less familiar to the general reader, although it has been well studied by Gregory Randall.[50] Located to the south of Chicago, just to the east of Interstate 57, Park Forest was developed by a group that called themselves American Community Builders, headed by Philip M. Klutznick, a former Federal Public Housing Authority commissioner who was also active in writing FHA publications on recommended forms for neighborhoods. Together with Caroll Fuller Sweet, a retired banker, and Nathan Manilow, builder and investor, the group hired Elbert Peets, well-known planner and author and garden city proponent, to prepare an overall plan (fig. 40). The new houses were intended initially as rental units for veterans and their families, but soon single-family dwellings were added for sale. Plagued by transportation difficulties and slow sales, the whole developed rather slowly until 1962, when it contained 8,500 dwelling units (housing about 28,000 people). Its eventual social composition was more upscale than that of Lakewood or Levittown, Pennsylvania: its "average adult male" inhabitant in 1950 had more than four years of college, and many household heads were professional people.[51] But in the 1950s, Chicago newspapers often spoke of Park Forest as a model for new planning.

Research and Methods

In adding to the work on the Levittowns, Lakewood, and Park Forest by looking at twelve other important developments, and by looking at design issues as well as society, I hope to get beyond the highly prejudiced critiques of the early years, and beyond the few special studies, in order to take a closer look at typical tract houses, their immediate environments, their formal character, and their attractions to their inhabitants. Were there commonalities among the tract houses of different places? Why were they built, and who designed them and their physical environments? Why did people like them, and why did people stay in their new communities? How do tract houses compare to other American dwelling types of earlier periods? How did the settlements themselves vary in planning, in relation to the size of the tract? How did they compare with other efforts at mass housing, in the United States and elsewhere? Who were the principal creators of the new designs? Did their design inspiration derive in any way from "high" architecture, or may the reverse have been true? My perspectives are those of the architectural and urban historian, but the questions I ask go beyond the questions usually asked within those specialties. This book can only be a beginning, however; many additional studies and reexaminations are needed, both specific and general.

The vast majority of housing developments in the first postwar years were quite different from the giant Lakewood or Levittowns, and from the well-planned

Park Forest; they were on smaller tracts, and contained smaller numbers of houses. There were thousands of these developments, a daunting number. My preliminary surveys show that they varied a great deal among themselves. Some were explicitly marketed to the well-to-do, though the majority were intended for low-income buyers, especially veterans. Some were quite large (four thousand houses or more), many were medium-size (twelve hundred to three thousand), and a great many were quite small (four to six hundred). The builders varied too: some of the builders, like Burns and the Levitts, had begun to construct and market single-family houses well before the war, but most plunged into the development business after the war without much education or training. The engineers who helped the builders lay out their developments ranged from the licensed "land surveyors" who invariably signed off on subdivision proposals to highly trained and broadly educated specialists. Houses varied somewhat in style, materials, and construction methods. In an effort to show variation as well as commonalities, I have selected a few developments to consider in detail, in full knowledge of the difficulties of sampling among a large number of places and types.

My focus on Los Angeles, Chicago, Philadelphia, and Boston unfortunately excludes examples of the new suburbs of the South and the Northwest: I avoided these because of constraints on my time and energy. I have also avoided most of the new communities of the Southwest, for similar reasons. But, by including Elk Grove Village in Chicago, built by the Dallas firm Centex, I have been able to take a brief look at postwar urban development in Texas. I also exclude the New York metropolitan area. New York City's suburban history is enormously complex, since it took place on a huge scale in three very different areas: New Jersey, Long Island, and lower New York State. A fair sampling of builders and communities from all three areas would overbalance the other builders and communities discussed here. And I question whether the suburbanization of New York City, the core of the East Coast "megalopolis," was very typical of the nation as a whole. In any case, other earlier writers have tended to focus on New York's suburbanization, in lower New York State, Long Island, and New Jersey: this means that we need now to look more carefully at other geographical areas.

Within each of the metropolitan districts dealt with here, I explored the areas outside the older cities by car and using maps, in order to locate sizeable (six hundred to about six thousand dwellings) developments begun between 1947 and 1959. Further exploration, together with newspaper searches, narrowed my examples to nine builders: three in or near Los Angeles, three near Chicago, two in the Philadelphia area, and one who worked near both Boston and Chicago. I selected these builders to demonstrate variations in sizes of their enterprises, and variations in backgrounds and methods. Of the builders, three were small firms constructing houses on small subdivisions (Vandruff near Los Angeles,

Stoltzners outside Chicago, Facciolo in the Philadelphia area); the others built up tracts that contained between one and seven thousand dwellings. Of these larger builders, three remained local (Bodek in Philadelphia, Cortese in the Los Angeles area, Hill in Chicago), their reputations tied to the construction of a single tract. Two others (Campanelli Brothers, based in the Boston area, and Centex, coming from Dallas to build in Chicago) expanded their businesses beyond their local base, attempting to become national in scope. Of these last two, Centex succeeded in its national aspirations, growing into a giant of postwar housing construction; Campanelli Brothers, in contrast, eventually withdrew from the housing business and became a successful firm of commercial builders based in Braintree, Massachusetts. Fritz Burns of Los Angeles is represented here primarily through the design and construction of Panorama City, but he was a longtime builder, locally well-known for his earlier, large Los Angeles tracts; his business remained based in Los Angeles, but he built elsewhere in the West, and he exerted great influence nationally in the postwar period through his leadership in the National Association of Home Builders (NAHB). These examples allow me to discuss varied building types and different models of the building enterprise, and to look at the impact of size on the character of planning the subdivision. I also find that regional variations were important, at least at the start of the process: local traditions played a part in house design, while local landholding patterns and land regulations greatly influenced the size and conceptualization of subdivisions.

The builders I focus on were one-man or (in two cases) one-family enterprises; their procedures depended upon the highly idiosyncratic personalities of their owners.[52] In most of these cases, I was able to locate subdivision records, and to interview the original builders or their children. In many instances I was also able to interview local planning officials. Often, growing community organizations have collected sales brochures and other pertinent documents. Indeed, community organizations in many of these places have become very active in the past ten years, establishing libraries, setting up house museums, collecting interviews from the builders and buyers, and in a few cases gaining "historic district" classification for their communities. I have supplemented this information through intensive study of the real estate articles and advertisements in the major metropolitan newspapers. Other important resources for me have been the publications of kit builders (Sears and Aladdin) and pattern-book publishers such as Garlinghouse Company.[53] These sources often inspired the builders discussed here. This selection of builders and developments should permit some generalizations about what was typical in the period.

To set these specific tracts in their context, it has also been necessary to look at VA and FHA guidelines for builders and lenders, which were national in scope. While it is not at all certain that most builders consistently read national

L. R. LIVING ROOM   K. KITCHEN
B. R. BEDROOM   D. DINING

41. FHA, Minimum House, 900 square feet, 1940, exterior. Federal Housing Administration, *Principles of Planning Small Houses*, July 1, 1940.

42. FHA, Minimum House, 900 square feet, 1940, plan. Federal Housing Administration, *Principles of Planning Small Houses*, July 1, 1940.

architectural magazines, they all paid attention to national lending guidelines. The FHA published guides to every aspect of building and development. In 1936 and 1940, the FHA's central office described standards for the building of a "minimum house" that would be about 650 to 900 square feet in plan. The earlier house included two bedrooms, a dining area, a kitchen, and a bathroom. By 1940, the living room had become dominant, and the dining area had been absorbed into the kitchen (figs. 41, 42). In plan and exterior appearance, this house provided the model for much of America's wartime housing. Many of the first postwar tract houses (such as the Levitt Cape and "ranch") mimicked this plan. By 1941, and continuing thereafter, FHA publications also urged builders to make their designs responsive to "function," echoing, perhaps, the discussions of small dwelling types that had been taking place during the previous fifteen years in Europe.[54] Other FHA publications offered guidelines for neighborhood design, contract specifications, construction methods, siting, and land planning. Often, the district organizations of the FHA added further specifications and advice to these sets of guidelines. For new and inexperienced builders, the FHA publications offered a comprehensive education in "how to do it."

Apart from its prescriptions about house planning, the most important FHA regulations were those relating to neighborhood design.[55] Beginning in 1936 with the pamphlet *Planning Neighborhoods for Small Houses*, reissued in an expanded version with revisions in 1941, and with supplementary provisions for specific states from 1946 to 1965, the FHA attempted to assert rules for the planning of new communities. These rules were derived from the teachings of Clarence Perry about neighborhoods, from nineteenth-century ideas about neighborhood revitalization, and from such traditions of garden city ideas as existed in this country.[56] American garden city planning ideas—from Forest Hills Garden to New Deal "Greenbelt" settlements, to Radburn, Reston, and Columbia—neglected the idea that workplaces should be embedded in new communities, an idea that the European Garden City movement held dear. FHA neighborhood planning guidelines repeatedly referred to Radburn, New Jersey, as a model (fig. 43). New

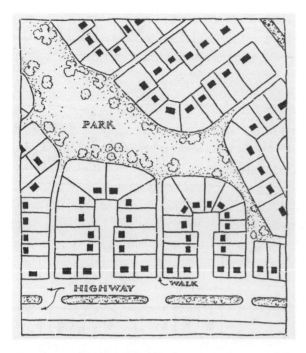

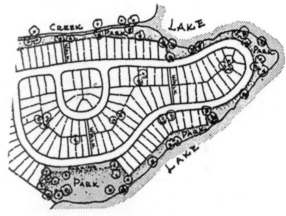

neighborhoods, the FHA urged, must be focused around parks, schools, and other community facilities; their streets should be curvilinear and organized for walking; the whole should be protected from through traffic by buffering roads around the perimeter (fig. 44). Furthermore, neighborhoods (or subdivisions—the distinction was not made clear) must be part of overall community planning, with a master plan to be carried out by local zoning officials.[57]

In the case of house design, the FHA or its local branches exercised significant control through the approval of mortgages, but its planning ideas had a less direct influence. Although the guidelines stated that "approved" neighborhoods would be favored in the granting of mortgages, few mechanisms for such approval existed. An indirect influence is very clear: FHA neighborhood planning ideas were held up as desirable by the NAHB (see the section on Fritz Burns in chapter 2), which offered prizes for neighborhood development; prize-winners were newsworthy, which was sometimes useful to the locality. But the implementation of FHA regulations was left to local zoning or planning boards, which often ignored them, and to individual builders, who often resisted providing open space or community facilities. Frequently, but not invariably, local zoning boards and planning officials required some provision for park spaces or spaces for schools as part of a subdivision plan. Many individual builders and their engineers turned to curvilinear streets and cul-de-sacs, however; perhaps this preference was derived from the FHA publications. And in a few instances,

43. Radburn, NJ, plan. Federal Housing Administration, *Planning Neighborhoods for Small Houses*, July 1, 1936.

44. Street design: "preserve natural features." Federal Housing Administration, *Successful Subdivisions*, 1941.

at least among my case studies, builders and engineers produced well-conceived overall master plans at the start of the building process (Panorama City, Lawrence Park, Elk Grove Village). In many other cases, builders were able to affect the ideas and regulations of local planning officials.

As part of a study of context—of the sources of builders' and buyers' ideas about their houses—I have made a systematic study of the main architectural and builders' magazines, and of the "home" magazines and books that proliferated in the postwar period. In the first ten years after the war, houses and housing were big news for Americans: new magazines had feature articles on the builders and their houses; huge numbers of books were devoted to "how to build a house" or "how to buy a house"; glossy magazines like *House and Garden* and *Better Homes and Gardens* promoted particular kinds of house design and interior design, and older professional journals for architects greatly expanded their readership with frequent articles on house design and construction. These magazines, and other popular periodicals like *McCall's Magazine, Woman's Home Companion, Saturday Evening Post, Collier's*, and *Parents Magazine* published frequent questionnaires gathered from new buyers.[58] Research institutes such as the Illinois Small Homes Council tirelessly collected information about specific building techniques, and about buyers' home preferences. Cornell University's College of Home Economics (within the School of Agriculture) spent several years studying kitchen design, and published their findings frequently.[59] Producers of home appliances and construction materials published their own studies of the housing boom. So did insurance firms and realtors' associations. The federal government created new boards and agencies, which studied the housing phenomenon: the Building Research Advisory Board, and the National Research Council, for example, or the Housing and Home Finance Agency. And so did educational institutions and a variety of nonprofit organizations. According to a report by the Building Research Advisory Board in 1952, 861 educational institutions, foundations, commercial laboratories, trade associations, and professional societies were publishing reports on their housing research. And when one of these magazines, organizations, institutions, or government offices issued a report, major newspapers across the country published a condensed version.

During the same years as these reports and publications, American museums were also focusing on some aspects of house design. Beginning with the famous exhibition on "The International Style" in 1931, the Museum of Modern Art in New York emphasized the role of house design in "modern architecture": for the most part, the abstract and austere house designs of émigré architect Ludwig Mies van der Rohe,[60] greatly admired by long-term curator Philip Johnson, set the standard of taste in house design for MoMA's exhibition policies. But other styles and issues gained a hearing. The museum also exhibited the architecture of Frank Lloyd Wright, and built exhibition houses displaying a range of styles: one by West Coast architect Gregory Ain and one by Gropius associated and former Bauhaus teacher Marcel Breuer.[61] Under the brief curatorship of Elizabeth Mock, disciple of Frank Lloyd Wright, MoMA architectural policy took a more practical turn, exemplified in Mock's publications *If You Want to Build a House* and *Tomorrow's Small House*. Nevertheless, the MoMA shows and publications never confronted issues of cost, nor did they ever make clear the large role that mass housing had played in Europe in the development of the modern movement. It is highly unlikely that MoMA's appeal ever reached very far beyond the architectural elites of the nation, and the students of Mies and Gropius at IIT and Harvard.[62]

If one looks for influential imagery that might have inspired the ideas of builders and buyers, a better choice might be American World's Fairs and other exhibitions featuring a "House of the Future" or a "House of Tomorrow." These notions had a long and very far-reaching popular history.[63] Beginning at least as early as the 1920s, the theme of a "house of the future" or "house of tomorrow" appeared frequently in exhibitions and newspaper articles. The electrical industries displayed electrified model houses from early in the century.[64] Henry Ford predicted a prefabricated "all electric house" in 1929, while in 1931 the Architectural and Allied Arts Exposition in New York City exhibited a factory-made house of aluminum, glass and rubber. Also in 1931, newspapers reported the views of realtors that the "house of the future" would be mass-produced, "made for use and pleasure" and not to satisfy "the whims of architects." In 1932, a "small house forum" held by the American Institute of Steel Construction predicted the mass production of a "nomadic house," full of new appliances and transportable by truck and rail.[65] Occasionally, exhibitions and newspaper accounts described housing achieved by International Style architects in Europe as houses "of the future," but for the most part, their emphasis was devoted to American technology and its prospects for dwelling design.[66] American World's Fairs of the thirties and early forties featured some version of "the house of tomorrow": visited by huge audiences, these exhibition houses also came to be well-known to newspaper and magazine readers, though they were not universally admired. The "House of Tomorrow" at Chicago's Century of Progress Exposition of 1933, for example, a circular, all-glass structure, was dismissed as "freaky" by the *Chicago Tribune*.[67] "Tomorrow Town" at the New York World's Fair of 1939–40, widely visited and reported and generally well liked, exhibited fifteen different houses, sponsored by an equal number of manufacturers, interest groups, and by the FHA. Prospectuses promised that there would be "no extreme or modernistic design" in Tomorrow Town.[68] A wood house (National Lumber Manufacturers Association), a plywood house (Douglas Fir Plywood Association), an all-electric house (General Electric Company), and a house of glass (Pittsburgh Plate Glass Company) received the most attention: the first three were greatly admired. The Pittsburgh

45. Pittsburgh Plate Glass
Company, house 4 (architects
Landefeld & Hatch),
World's Fair 1939–40,
Flushing Meadows, NY,
exterior. Gottscho-Schleisner
Collection, Library of
Congress.

46. Pittsburgh Plate Glass
Company, house 4 (architects
Landefeld & Hatch),
World's Fair 1939–40,
Flushing Meadows, NY,
interior. Gottscho-Schleisner
Collection, Library of
Congress.

Plate Glass house, despite promises in the fair's prospectus that there would be "no extreme or modernistic design" in Tomorrow Town, closely resembled contemporary International Style houses (figs. 45, 46). The commentator in the *New York Times* described it as "the fish-bowl home," but it may have prefigured, or influenced, the use of large glass areas in the houses of the fifties and sixties. A model kitchen also looked ahead to some of the kitchens of the fifties and sixties (fig. 31). Other model houses featured new materials: plywood siding, asbestos siding, asphalt shingles, materials that would become familiar in the tract houses of the postwar period. A "motor home" had its main entrance through the garage.[69] Thus, even before the beginning of war in 1941, a "future house" built of modern materials and modern but not "modernistic" in design, with space for at least one automobile, was a theme familiar to virtually all Americans.[70]

During the war, especially in its last years, newspapers, exhibitions, and advertisers took up the theme. The house of tomorrow, writers, manufacturers, and exhibitors agreed, would be "all electric," with electric, "streamlined" kitchen appliances, built-in radios and television sets, automatic household-wide vacuuming systems, air conditioning, kitchens "that cook by radio frequency—radionics." New materials including plastic fabrics and aluminum and fiberboard panels would be used in the construction of small, mass-produced, relatively inexpensive dwellings, heated by radiant heat. There would be plenty of glass (but not too much)—in doors and windows.[71] The theme of "tomorrow's house" had a significant afterlife in the postwar period, even as its promises were being fulfilled in American tract houses. Fritz Burns's "research house" of 1946, designed by Wurdeman and Becket (figs. 47, 48), erected at Highland Avenue and Wilshire Boulevard in Los Angeles as an exhibition, contained a built-in radio system and a multitude of all-electric appliances (disposal, blender, dishwasher, washer/dryer, home freezer). It also featured the storage wall that Burns had used in many of his houses, and an outdoor patio heated by radiant heat along with an outdoor barbecue. It was visited by thousands, and published in national magazines.[72] Usually, though, the phrase was used to suggest something extremely modern, perhaps not yet buildable. Monsanto's "House of the Future" at Disneyland in 1957, for example, was built of intersecting plastic pods: this was titillating but not an inspiration to builders or buyers. Yet the idea of a house of the future persisted: when Kimball Hill opened his Housing Research Laboratory in Rolling Meadows outside Chicago in 1958 (see below, chapter 4), one of the houses was billed as an "extremely modern 'House of Tomorrow.'"[73]

Closely related to the World's Fairs, with their emphasis on building technology, were the home shows of the postwar period. These were exposition-like shows, frequently sponsored by local Home Builders' Associations in conjunction with various manufacturers. Here one could see the newest techniques and materials: wall coverings, stud construction, and insulation were displayed,

47. Fritz Burns with architects Wurdeman and Becket, Research House, Los Angeles, 1946, exterior. Maynard Parker photographer.

48. Fritz Burns with architects Wurdeman and Becket, Research House, Los Angeles, 1946, patio. Huntington Library, Maynard Parker photographer.

together with kitchen and bathroom appliances, and new kinds of tools for do-it-yourselfers. Sometimes, too, a copy of the newest house by a local builder would be featured, as was the case with both Burns and Vandruff in Los Angeles (see chapter 2). These shows go back at least to the 1930s, but became much more numerous after the war. Both builders and buyers visited them eagerly. As did "fixer-uppers."[74]

Some writers see the idea of "the house of the future" or "the miracle house" as propagated by big business (and especially by manufacturers of household appliances and equipment), and as antithetical to the interests of small builders.[75] But, as we will see in the successive chapters on individual builders, merchant builders prided themselves on the household equipment they provided and formed close connections with appliance manufacturers, who helped them pay for their advertising.[76] If postwar builders did not adopt some form of "high-style modernism," it was because they saw that buyers shared the views of newspaper commentators on the World's Fair houses—their amenities were welcome, but many of their forms seemed foolish or alien. The great majority of Americans saw the split-level or the ranch as the true "modern" house.

Making use of this flood of published information and exhibited imagery is a complicated process. The reports published by research organizations offer various kinds of "hard" information: numbers of houses in certain locations; the expressed preferences of certain builders and buyers. Beyond that, however, these materials need to be treated by scholars with careful discrimination as to who read what, when, and why. Very few of the builders I have focused on read professional magazines for architects, though they would sometimes pick up a special issue on builders. Nor did they pay much attention to the glossy home magazines. Experienced builders, and most new ones as well, read the magazines that were most oriented toward construction issues—magazines such as *American Builder and Building Age*, *Construction Methods and Equipment*, *American Builder*, or *Practical Builder*; they also turned to pattern books, as builders so often had in the past. Both experienced builders and new builders paid very careful attention to the handbooks and guidelines of the FHA and the Veterans' Administration. As for professional architectural periodicals, too often historians, especially architectural historians, have substituted the study of houses published by *Architectural Forum* or *Architectural Record* for a study of what was actually built, leading to some extreme distortions. What was published and what was built were often quite different. When starting to build, builders liked to do their own research into what buyers wanted. Buyers certainly did not read the professional architectural magazines, and almost certainly they avoided the expensive popular magazines.[77] Buyers had available to them a vast array of books and articles on the theme of "planning to build" or "how to buy," but the buyers I was able to interview do not remember reading anything like this. When these young families found that they badly needed a house, they looked in the newspapers, visited the houses advertised, and bought their houses: their selections, in other words, were rather simple and straightforward. And overarching all these issues is one of *timing*: most of the fundamental changes in house and community design after World War II took place within a very brief period, between 1945 and about 1952. After the latter date, it rarely makes sense to speak, for example, of the possible influence of a publication, museum show, movie, or television program upon a particular major design feature.[78]

A thorough study of newspapers, including articles on development and advertisements for new houses, can reveal a great deal about what was actually built, and considerable information about the buyers.[79] Contemporary newspaper reporters often interviewed the inhabitants of the new communities that were springing up around their cities; such articles are extremely useful. The great manufacturers of household equipment—Honeywell, Westinghouse, Hotpoint, Norge, and especially General Electric—featured contemporary builders' houses in their advertising and sometimes partnered with them in promotional schemes, or in discovering land for development. Their role is significant, but again, their advertisements are not always representative.

As for the roles of other media in affecting housing design preferences and choices, I do not think that television had much part in affecting house types or buyers' choices. As I explain in chapter 5, TV programs seem instead to have drawn upon postwar excitement about housing to produce prototypes that were far more elaborate than what was actually being built. Movies had a much broader audience in the first decade after the war, that is, during the years when the first design decisions were being made. But, as with TV, their themes were suggestive of excitement about the new houses, rather than playing any causal role. Nevertheless, given the flood of publications, reports, museum displays, and World's Fair exhibitions, neither builders nor buyers could have remained unaware of the intense public interest in their new houses and settlements.

It is my contention that the people who "made" the tract house developments—who shaped house design and overall layout—were the builders themselves, in concert with the engineers and above all, with the buyers. Builders learned from and competed with each other, visited each other's developments, assessed each other's markets and profits. But, more than anything else, they interacted with the buyers, by testing the market through model homes, hearing buyers' preferences through their salesmen, and sometimes doing their own surveys of buyers' opinions. The buyers, on the other hand, reacted to the houses that they could see and visit and voted with their pocketbooks and moving vans. They found their new houses through word of mouth (family, friends, buddies from the service) or advertisements in the newspapers; or sometimes through a new employer. They were even less likely than the builders to read glossy home design magazines or architects' publications, though of course they read some of the most popular magazines like *Parents Magazine*, *Popular Science*, *Saturday Evening Post*, and *Readers' Digest*.[80] They were faithful newspaper readers and enthusiastic moviegoers; television was much less important to them in the early years of tract house development. Above all, they were influenced by their life's experiences, by experiences of immigration, depression, and war; by housing traditions that included farmhouses, workers' tenements, bungalows, and war housing. These traditions were important to the builders too. They understood each other well, the builders and buyers, for they came from similar backgrounds and shared many of the same viewpoints. Thus, I have attempted to convey the life stories of each whenever possible.

My case studies of builders and their developments are organized regionally: Los Angeles and Southern California (chapter 2); the Philadelphia and Boston metropolitan areas (chapter 3); and the Midwest and Southwest, represented by four builders in the "Golden Corridor" area northwest of Chicago (chapter 4). Chapter 4 deals with builders whose work evolved within local Chicago traditions, and also with builders who came to Chicago from outside, from Dallas and Boston. In all these chapters, the emphasis is on the builders as individual entrepreneurs: on who they were, why they built, how they organized their firms, how they acquired land, what house forms and street arrangements they chose and why. Their firms ranged in size from one-man and one-family operations to a large corporate entity dominated by a single individual. Often, their ideas came from their strong local roots, but they also paid a great deal of attention to other builders' work and to the development of markets nationwide. Thus, over time, we will see their house forms and street layouts become more and more detached from their particular region. The regional organization of my text does some violence to chronology, however. In the chapters on Chicago, for example, I treat a later building firm, the Stoltzners, before an earlier one, Kimball Hill, because the Stoltzners were a smaller firm, and worked closer to the urban core. Ralph Bodek in Philadelphia precedes, in my text, the earlier Campanellis in Boston. I will try wherever possible to make clear the actual time sequence of events in house design while also stressing regional differences.

The three specific case study chapters are followed by two more general chapters. Chapter 5 analyzes the ideas and motives of the buyers of tract houses within this early postwar period. It depends on specific evidence gleaned from interviews with original owners of houses within my case studies; it sets the choices of these buyers within the broader context of the history of modest dwelling types from the 1920s onward. It also emphasizes the impact of World War II on popular ideas and attitudes in the first postwar years. Chapter 6, the conclusion, returns to issues of authorship, and then discusses the successes and failures of tract houses as mass housing.

My account stops about 1965. The tract house developments of the first two decades after World War II form a special chapter in the history of American housing and urban growth. After the 1960s, new developments shrank in size as large parcels of agricultural land became less and less available (and more and more expensive). The tract house, on the other hand, became larger and larger and more complex in plan in response to changes in taste and changes in population. New buyers in tract house developments came to be more affluent and more demanding of certain amenities. Federally subsidized mortgages, so prevalent in the earlier period, also shrank in number and increased in cost, in response to the decreasing number of veterans (either from World War II or the Korean War). Increasingly, the roles of builder and developer came to be separated, with the developer finding and financing the land and laying out the streets and sewers, while selling off individual parcels to individual builders or, sometimes, to architects. Nonetheless, the innovations of the fifties continued for a long time: the "open-plan," large, informal, and rather undifferentiated living spaces (including the kitchen), intimacy with the outdoors via large windows or patio doors, small and relatively private bedroom areas, efficient arrangements for built-in storage, a visually dominant garage, a high level of sophisticated household equipment. The lifestyle that evolved in tandem with the new kinds of houses—neighborly, informal, focused on the nuclear family with young children, oriented to the outdoors, committed to property ownership and to the local community—has also endured.

CHAPTER 2

West Coast Builders
Los Angeles and Orange County

The transformation of Los Angeles and its surrounding areas in Orange County, from a small township of 11,200 in 1880 to the world's largest megalopolis in 2000,[1] began and continued with land speculation (fig. 49). After the end of the Spanish and Mexican periods (late eighteenth century to the 1840s), the arrival of the railroad and the spread of irrigated agriculture drew thousands of new settlers to Southern California. As the old Spanish and Mexican land grants were broken up into smaller and smaller pieces in the later nineteenth century, land-hungry investors poured into the area, from the eastern, southern, and midwestern United States. Some farmed (cattle, oranges, beets, beans); others built; some, like Henry Huntington, creator of the Pacific Electric streetcar system, did both. By the end of the century, oil, too, attracted investors and new settlement.[2] In the late nineteenth century, and on up through the 1920s, real estate represented a major part of the city's economic activity; the real estate boom was interrupted only by the Great Depression. By the later 1930s, Los Angeles had become a center for West Coast garment industries (staffed by Mexican and Chinese immigrants), and for the development of the nation's new media industries: motion pictures from the early twentieth century, then radio and television. With the beginning of the war in the Pacific in 1941, new air and naval bases in and around Los Angeles, together with vast new armaments industries, drew millions of new residents, of all races and ethnicities. And with the laying down of the a new highway system based on the Los Angeles Master Plan of 1941, the scene was set for renewed explosive growth in the postwar period. The population increased tenfold between 1890 and 1920, doubled between 1920 and 1940, and doubled again from 1940 to 1960, when it reached about two and a half million. Some of this increase was due to the annexations (of both unincorporated towns and incorporated cities) that increased the size of the city from 28 square miles in the 1890s to 469 square miles in 1932. Los Angeles was larger in area than most other cities in the world in the twentieth century, and larger in both population and geographic extent than all other US cities but New York in the same century. Huge, sprawling, and diverse, composed of ethnic enclaves, historic neighborhoods (some long-established), multiple cities, towns, and communities (some very recent), Los Angeles has often seemed "incomprehensible to outsiders."[3] Perhaps as a result, the history of housing and urban development in the Los Angeles megalopolis has tended to be written by local specialists, and to be comparatively neglected by non-Californians. This has been true of the area's architectural history, too.[4] Yet Los Angeles provided American housing— and American architecture—with many innovations, and almost every innovator in Los Angeles building "came from somewhere else."

Fritz Burns and the "California Ranch House"

Fritz Burns (1899–1979) was certainly not "typical" of American builders in his accomplishments: through his work and contacts in Los Angeles, together with his leadership in the National Association of Home Builders (NAHB), he was for a while (ca. 1942–55) a dominant force in the nation's housing industry. But he belongs at the beginning of this account: his wide-ranging significance has not been fully understood even by California scholars, and certainly not by architectural historians, or historians of housing. If American builders in other parts of the country were looking to any models outside their own regions, or to any national design authorities besides the FHA, it was to Burns's work and to the standards and goals set by the NAHB. If they were reading magazines with a national circulation, they were reading NAHB publications and those that were most directly influenced by the NAHB.

The NAHB was founded by Burns and other leading builders in 1942, as a breakaway organization from the National Association of Real Estate Boards (established in 1908). Among the other early leaders of the organization were David Bohannon from San Francisco, J. C. Nichols of Kansas City, and William J. Levitt "of Long Island."[5] In 1942, building materials were scarce, and private builders were jockeying for government contracts to build war housing. Leading politicians and government administrators wanted to give the tasks of building

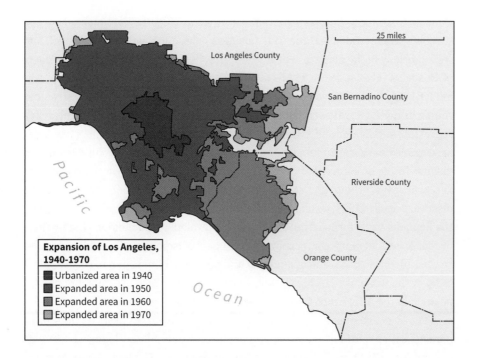

Expansion of Los Angeles, 1940-1970

■ Urbanized area in 1940
■ Expanded area in 1950
■ Expanded area in 1960
■ Expanded area in 1970

49. Los Angeles, map of development. Nathanael Roesch from census data.

war housing to public housing agencies. In the early 1940s, Burns success-fully led a lobbying effort against the "socialistic" plan of the War Production Board to restrict all defense contacts to public agencies.[6] Absorbing the earlier National Home Builders Association in 1943, the NAHB rapidly became the lead-ing trade association for builders and members of building-related enterprises. Chief among its publications was the *Correlator*, a monthly journal for members, renamed the *Journal of Homebuilding* in 1957.[7] The *Correlator*, and its successor, published NAHB prizes, house designs that its editors approved of, and a large amount of information about building products. It reported extensively on the annual conventions held in Chicago and New York, as did the newspapers of New York, Chicago, and Los Angeles. The organization soon established its per-manent headquarters in Washington, DC, and proved to be an effective lobbying organization there. Fritz Burns was the organization's vice chairman in 1943, and in 1945 was made its "honorary president." With centers in three major metro-politan areas and a leadership drawn at least in part from California, the NAHB established a high profile among the nation's builders. In addition to its prizes for neighborhood planning, the NAHB sponsored competitions in house design, and supported college-level degree programs for home builders.

Fritz Burns was twice a millionaire when he took over leadership of the NAHB, but he came from very humble beginnings. He was raised by Catholic German and Irish immigrant grandparents in Minneapolis; at an early age he went to work for a Minneapolis real estate firm. Unenthusiastic about formal schooling, he attended a three-year business course instead of high school, and served briefly in the army in World War I. In 1919, he enrolled in Wharton School of Business (University of Pennsylvania) for a year and then began prospecting for land (for Dickenson & Gillespie, a Minneapolis firm) along new streetcar routes in the East, Midwest and Far West. He soon settled in Los Angeles as a real estate subdivider and salesman (he was not, at this point, a builder); by 1929, his extraordinary skill at finding and selling land had brought him his first million dollars. In the stock market crash and early years of the Great Depression, he lost nearly everything, and eked out a living as a kind of beachcomber. But the discovery of oil in 1934, on one of his few remaining parcels of beach property, laid the financial basis for his future career as a developer and builder. And by then, of course, he had many contacts and a great deal of experience in the Los Angeles real estate market. As land acquisition and home building began to recover after 1934, in the wake of FHA legislation, Burns was well placed to gain a dominant position in the future development of the Los Angeles metropolitan area.

The decisive events in this future career were three: first, Burns's partnership with Fred Marlow, the young engineer and land developer who in 1934 became the FHA's first district director in Southern California and Arizona; second, Burns's early role in the NAHB (1942 and 1943ff.); and third, his collaboration with Henry J. Kaiser from 1945 on. When Burns and Marlowe joined together as developers from 1937 to 1947, Marlow was forced to resign his post with the FHA, but he retained extraordinary influence on planning and building operations in Los Angeles. From Marlow, Burns gained an intimate knowledge of FHA mortgage policies, and FHA guidelines on housing design and street layout. Together, Burns and Marlow laid out and constructed, in quick succession, four important developments: Windsor Hills, 1938–41 (1,500 lots, for which they claimed to have built most of the houses themselves),[8] Westside Village, 1938–40 (788 houses), Toluca Wood, 1941–(400 houses), and the first phase of Westchester, 1941–45 (669 single-family dwellings) in Los Angeles.[9] In 1941, in collaboration with three other builders, they captured the commission for a huge project for defense housing at Westchester: here Burns and Marlow erected a total of 998 dwelling units (669 single-family dwellings) between 1941 and 1945. Immediately after the war's end, in collaboration with Kaiser, Marlow and Burns added another large section of single-family houses to the Westchester development (1945–52, about 1,300 dwellings). In 1947, Kaiser Community Homes began the Panorama City development in the San Fernando Valley near Burbank; this became a self-contained community of about three thousand single-family dwellings, with great influence across the United States. Its houses were widely known, as was the overall plan, for which Burns received a neighborhood planning award in 1949 from the NAHB.[10]

Burns's views and practices changed greatly from 1938 on. During this later period of his career, he evolved from a land developer into a merchant builder with a large role in house design, and moved away from prewar marketing policies that favored the well-to-do. At Windsor Hills (1938–41), a rare hilly site, Burns and Marlow laid out the streets and infrastructure, platted the fifteen hundred lots along curvilinear streets, and promoted and sold the development and its individual houses. But they contracted out the actual house designs and house building to a variety of contractors and architects: to a considerable extent they still acted as subdividers and salesmen, which had been the extent of Burns's role in earlier developments. Marlow introduced new kinds of heavy grading equipment in clearing and grading the land, so that each of the houses rested on a relatively level lot.[11] Paved streets, sidewalks, and drives for the one-car garages were provided; the sidewalks were separated from curbs by manicured grass strips. The look was glossy.

The houses themselves, as Burns and Marlow presented them in their sales brochures, were relatively expensive and elaborate: most frequent was a squarish three-bedroom, one-story house with hip roofs, raised above a garage that was dug into the hill—a prototype of later split-levels, the "La Brea." The more expensive houses (three bedrooms, costing $5,250–6,500, $78,000–96,000 in 2010 dollars) were advertised in sales brochures as offering "stability, prestige and social assurance"; there were references to restrictive covenants. The plans of the houses were relatively formal, with a dining room clearly separated from the living area. But there were also some more modest houses ($1,450–4,000, $21,500–59,000 in 2010 dollars), including an "early California ranch house" and a "Moderne" design (figs. 50, 51); these boasted "Pullman lavatories," "all gas kitchens," and a "superabundance of cupboard space." Sales brochures emphasized construction, which consisted of heavy wood framing on a reinforced concrete slab. The builder of most houses was Joseph Schulte, whom Burns would later make director of his Research Division for Housing.[12] Burns carried on extensive market research in order to influence the choices of Schulte and the other individual builders; he continued this practice in all his later developments.

At contemporary Westside Village (1938–40), at Toluca Wood in 1941, and at Westchester from 1941 to 1943, Burns and Marlow acted as their own house designers, and planned and executed every aspect of the developments themselves, together with their own employees.[13] At around $3,000 ($44,500 in 2010 dollars), the houses of Westside Village and Toluca Wood were less pretentious than those at Windsor Hills; sidewalks, lights, curbs, and finished driveways were not provided as part of the purchase price.[14] (There were also no sidewalks at Toluca Wood.) Westside Village marks the beginning of Burns's efforts at mass building: he and Marlow laid out a "staging area" "where suppliers delivered materials that workers precut and preassembled for eventual trucking

50. Fritz Burns and Fred Marlow, "Moderne," Windsor Hills (1938–41), Los Angeles, exterior and plan. Windsor Hills sales brochure.

51. Fritz Burns and Fred Marlow, "Early California Ranch House," Windsor Hills (1938–41), Los Angeles, exterior and plan. From Windsor Hills sales brochure.

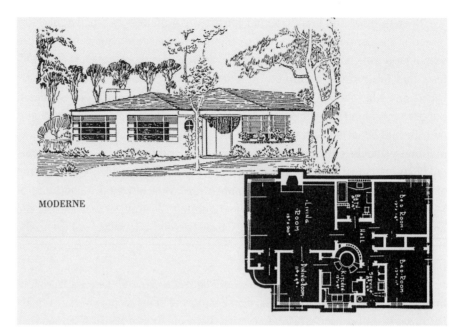

MODERNE

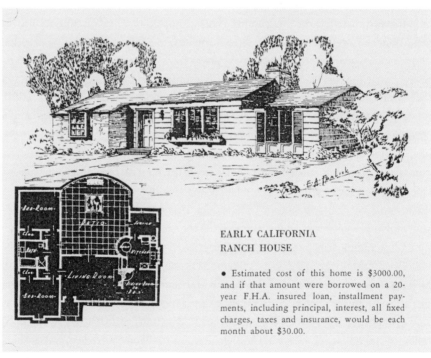

EARLY CALIFORNIA
RANCH HOUSE

● Estimated cost of this home is $3000.00, and if that amount were borrowed on a 20-year F.H.A. insured loan, installment payments, including principal, interest, all fixed charges, taxes and insurance, would be each month about $30.00.

throughout the construction site."[15] Both developments included two- and three-bedroom houses, with 820 to 1,200 square feet of living space (exclusive of garages). They were of wood frame construction, finished in stucco, in several different models of exterior design.[16] But at Westside Village, Burns introduced a standardized plan, which he then continued to use until 1947. This radically simplified plan contained an L-shaped living-dining room, wrapped around a large "eat-in" kitchen at the rear, with the two bedrooms to the right and the garage at the left. The bedrooms and bath were accessed rather directly from the living room; there was no foyer or hall (fig. 52, two-bedroom plan).[17]

Yet despite the minimal simplicity of the new plans, the low cost of the houses, and Burns's 1943 description of himself as always devoted to "the construction of homes in the lower price brackets," Westside Village and Toluca Wood were still marketed as little country estates.[18] Burns's promotional pamphlets showed inhabitants wandering the streets of Toluca Wood on horseback. White picket fencing surrounded the tiny front yards; residents played croquet and badminton or relaxed on a shaded lawn (fig. 53).[19] (At this time, Burns frequently spoke and wrote of the need for separating the classes in new housing developments.)[20] The first phase of Westchester, on the other hand, contained war housing, intended primarily for employees (male and female) at nearby Douglas Aircraft, which was marketed differently.[21] At $3,890 to $4,790 in 1942 ($52,000–64,000 in 2010 dollars), nine models (including the Rancho, Suburban, Cape Cod, Victory, and Defender) promised particular bathroom fixtures, electric water heaters, "easy housekeeping," and, if desired, full furnishing, to "the families of war workers," appealing, by implication, to women workers. These "compact and economical" houses were billed as "the low cost housing triumph of the century"; and this time, they came supplied with sewers, paved streets, sidewalks, and driveways (fig. 54).[22] Government financing helped to provide these amenities, but it is also clear that the status of the Marlow-Burns portion

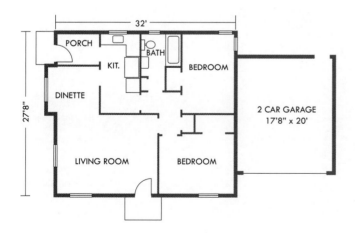

52. Fritz Burns, Westside Village, Los Angeles, 1938–40, two-bedroom model, plan. Nathanael Roesch.

of Westchester as part of a much larger planned community also contributed to their inclusion.[23] In Westchester, Burns began to think of himself as a "community builder" for low-cost homes.

In May 1945, two weeks after VE Day, Fritz Burns and Henry J. Kaiser announced the formation of their new partnership, Kaiser Community Homes (KCH). Over the next eight years, KCH constructed more than 5,000 houses, most of them in the Los Angeles area, and about 1,300 of them at Westchester in the second phase of its development. Nourished by the continuing presence of Douglas, Hughes, Northrup, and North American aircraft manufacturers, and by the growth of adjacent Los Angeles Municipal Airport, Westchester reached a population of approximately 25,000 in 1948 and contained about 8,000 dwelling units by 1953. Of these, Burns and Marlow, and Burns, Marlow, and Kaiser, were responsible for building about 2,500, over both eras of Westchester's development.[24]

At first, KCH seemed an unlikely partnership. Kaiser was an industrialist of national and even international fame. He was one of the principal builders of the Hoover, Bonneville, and Grand Coulee Dams; during the war his West Coast companies had constructed some 1,500 ships, a substantial portion of the US fleet.[25] His shipbuilding had made him something of a national hero, and he gained

53. Fritz Burns, Toluca Wood, Los Angeles, 1944, view of front yard. Toluca Wood sales brochure, Fritz B. Burns Papers, Loyola Marymount University.

54. Westchester, early street view. "Dick" Whittington Studio, Huntington Library, San Marino, CA.

great influence in Washington. He had also constructed the country's largest tracts of war housing: the best known is Vanport, Oregon, a settlement of 10,000 units (and a total population of 42,000) that housed workers in nearby Kaiser shipyards.[26] Two further tracts furnished 16,000 units of housing for workers in Kaiser shipyards at Richmond, California.[27] Kaiser, in other words, was used to large-scale thinking and doing. He was also a man of considerable social conscience, of a practical and efficient kind: Vanport provided round-the-clock day care services and comprehensive health care for Kaiser workers (presumably intended—at least in part—to increase their productivity). He had founded Kaiser Permanente, one of America's first HMOs, for workers on the Grand Coulee Dam, and continued to endorse the notion that working-class settlements should have access to full health care coverage.

In 1944, Kaiser began to search for peacetime outlets for his industrial might. He developed his cement and steel operations, began producing aluminum and gypsum, and started manufacturing automobiles and a variety of household products. And he decided to build low-cost houses, which he believed could be prefabricated, whole, out of steel, aluminum, or plastic.[28] He thought that these new dwellings could be produced at the rate of ten thousand per year, and that they would form great new towns, "complete communities," "ideal communities [of] work, of worship, of learning and of play." The first ads for KCH (fig. 55) showed apparently infinite numbers of such dwellings stretching across the nation. Kaiser's grandiose plans for postwar housing were jubilantly announced in the nation's newspapers, and helped to produce widespread belief, for a few years after the war, in the possibility of virtually instant housing and new towns.[29] These ideas led him to Burns.

55. Kaiser/Burns advertisement, ca. 1946.

56. Fritz Burns, Construction, Westchester, Los Angeles, 1941. University of Southern California.

In 1945, Burns had never built a housing development of more than a thousand units, and he had built them by relatively conservative methods and certainly without off-site prefabrication. On the other hand, Burns had a presence in the capital, as honorary president of the NAHB, and he was beginning to be known nationally as the champion of free enterprise within the housing industry. He was already (before the Levitts) one of the largest builders of houses in the country, and his war housing at Westchester I had set a much higher standard than war housing anywhere else. There is no evidence that Burns ever subscribed to Kaiser's plans for huge-scale construction or prefabrication; rather, Kaiser gradually adapted his ideas to Burns's construction methods, which proved to be much more efficient and economical (fig. 56). Their houses at Westchester II resembled very closely Burns and Marlow's earlier houses at Westchester I, with the significant exception that they provided attractive prefabricated storage walls between the bedrooms, setting a new standard for closet space in new dwellings (fig. 57). KCH houses at Westchester II came to be almost universally known throughout the building industry by 1947, largely perhaps because of the enormous publicity surrounding Kaiser's claims.

Neither the second phase at Westchester, nor the other (rather small) early developments built by KCH afforded an opportunity for community planning.[30]

The only such opportunity they had, in fact, was at Panorama City in the San Fernando Valley, which they began to develop in 1947 and completed in 1952. Panorama City spread over 800 acres, and eventually contained about 3,000 dwellings, of which about 2,000 were constructed by KCH. Burns had been negotiating to buy the "Panorama Ranch," a dairy farm, since August 1944; in 1947, Burns had purchased the first 400 acres above Roscoe Boulevard in what was then the Van Nuys district of the San Fernando Valley, from the Panorama Ranch. Another 400 acres, south of Roscoe, was purchased not long thereafter (from a different landholder); KCH developed the eastern half of this second tract, while the western half was developed by a closely associated firm.[31] Housing construction began in 1948: the KCH portions of Panorama City totaled 2,500 housing units by the end of 1950. (Some of these were "duplexes," that is, twin houses.) The location was quite distant from downtown Los Angeles, and separated from it by the Santa Monica Mountains. But Lockheed Aircraft in Burbank was six miles away, and the opening of a new General Motors plant, announced in 1945 (it did not actually open until February 1948) was expected to provide 1,500 new jobs. Schlitz and Anheuser-Busch soon established nearby facilities that employed over two thousand workers.[32] Burns and Kaiser also envisioned a large new shopping center located along the western edge of the city: begun in 1950, this complex housed "eighty retail stores and some of LA's first major department stores. . . . San Fernando Valley residents . . . made it their virtual downtown."[33] Panorama City's population was therefore drawn from workers and management in nearby manufacturing industries, but also from the service industries of the shopping center. It also attracted quite a number of residents who worked in the entertainment industry in Burbank and Hollywood. Over time and partly as a result of his involvement in war housing, Burns's earlier insistence on building only for the white middle and upper middle classes had faded away. Now, he rejected economic and social stratification in new neighborhoods as "un-American." And, according to salesmen interviewed by James Keane, "by 1949 Burns' sales crews did not enforce racial restrictions."[34]

The first plan of the new community (fig. 58), published in 1946 by the Los Angeles City Planning Commission, showed the streets above Roscoe Boulevard, reaching to Osborne in the north, and stretching from Van Nuys Boulevard in the west to Woodman Avenue in the east. This is the part of the plan that has been most extensively studied so far; Greg Hise has shown it to be a collaborative effort of KCH engineers and Planning Commission members.[35] The curvilinear character of the streets marked a radical break from the traditions of grid planning in Los Angeles and Orange County. The actual development was much larger than the plan published by the Planning Commission, however: it followed a plan that I have derived from the tract maps of 1948–50 (fig. 59).[36] The second plan shows a community almost double in size, and reaching beyond Woodman in the east to include an area that Kaiser had set aside for a hospital.[37] Roscoe Boulevard was not yet a major through road, and the later layout shows a great deal of consistency in terms of north-south street arrangements, so I think it is correct to look closely at this later plan.[38] The engineer who laid out the streets in both the north and south portions of the community was Thomas A.

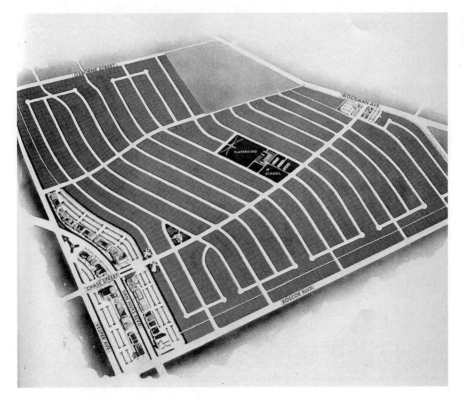

58. Panorama City, first plan, 1946. Los Angeles City Planning Commission.

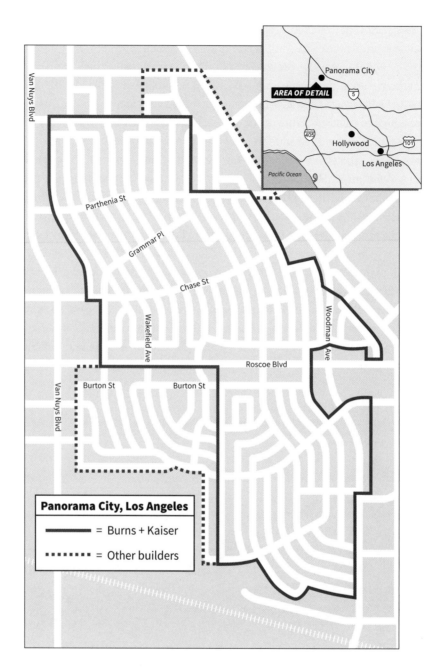

Panorama City, Los Angeles

— = Burns + Kaiser

••••• = Other builders

59. Panorama City, plan based on official tract maps, showing final boundaries, and areas developed by Burns and Kaiser. Barbara Miller Lane and Nathanael Roesch.

Jordan of the Los Angeles Engineering Service Corporation, a man of long experience in planning, and the author, among others, of the plan for Hollywood Hills in the 1940s.[39] The Panorama City plan is a rather curious affair, a kind of bent and twisted version of a typical Los Angeles grid, with most of the long north-south streets forming T-intersections before they reach the major boundary thoroughfares. At the center of the northern section, eleven acres were set aside for a school and playground facilities; other parcels were sold at cost to churches and private schools.[40] No parks were included in the plan, aside from the central area around the school.

The site of Panorama City is flat, so these street arrangements were dictated by contemporary concerns with street and neighborhood planning, rather than by site-specific considerations. In 1936, 1938, and 1941, the FHA had published guides to successful neighborhood planning, which emphasized the importance of open space, community facilities, and streets protected from through traffic. Radburn, New Jersey, with its curving streets, had been held up as a good model in these publications (fig. 43).[41] The importance of curving streets had been endorsed by the NAHB at an early date; many of the larger builders of the first postwar years adopted these patterns in their housing developments.[42] Burns and Marlow had employed slightly curvilinear plans (on a much smaller scale) at Windsor Hills in 1938, where curves were required by the hilliness of the site, and in the second phase of Westchester. Whatever the proximate sources of the Panorama City plan, it won Burns a prestigious award for neighborhood planning from the NAHB early in 1949.[43]

At Panorama City, one can already observe the full-fledged sales and advertising techniques that would be characteristic of tract house marketing in the fifties and sixties. Full-page ads invited readers to showings of model homes, listed their contents, and offered exterior drawings. When one "unit" of houses was sold out, the next would be "opened" with a "new line" (seldom different from the older one). Repetitive phrases and slogans gave readers mottos to remember: Panorama City offered "homes for the thrifty" with "innovations never before found in any house"; it contained "22 miles of homes"; it was "a city where a city belongs." And Burns was a magnificent huckster: low-flying aerial photographers took pictures of moving vans converging on a single street (the presence of the vans had been artfully orchestrated beforehand); an early house at Panorama City (fully furnished) was given away as a prize on Art Linkletter's nationally popular *People Are Funny* radio show.[44] Next to the sales offices, there were fifteen model houses on display, fully furnished by Barker Brothers furniture company, where potential purchasers could make their choices among different exteriors, plans, rooflines, and exterior and interior finishes. One could visit the models during the day, of course, but also during "moonlight tours." The models had names: the Coronado, the New Englander, the Windsor; and the best-selling two- and three-bedroom "California ranch house" series—the Coronado, the Del Mar, the Catalina, and the Ramona—designed for KCH by architect Welton Becket.[45]

In his earlier housing developments, Burns had not used an architect (though many participated at Windsor Hills); unlike many other states, California did not require an architect's signature as the legal precondition for a building permit. Howard Hunter Clayton, a Los Angeles artist, had appeared as a "designer" in the earlier Burns developments, but Burns was proud of his own standardized house plans as he developed them at Toluca Wood, Westside Village, and Westchester (fig. 52). Early sales at Panorama City were slow, however, and Burns had already become acquainted with Welton Becket in building the "Research House" of 1946, which had received immense local and national publicity.[46] It seemed that Becket's name might help sales. Becket, then, was brought in, in the summer of 1948, to "collaborate" in the design of KCH's new California ranch house models at Panorama City.[47]

Becket's ranch houses largely abandoned Burns's earlier standard plan, merging the earlier dining ell into an expanded living room (fig. 60).[48] The storage walls developed at Westchester were retained, but the interior spaces were, within their very small footprint (750 square feet), much more open. The "Ramona Ranch" version featured a slanted, gable-shaped ("cathedral") ceiling with exposed rafters over the main living space. The ceilings were "tongue & groove planks of Douglas fir, with beams and planks finished in desert colors to bring out the natural beauty of the wood."[49] Even more important, the external profile was exceptionally low,[50] with a sweeping gable roof, so that the Ramona Ranch now for the first time took visual advantage of the low and spreading proportions implicit in the ranch house type (fig. 61).[51] The ads recognized these formal changes, pointing out the "fresh, clean, sweeping lines and good form of the 'new look' in architecture."[52] From the beginning of 1949, the great majority of

60. Welton Becket, plan for "California Ranch House" series, Panorama City, 1948. Nathanael Roesch from original in Welton Becket Archive.

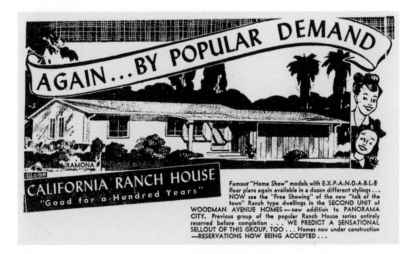

61. Fritz Burns with Welton Becket, Ramona Ranch, 1948–49. Restored by Nathanael Roesch from a newspaper advertisement of September 1949.

houses at Panorama City followed some of these features of Becket's pattern.

Because Fritz Burns adopted the ranch label for his earliest tract houses, at Toluca Wood in 1941 and in the first phase of his Westchester houses (1941–44), some writers see Burns as the originator of the ranch house form of the 1950s.[53] But Burns's earlier houses were not well known outside California at the time, nor were they, at least before the war, intended for lower-income buyers. And while it is possible to find isolated occurrences of large one-story houses with attached garages described as "ranch" houses on the East Coast and Midwest from about 1941, these were not yet serving as models for new tract houses.[54] But the California ranch house series at Panorama City represented a turning point in the development of the ranch house, in both California and the nation. Let us consider the broader evolution of the ranch house in the United States to pinpoint the role of the Panorama City ranches.

The Development of the Ranch House

In contrast to other postwar house types, the ranch house has attracted enormous attention in many different spheres. Architectural historians have debated its formal origins at length, and writers for newspapers, magazines, and the Internet have written and posted reams of commentary on its history. This interest is partially due to the popularity of what one might call the ranch house revival today. Ranch houses of the 1950s are now attracting young buyers who are busy restoring them. New popular magazines, like *Atomic Ranch*, celebrate the type. Partly in consequence of this "retro" enthusiasm, ranch house developments like that at Panorama City are attaining historic district status. Another reason for the widespread interest is that the development of the ranch house raises important questions about the connections between "high" architecture, "vernacular" architecture, and tract house building, and about the relations between regional architecture and American architecture as a whole. Can we trace the origin of the ranch house back to an indigenous California vernacular architecture? Can we argue for the decisive influence of Frank Lloyd Wright, perhaps the greatest of American architects, and one who was, generally speaking, independent of regional traditions? Or on the other hand, to William Wurster, the modern reinterpreter of California traditions before he became dean at MIT? Or to Cliff May, influential California builder turned publicist? How "modern" was (and is) the ranch house? Did it have affinities with the International Style of modernism? The questions, at every level of scholarship and popular writing, go on and on.

In order to understand the evolution of the ranch house in tract house developments it is necessary first to separate the history of the name and the history of the house type. The ranch house label for the one-story single-family dwelling has its roots in the Southwest (and especially in California), where the original Spanish land grants were known as "ranchos." As these huge pieces of land were broken up and sold, the original label was often retained for the subsequent parts. Thus a new parcel would have a legal description showing its origin in one of the original ranchos. The dwellings of the original ranch owners mostly had two stories, though their employees often lived in one-story housing. In the twentieth century a house on one of the subsidiary parcels slowly acquired the label "ranch house" too. As noted above, one of the architect-builders affiliated with Burns at Windsor Hills in 1938 labeled his houses "old California Ranch" (fig. 51); thereafter, Burns began to describe his small development houses as "ranchos."[55] For Burns and his builders, the term seemed to have the same kind of resonance as "farm" or "estate" had for East Coast builders: it suggested affiliation with an older, and much grander, housing tradition.

In the rest of the country, a wider audience also learned about "ranch houses." In 1931, *House Beautiful* began to apply the label to a variety of houses that appeared to draw upon an indigenous California housing tradition, and the nomenclature was picked up by the *New York Times* in 1935 and by *Architectural Forum* in 1937. During the thirties and early forties, excitement about California and "the West" grew throughout the nation, bringing with it enthusiasm for all things western, including the idea of the great ranch. As the original ranchos had been broken up early in the twentieth century, some had been equipped with resort-like facilities for visiting sportsmen, who could see themselves, when on vacation, as cowboys or as hunters in the wilderness.[56] Increasingly in the twenties and thirties, owners of parts of the old ranchos established "dude ranches" that offered vacations on horseback to athletic and wealthy people; these were imitated, first in the Midwest, and then on the East Coast. By the forties and fifties, dude ranches were a winter vacation spot for middle-class sportsmen and their families too. The vacation dwellings of the dude ranches featured "western" or "southwestern" themes: Rancho Nezhone in Arizona, for example, refurbished its resort in 1944 with "Spanish-style furniture" and a barbecue pit. Others placed adobe buildings around shuffleboard courts.[57]

During the depression and war years, too, westerns like John Ford's *Stagecoach* (1939) dramatized settings in the West in which the good, personified as a cowboy, usually acting alone, triumphs over evil. Westerns helped to spread enthusiasm for ranches and images associated with them throughout the nation. Thus, excitement about western traditions and mores grew from the 1930s onward, and increasingly the glamour of Hollywood—its movies, their plots, their stars—enhanced this excitement. The western movie became a national favorite. Actual experience of California broadened as well: during the war, servicemen bound for the Pacific shipped out from California bases, their families in tow. Each of the builders discussed in chapter 3 had had some experience in California.

Thus, when the Levitts adopted the "ranch" label for their first houses in Long Island that were offered for sale, houses that bore no resemblance to any California tradition, the label already had a good deal of resonance across the nation. The "ranch house" label for builders' houses was especially common in the Midwest during the middle forties, right after the war. Some of these houses were quite similar in plan to the typical ranch house of the fifties, but lacked the garage that gave the later type its distinctive profile.[58] Quoting a survey of buyer preferences, the *Chicago Tribune* reported a midwestern and western preference for one-story houses in January 1946; among one-story models the largest vote nationally went to the "Cape Cod" cottage, but the second largest went to the "ranch house."[59]

Long before the ranch house *name* gained resonance, the one-story house *type* (without any particular association with ranches) had a long history in the United States. A one-story adobe tradition existed throughout the South and West, evolving from modest prototypes used by farmhands during the period of Spanish settlement. Cape Cod cottages, small one- or one-and-a-half-story houses with very simple plans, had been built in New England from the seventeenth century onward, and experienced several revivals.[60] The one-story bungalow was popular in Chicago and other midwestern cities, and in Southern California in the first decades of the twentieth century.[61] Also prevalent from the nineteenth century on, especially in the Midwest and Far West, were simple urban workers' cottages, sometimes one-story at ground level, sometimes a main story set above a ground-level basement.[62]

In the first few years after World War I, the one-story house came to be seen as a good low-cost alternative to the larger two-story houses of most American cities and suburbs. In 1923, the Home Owners Service Institute published a great number of these in *The Book of a Thousand Homes: Volume 1 containing 500 plans of Moderate Cost.* Some of these houses had a simplified floor plan, without dining room, parlor, or porch, foreshadowing the ranch house of the 1950s. With the onset of the Depression, the attention of builders turned again to one-story houses as an inexpensive housing alternative, especially in warm climates, where, it was argued, the builder could avoid excavating a basement.[63] President Hoover's "Own Your Own Home" campaign encouraged the idea that home ownership by low-income people represented a bulwark against socialism, and his administration (1929–33) encouraged the growth of such small-house organizations as the Better Houses in America group and the Home Modernizing Bureau.[64] Hoover also helped to introduce new long-term mortgages to stimulate house construction. In 1934, the Division of Subsistence Homesteads of the Department of the Interior began to provide farmsteads to new settlers under the title "Rurban Homes." Small settlements (ca. 200 houses) were constructed under this program at El Monte, California, Gardendale Homesteads, Alabama, and Jersey Homesteads, Hightstown, New Jersey, settlements that may have provided models, both formal and in construction methods, for later one-story houses.[65] Kit builders and pattern book publishers like Sears Roebuck, Aladdin, and Garlinghouse were quick to respond.[66] In 1940, nearly all Aladdin models were small, one-story dwellings.[67]

It was only after the United States entered the war, however, that large-scale housing tracts were needed—for defense industries and at the bases of the armed services. In these tracts, speed of construction was essential, and it is here that we can see the beginning of important innovations in materials and

62. Levitt brothers, Oakdale Farms, Norfolk, VA, 1942–43, two-bedroom house exterior. *American Builder*, June 1942.

63. Levitt brothers, Oakdale Farms two-bedroom house, plan. Nathanael Roesch from *American Builder*, June 1942.

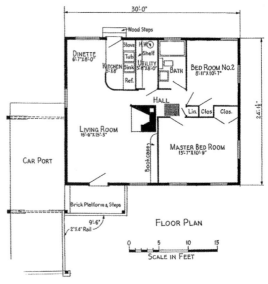

64. William W. Wurster, Miller House, Carmel, CA. 1935. Wurster, Bernardi & Emmons Collection, Environmental Design Archives, University of California, Berkeley.

construction methods.[68] The Levitts' housing of 1942–43 at Oakdale Farms and Riverdale, at the naval base in Norfolk, Virginia, was probably the most progressive of its time in these areas.

At Oakdale Farms, the 700-square-feet houses, with two bedrooms and an attached carport, were erected on a brick subfloor with no basement; at Riverdale, 630-square-feet row houses (duplexes) were built of concrete block on concrete slabs. The Riverdale duplexes had a combination dining area and kitchen, and were extraordinarily compact.[69] The Oakdale houses, with their attached carports, had something of the look of later ranches, but neither the slab construction nor the name (figs. 62, 63). The Levitts did not actually build anything resembling the typical ranch houses of the forties and fifties until they began Levittown, Pennsylvania, in 1952.[70]

In the thirties and early forties, a few leading American architects responded to nationwide interest in house design by elaborating on the one-story house. On the West Coast, R. M. Schindler (Schindler/Chase House, 1921–22) and Richard Neutra (Miller House, ca. 1937; "Small House in an Orchard," ca. 1939) were influenced by European modernism, which of course gave great prominence to house design. On the West Coast, too, William Wurster designed rustic-looking one-story dwellings, houses that California architectural historians often cite as precedents for the ranch house (fig. 64).[71] On the East Coast, Royal Barry Wills (1895–1962) spearheaded a popular colonial revival movement in both small and medium-size houses (fig. 65). Devoted primarily to the Cape Cod cottage type, Wills was greatly admired in Massachusetts for his craftsmanship, and had some national reputation via articles in *Life* magazine and *Saturday Evening Post*.[72] From 1939 on, he also published well-received books about one-story colonial house types.[73] Frank Lloyd Wright had drawn upon midwestern American

65. Royal Barry Wills, one-story house, ca. 1937. *Pencil Points*, February 1937.

66. Frank Lloyd Wright, Jacobs House, 1937. Photo by Guerrero.

traditions in his prairie houses, but by the time he came to build his one-story Usonian houses (1936–39) (fig. 66), he had transformed these traditions into his own truly modern yet personal idiom. Of all those American architects who are said to have elevated domestic architecture to the status of a high art in twentieth century, Wright was the most prolific, published, and innovative and the one with the largest national reputation by war's end.[74] It is possible to suggest some connection between the work of these architects and that of the builders I have studied, but it is never obvious that the connection amounted to "influence." While Wright and other prominent architects sometimes engaged with the problems of small house design during depression and war, their accomplishments in this design type were not great, and they sought above all to build large houses for wealthy patrons; their houses were therefore not easily seen as models for small or inexpensive dwellings. It is more likely that these architects, so often seen as providing inspiration to tract house builders, were instead responding to the same economic needs and cultural forces that produced American small house types in the first place. The architects of the fifties and sixties, however, learned from their elders, and at the same time from the builders who were successfully developing new types of mass housing.

Between 1946 and 1948, the picture changed. In 1948, the Garlinghouse pattern book series included a volume solely devoted to *Ranch and Suburban Homes*;[75] the same year, the Aladdin catalog noted that "present day homebuilders have shown a tremendous interest in Western Ranch House Architecture" (32).[76] Early in 1948, Kimball Hill began producing minimal-size ranch houses in the Park Ridge Manor section of Chicago; by mid-1948, the young Chicago architect-builder A. J. Del Bianco was making a reputation as a specialist in ranch houses. By the end of 1948, a Philadelphia builder was offering a "one-story ranch house [with] modern brick fireplace . . . and interior wood paneling."[77] In 1949, Broomall, Pennsylvania, builder Frank Facciolo was marketing his "California Cliff House," a flat-roofed "ranch," the Campanellis were building ranch houses outside Boston, and ranch houses dominated the market, according to advertising and newspaper reports, in suburban Chicago, New York, New Jersey, and Washington. Occasionally the houses were described as "Californian" or "western," but usually the label "ranch" appeared as well. In the summer of 1949, the *Washington Post* characterized this distinctive new kind of house: "The low, rambling, many-windowed house [is] today's successor to the substantial home of yesterday. This 'ranch house' seems stark in its severity, humble in its crouching pose at first glance. It is not self-sufficient nor withdrawn like the houses of the past, . . . because the modern family's life is closely tied up with the community. It is not imposing nor decorative because 'face' is now sought by other means than the towering mansion. Light, air, convenience, comfort, economy— these are the goals of today's householder."[78]

Perhaps this union of the type and the name would have occurred naturally, but the writings of California builder Cliff May in 1946 played a major part in the process. Collaborating with *Sunset* magazine, Southern California's popular magazine depicting "western" lifestyles, Cliff May (1909–89) published a small book called *Sunset Western Ranch Houses* in 1946. An instant bestseller, it sold about fifty thousand copies the first year, and many subsequent printings and separate editions followed between 1946 and 1955.[79] This publishing success led May to become a consultant to *House Beautiful* magazine in 1946; the magazine published his work lavishly from 1948 onward. May's life and work have been the subject of so much adulatory writing, from so many points of view, that it is hard to untangle the sequences of his career and possible influences.[80] The book of 1946 (unlike his later books, published in the late 1950s) did not foreground

May's own work, but examined some aspects of the history of California ranch houses, and then sought to connect that history to the work of California architects and builders of the 1930s and 1940s.[81]

Cliff May was born in San Diego, and grew up in adobe houses built by former rancheros. He began his career as a furniture designer, and then, in the early thirties in San Diego and Los Angeles, began to build custom houses at least partially modeled upon the dwellings of his youth.[82] In 1939, he began his first small housing development, Riviera Ranch, in Los Angeles. During the war, he built barracks for defense workers. His design and workmanship were greatly respected in the Los Angeles area; in 1940 he became president of the Los Angeles division of the Building Contractors' Association. But his major achievements as a builder occurred only *after* the publication of *Sunset Western Ranch Houses.* In 1950, he began to develop, together with his architect and partner Chris Choate (1908–81), a system of prefabricated wall systems that the two marketed for low-cost houses until 1955.[83] We will meet him again later in this chapter, collaborating with builder Ross Cortese and again with Choate, using these wall systems to create a housing development near Lakewood.

Sunset Western Ranch Houses began with a brief history of the nineteenth-century houses of the original ranchos, a history that emphasized one-story

67. Machado House, San Diego, CA, 1830–35. Cliff May, *Sunset Western Ranch Houses*, 1946.

68. Cliff May, designer, ranch house. May, *Sunset Western Ranch Houses*, 1946.

examples (fig. 67). May then laid out a longer analysis of why these forms were appropriate to the present. The latter parts were illustrated by drawings and photographs of May's own early houses, together with some by other California architects, especially William Wurster.[84] Some of the houses of his own that he chose to illustrate were modest in size, but many were large and "rambling," surrounded by extensive landscaping (fig. 68). Some had stables and horses, others were appropriate to "city" lots of sixty feet. A great deal of wood appeared on the interiors; some living rooms had cathedral ceilings with boards and rafters showing; in others, the walls were paneled in wood. Many had continuous spaces for living, eating, and cooking (fig. 69). Nearly all had a "barbecue" in the kitchen or patio. The western ranch house as adapted to the present, the author said, provided informally planned "livable space," gardens that are "not stage sets" but "designed . . . to be lived in"; and, by spreading out "like an oak tree," made possible both "spaciousness [and] indoor-outdoor living." May addressed the book to builders: by using these forms, today's builders could be satisfied that they have achieved "the most pleasant, comfortable living possible from the [available] materials and money."[85] In its 1946 edition and its later printings up to 1955, *Sunset Western Ranch Houses* came to be very widely known. Its illustrations and ideas could inspire large and elaborate rambling structures (and some of May's future designs would be of this type),[86] but also could appeal to builders who wanted to build more modest structures. The book also appealed powerfully to the desire among postwar buyers for an informal lifestyle (see chapter 5). May provided a wide public, builders and buyers alike, not so much with models for modern ranch houses, but with an attractive set of ideas about them.

69. Cliff May, designer, kitchen/dining area. May, *Sunset Western Ranch Houses*, 1946.

Fritz Burns adapted May's ideas for a builder's market in the "California Ranch House" series at Panorama City, and especially in the "Ramona Ranch," the version that sold best and received the most publicity.[87] A model of the Ramona Ranch was constructed for the 1949 Home Show, and attracted six thousand visitors per day in mid-June; it was re-erected in Panorama City for "moonlight" showings during National Home Week in September.[88] The house was first published nationally in *Architectural Forum*'s April 1949 issue on "The Builder's House." Then, in October of the same year, *Better Homes and Gardens* gave the building a five-page full-color spread and put the living room on the cover of the issue (fig. 70).[89] While my research indicates that builders rarely read architectural magazines and only occasionally consulted publications like *House Beautiful* and *Better Homes and Gardens*, it seems likely that they would have read special journal and magazine issues devoted to builders' houses. Some buyers may also have read the *House Beautiful* and *Better Homes and Gardens* issues, or at least have heard of them through realtors.[90]

The Ramona Ranch was far more appealing than earlier Burns houses and different in design. It hugged the ground and was longer and thinner, so that its profile was more elegant (fig. 61). The space was used with great efficiency. The attached two-car garage was billed as convertible into an extra bedroom or recreation room. But the most unusual features were the interior sloping ceilings

70. Fritz Burns with Welton Becket, Ramona Ranch, living room, 1948–49. *Better Homes and Gardens*, cover detail, October 1949.

71. Fritz Burns with Welton Becket, Ramona Ranch, 1948–49, patio, *Better Homes and Gardens*, October 1949.

with exposed wood rafters and tongue-and-groove planks of Douglas fir (fig. 70).[91] Modern-looking furniture with a hint of rusticity complemented the wood ceilings and the wood paneling (vertical grain Douglas fir) between living room and kitchen. At the rear, behind the garage, was a paved patio and planting bed (fig. 71).[92] Public attention focused on the Ramona Ranch partly because of its low price (ca. $8,000 for the two bedroom, $73,300 in 2010 dollars) and elegant looks, and partly because of its name and associations.[93]

Ramona was the title of a popular romance by Helen Hunt Jackson, first published in 1884. Jackson's fictional Ramona was the adopted daughter of a Southern California Mexican ranchero family, half American Indian and half Scots herself, who falls in love with an American Indian sheepherder, and marries him. After an idyllic interlude in Ramona's husband's village home, they are driven out by Anglo usurpers; the husband is murdered, and Ramona returns to her adoptive family, with whom she moves to Mexico City. The novel is important not only in its romantic theme, and in its homage to both the Indian and Hispanic

72. Home of Ramona, fruit box label, early twentieth century. Huntington Library.

populations of the early years of Southern California, but also because of its vivid descriptions of local places. The Ramona story gained a cult following in the subsequent century, with tourists from all over the country searching for "Ramona's grave," "Ramona's marriage place," and "Ramona's ranch." Entrepreneurs of tourism took advantage of the cult, so that several specific ranch houses have come to be known as Ramona's ranch.[94] Merchandisers from perfume companies to fruit packagers used a great variety of "Ramona" images to market their products (fig. 72). By 1936 no fewer than five movies had been devoted to the Ramona story.[95] If, as is often alleged, Fritz Burns's sales agreements prohibited not only African Americans but also Mexican Americans as buyers in Panorama City, this choice of name may seem particularly cynical.[96] But because of Ramona's romantic story, the name sold houses, and Burns was a gifted merchandiser.

Not all "ranch houses" after the Ramona Ranch displayed the same rustic qualities. But the Ramona Ranch of 1949, and the *Sunset* publications of 1946–55, firmly fixed the ranch house idea in the public mind, and in attitudes of builders and realtors. The label "ranch house" endowed the older small one-story house type, now with its attached garage and larger lot, with the flavor of wide-open spaces, "western" informality, rugged individualism, "indoor-outdoor living," the romance of Hollywood and its cowboys, and the lure of California.

Orange County: Vandruff, Cortese, and Disneyland

Burns and Kaiser were the first in the LA area to develop the ranch house as a prototype for mass housing. In the twenty years after Panorama City's California ranch house series, the ranch house appeared in houses for all income levels,

taking over the urban landscape of Los Angeles and Orange County. In its larger and more luxurious versions (fig. 73), it swelled to over three thousand square feet and sold for high prices. (Such a house looked like a ranch from the street, but the rear would have two additional wings, forming a U, with the relatively small lot almost entirely built over.) In its least expensive versions, as in the Mexican American suburb of Pico Rivera, it was a tiny L-shaped structure not much bigger than the Ramona Ranch, and sometimes on a smaller lot (0.16 acres at Pico Rivera, for example). Low to midprice models covered acre after acre of Orange County from about 1955 to 1970. Built by a great many different builders, they closely resembled one another (fig. 74); most of them added a bedroom (sometimes two) and a half bath in the fifties, but lot sizes remained comparable to those in Panorama City.

The most rapid growth of the fifties and sixties in the Los Angeles area took place to the southeast of the city, in the western portions of Orange County. The location of oil industries in Huntington Beach, together with the establishment

73. Ranch house, Tarzana, CA, ca. 1960. Photo by the author.

74. Ranch houses near Buena Park, CA, late 1950s, modern view. Photo by the author.

of the Los Alamitos Naval Air Station and the Santa Ana Army Air Base, gave the county great importance in the war effort; after the war, veterans often wanted to return there. With its miles of beaches and fruit trees, Orange County already in the forties seemed like a resort area. With the opening of Disneyland in Anaheim in 1955 and the contemporaneous growth of Knott's Berry Farm in Buena Park,[97] the western part of the county took on the appearance of a major recreational center, and in fact much of its future growth was fed by tourism. Aerospace firms and light industry began to locate in the county in the later 1950s, further fueling growth. Population grew sevenfold from 1950 to 1970.[98]

In Orange County, at least in its western portions, the old ranchos had been much more fully broken up in the early twentieth century than was the case in Los Angeles County. Larger tracts were scarce by the fifties, but smaller ones changed hands with great rapidity. In the fifties, there was a great deal of annexation competition, with older towns like Anaheim and Long Beach absorbing new territory, while newer towns along the county border like Buena Park were incorporated and proceeded to annex neighboring parcels. These newly annexed parcels were then developed by small builders in collaboration with town officials. In contrast to Los Angeles County, the establishment of countywide supervision of the development process in Orange County proceeded only rather slowly. But a dominant street grid, laid out earlier in the century, reached from Lakewood and Long Beach in the west to Santa Ana in the east, and thus controlled the pattern of growth to some extent. In this context, a large number of small builders began (and sometimes quickly ended) their careers in the mid-fifties, building small developments of rather uniform-looking ranch houses with evocative names like Lucky Western Homes, Enchanted Park, Happy Homes, Rancho La Palma, or Circle Arrow Ranchos.[99] The interior streets within each tract were occasionally curvilinear, but most were not. Some of these builders, like William L. Lyon, grew large and became major home builders in other locations; others lapsed into obscurity. Most of the ranch houses in Orange County were larger than those at Panorama City (usually three and four bedrooms, with one and a half to two baths); prices were higher and increased over time with inflation.[100] Many attempted to offer some version of luxury, or at least the appearance of luxury. And some drew inspiration from nearby Disneyland and its fantasies of past and future.[101]

Cinderella Homes

Cinderella Homes (1955–61), owned by Jean Valjean Vandruff (1922–), was an example of this type.[102] It is also one of the smallest among my case studies. Jean Vandruff grew up in a family of poor Oklahoma ranch hands and tenant farmers.[103] As a teenager, he took a course in sheet metal work, which allowed him to leave home in 1941 and work for the Douglas Aircraft plant in El Segundo, just south of the areas of Westchester that Burns began to develop at that time. One brother joined him there, and his parents left the farm for work in war industries in San Pedro at about the same time. Vandruff then enlisted in the Army Air Corps, which trained him as a pilot; in the last year of the war he flew bombers in the Philippines, Borneo, and the South Pacific. Returning to Los Angeles, he attended architecture school at USC for two years, then left to try his hand as a builder of custom homes. (He obtained a builder's license.) Soon (1950) he formed a partnership with his elder brother Shannon; together they obtained commissions for about six custom designs per year. Between 1955 and 1957, the brothers were able to acquire three tracts of land in Anaheim, partially contiguous, from portions of what had once been Rancho Los Alamitos.[104] Here they turned to the speculative building of what they called "Cinderella Homes"; they constructed 869 dwellings in the three tracts, laying out the streets on a modified grid within the larger grid of Anaheim's streets and roads, curving some of the interior streets, and adding a few cul-de-sacs (figs. 75, 76).[105] Thereafter,

75. Cinderella Homes, subdivisions in Anaheim, CA, 1955–57, map. Nathanael Roesch.

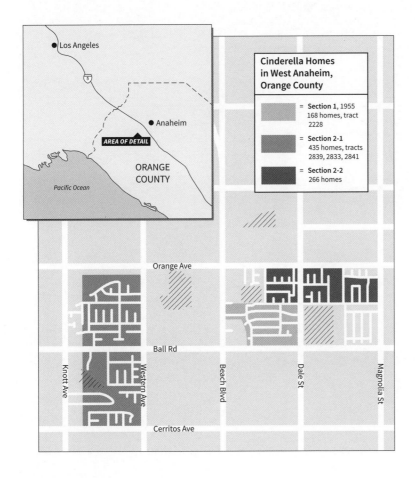

the brothers were not able to find further tracts of an appropriate size; for several years they "franchised the name, plans and specifications" to builders as far away as Houston and Wichita, Kansas.[106] Their partnership ended in 1961; both went on to different work. One of the Cinderella Homes was featured at the Los Angeles Home Show of 1956, whose advertisements praised this "California ranch house" for its look of "relaxed luxury."[107]

The Vandruff house displayed at the Home Show was not large: it had only 1,154 square feet of living space in its three bedrooms, living room/family room, kitchen, and one and three-quarters baths. An attached garage could accommodate two cars. But it appeared quite large because of the proportions and its length. Vandruff negotiated a wider lot dimension of seventy to seventy-two feet with the Anaheim authorities (this width became standard in Orange County thereafter), so the houses stretched a full sixty-two feet along the street side (fig. 77). An exceptionally low front roofline and large roof overhangs enhanced the

76. Orange County tract map 2228, showing detail of Cinderella Homes street layout.

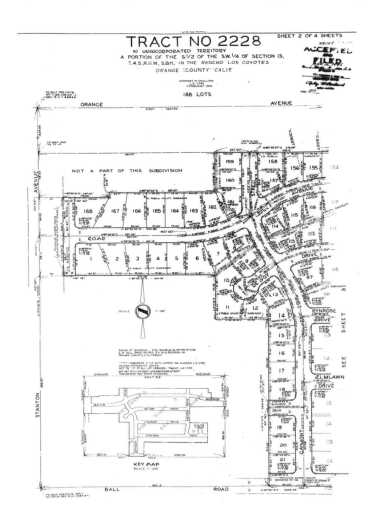

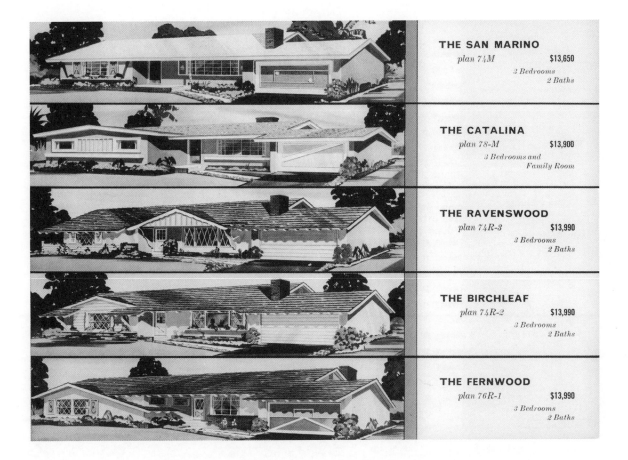

THE SAN MARINO
plan 74M $13,650
3 Bedrooms
2 Baths

THE CATALINA
plan 78-M $13,900
3 Bedrooms and
Family Room

THE RAVENSWOOD
plan 74R-3 $13,990
3 Bedrooms
2 Baths

THE BIRCHLEAF
plan 74R-2 $13,990
3 Bedrooms
2 Baths

THE FERNWOOD
plan 76R-1 $13,990
3 Bedrooms
2 Baths

77. Jean Valjean Vandruff, Cinderella Homes sales brochure, 1955–57, five models.

appearance of length. Some models also had a large gable over the bedroom wing (fig. 78). Shingles on the roofs and extensive wood on the interior were noted in the ads as among the many "custom" features: these houses, said the ads, looked like much more expensive custom-built homes. Vandruff's plans were unusual in several respects: there was no formal dining room; a generous living room (twenty feet) continued on into a family room that was itself continuous with the kitchen (fig. 79). There were eating areas in both the family room and kitchen. A floor-to-ceiling fireplace constructed of "used brick" dominated the living room. A continuous band of waist-high windows opened the living room to the street. Exteriors were painted in pastel colors, and great attention was paid to the colors of the appliances and bathroom fixtures. Advertisements also promised "wood floors, formica counter tops, TV in kitchen, walk-in closets, sliding glass patio doors at rear, 34 different exteriors, 4 floor plans."[108] The first group of 168 sold out in three and a half weeks, according to the *Los Angeles Times*.[109] Prices initially ranged from $13,650 to $14,650 ($109,000–117,000 in 2010 dollars). Ads also described the Cinderella Home as a "California ranch."

The "Cinderella" name suggested a storybook outcome for the poor girl who marries a prince and achieves her dream. In the ads, the new home is presented by a young woman, dressed for the ball like Cinderella in the movie, wearing glass slippers and holding a golden key (fig. 80). Disney's animated film of the same name had appeared in 1950; through the movie and the book based on it, images of the royal palace and the ancient-looking village nearby came to be familiar to a wide public. When Disneyland opened in Anaheim in 1955, the "Circus Train" ride passed by replicas of the Cinderella village and the royal castle from the film, located within the Fantasyland section. The Cinderella Homes did not resemble any of these buildings very closely, but the low roofs and the occasional dramatic gable were suggestive of the thatched huts of the Cinderella village near the palace in the movie, and curlicue-like ornament on the exteriors and the fireplaces recalled some of the medievalizing decorative features of Cinderella's cottage in the film and the book about it published at the same time.[110] The fantasy element of the story, "your every wish for a home . . . come gloriously true" as Vandruff's ads put it, pervaded Vandruff's promotional materials.[111] The

78. Fernwood model, detail of Cinderella Homes sales brochure, 1955–57.

79. Plan 78-R-1, detail of Cinderella Homes sales brochure, 1955–57.

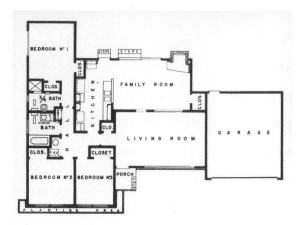

plan 78R-1 **$14,250**

your every wish for a home
...come gloriously true,

Cinderella ESTATES

built by **VANDRUFF**

presence of Disneyland four miles to the east must have given the house name additional resonance in buyers' minds. A look at the streets of Vandruff's developments today, however, suggests that most of the houses were actually plainer than the advertisements and presentation materials suggest.

Joseph Mason, author of a history of housing that was influential in the eighties, complained about the "Cinderella or Disney World" look, and said that it soon disappeared in tract housing.[112] But the Cinderella model was replicated by many other builders in Orange County in the later fifties, and versions of the gables occurred often in tract houses of the later fifties and early sixties elsewhere in the United States.[113]

Ross Cortese and Rossmoor

Subtler references to Disneyland, and to contemporary Disney movies, were also evident in Rossmoor, the only development in western Orange County during the fifties that was comparable in size to Panorama City. Rossmoor (1956–62), located on the twelve hundred remaining acres of Rancho Los Alamitos, next to the Los Alamitos Naval Air Station and about six miles west northwest of Disneyland, was a planned community of thirty-five hundred dwellings, designed and

81. Rossmoor, entrance.
Photo by Maynard Parker,
ca. 1956.

developed by Ross Cortese, later known for the creation of a series of successful retirement communities called Leisure Worlds. Just as Disney had his designers surround Disneyland with a berm, a raised earthen barrier, Cortese surrounded Rossmoor with a wall, and advertised the community as a "walled city."[114] Brick piers at the entryway to Rossmoor (corner of Rossmoor Way and Los Alamitos Blvd.) suggested a gate, although they did not function as one (fig. 81).[115] Perhaps, like Disney, Cortese was trying to create the image of a "controlled community," manageable and orderly, within the rather chaotic development pattern of Orange County.[116] When Cortese turned to the creation of the Leisure Worlds, he again walled them off from their surrounding communities and provided them with gates—real ones.

As among the Cinderella Homes, some of the models at Rossmoor were strongly suggestive of the storybook villages of contemporary Disney imagery. With their cedar "shakes" (shingles that appear handmade), turrets, dovecotes, broken rooflines with extended overhangs, densely mullioned windows, and eccentric shapes, they shared with the films a nostalgia for ancient towns and houses that had never really existed (figs. 82, 83, 84). The Farm House model, advertised with fantastic-looking roofs and a barn-like garage in front, evoked something of Cinderella's village, and even of the dwarf's cottage in *Snow White* (fig. 85).[117] The roofs and protuberant nooks of the Salem implied village-like and barn-like reminiscences (fig. 82). These four houses (Farm House, New Englander, Plymouth, and Salem), among the earliest at Rossmoor, were also, at the beginning, the most aggressively marketed: "Live like a country squire . . . recapturing the cherished spirit of bygone days" urged one of the earliest advertising brochures.[118] There were many other models, as well, though, and these predominated after the first few months of building and advertising: the

82. Rossmoor sales brochure, cover showing "Salem" model, ca. 1956.

83. Rossmoor, Plymouth exterior. Photo by Maynard Parker, ca. 1956.

El Dorado (fig. 86) and Golden Estates models with a shallow-pitched roof and large glass areas, were especially frequent and popular.[119] The Starlite boasted flat roofs and unadorned surfaces. Cortese's advertising described all the models as California ranch houses and spoke of them all as "modern." Yet the names, especially of some of the earliest models—Salem, Mayflower, Providence, Plymouth, New Englander—referred to a different kind of reality, that of the earliest periods of colonial North American history.[120]

The new settlement was explicitly upscale: advertising targeted "Executives"; "luxury model" houses had two bathrooms and three to four bedrooms with an optional additional family room. Lot sizes varied from 67 feet to 83 feet wide and from 102 feet to 124 feet deep; the houses were packed in very tightly on their lots.[121] The earliest models had detached garages and were relatively

84. Rossmoor, New Englander exterior. Photo by Maynard Parker, ca. 1956.

85. Zachary Silvia, Rossmoor, Farm House model, ca. 1957, from sales brochure of ca. 1958.

close to the street; later models, with attached garages, were L-shaped, with one of the bedrooms behind the garage, so that the main wing was rather distant from the street. Prices started at $17,500 in 1957 ($135,800 in 2010 dollars), considerably more expensive than surrounding houses in Buena Park and Anaheim, including Cortese's earlier houses built by Frematic Homes. Plans were innovative, with more than half of the standard plans featuring a nearly continuous dining-kitchen-playroom area (fig. 87).[122] This was reminiscent of the continuous family room–kitchen at Cinderella Homes, but much larger. Inside, the finishings of the early models included exposed beams, a brick fireplace wall, mahogany paneling, and old-fashioned looking cherry cabinets in the kitchen.[123] In subsequent models, some of these details were moderated to create lighter, slicker-looking rooms, as in the glamorous photographs by Maynard Parker (fig. 88), but the fireplaces and exposed beams continued.[124] In addition to the ubiquitous fireplaces, all models offered forced-air heating, despite the warm climate. Advertising for all the houses laid great emphasis on the bathrooms and kitchens, the latter equipped by Westinghouse, and billed as "the Betty Furness beautility kitchen."[125] The kitchen featured a central island with a cooktop with copper hood above, and very up-to-date electric appliances; these were tinted in a choice of turquoise, pink, or yellow (fig. 89).[126]

Taking a leaf from Fritz Burns's array of marketing strategies, Cortese organized a giveaway of a fully furnished house on the *Queen for a Day* television program: an unemployed single mother of four from the nearby town of Downey

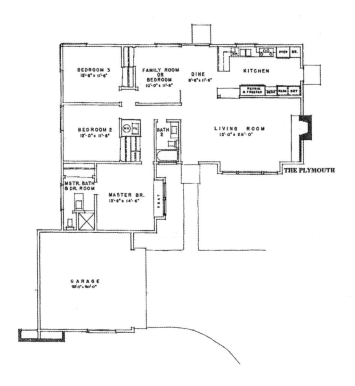

BEDROOM 3
12'-6" x 11'-6"

FAMILY ROOM
OR
BEDROOM
10'-0" x 11'-6"

DINE
8'-6" x 11'-6"

KITCHEN

BEDROOM 2
12'-0" x 11'-6"

BATH
2

LIVING ROOM
15'-0" x 26'-0"

REFRIG.
& FREEZER

DISH

WASH DRY

THE PLYMOUTH

MSTR. BATH
& DR. ROOM

MASTER BR.
13'-6" x 14'-6"

GARAGE
20'-0" x 20'-0"

87. Rossmoor, Plymouth, plan,
ca. 1956. Nathanael Roesch
from sales brochure of ca.
1958.

won the New Englander model, and was driven to her new acquisition in a gold Cadillac.[127] Other advertising campaigns involved visits from Betty Furness, spokeswoman for Westinghouse, to promote "her" kitchen.

Construction proceeded rapidly as sales increased. According to Heidi Cortese, Ross Cortese had already assembled a construction team in his earlier ventures, and kept them working year-round at Rossmoor. The houses appear to have been conventional "stick-built" dwellings on concrete slabs; rather than radiant heat, however, Cortese employed hot air heaters.[128] The original site plan was a sophisticated one, with figure-eight-shaped north-south loops embracing shopping centers and schools, and other internal streets, mostly curvilinear, forming different neighborhoods for the new houses (fig. 90). The development contained a central area, intended for public buildings at a later date, school sites, and parks. Just south of the new Santa Ana Freeway, Rossmoor was accessible to downtown Los Angeles to the west ("29 minutes," according to the ads), and to Santa Ana to the east. Cortese sometimes styled himself "the creator" of the plan, but in fact the designer was Kenneth F. Mitchell, "former head planner of the LA FHA office."[129]

Ross Cortese (1916–91) was the child of immigrants from a rural area of Calabria in Italy who came to Ohio to work on a farm. Ross and his six younger siblings accompanied their parents to Glendale, California, in the late twenties.

88. Rossmoor, New Englander, living room. Photo by Maynard Parker, ca. 1956.

89. New Englander, Kitchen. Photo by Maynard Parker, ca. 1956.

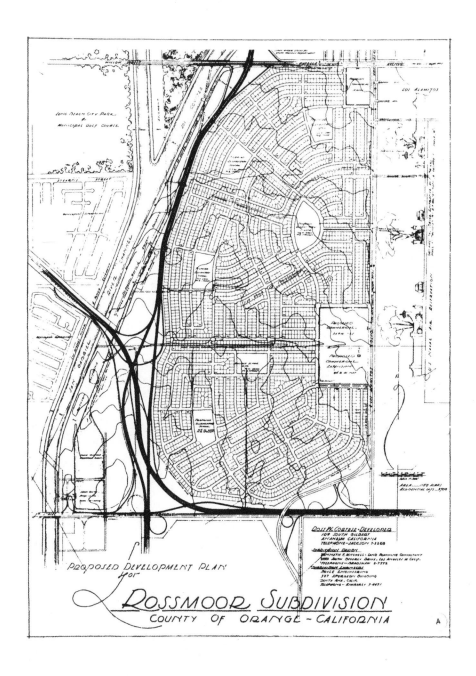

PROPOSED DEVELOPMENT PLAN
for
ROSSMOOR SUBDIVISION
COUNTY OF ORANGE - CALIFORNIA

90. Rossmoor, subdivision plan, ca. 1959. Brochure on proposed shopping center, Heidi Cortese Papers.

Dropping out of elementary school, Ross worked first as a farm laborer in Orange County, and then soon began to familiarize himself with the real estate business.[130] In 1939 he met and married Alona Marlowe, herself a builder; together they built small apartment buildings and remodeled older houses. Cortese served in the army, where he studied architectural drafting. Not much is known about his life between 1945 and the early fifties, but during these years he and his wife were already building individual single-family houses and assembling larger property holdings.[131]

In 1951 or 1952 we find Ross Cortese developing eight hundred parcels at the southern fringe of Lakewood.[132] Here he joined with Cliff May and Chris Choate, both of whom he had come to admire, to build the Lakewood Rancho Estates, a group of three- and four-bedroom ranch houses, styled "the Californian," set at right angles to the street on very narrow lots (fig. 91). Each had low-pitched gabled roofs, large glass areas, and a generous patio (fig. 92).[133] The houses were constructed from prefabricated panels, according to a system developed by Choate in the early fifties, and promoted by Choate and May, as partners, for several years.[134] Thus Cortese can be seen as Choate and May's most important patron in the early fifties. In 1955, he moved on to Anaheim,

91. Group portrait, from left to right: Ross Cortese, Cliff May, and Chris Choate. Cliff May Papers, Art, Design & Architecture Museum, University of California, Santa Barbara.

92. Lakewood Rancho Estates, four-bedroom model, brochure ca. 1952. Cliff May Papers.

IMAGINEERED FOR YOU

Here you'll discover a distinct kind of home that introduces a new day in western living. The builder, Mr. Ross W. Cortese, and his team of designers have created a home that answers your needs for indoor-outdoor family life. Their combined talents in design and construction make possible this spacious home at such reasonable cost... with its luxurious open beam interiors, its unique built-in kitchen, its many quality features. Contemporary in spirit—here is a home that opens your door on tomorrow!

93. Ross Cortese, Chris Choate, and Robert Jones, Frematic home, Anaheim, CA, exterior view. Illustration from a builder's sales brochure of 1955.

and built, again in collaboration with Choate and members of Choate's firm, a development of "Contemporary Ranch Style" homes. In Anaheim, Cortese and his collaborators created a building firm called Frematic Homes. Frematic houses resembled the houses produced by May and Choate's panel system, and may have been constructed in the same manner (fig. 93). Like the Lakewood Rancho houses, these too were very modern-looking and already displayed the kitchen equipment that Cortese would use so successfully at Rossmoor.[135] They were designed, according to the *Los Angeles Times*, by Robert G. Jones, an architect and builder who was a member of Choate's staff.[136] Cortese won the NAHB Award of Merit for Residential Design in 1955 for the Anaheim houses constructed by Frematic.

Meanwhile, Cortese was negotiating with the Irvine Company to buy its twelve-hundred-acre portion of the former Rancho Los Alamitos.[137] After the completion of Rossmoor, Cortese went on to develop his enormously successful 6,750-unit retirement community at nearby Seal Beach, called Leisure World.[138] Thereafter he devoted himself to building replicas of Leisure World, in New Jersey, Maryland, and California, with greater and lesser success. Leisure World at Seal Beach, which consisted of apartment units, was also characterized by elegant design principles clearly inspired by the Lakewood and Anaheim houses, as well as by the more "modern" models at Rossmoor. It was constructed with a panel system that was almost certainly based on that developed by Choate and May.[139]

The development of house design at Rossmoor as described here leaves many questions unanswered. Why did Cortese shift away from the modern-appearing designs at Lakewood and Anaheim to the early fantastic exteriors at Rossmoor, and then shift rapidly back again? Advertisements described Earl G. Kaltenbach, Jr. as the architect at Rossmoor, and Kaltenbach had been the designer of the original Disney Tomorrowland, with its futuristic House of Tomorrow. His houses in the Los Angeles and Orange County area were uncompromisingly modernist, although many articles that discuss his work stress his commitment to natural materials and traditional detailing. On the other hand, Kaltenbach's role in design at Rossmoor is by no means clear, since all of the plans and elevations were produced by Frematic, and Chris Choate's name also appeared, as "designer," on many of them.[140] Some sources suggest that Chris Choate formed a continuing collaboration with Cortese at Frematic, and went on to work at Rossmoor and the Leisure Worlds. Others point to an involvement of some members of Choate's staff. But Choate was certainly no advocate of fantasy and nostalgia either.[141]

Did Cortese himself decide to overdecorate and overcomplicate the earliest houses because a more "modern" exterior seemed cold and unfamiliar (a not infrequent concern among builders at the time)? Or because he wanted to differentiate Rossmoor from its surrounding areas? Or because the more modern houses looked too inexpensive, and Cortese feared they would not attract buyers to "executive row"? The Rossmoor houses sold for 20 to 30 percent more than houses in the surrounding areas of Orange County and were advertised as upscale. Through Alona Marlowe and her family, Cortese had many connections to Disney's staff and design ideas, connections that reached far beyond Kaltenbach's role at Tomorrowland.[142] Was Cortese captivated, at first, like Vandruff, by the Disney aura—by Disneyland's combined appeals to futurism and nostalgia for a fantasized past—but then gradually thought better of it? Cortese may also have felt some nostalgia of his own for the rural areas that he remembered from his boyhood,[143] But, like other builders, he wanted above all to sell houses; he must have found that the more "modern"-looking ranch appealed to his Orange County buyers more than the earlier, rather fantastic-looking models.

Fritz Burns, Jean Vandruff, and Ross Cortese all saw themselves, and presented themselves, as creators of the California ranch house. Vandruff glamorized Burns's working-class version by fantasy elements drawn from Disney; Cortese developed upscale models that looked glamorous because of their design (and because of the photographs of Maynard Parker); he also drew upon some rural and fantasized prototypes. In the later fifties, Vandruff's and Cortese's houses may have done as much as Cliff May's later work to popularize the ranch house form among affluent clients and their architects and builders. But it was Burns and the earlier May, working with Choate, who convinced the builders of modest housing that the California ranch house could be an important model for them. On the East Coast and in the Midwest, as we will see in the following chapters, builders sometimes gave their houses a "California" label, but they also developed their designs out of their own local traditions.

CHAPTER 3

East Coast Builders
Philadelphia and Boston

In its growth patterns, the Philadelphia metropolitan region was almost entirely different from Los Angeles and Orange County. One of the nation's earliest cities (1682), and for a time its capital, Penn's planned city grew steadily over the centuries. In the nineteenth and early twentieth centuries Philadelphia was the third largest city in the United States (after New York and Chicago). It was a major port and center of shipbuilding almost from its inception, and later became preeminent in locomotive manufacture and textiles. It was also a center for printing, bookbinding and publishing, and education, housing some of the nation's leading universities, medical schools, and hospitals. After 1945, these focuses continued, but both manufacturing and service industries began to disperse to suburban areas. In the 1950s, the rate of growth of the city itself slowed dramatically, while that of the metropolitan area increased rapidly. Outside the city limits, however, postwar development followed a different path from that of most other American cities.

Like other eastern cities, Philadelphia had initially expanded with the aid of trolleys and streetcars, but its railroad commuter suburbs proliferated from the 1890s, growing outward from the old city especially along the "Main Line" of the Pennsylvania Railroad (leading to Chicago).[1] In the postwar period, as a result of the increasing use of the automobile, the railroad suburbs themselves grew outward from their railroad stations, responding to some of the increased need

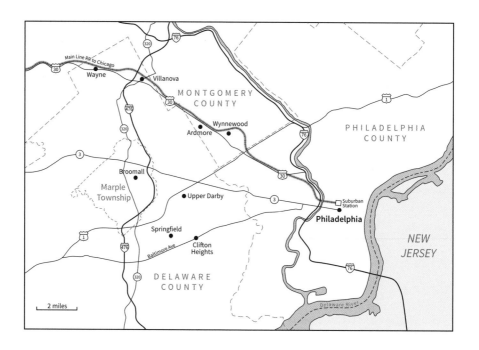

94. Philadelphia metropolitan area, map. Nathanael Roesch.

for housing.[2] With the addition of new housing stock by a multitude of very small builders, these older commuter suburbs grew into significant towns, which continued to rely to a great extent upon the railroads. The growth of these railroad commuter towns therefore siphoned off some of the postwar growth that elsewhere depended entirely on the automobile. Another difficulty that hampered development after World War II was the scarcity of large tracts of farmland close in toward the city. Landholding in the metropolitan area was frequently in the form of large estates, purchased in the nineteenth or early twentieth centuries by Philadelphia's commuting upper classes and elites, who built for themselves historicizing mansions on a huge, manorial scale. These owners were not in a hurry to sell.[3] Between the estates, landholdings were small, while on their periphery was an area of lush and productive farms of medium size, whose owners also were not eager to sell. A builder in the Philadelphia area therefore faced exceptional constraints created by the patterns of land use.[4] Perhaps as a result, the city's financial interests had little experience with larger scale development, and remained relatively uninterested in investing in housing for a long time after the war.

For many years, eastern Pennsylvania did not develop a high-speed road system to help automobile-based population growth. The first stretch of the Schuylkill Expressway (Route 76) opened only in 1951, with short segments opened over the next ten years. The segments of the Pennsylvania Turnpike

(Route 276) closest to the urban area opened in 1954, 1956, and 1957; Interstate 95, connecting Philadelphia to other cities along the eastern seaboard, was begun only in 1958.[5] Traffic analysts and urban planners recognized the need for a ring road around the old city, connecting older routes to the north, south, and west, but this "Blue Route" (Route 476) was not begun until the seventies and not completed until the nineties. (The delay was caused primarily by the objections of relatively small property owners and the older towns that lay in the path of the proposed routes.) All of these high-speed highways except the Blue Route occupied the transportation paths of much older and smaller roadways; these abutting roadways therefore had to serve an increasingly large flow of automobile traffic during construction of the faster routes; the frequent result, by the end of the fifties, was gridlock. For all these reasons, the automobile-oriented suburbs of the postwar era tended to be small and exceptionally widely dispersed. Zoning and planning practices were also extremely diverse, with older railroad communities having old and well-developed ordinances, while newer areas sometimes lacked any regulation whatever (fig. 94).[6]

The most significant growth in the Philadelphia area in the early years after the war took place in Delaware County, to the southwest of the old city, and especially in Marple Township, in the northwest corner of the county; here the population grew fourfold between 1950 and 1960 (from ca. 5,000 to ca. 20,000—rounded numbers; ca. 2,000 in 1940).[7] Marple Township was far distant from the commuter towns of the Main Line, and, though relatively close in to the city, remote from major transportation routes. The area had not been among the most attractive for upper-class owners, but some of its farms were sold off to the estates of elite families in the 1920s and 1930s, and some of these came back onto the market after the end of the war. Here, postwar builders were able to assemble a few substantial tracts of land. One of the smaller of these builders was Frank Facciolo; the largest of them was Ralph Bodek. Both Facciolo and Bodek were strikingly innovative in their housing and siting designs. And both asserted a curious debt to California houses. Facciolo claimed that the flat-roofed masonry-clad house at his Rose Tree Woods development (1949–54) that was described by him in advertisements as the California Cliff House (fig. 95) evolved from a house he had seen in San Francisco shortly after the war.[8] Bodek always said that his early split-level house at Lawrence Park (1954–62 or –63) (figs. 7, 107) was a reworking of a split-level house he had seen while serving at a naval air station near Los Angeles during the war.[9] There is no obvious Californian prototype for either design; both builders were probably tapping into the romance of California in the postwar period. They may also have thought of California builders and building as exceptionally innovative, and therefore as offering models for a new kind of housing in the East.

In this image:

California Cliff House

IN BEAUTIFUL
ROSE TREE WOODS
FOR COUNTRY LIVING
SAMPLE HOUSE OPEN DAILY 1-9 P. M.
SAT. & SUN. 9 A. M. TO 9 P. M.
DIRECTIONS—From 69th St. drive out West
Chester Pike to Howard Johnson's, Broomall,
turn left ¼ mile to Furnished Sample.

Stone-front, fireproof concrete masonry construction
Radiant heat ● living room with 13-ft. picture window ●
ceiling-high stone fireplace ● dining room ● 3 bedrooms
● tile bath ● Lot sizes average ½ of an acre.
STOP OUT OR WRITE FOR FREE BOOKLET

FRANK FACCIOLO, Agent
8 W. BALTIMORE AVE. LANSDOWNE
MAdison 6-2810

GENERAL ⒼⒺ ELECTRIC
All-electric Kitchen

95. Frank Facciolo, "California Cliff House." restored by Nathanael Roesch from a newspaper advertisement of September 1951.

Frank Facciolo's Idiosyncratic Ranch Houses at Rose Tree Woods

Frank Facciolo (1924–2002) grew up in Clifton Heights, a late nineteenth-century suburb in Delaware County, six miles west of center-city Philadelphia. Clifton Heights, working class and lower middle class, was populated by twin houses and row houses, and served by the local trolley system. Facciolo's grandfather had brought his family from Italy to the Pennsylvania mining districts north of Philadelphia in the 1890s; soon the family had become farmers in the same area. Facciolo's father and uncles went into the building trades in the Philadelphia suburbs (especially masonry and plastering); they also began to purchase small properties. The young Frank attended Villanova University, receiving a bachelor's in economics in 1945. He was enthusiastic about modern architecture from an early age. Almost immediately after graduation he obtained a license as a real estate broker, and began to look for land that he could build on.[10]

In 1948 Facciolo established his own construction firm and a separate building and development firm (Facciolo and Barrett).[11] By 1949, he had assembled about two hundred acres, in the midst of an estate district.[12] His first purchases in Marple Township were adjacent to the Paxon Hollow Golf Course, and were part of a tract formerly owned by Atwater Kent, the prominent Philadelphia engineer and radio manufacturer.[13] Here he began to build the California Cliff Houses (locally called "the flattops," although in fact the roof had a gentle slope),[14] constructing identical ranch houses over a period of several years. Five years later he purchased a contiguous segment from Allendale Farms,[15] permitting him to add another large group of houses: at about this point, Facciolo and Barrett shifted to the split-level form for their houses, perhaps partly in response to the popularity of the new houses in Lawrence Park, but also in order to accommodate the hillier areas of the property.[16] He called the whole settlement Rose Tree Woods.[17] The area was heavily wooded with both flat and hilly sections. A steep ravine ran north-south in the center along a small creek called Trout Run. A significant proportion of the land was therefore unbuildable; Facciolo left these sections wooded, except for a swimming club for which he donated twenty acres in 1956. (His firm also did the grading and clearing for the club.)

In the earlier part of Rose Tree Woods, the California Cliff Houses sat not on cliffs but on level ground, each on a lot of about one-third acre. Like almost all tract houses of the period, the long axis of the house was parallel to the street. Front setbacks were relatively shallow by older suburban standards, but backyards were exceptionally deep.[18] Facciolo retained as many trees as he could along the backs of the properties, and helped new owners obtain ornamental shrubs.[19] New owners prized these wooded lots highly.

96. Facciolo, "flat tops," Rose Tree Woods, Broomall, PA, modern street view. Photo by the author.

97. Facciolo, "flat top," Rose Tree Woods, Broomall, PA, modern view. Photo by the author.

The Rose Tree Woods ranch houses were constructed of finely cut, narrow stones in horizontal courses on the front, while sides and rear were built of concrete block finished in stucco (figs. 96, 97, 99). Interior bearing walls were masonry, and a large (ceiling height and ten feet wide) fieldstone fireplace dominated the living room interior. Some of the interiors had gently sloping exposed beams. A large picture window in the living room and another at the corner of the house brought light into the interior. These windows, and the banded windows elsewhere, were trimmed in dark-stained wood. Inside were a living room, a dining room, a utility room, two or three bedrooms, one bathroom, and a one-car garage (fig. 98).[20] The houses were built upon a concrete slab with radiant heat. A floor-to-ceiling masonry fireplace wall in the living room appears to have been a gesture toward Frank Lloyd Wright. The original asking prices were $12,000 ($109,000 in 2010 dollars) for the two-bedroom house and $12,800 for the three-bedroom; soon, however, Facciolo raised the prices to $14,000 ($117,000 in 2010 dollars) and $14,750.[21] The houses had one thousand to eleven hundred square feet of living space.

Facciolo employed a young architect (David Scott) to draw up the plans and working drawings.[22] But there is every likelihood that the plan and exterior form were his own. The flattops were shockingly different from all housing norms in the Philadelphia area, where old colonial traditions (the "farmhouse colonial") had been continued for centuries in two-story houses with a variety of "colonial" or neoclassical details. From the 1890s, a number of other historical styles had appeared in Philadelphia's suburban housing: small "late Victorian" houses that were built by tract builders near the principal Main Line railroad stations and large revivalist mansions custom-built nearby, designed by well-known architects for the elite, often in medievalizing styles. The one-story free-standing house was virtually unknown in the Philadelphia area. Thus it is interesting to speculate about how Facciolo arrived at his radical design.

Facciolo must have seen one-story houses built on concrete slabs on his trip to California, and some of these could have been flat-roofed. But these California houses were not clad in masonry, nor did many use radiant heat.[23] Radiant heat and slab construction were being used by the Levitts in the late 1940s, but there is no evidence that Facciolo ever visited Levittown. For slab construction and radiant heating, there was a much closer model for him to look at: Frank Lloyd Wright's Suntop Homes of 1939 in Ardmore, Pennsylvania, only a few miles north of Broomall.[24] And there is more than a hint of Wright in the window patterns, window trim, and stone fireplaces of the Rose Tree Woods houses.[25] As to the sophisticated-looking masonry work, Facciolo also could have seen Wright's Falling Water, a three-hour drive to the west of Broomall. Late in his life, Facciolo told a newspaper reporter that Wright's Broadacre City houses provided an inspiration for his own Rose Tree Woods houses, but almost certainly he was misremembering, since these illustrations to Wright's Broadacre City were not at all well known at the time Facciolo began to build the flattops.[26] Probably Facciolo was simply remembering that he had an interest in Wright in his youth, an interest that could have been nurtured by these local examples. Probably, too, the flattop's masonry drew upon the strong traditions of skilled masonry work

98. Facciolo/Scott, "flat top," plan, 1953. Nathanael Roesch, from plan lent by Marple Township Zoning Office.

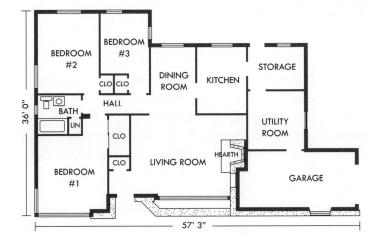

99. Facciolo, own house, Rose Tree Woods, 1956, interior showing living room fireplace (similar to his speculative houses), modern view. Photo by the author.

100. Facciolo, own house, Rose Tree Woods, 1956, exterior, modern view. Photo by the author.

among the Italian construction trades in the Philadelphia area, traditions that were being carried on among his extended family.[27] Nevertheless, the combination of forms, materials, and construction used by Facciolo in the first Rose Tree Woods houses remains unique in its era and location. And the design of these early houses continued to be Facciolo's favorite: the large house he built for himself and his family in Rose Tree Woods employed similar forms and materials, combined with a pitched roof (figs. 99, 100).

Because the Facciolo developments in Rose Tree Woods were carried out over a long period of time, piecemeal, and because the site was difficult, the area does not have a coherent site plan. Curving streets turn back upon themselves in small groups; there are few through streets, and many cul-de-sacs (figs. 101, 102). Perhaps by these accidents of timing and topography, the overall result bears some resemblance to the prescriptions of the FHA as to neighborhood planning. On the other hand, Facciolo employed the engineering firm of Damon and Foster, which had been the leading civil engineering firm in the Philadelphia area since the early 1900s. H. Gilroy Damon, the head of the firm at this time, was a highly educated and cultivated man, who may have had some influence on the site planning. Certainly he did have an influence at Lawrence Park, as we will see.

Frank Facciolo went on to build a number of smaller developments in the Philadelphia area between the middle 1950s and the early 1970s, and he continued building houses at Rose Tree Woods throughout that period, now on the hillier parts of the site. From the later 1950s, he built split-levels, somewhat more expensive than Bodek's and more lavish in the use of masonry (fig. 103). But he returned to the flattop model only once, in a very small development near Wayne, Pennsylvania (Waynewoods, 1954–56), now with a pitched roof to accommodate air conditioning (fig. 104). He came to be prominent among area builders, and was, for a time, president of the Home Builders' Association of Philadelphia and Suburban Counties. Although when Facciolo began building in Rose Tree Woods he had succeeded in getting generous zoning variances from the Township, in successive decades he was often in conflict with local officials.

101. Modern street and lot plan of Rose Tree Woods. Nathanael Roesch from modern zoning plan at Marple Township Zoning Office.

102. Facciolo, subdivision plan section "B," 1954, showing street layout and locations of houses. Plan lent by Marple Township Zoning Office.

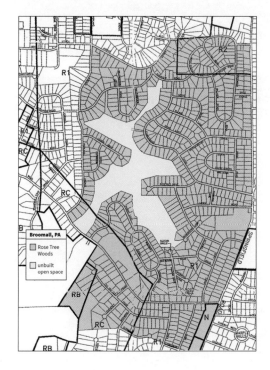

103. Facciolo, split-level house, Rose Tree Woods, ca. 1960, modern view. Photo by the author.

104. Facciolo, house at Waynewoods, Wayne, PA, 1954–56, modern view. Photo by the author.

105. Frank Facciolo stands in the middle of Sproul Road across from his Rose Tree Woods development, *Philadelphia Inquirer*, February 9, 1997.

Facciolo liked to think of himself as a "man of the people" (fig. 105). Toward the end of his career as a builder, he lamented the pressures created by recent local zoning and rezoning, which, he said, made it impossible in his later years to build housing for low-income and moderate-income people. "We had mobility in housing [when I started building]. Now a man's ability to elevate himself in housing is limited as a result of these zoning methods."[28]

Ralph Bodek and the Pennsylvania Split-Level

When Ralph Bodek (1914–98) began Lawrence Park in Marple Township, he had a good deal more experience in the building and construction business than Facciolo had. The son of Joseph and Jenny Bodek, he was descended from Austrian and Polish Jews who had come to this country at the beginning of the twentieth century and settled in the Philadelphia area. He married Leona Rosenthal in 1935. Joseph Bodek had built a number of apartment buildings in the city and its near suburbs, while Leona's father owned a prosperous trucking company. Ralph grew up as a not very observant Jew, in one of the family apartment buildings, in the inner suburb of Upper Darby. Both families were well to do and well educated; a cousin, Gordon Bodek, distinguished himself at the University of Pennsylvania.[29] Ralph Bodek attended Penn as an undergraduate, joining one of the better fraternities there; he went on to the Wharton School of Business, receiving a bachelor's in economics in 1937. Thereafter he worked for his father helping to manage the apartment buildings until he began his war service. Bodek became an officer in the naval air force, stationed at Alameda and Sunnyvale, California; it was here that he began to think of becoming a builder himself. Returning from the war, he tried out jobs in journalism, and also continued to work for his father. Soon, however, he began to build on his own, using his father's and father-in-law's contacts to obtain building loans.

After the war, Ralph and Leona Bodek purchased a large and expensive house in Wynnewood near Philadelphia, at a time when local social attitudes in the Main Line suburbs were generally anti-Semitic. Between 1948 and 1952, Bodek constructed six relatively small developments of row houses and twin houses in the near suburbs of Philadelphia.[30] In the process, he built up a team of construction supervisors, a cadre of employees among the building trades, and a series of connections with local sales agents and furniture makers. Soon he was able to assemble enough financial support to take advantage of the rapid development of the farmland around Springfield, ten miles southwest of Philadelphia, a very old farming community that developed as an industrial area in the early nineteenth century and then had grown rapidly in the early twentieth century. Springfield was one of the few communities near to Philadelphia and connected to it by good transportation routes (trolleys), that was still, at war's end, surrounded by small farms. Bodek purchased 169 acres at the edge of the old town and built 600 houses on one-fifth-acre lots. The houses were two-story all-brick construction, boxy-looking center-hall layouts with colonial-looking trim around the doors and windows; each had three bedrooms, one bath, but no garage; they sold for $12,900 in 1952 ($106,148 in 2010 dollars), substantially less than Facciolo's contemporary flattops, and they sold well (fig. 106).[31] Bodek called his first major housing development Colonial Park.

Building on his success in Springfield, Bodek went on to a much riskier venture: the development of Lawrence Park in Broomall, a town within Marple Township. Here Bodek purchased the 600-acre Robinson Tract in April 1953 for $900,000 (about $7 million in 2010 dollars), renaming the tract after Lawrence Road, which ran through it. The Robinson Tract had been part of the estate of Samuel Robinson, cofounder of Acme Markets in 1917, who had assembled the Broomall property in the 1930s.[32] A series of negotiations over the sale of the property in 1952 had led Marple Township zoning officials to rezone the entire tract, specifying that about a quarter of the land would be dedicated to industrial and commercial development, and a further large section would be reserved for parkland and schools. Bodek and his backers liked these arrangements, realizing that they would be able to sell off large parcels for an industrial park and shopping center. His plans, developed over the course of the following year, called for 1,200 homes to be erected on 420 acres, a light industrial area on 150 acres, 60 acres for parks, 30 acres for a shopping center, and 12 acres for schools.[33] But the tract was, at this point, far distant from major transportation

106. Ralph Bodek, house at Colonial Park, Springfield, PA, ca. 1952. Photo by the author.

routes, and there was certainly no guarantee that it would support residential, commercial, or industrial development. It was also hard to build on: it was very hilly, and bisected by an even steeper and larger ravine than that which lay at the center of Rose Tree Woods (located just across Lawrence Road).

Along Lawrence Road, Bodek built three model houses, fully furnished, for prospective buyers to choose from. These were the small, compact, split-level houses that would dominate the whole development over the next nine years. Like Bill Levitt, Bodek built and rebuilt, and rebuilt again the first of these model houses, working with his foremen and their workmen, until he was satisfied by it. He then hired a young architect to produce the "working drawings" that were required by Broomall building officials; he always claimed, however, that the design was his own (figs. 7, 9, 107).[34] The houses were masonry and frame construction, with brick and stucco on the exterior, asbestos shingles, and asphalt roofs. Each contained about 1,600 square feet of living space within a footprint of only 1,100 square feet; their lots ranged from 6,534 square feet to 8,064 square feet. The exteriors derived a certain colonial flavor from their shutters and central entry, but in most respects they appeared novel and modern. Inside were three rather small bedrooms (12 feet 9 inches × 13 feet 6 inches, about 10 feet × 10 feet, and about 8 feet × 10 feet), a continuous L-shaped living-dining room,

108. Lawrence Park, living room interior. National Association of Home Builders, *Correlator*, 1955.

109. Lawrence Park, recreation room interior. National Association of Home Builders, *Correlator*, 1955.

kitchen, and a tiny "recreation room" (with built-in television or radio), at the bottom level, leading to the one-car garage (figs. 108, 109). Later models sacrificed the garage and provided a larger recreation room. There were hardwood floors throughout, except in the kitchen (linoleum) and bathroom (tile).[35] The living room, with its six-paned picture window, faced toward the street. On most parts of the hilly site, the houses were dug into the sloping ground so that the living area had access to the back, but the recreation room did not. The full price in 1954 was $14,990 ($121,000 in 2010 dollars) including air conditioning; most buyers, however, did not elect this option, and paid about $1,000 less ($113,000 in 2010 dollars).[36]

Bodek believed that he derived the split-level from a house he had seen in California. It is true that he could have seen many varieties of split-levels in California, though none that closely resembled the ones in Lawrence Park. He also believed that he "invented" the split-level house in its modern and most popular form. Certainly Bodek built and rebuilt his model to his own satisfaction: there is no doubt that the design was at least partially his own. On the other hand, split-levels were coming into fashion in many places in the middle-Atlantic states in the 1950s, and local developers around Philadelphia were building them at least as early as 1952.[37] Thousands upon thousands of such houses were built, as the form gained in popularity, even for larger houses and lots.

Origins of the Split-Level House

It is difficult to trace the antecedents of the split-level house: it appeared quite suddenly as a low- to medium-cost housing type in the early 1950s, in many places and in many varieties. Expensive houses had long been built on more than one level in hilly areas, especially in California.[38] And on hilly sites from the later 1920s through the 1930s, architects and builders of moderately priced houses often dug the garage into the hill at street level, with a one- or two-story house above it, entered through the garage, or by a steep exterior stair (fig. 110).[39] Architectural and house design magazines began to praise the "split-level" design in 1939, but often their examples sprawled over many levels.[40] Yet by 1949, a compact yet dynamic and "modern-looking" version was under construction in Queens, Teaneck, New Jersey, and in several sites on Long Island (fig. 111).[41] By the fall of 1951, a 2,000-square-foot model appeared in many parts of Bergen County, New Jersey.[42] In the Chicago area, the *Chicago Tribune* reported a "surge of popularity" of the type in mid-1951 (June 26, 1951); ads for split-level houses were frequent from 1953 onward. In the mid-1950s, the Garlinghouse Company published an entire volume on split-level houses from the East and Midwest.[43] Split-levels appeared in the Philadelphia area papers only from the mid-1950s (especially from 1954, with the building of Lawrence Park), and in the Boston area a few years later; they were virtually absent from Los Angeles reporting.[44] In the 1950s and 1960s, the type was rather specific to individual regions: it was especially prevalent in the New Jersey suburbs of New York, the suburbs of Washington, DC, and Philadelphia, and the suburbs of Chicago.

Many builders disliked the split-level form since it was harder to build than the one-story ranch, and because it had some resemblance to more traditional two-story houses, it usually seemed more conservative looking.[45] The Levitts, for example, did not use this form, at least in the early postwar years, perhaps because of its greater construction expense; and, according to Herbert Gans, they were openly contemptuous of its looks.[46] But it was popular in hilly areas of the East Coast, and, because its partial basement offered the possibility of a more conventional heating system than the radiant heat on which the ranch

110. Ralph I. Williams, Welland Road, Blake Park, MA, 1940. Photo by Ken Liss.

111. Berne Company, split-level house advertisement. *New York Times*, October 23, 1949.

112. Bodek, Lawrence Park, "ranch-style split," ca. 1962. Photo by the author.

houses depended, it made considerable headway in the colder portions of the Midwest, on flatter sites.[47] When, in the mid-fifties, a family room or recreation room became popular, the split-level house accommodated this space easily, by widening the basement level that contained the garage. With the ever-increasing popularity of the ranch house type, however, builders in the later 1950s increasingly concealed the levels of the split-level house, putting the living room at entry and grade level and excavating lower levels in the rear, and sloping the roof very gradually from front to back, so that the two levels in the rear were not visible from the street. This version came to be known as the "ranch-style split" (fig. 112).[48] On relatively flat ground, a "front-to-back" split-level arrangement served some of the same purpose, partially obscuring the wing at the back (fig. 26). Like the ranch house, the split-level increased in size over time (fig. 27), but its plan was less flexible, and thus harder to expand.

No one else but Bodek built as many split-levels in a single place in the 1950s, however, and no one else built them as compactly and for as low a price. Thus, Bodek may be said to have popularized the split-level house for lower-income buyers, and to have played a major role in the ensuing development of this house form, which came to predominate in the Philadelphia area in the nineteen fifties and sixties.

* * * * *

Fulfilling his original plan, Bodek erected approximately 1,200 houses at Lawrence Park between 1954 and 1963, taking ten years to complete his original proposal. He tended to obtain building permits at the rate of 80 to 120 houses at a time, a slower pace than many of the builders considered here; he then built them in groups of 10 to 20.[49] He did not assemble a year-round workforce, but employed a few permanent foremen, some of whom went on to become local builders themselves;[50] together he and his foremen drew upon the numerous local subcontracting firms that he and his father had employed over the years. Bodek insisted that his draftsmen provide extremely detailed working drawings for the foremen to work with (fig. 113). The houses were conventionally framed up, and while a number of new materials were employed (including asbestos shingles), there were no "prefabricated" elements. Bodek was attentive to quality, often checking over the houses together with his foremen to make sure they met his requirements. He was also demanding and punctilious in his specifications for materials.[51]

Street patterns at Lawrence Park shifted and changed somewhat over time, according to the requirements of new groups of houses. Street names also changed.[52] There is no record of an initial overall master plan, but early drawings of the principal core of the development by Damon Engineering, when compared with the final street layout observed in contemporary atlases, show that Bodek and his engineers planned Lawrence Park in a series of three roughly concentric ovals, with both a park and an elementary school at the center (fig. 114). To the southwest was to be the new shopping center, opened in 1957, and to the southeast the industrial park (sewer plans 1955, opened in 1961) would be located.[53] Streets that connected the ovals sloped sharply toward the central area. Only three streets connected across the main thoroughfare, so the whole was private

113. Bodek, basic house, working drawings (unsigned), section through kitchen, partial view. Nathanael Roesch, from larger drawing lent by Marple Township Zoning Office.

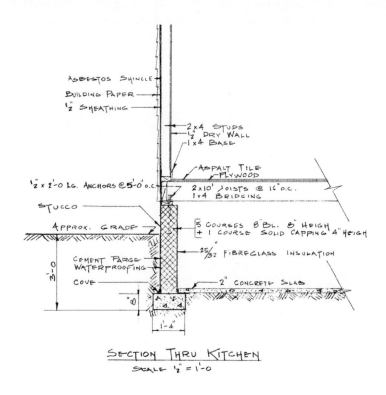

and inward-looking, and without much traffic. The plan was dictated to a certain extent by topography, since the hilly sections surround the areas that were planned for park and school. On paper, it is rather formal-looking, and owes a great deal to the training, experience, and insights of H. Gilroy Damon, Bodek's engineer. But "on the ground," the plan offers a visual sense of focused community together with a certain informality (fig. 115). The sense of informality is heightened by the changing character of the house exteriors: gradually, masonry replaced both brick and siding or shingles, and rooflines shifted to an asymmetrical gable (fig. 25). Since the new residents tended to replace the garage with an expanded recreation room, the later models built this feature in, omitting the garage. The later models were also larger (two and a half baths), with a "cathedral ceiling" in the living room; they were also more expensive.[54] In the later phases of the development, the houses shed most of their earlier "colonial" references.

Bodek proved to be an inspired merchandiser—almost as much of a huckster as Fritz Burns. He succeeded in obtaining a two-page advertisement in *Life* magazine (September 6, 1954, with the help of Hotpoint). He adopted the technique of displaying model houses, fully furnished, from which prospective purchasers could select the furnishings and appliances they wanted. Opening day for the model houses was celebrated with parties, balloons, and a blimp; twenty thousand prospective buyers attended.[55] In 1955, with great fanfare, he donated twelve acres of land to the Marple School Board for the new elementary

114. Bodek, and Damon & Foster Engineers, Lawrence Park, preliminary subdivision plan, July 1954.

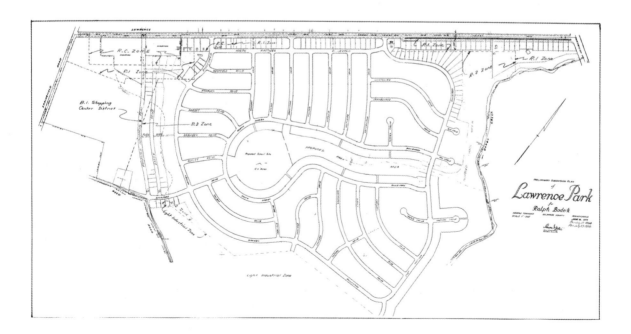

115. Lawrence Park, modern street view. Photo by the author.

school (built 1957–58, by Bader, Young, and Schultze); by 1956, about eight hundred families had moved into Lawrence Park. In the same year, he was able to sell off some of the rights to develop the shopping center and industrial park (though he retained a financial interest in both); the shopping center opened a year later, and drew many more purchasers to Lawrence Park.[56] Many of the residents of Lawrence Park were also attracted by the presence of the new St. Pius X parish, which had begun right next to the development in 1955, and which now opened new parochial schools.[57]

Bodek shouldered aside the young architect who drew his initial house plans, but he formed strong relationships with three engineers. The first was H. Gilroy Damon (d. 1981), the most senior and influential civil engineer in Delaware County and the surrounding Philadelphia metropolitan area. Damon had been trained in engineering at Cornell; he then worked for urban designer and housing designer John H. McClatchy in the development of Philadelphia's Sixty-Ninth Street area and subsequently joined the Sharon Hill firm his father had established around 1900.[58] He held a series of official positions in the township and county, so that in official debates, his was often the last word on what should be built, and how. From 1928 to 1932, he had collaborated with leading East Coast planners on an important regional plan for the contiguous urban areas of Pennsylvania, New Jersey, and Delaware. This plan had no government backing and therefore little concrete result, but its emphasis on neighborhood design, open spaces, and the inclusion of recreational areas and schools had a broad influence in the thirties, forties, and early fifties.[59] In 1954, H. Gilroy Damon, Jr. took over the leadership of the firm after his father's retirement; he then worked very closely with Bodek on the plan for Lawrence Park, and was the second of the engineers mentioned above. It is likely, therefore, that many of the more community-oriented features of the plan can be attributed to the Damons.

The third engineer to whom Bodek drew close was Claude De Botton, a young assistant who joined Bodek's firm in 1957. De Botton, an émigré from Egypt whose Jewish family had fled the Nazis, trained at the University of Pennsylvania in civil engineering and at Drexel University in architecture. Bodek admired De Botton's expertise when he met him through his Penn fraternity, and moved quickly to hire him. For a few years (1957–60), De Botton took over the general supervision of construction at Lawrence Park; he also designed a number of the new exteriors and plans that were employed among the houses in the later years of the development. The two men formed a short-lived but intimate relationship, with De Botton seeing Bodek initially as a mentor, and Bodek relying more and more on De Botton's contributions. After their friendship ended, De Botton became a local developer himself.[60]

It is not clear that Ralph Bodek thought of himself as a "community builder" when he began the Lawrence Park development, but clearly even at the start he had some notion that it must have a school, open space, and proximity to shopping and to industrial employment. The design of the community itself—at least the original design—had many of the best features of community design as they were understood in the mid-1950s. This design was certainly partly a result of the terrain, but also almost certainly partly a result of Bodek's interactions with his engineers. In the end, however, the central area was not made over into a park, and did not house the new elementary school (this was ultimately built at the western end of the development); the visual focus on the center simply leads the eye to a central piece of rough and undeveloped land. Bodek was willing to give up his plans for the central area of Lawrence Park in order to realize the profits he needed.

Many builders of the postwar period engaged in some kind of market research: sometimes they would build a few different models and calculate which ones sold better; sometimes they would use questionnaires filled out by buyers or prospective buyers to get an idea of what they should be building next. Ralph Bodek was the earliest of the builders discussed here to attempt the latter kind of research. In 1955 he commissioned a study of Lawrence Park buyers to be conducted by a seven-member market research team from the University of Pennsylvania; he published the results in 1958 as *How and Why People Buy Houses.*

This survey was a curious affair, restricted as it was to seventy-eight buyers of split-level houses in Lawrence Park *about a year after* they had made their house purchases. The explicit preference of the buyers for the split-level house type was therefore utterly predictable. Nor did the interviewers ask the buyers very penetrating questions about themselves: we do not learn their incomes, or very much about their work, their veteran statuses, or their previous housing experiences. The Bodek study focused above all on *how* people had found the house that they chose, and under this heading, it arrived at some interesting conclusions. Some of its characterizations of their searches are also useful, if we remember their status as satisfied new home buyers in a new split-level community.

Bodek's study concluded that house buyers searched specific locations that provided acceptable commuting distances (by automobile) to their workplaces. They found likely houses above all through newspaper advertisements, but also often either through friends and hearsay, or just by driving around and looking for sale signs. To his chagrin, very few were even aware of the advertising in *Life* magazine of which Bodek was so proud. He also found that a majority of buyers preferred a new house to an old one, and preferred to move into a new community rather than an established, older community. As part of their decision-making process, buyers had consulted family members and acquaintances in the building trades, rather than "experts." Other issues that were found to have affected their choices were: lot size (especially the space between houses), characteristics of the kitchen (they wanted a "modern kitchen"), and number of bedrooms (they wanted three). Scarcely any had been seeking a house that was all on one floor (again, quite predictable, since they were all new owners of the split-level type, and since, in any case, low-cost ranch houses were scarce in the Philadelphia area at the time). Most rejected air conditioning, which Bodek had thought would be a great attraction: they were suspicious of it, thinking it would be hard to control.

Beyond these rather limited findings, Bodek's study was unusual for its focus on "irrational" or emotional features in the buyers' choices. The book is subtitled *A Study of Subconscious Home Buying Motives.* The research team proposed to identify these motives by including in the interviews a "free association" component, in which the interviewees were shown pictures of "specimen houses" (a row house, a twin house, a two-story colonial house, a typical Bodek split-level, and a ranch house), and asked for their reactions. From this feature of the interviews, Bodek arrived at a number of conclusions about buyers' attitudes to social status. The row house, he said, was seen as a house for low-income families; the twin was identified with "the low-middle-income group, with laborers

and low white collar workers predominating"; the ranch house, he said, was seen as "very modern," "rather advanced and sporty," "not quite respectable." The ranch house model that Bodek showed in the book was his own early and very conservative version, hardly "sporty" (fig. 116), but one wonders whether the respondents were also encouraged to compare the nearby Facciolo flattops to their own rather staid-looking split-levels.

According to Bodek, the dominant house type in the Philadelphia suburbs at this time was the two-story colonial. This type, Bodek believed, caused status anxiety: it was "at the top of the social scale," seen as occupied by "upper-income professional people and executives." "Many would like to be similar to these people," he argued, "but they believe that they really cannot be like them. Therefore, they look for some intermediate social position. . . . The split-level home fills the bill."[61] It is hard to avoid the conclusion that these attitudes were as much Bodek's as his buyers', and that his conclusion contains a considerable portion of self-justification. It is also worth remembering that Bodek had begun to abandon the colonial references in his Lawrence Park split-levels by the time his book was published and that he began to build ranch houses in Lawrence Park soon afterward.[62]

At about the same moment in time as Bodek began to build ranch houses, Frank Facciolo started constructing split-levels. The configuration of their sites contributed something to these shifts: in the later fifties Facciolo was moving on to the hillier sites in Rose Tree Woods, while Bodek was exploiting the flatter areas of Lawrence Park. But they both were unquestionably trying to broaden their appeal among buyers. Facciolo, ever the proponent of "houses for the working man," built more expensively; in reality, it was Bodek's houses that appealed more strongly to working-class and lower-middle-class people.[63] Lawrence Park has also retained its original visual identity over time to a greater extent than Rose Tree Woods. The split-level with a "modern" look, and the ranch house with some conservative flavor, both deeply influenced by Bodek, subsequently dominated suburban development in the Philadelphia metropolitan area, growing larger and larger as they were sought out by more affluent buyers.

Campanelli Brothers and the New England Ranch House

Boston was older than Philadelphia and equally important politically in the colonial period. Its early development was in many ways similar. One of the world's most important ports in the eighteenth and nineteenth centuries, Boston was also a major center for manufacturing, especially in the garment and leather goods industries. To an even greater extent than Philadelphia, the Boston region gathered together the nation's oldest institutions of learning, and a large segment of its publishing enterprise. Partly because of its flourishing port, the city came to be one of the country's largest focuses of immigration in the nineteenth century, and developed very sizeable Irish, Italian, Polish, Russian, and Chinese enclaves, both inside the original city boundaries and in the early streetcar suburbs. (Its Catholic and Jewish populations were correspondingly large.)

To a greater extent than Philadelphia, however, the Boston region became a center for science and technology, so much so that in the years right after World War II it was thought of as the nation's most important site for high-technology enterprises. This was partly a result of the enormous influence of MIT in the development of American technology, which laid the basis for extensive collaboration with government defense efforts during World War II. The Radiation Laboratory at MIT developed radar and LORAN, while the MIT-affiliated Lincoln Laboratory near Lexington introduced sophisticated electronic systems of air defense. Already existing electronics companies like Raytheon (Cambridge, Newton, and then Waltham) joined in the development of defense systems, including new kinds of weapons during the war, as did older weapons-producing centers such as the Watertown arsenal. This wartime experience established a basis for the clustering around Boston of government laboratories and electronics industries after the war. Increasingly, high-tech enterprises located their offices along the new ring road around Boston, Route 128, begun in 1936 and rapidly extended in the first few years after the war (Wang Labs in 1951, Natick Labs ca. 1952). The beginning of the Massachusetts Turnpike in 1957 leading west and the development of Interstate 95 to the south meant that in the 1950s the hinterland around Boston developed an unusually efficient highway system.

The same could not be said of Boston's railroad system. Unlike those in Philadelphia, Boston's long-distance railroad links were exclusively to the north and south, and the commuter rail systems that fostered commuter suburbs in the Philadelphia area were largely absent. Instead, suburban growth outside the area of the earliest streetcar suburbs centered on the towns and villages that had populated the Massachusetts landscape since the colonial period. With the development of high-speed automobile arteries in the postwar period, new road building tended to link these older population centers; suburban growth therefore developed along the new roads, clustering to a certain extent around the older communities, but not radiating out from railroad commuter nodes as it did in the Philadelphia area.

Another difference from the Philadelphia area was the pattern of landholding in the Boston area. Massachusetts farms, like those of New England more generally, were relatively small and by the mid-twentieth century quite unproductive. They were also located rather close in toward the city, often bridging the path of Route 128. By the 1940s and 1950s, therefore, farmers were eager to sell, and the basis was laid for automobile-based suburbanization. But the parcels that builders and developers could acquire were correspondingly small, and rarely contiguous. Hence, individual building tracts in the Boston area were small and lacked continuity with one another.

Colonial architectural traditions were as venerated in the Boston area as they were around Philadelphia. But around Boston and unlike Philadelphia, a powerful element in the tradition was the modest wooden cottage, one to one and a half stories high, clad in boards or shingles without much embellishment.[64] This kind of house design, often called the "Cape Cod Cottage," was the basis of a widespread revival on the East Coast in the 1920s and 1930s, and provided the model for the first Levitt houses on Long Island.[65] Boston-area builders in the postwar period also used the Cape to a certain extent, but soon abandoned it in favor of the ranch house type introduced by the Campanellis.[66] Without basements, heated by radiant heat, apparently unsuited to the cold New England climate, Campanelli ranches were wildly popular. From Needham to Natick, Framingham to Brockton, Peabody to Hingham, ranch house residents spoke (and speak) with great affection of their "Campis."[67]

In the Boston metropolitan area, a single firm—Campanelli Brothers—dominated the market in suburban houses after 1948. Four brothers created a construction company in 1946 or 1947 that transformed itself rapidly into the leading home building enterprise in the Boston area (I include in this area Brockton, MA, and Warwick, RI). Ultimately, Campanelli Brothers gained a national reputation, and built extensively in Florida and Illinois. We will return to their work in Chicago in the next chapter. In the 1950s and 1960s, the firm built thousands of houses (8,500 to 12,000) in twenty-one different locations around Boston, battling fragmented property holding and often hostile zoning boards in the process (fig. 117).[68] From a very early date, perhaps earlier than any other

117. Campanelli subdivisions
near Boston 1950–65, map of
locations. Barbara Miller Lane
and Nathanael Roesch.

American builder in the East, they specialized in ranch houses with an open plan, erected on slabs and heated by radiant heat; they built these houses to fit all incomes and site requirements. The Campanelli brothers had no prewar experience or training in the building business, and little formal education, yet they devised construction and design processes that permitted them to design and build quickly and sell with great success. They were aided in their rise from a small construction business to leading builders and developers by a strong management team and by important close associates: the Natick realtor Martin Cerel and the Quincy engineer Bradford Saivetz.

The Campanelli brothers Michael (1912–74), Joseph (1918–2007), Nicholas (1921–2013), and Alfred (1924–2003), together with their sister Ann (d. 2012), were the children of Francesco Campanelli and Lisa Marie Colondono Campanelli (fig. 118). Around 1915, Francesco (Francis) and Lisa Marie emigrated from a tiny and ancient mountain village in the Italian Apennines, and settled in Brockton, Massachusetts.[69] Francesco, a former shoemaker, worked in the flourishing

FIELD OFFICE
CAMPANELLI BROS. INC. &
BRAINTREE LAKEVIEW REALTY & INC.
NATICK BUILDERS CO. INC.

118. The four brothers at their field office ca. 1950. Left to right: Nicholas, Alfred, Michael, Joseph.

shoe manufacturing industry of Brockton. The family lived in an old "triple-decker" apartment building in Brockton. When Francesco died in 1927, Michael (who was in his early teens) left school in order to help support the family; soon the other brothers followed suit. Some of them worked at the Quincy shipyards before the war. The family was extremely close-knit. When war came, Joseph, Nicholas, and Alfred joined the navy, serving in the Pacific,[70] while Michael continued in the Quincy shipyards.[71] At war's end, the brothers decided to open a construction and real estate business; Michael, who had acquired some property in Braintree and opened a grocery store there, was the financial planner for the new firm, but Joseph, Nicholas, and Alfred were the innovators in the business. (Later they were joined by Salvatore [Sully] De Marco, Ann's husband.) Having done some work with poured concrete during the war, they began by pouring footings for new buildings, and then branched out to build houses on slabs.[72] Some of the brothers' first groups of houses were built on previously platted land in Warwick, Rhode Island, not far from the family home in Brockton. Here, from 1946 or 1947 on, they made a significant name for themselves as builders of ranch houses; indeed the designs of most of their later ranch house models can be traced back to the community known as Governor Francis Farms in Warwick. Meanwhile, Michael began to acquire small plots of land in proximity to his store in Braintree. The brothers' first housing development on their own land, begun in 1947 or 1948, numbered twenty-five ranch houses on slabs near Lakeside Drive in Braintree, and was called Braintree Dam (1948 to about 1953).[73] At about the same time, the brothers began to prospect for land in Natick, Massachusetts: here they built another of their earliest developments, the small Beaconsfield (about 130 houses, ca. 1949–51). Like Governor Francis Farms, this was on already-platted land.

Over time, the Campanellis built four or five different developments in and around Warwick, totaling about 200 houses. In Warwick, the first group was erected behind the Aldrich High School, from about 1948 to 1955. The second was at Governor Francis Farms, where some 135 houses were built between 1948 and 1956.[74] The third was Sheridan Park off Main Avenue.[75] The fourth was off Buttonwoods Avenue, due east of Buttonwoods shopping center, with Warwick assessor's dates of 1955. An early resident of Governor Francis Farms visited another Campanelli development in Barrington, Rhode Island, and described it as under construction in 1950.[76] I have succeeded in locating three of these subdivisions.

Governor Francis Farms, on a property belonging to the Brown family, descendants of early nineteenth-century governor John Brown Francis (1833–37), was an attractive site near the water (on the Gaspee Peninsula between two coves), about seven miles southeast of Providence. It was laid out by Warwick landscape architects Edwin Prellwitz and J. D. Graham in 1938 as a community of relatively modest dwellings.[77] The settlement developed slowly during the war. In the 1930s the Brown family added to it, as Providence/Warwick airport construction began to develop toward it. From 1938, building development was supervised by Roswell B. Liscomb, a forward-looking realtor/developer, but was still under the control of the Brown family, the landholders, who constituted a Board of Directors. This board's approval was needed for each new lot and building design. Building proceeded after 1945 relatively rapidly; by the 1980s the houses numbered "more than a thousand."[78]

It was Liscomb who invited the young Campanellis to the site after the war. Shortly thereafter, the Brown family donated land for a new school to the growing community, and land for a shopping center. Liscomb took charge of the advertising: in his firm's publications, the style of the houses was labeled as "semi-colonial ranch," and the Campanellis were described as "Gaspee Builders," and as "one of the largest building organizations in New England," one that can, because of the size of its operations, "pass along large savings" to the buyer.[79] Liscomb's advertising also described the "sensible deed restrictions" at Governor Francis Farms as attractive to banks.[80] Before the war, the Governor Francis Farms board had actively discriminated against Jews, Portuguese, Eastern Europeans, and Catholics, against all, in other words, who were not seen as

119. Campanelli Brothers, Governor Francis Farms, Warwick, RI, early model, exterior, modern view. Photo by Diane Brannon.

120. Campanelli Brothers, Governor Francis Farms, Warwick, RI, early model, plan. Nathanael Roesch, from sketch by current owner.

"white Anglo-Saxon Protestants." But in the postwar period, these restrictions were abandoned: Liscomb and the board at that point simply vetted new buyers for financial stability and apparent commitment to the purchase.[81]

The first model houses built by the Campanellis at Governor Francis Farms between 1948 and 1952 established the house forms that Campanelli Brothers would follow for many years thereafter (figs. 119, 120, 121, 122). The houses in figures 119 and 121 were three-bedroom, one-bath dwellings, long and low and simple in outline, with a hip or gabled roof, an attached one-car garage, a relatively large living room (14 × 18 feet or 12 × 16 feet) with a fireplace, and a dining ell leading to the kitchen. The living room was at the front in figures 119 to 121, and the kitchen at the back, but the third of the models of this early period (fig. 122) was an L-shaped house: here, the arrangement was reversed, with the living room placed at the rear. The houses, advertised by Liscomb as "all electric," had up-to-date kitchen and laundry equipment (GE washing machine and dishwasher), and the Campanellis offered a choice of colors for walls and fixtures.[82] Their early version of the ubiquitous picture window was a bow window or a multiple-paned "western style" window;[83] by 1952, this had been replaced by the tripartite picture window typical of the fifties, as in figure 121.[84] Sometimes, as in figure 121, a small projecting gable framed the entry door.[85] There was about 1,000 square feet of living space in these early houses. The only obvious "colonial" motif in the houses was the window shutters. As a sales brochure published by Liscomb's office makes clear, the Campanellis continued to build these three models in Governor Francis Farms throughout the early fifties.[86]

The Campanellis used the same forms and plans elsewhere too, in concurrent work at Braintree and Natick, and in their later work in Natick, Needham, Framingham, Holbrook, and Brockton (figs. 123, 124, 125; fig. 6). It is therefore hard to be sure that the Warwick houses were unequivocally the first of their types for the Campanellis. But we can conclude that the firm created and popularized a sophisticated New England version of the ranch house at a very early date—at

121. Campanelli Brothers, Governor Francis Farms, Warwick, RI, early model, modern view. Photo by Diane Brannon.

122. Campanelli Brothers, Governor Francis Farms, Warwick, RI, early model, L-shape, modern view. Photo by Diane Brannon.

123. Campanelli Brothers, house, Westfield, Natick, 1954, exterior, modern view. Photo by the author.

124. Campanelli Brothers, house, Westfield, Natick, 1954, plan.

least as early as 1949—at a time when the ranch house type was extremely rare in all other places except Chicago and Los Angeles. Their designs, despite their sometimes slight "colonial" flavor, were widely understood as revolutionary. As one early resident remembers, "We were willing to wait for it," because "it was a whole new kind of house; it seemed right for a whole new time."[87]

Now advertising themselves as "New England's largest builders of quality ranch homes,"[88] the Campanelli brothers moved on from Warwick and Braintree to acquire land in Natick, much nearer to Boston. Initially they found only a rather small and already platted land parcel near the center of town. Working for the first time with Bradford Saivetz, together with a local realtor,[89] they built sixty-six houses in Beaconsfield in 1950–51 and added another sixty-five in the next three years. The firm's success began to take off in Natick, and then in neighboring Framingham: in Natick they built, in quick succession, subdivisions called Wethersfield and Westfield, totaling about 1,500 houses between 1950 and about 1955, and, in Framingham (in subdivisions called Fairfield, Elmfield, Pinefield, Cherryfield, Ridgefield, Longfield, Woodfield, Deerfield, and Greenwich), a total of about 2,600 houses between 1953 and about 1966.[90]

During the same period of time, they also built small groups of houses (200 or fewer) at Braintree, Newton, Needham, Wayland, Beverly, Hingham, Danvers, Chelmsford, Hudson, Ipswich, Peabody (ca. 300), Raynham, Sudbury, and Westford. In 1956, they launched a series of subdivisions in their hometown of Brockton, building more than 2,000 houses there by about 1965. The houses at Beverly, Hingham, Danvers, Chelmsford, Hudson, Ipswich, Peabody, Raynham, Sudbury, and Westford (most on the more affluent "North Shore" of the metropolitan area) were larger than the early houses, with three to four bedrooms, two or more bathrooms, two-car garages, and large kitchens with eating areas,

125. Campanelli Brothers, Ridgefield, Framingham, L-shaped house 1955 (advertised as "the Enchantress"), modern view. Photo by the author.

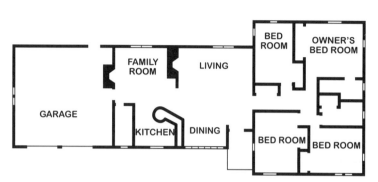

FAMILY ROOM · LIVING · GARAGE · KITCHEN · DINING · BED ROOM · OWNER'S BED ROOM · BED ROOM · BED ROOM

126. Campanelli Brothers, El Dorado, Hingham, plan. Restored by Nathanael Roesch from a newspaper advertisement of October 1957.

127. Doris Campanelli showing interior (note pine paneling and plaster ceiling).

sometimes continuous with family rooms or living areas (fig. 126).[91] The houses at Brockton (figs. 6, 8), on the other hand, were smaller than those at Warwick and much less expensive. Working with local suppliers, the Campanellis developed some very popular interior finishes and kitchen designs (fig. 127).[92] One of their best-liked kitchen appliances was the GE "wall-mounted refrigerator" (fig. 128, plate 2).[93] One buyer in Brockton says that this refrigerator was a major factor in his family's choice of house, "because it gave us so much more counter space" (Mr. KC). The firm developed a particularly close relationship with General Electric, winning citations from that company for the volume of its purchases.[94] The local GE representative was active in looking for land for the Campanellis.[95] Many of the houses, in all price ranges, had an exterior patio, often stressed in advertisements (fig. 129).

The brothers continued to experiment with new models, testing the market. A house type with a sweeping front gable, supported on short masonry piers and somewhat resembling the Cinderella Homes in Anaheim (1955–57), advertised as the Californian, appeared in some of the Framingham and Brockton houses (figs. 130, 131) in ads of 1958 and 1959. In the more affluent communities, in the early 1960s, the firm added to its roster of house types a "mid-level split" and a more conventional split-level; at this time they also built some two-story houses (fig. 132).[96] Overall, however, the brothers continued to build ranch houses, with plans and external styles that did not change very much. The ranches in more affluent neighborhoods had more bedrooms and baths, but were otherwise quite similar to the earlier and smaller models.

In Natick and in many subsequent areas around Boston where the Campanellis built, there were conflicts with the local planning and building authorities. These were bodies that had little or no experience with new housing

128. GE wall-mounted refrigerator, advertisement, detail, *Saturday Evening Post*, November 20, 1956.

129. Campanelli Brothers, patio from living room of L-shaped house in Holbrook. Restored by Nathanael Roesch from advertisement of May 1956.

THERE'S NO HOME LIKE THE"

Fairfield

AT HOLBROOK. MASS.

$16.98 per week
$67.00 Mo. Princ. & Int.
G. I. NO DOWN PAYMENT
30 year mort. @ 4½%
Easy non-G.I. financing
$13,400

130. Campanelli Brothers, house with giant cross-gable, Framingham, 1955, modern view. Photo by the author.

131. Campanelli Brothers, "The Californian," Brockton. Restored by Nathanael Roesch from newspaper advertisement of February 1959.

VETERANS - *Nothing Down!*
SEE THIS TERRIFIC VALUE NOW.

$14,990*

*THE CALIFORNIAN
Brand New, Conventionally Constructed, Architecturally Designed
3-BEDROOM RANCH HOMES
With Garage • 1½ Baths

construction; often, these boards were obstructive, failing, for example, to issue building permits in a timely manner. Often too, the future neighbors of prospective developments looked for opportunities to thwart the new developments. Bradford Saivetz, along with Martin Cerel, represented the Campanellis at public hearings, in Natick and other local communities, supporting policies and legislation to protect the new builder.[97] Working with the local Home Builders' Association and with Cerel, Saivetz and the Campanellis also pushed through at the state level new legislation that protected builders against the adoption of planning changes during the period of construction.[98]

New England's Greatest Selection of New Homes . . . In Framingham!

"The Most Popular Suburb." *Deerfield III*
AT-FRAMINGHAM CENTRE

No matter what type of home you're looking for . . . DEERFIELD III has it! A terrific selection of big split-entry ranches with FULL BASEMENTS, magnificent traditional colonials with FOUR spacious bedrooms . . . the ever-popular and all-new L-SHAPED designs (with 7 double-size rooms!) . . . and a fantastic variety of rambling ranches! There's SOMETHING FOR YOU . . . in New England's MOST POPULAR Suburban community! Drive out today with the family . . . have a free Pepsi, and be our guests!

The CARVER $23,990
9 Room Colonial with Attached Garage

The GLENWOOD $18,990
Full Basement Center-Entrance Ranch

PRICES START AT
$16,990
GI'S NO CASH DOWN Non-GI's Little Cash Down

Your Choice of Many, Many Architectural Designs!

PLENTY OF CHOICE WOODED SETTINGS NOW AVAILABLE

The HAMPTON $19,990
7 Room L-Shaped Home with Attached Garage

The BEDLINGTON $16,990
Budget-Minded Families will love this dream home

DIRECTIONS: Route 9 WEST to traffic lights in Framingham Centre (1½ miles beyond Shoppers' World). SHARP RIGHT at the ESSO sign onto Edgell Road and follow road about 4 miles to Harrington Road and Deerfield III (watch for yellow arrows along the route). From Sudbury, take Nobscot Road off Route 20 which becomes Edgell Road in Framingham and watch for yellow arrows.

The RENWICK "B"
$19,500
Fabulous Bay View Window Ranch, New and Exciting!

The MASON $17,990
Brick-Front Rambling Ranch with Front Porch

Means MC Confidence MARTIN CEREL *Realtor*
INCORPORATED
Natick, Massachusetts • OLympic 3-3000   CAMPANELLI BROS. INC., Builders

There is no conclusive evidence as to how and why the Campanellis created their version of the ranch house. Campanelli family members consistently emphasize that house design, for them, was "market-driven"—that is, they built what they learned would sell.[99] And it is certainly clear that they built increasing numbers of ranch houses because they sold extremely well. But it is also obvious that the Campanelli ranch houses themselves helped decisively in creating these market preferences, so the issue of the Campanellis' inspiration remains. The brothers visited Levittown, Long Island, in the late 1940s, and observed the construction techniques used there, but the true ranch house was not yet being built by the Levitts. It is possible that the Campanellis saw and read the 1949 *Better Homes and Gardens* issue on the Ramona Ranch, or Cliff May's 1946 publication *Sunset Western Ranch Houses.* (Given their lack of schooling, and their early self-identification with construction rather than architecture, it seems very unlikely that they would have read the articles on the ranch house published by the professional architectural magazines in the later 1940s.)

132. Campanelli Brothers, Framingham, Deerfield, six models. Restored by Nathanael Roesch from newspaper advertisement of July 1961.

In many respects, the Boston metropolitan area was something of a hotbed of housing innovation. Royal Barry Wills, the well-known popularizer of modernized colonial Capes, had centered his practice in the Boston area, and was beginning to build one-story houses (fig. 65). Already in the 1940s, Gropius protégé Carl Koch had begun building modernist-looking houses in the Belmont area (Snake Hill), and soon after the war he began to promote the "Techbuilt" prefabrication system for small houses, which won a good deal of local and national acclaim.[100] William Wurster, a practitioner of the ranch house form long before it became well known outside California (fig. 64), was dean of architecture and planning at MIT from 1945 to 1950, and it is not unlikely that his work was written up in Boston-area newspapers.[101] In 1947, the Architects' Collaborative (TAC, of Cambridge, MA), under Walter Gropius's leadership, introduced a group of flat-roofed modern houses in Lexington (Six Moon Hill, twenty acres, occupied by TAC members); perhaps the Campanellis visited these (though they never built a flat-roofed house). And in 1951, TAC built a larger and better-known community in Lexington, Five Fields (1951–57): here eighty acres were built up with pitched roof "ranch" houses, which could have been attractive to the Campanellis.[102] But perhaps, like Facciolo and Bodek, one or more of the Campanellis simply "saw something" he liked while serving in the navy, something that provided a model for the early ranch houses. The "Californian" label for figure 131 indicates that they made some connection between ranch houses and California.

As time passed, as the business flourished, and as further variations in design were introduced, it is possible that some members of the firm consulted national magazines; the most likely stimulus of this sort would have been the *Correlator*, the monthly publication of the NAHB, which contained not only design ideas but also long sections on building construction and technological innovations. And we know that by the mid-fifties the partners liked to attend the larger home shows, especially in Chicago, but perhaps also in New York.[103] But, at least in the early years, the Campanellis were much more likely to turn to local and personal acquaintances for advice: one of these was builder and developer Charles Brustin (1913–90), who introduced them to Bradford Saivetz; another was architect Ralph I. Williams (1916–2006, an acquaintance of Brustin and Saivetz; fig. 110), whom they hired to produce working drawings for their earliest houses, before they added two other local architect/draftsmen to their permanent staff.[104] Brustin, according to Saivetz, helped them to see how to divide the tasks of building into smaller tasks appropriate to the various subcontractors.[105] Realtor Liscomb at Governor Francis Farms may also have played a part in helping to form their early designs. Nicholas Campanelli, though, has always stated most emphatically that the brothers designed the houses themselves, and that architects were useful to them *only* for making the working drawings. (As one Campanelli ad put it, "The best architects a builder has are today's home buyers

and prospective buyers.")[106] Whatever the explanation for their preference for the ranch house type (sometimes with a trace of colonial detailing), it is clear that they were devoted to it: the ranch continued to predominate in their East Coast building during all the years that the firm continued to build houses (up to the early seventies). The family house in Brockton, built originally for their mother (ca. 1955) and then expanded as a residence for Nicholas Campanelli and his family, was a larger-scale version of the ranch houses they were building throughout the Boston suburbs (figs. 133, 134).[107]

Campanelli houses in the Boston area were finished with shingles or horizontal siding (usually asbestos, sometimes wood), and solidly built. The Campanelli brothers modeled their use of concrete slab construction on the practices of the Levitts, but their designs were very different from the early Levitt designs. And although the brothers employed relatively large-scale building methods— clearing several blocks at once, pouring multiple slabs at once, using each group of construction workers in sequence, and buying precut lumber from nearby lumber yards[108]—most of their developments were relatively small in scale and slow in construction. Usually the Campanellis waited until a first small group of houses was built and sold before starting the next group: in this way they avoided debt and attracted the support of local banking enterprises.

The Campanellis found land for their developments from a variety of sources: the previous uses of their tracts included, in addition to small farms, a golf course, a tree farm, a disused airport, a gravel pit.[109] The piecemeal character of their developments, largely the result of the character of landholding in the Boston metropolitan area, meant that, in order to maintain consistent crews and to develop relations with their suppliers, they had to constantly expand the number of places in which they built. This is turn made the firm especially dependent upon

133. Campanelli Brothers, Nicholas Campanelli house, Brockton 1955ff.

134. Campanelli Brothers, kitchen interior, Nicholas Campanelli house, Brockton 1955ff.

135. Left to right, standing: Bradford Saivetz, Nicholas Campanelli, Martin Cerel.

Opposite:

136. Bradford Saivetz for Campanelli Brothers, plot plan, Wethersfield. Restored by Nathanael Roesch from plan in Middlesex South, Registry of Deeds, Cambridge, MA.

137. Bradford Saivetz for Campanelli Brothers, plot plan, Brookfield Heights. Restored by Nathanael Roesch, from plans in Brockton Engineers' Office.

their real estate brokers to locate new sites, and on their engineer to lay out the plot plans and streets in a great variety of settings. They first worked with the engineer Bradford Saivetz at "Beaconsfield" in North Natick (1949–51),[110] and began their long relationship with broker Martin Cerel shortly thereafter (fig. 135).

Bradford Saivetz (1923–), who describes himself as "the fifth brother," worked as the Campanellis' engineer on all their housing in Massachusetts from 1950, and on many of their commercial properties thereafter.[111] He also played an important part in their work in Chicago, and in some of their enterprises in Florida. Saivetz sees his special talent as the ability to get a maximum number of lots out of a particular tract, and in this he was very effective. In the Boston metropolitan area, where by necessity he was working with a multiplicity of local ordinances and traditions, Saivetz's plans were consistent and distinctive, both for their efficient use of land and for their gently curving streets (modeled, he says, on the curvilinear street patterns of small New England towns) (figs. 136, 137).[112] His engineering firm came to be quite prominent in Massachusetts; ultimately it worked for some of the largest housing builders and commercial enterprises in the country.[113]

Born in Peabody, Massachusetts, Saivetz was the grandson of Jewish immigrants from Eastern Europe; his paternal grandfather operated a kosher butcher shop, and his father provided meats from local dairy farms to local kosher enterprises. It was a large and closely knit family, not very well off, but living on properties large enough to grow big gardens. Saivetz attended engineering school at Northeastern (both before and after the war), and, after a stint in the Marines, set up his own surveying and engineering business in 1948 (in Quincy, MA). Like the brothers, he was still in his twenties, and eager to participate in

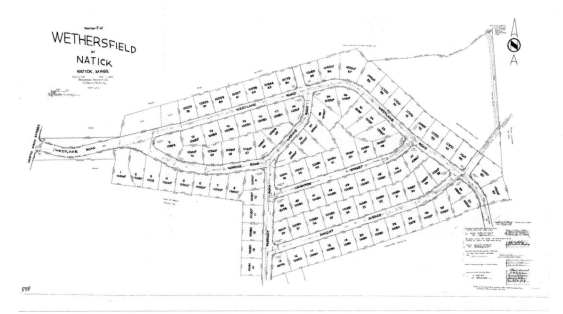

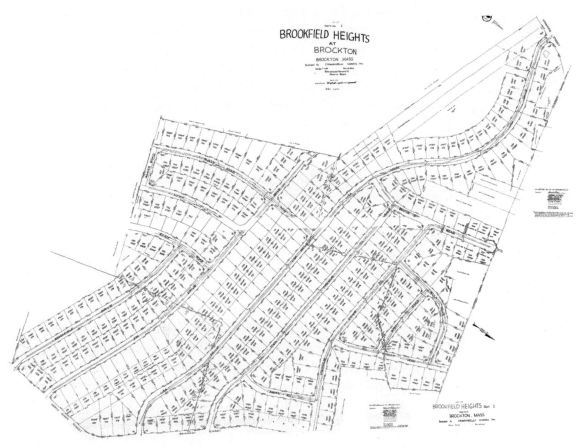

the land boom then beginning around Boston: his first jobs involved housing.[114] Like other veterans who swelled the ranks of civil engineers in the first post-war years (and unlike the leaders of long-established firms like the Damons of the Philadelphia area discussed above),[115] he was hugely enthusiastic about new technologies, and quick to adopt new methods. His firm early employed new cal-culators that had been developed during the war and was one of the first in the Boston area to use a computer, greatly simplifying the complex task of laying out many house plots at once. He saw himself, as the Campanelli brothers probably also did, as helping to solve a critical housing shortage for returning soldiers, especially those of low income, and as "fighting ignorance in order to achieve a better future."[116]

The other principal actor in the rise of the Campanelli firm was Martin Cerel (1908–87), a realtor based in Natick.[117] Cerel was an extraordinary—perhaps unique—figure in the history of postwar tract housing: a finder of land and financing, a facilitator of new kinds of design, construction, and development, full of ideas and successes in bringing new enterprises to Natick, but a man who did not own most of the land with which he dealt, and did not invest in most of the housing developments that he advertised.[118] He was a broker, par excel-lence, a genius at advertising and networking. New tracts, whether designed and developed by the Campanellis or by other builders, were advertised as "another Martin Cerel community." As a result, those who wrote at the time, and those who have written later about housing development around Boston, have assumed that Cerel was the developer and/or designer of vast expanses of new housing. Cerel was indeed eager to educate the public as to the nature of subdivi-sion planning and design, but he did not, himself, perform these functions.[119]

Martin Cerel was the son of a Lithuanian Jew who owned a store in Med-way, Massachusetts.[120] After his mother's early death, Martin left school without graduating and clerked in his father's store. Shortly before the second Word War, the elder Cerel began a real estate business, Joseph Cerel & Son, Residential, Village and Farm Properties, with offices in Medway and Natick. Joseph Cerel came to be expert at finding small farms and village properties, which he bought or optioned and then resold (sometimes after some renovation). His three sons worked with him throughout the war, but it was Martin who took over the Natick part of the business and the local know-how and contacts that came with it. After the war, Martin was quick to ally himself with local builders, and especially with an enterprise called United Homes, for which he served as the treasurer, and for which he put together some large parcels in Natick and Wellesley between 1945 and 1949. These developments, which his advertising described as "Sherwood-at-Natick," "Stratford-at-Natick," and "Pelham-at-Natick," were very successful. Sherwood featured a small two-story house with some half timbering; Strat-ford, "an expandable Cape Codder"; Pelham, a modified Cape, which Cerel

advertised as a "ranch" (fig. 139). This Pelham "ranch" was an almost exact copy of the Levitt "ranch" being built on Long Island at the same time (fig. 19), and it is clear that there was a good deal of contact between United Homes and the Levitt enterprise.[121] Further United Homes developments in the Natick area followed between 1950 and 1952; all were Capes or two-story quasi-colonials with full basements.[122]

At this time, Cerel built up the staff of his office on Route 9 in Natick to include a large roster of salesmen, together with artists, a writer, and a photo lab, in order to create copy for his ubiquitous newspaper ads.[123] An ebullient host, he began to entertain local bankers and businessmen at a weekly office luncheon prepared by his own chef. And he began to use several characteristic marketing devices: the developments displayed fully furnished and equipped model houses, which offered several choices of wall coverings and flooring; each group of houses was sold in sections, with one advertised as "sold out" before the next was marketed; the opening of each section was celebrated with carnivals, pony rides, balloons, and prizes.[124] Such was Cerel's growing reputation that he became president of the Home Builders Association of Greater Boston in 1952.[125]

As a result of his increasingly diverse and important contacts, Cerel was able to broker the location of new industries and commercial enterprises in and near Natick.[126] He played an important role in obtaining land for Shoppers' World, the immense new indoor shopping mall in Framingham that opened in 1951,[127] and for the Natick Industrial Park, which included, by 1954, Ford Motor Company offices, Carling brewery, and Natick Labs, established by the Army Quartermaster Corps.[128] Shoppers' World was a prominent feature of all Cerel's South Shore housing advertisements after 1951, and the employees of Natick Labs and the other Industrial Park components bought into several of the Campanelli developments that Cerel was advertising and marketing in the mid-fifties.[129] By 1957, Cerel was a very wealthy man.[130]

But despite Cerel's undoubted services to the economic development of Natick and Framingham, and despite his habit of advertising each new housing development as "a Martin Cerel community," there is no evidence that he had either design ability or an overarching sense of community building. He did not design streets or houses, or commercial and industrial complexes, or participate in their design. He understood the importance for new housing of the proximity of industry and commerce, but he did not have any clear ideas about how to connect new enterprise to the housing developments themselves. His thinking about housing developments was always that of the real estate salesman: he wanted, simply—to sell houses.[131]

During the years of close collaboration with the Campanellis and Saivetz, Cerel's advertising changed to mirror the economies of the ranch house and

139. Martin Cerel, "ranch" advertisement (for Pelham Cape). Restored by Nathanael Roesch from newspaper advertisement of April 1949.

140. Martin Cerel, own house, Natick, 1953ff.

its appeal to new markets. His ads for the inexpensive Pelham Capes (which he called ranches) had featured an image of a cowboy, and exhorted new buyers, "Look here, pardner!" "Stake your claim" to "a touch of Texas" (fig. 139),[132] while his ads for high-end houses at Wellesley-at-Natick spoke of "small estates" where new owners could "live like a country squire."[133] Now, for the Campanelli houses, his publicity depicted a "modern, rambling ranch home," with a "22 ft. fireplaced living room," a "dream kitchen," a "huge recreational garage," a house where "everything's new," offering "a new concept of living." Now he emphasized the proximity not of golf courses, but of shopping and "ultra-modern" schools. Every ad now began with the price—$14,990 for GIs for a three-bedroom, one-and-a-half-bath house with a one-car garage in Westfield-at-Natick ($122,000 in 2010 dollars), for example.[134] Cerel saw the Campanelli ranch houses not merely as superbly marketable, but also as glamorous: in 1953 he modeled his own luxurious house in Natick on the Campanelli designs (fig. 140).[135] Later, when the Campanellis took over their own advertising, they continued to emphasize the theme that the Campanelli ranch house was a revelation of a "new way of life." New houses in and around Brockton, for example, were advertised as part of—or perhaps the cause of—the rising sun (fig. 141).

The relationship with Cerel continued for a number of years on a lesser scale, on smaller properties in Peabody, Deerfield, Bellingham, Danvers, and Ipswich, but after 1955 the Campanellis began to use other real estate brokers to find available tracts, while Cerel began to work with other builders in addition to the Campanellis.[136] In 1956, the Campanellis briefly joined Cerel and construction magnate and developer Lou Perini (owner of the Boston Braves) in an ill-fated attempt to create a new suburb in West Palm Beach, Florida.[137] The Campanellis' portion of this development plan was restricted to the design and building of a new (and separate) community for African Americans, mandated by the

141. Campanelli Brothers:
Brookfield at Holbrook,
showing sunrise. Restored
by Nathanael Roesch from
newspaper advertisement
of October 1959.

planning office of West Palm Beach. Ultimately, the new suburb for whites was also developed successfully, but the Campanellis withdrew rather quickly from the enterprise, and Cerel lost money during the planning phase.[138]

During the initial years of collaboration with Cerel, while working in Natick and Framingham, the Campanellis had built up their firm. By 1957, their firm had surpassed Cerel's in size, and followed many of the same practices that he had employed at United Homes. Each new development was heralded by model homes, and, after all of the land in a subdivision was prepared and cleared, construction continued in segments of the overall subdivision, awaiting sales. Now the Campanellis themselves designed the newspaper advertising (under the direction of Sully De Marco), using ever more complicated drawings, together with a wide range of photographs. (The Campanellis were the first East Coast builders I encountered to include house plans in their advertisements.) Their wives and children now appeared in publicity photos (as Cerel's also did), to advertise Campanelli houses and house interiors (figs. 127, 133, 134). The firm added a draftsman and a junior architect, to prepare advertising copy and draw up the building proposals.

The brothers themselves spent a great deal of time on site, and they also had a staff of foremen whom they employed full-time, year-round.[139] These were loyal and devoted men who worked for the company for many years, often until retirement.[140] Subcontractors varied, since actual building operations were seasonal; again, however, the firm employed the same tradesmen year after year, building up long-term loyalty. The company came to be known as service-oriented: foremen or other employees visited new buildings periodically during the first year or so after construction, and problems were usually resolved without charge.

During the height of the building season, the partners met each week (on Thursdays) with all the men on their staff (architects or draftsmen, engineers, foremen, subcontractors, advertising people, and sometimes bank representatives); the meetings continued during the rest of the year for a smaller group. This method of administration kept the brothers in close touch with all aspects of the operation, and it kept them in touch with each other too: a governing principle within the firm was that no decision on any significant financial, marketing, or design issue would be taken without the explicit agreement of all four brothers.[141] This tradition continued, with modifications created by distance, when the brothers began working in Illinois and Florida.[142]

Throughout the history of the firm, Campanelli Brothers remained a tightly knit organization intimately tied to the family (fig. 142).[143] Decision making continued to be closely controlled by the brothers despite increasing reliance on their senior staff. Most of the brothers sometimes served as foremen, and they and their children (and those of Ann and Sully De Marco) participated in construction work (fig. 143). The task of naming streets, intractable for many builders, was solved by the partners and the "fifth brother," Brad Saivetz, by always using family names. Joseph, Michael, Nicholas, Ann, and Alfred streets or roads appeared in nearly every development, as did Lisa and Francis (their mother and father). Bradford Saivetz, and his family (his wife Temi and their children Richard and Ruthellen) too gave their names to streets and roads in more than a dozen developments from the South to the North Shore. Through the repetition of these street names in place after place (and also by the repetitive addition of "field" to the name of nearly all developments), residents in the Boston metropolitan area came to have an almost intuitive sense of which housing groups had been built by the Campanellis.[144]

The Campanellis, like other builders of the time, combined traditional American building methods with new materials and techniques, building fast

142. Campanelli family portrait. Back row, left to right: Joseph Campanelli, Sully DeMarco, Michael Campanelli, Nicholas Campanelli. Front row, left to right: Clara Campanelli, Ann DeMarco, Lisa Marie Campanelli, Josephine Campanelli, Doris Campanelli.

and inexpensively. But, because of their highly qualified foremen, and their close attention to materials, details, and supervision, their houses gained an impressive reputation for their excellent construction. Initially, this reputation was local, but it soon became national and even international. In late fall of 1955, Alfred Campanelli guided Soviet housing experts through the company's recent housing in Peabody, demonstrating methods of construction and design.[145] One of the earliest families to move into the Campanellis' subdivision in Chicago (in 1960) bought their house because a friend living near Boston had told them of the firm's reputation.[146] In their hometown of Brockton, the Campanellis became local heroes: here they established scholarships for local high school students and endowed the sports stadium for the Brockton Rox baseball team (named after fellow Brockton-hero Rocky Marciano).[147]

But the Campanellis were never able again, on the East Coast, to approach the size and scale of the developments in Natick and Framingham. In 1957, they began an intensive land search in other states and ended up building one of largest developments of the fifties in the Golden Corridor of Chicago, where they were finally able to acquire large tracts of land (400 acres initially; ultimately 1,500 acres). They built there until the early 1980s; then they stopped constructing houses and negotiated the transition to commercial building. Unlike Centex, the largest building firm discussed here (and the Campanellis' rivals in Chicago's Golden Corridor), the Campanellis did not seek to become a national house-building firm in the long term.[148] Instead, they continued (and still continue) as a highly successful commercial and industrial construction company. We will meet them again in Chicago.

CHAPTER 4

The Builders of Chicago's Golden Corridor
Midwestern Ranches and Splits

From 1890 to 1980, Chicago was the second largest city in the United States, reaching its highest population of 3.6 million in 1950. (Its metropolitan region exceeded 5 million in 2000.) Its continued explosive growth had a great deal to do with geography and transportation: Chicago sat at the confluence of lake and river traffic from the north, south, west, and east, traffic that connected with Chicago's extensive railroad network, built up from the 1840s onward. As a result, early on Chicago became the hub of the US railroad network, the trans-shipment point for goods from all directions.[1] Located in the midst of rich grain fields and large-scale cattle industries, and serving also as the entrepôt for the shipment of timber from the north, the grain and timber trades (and the meat-packing industry) defined the economy of the city at an early date. Gradually, cattle and hogs from the ranches of the West and Southwest were transported to the city for processing. During the same period, the importation of iron ore from Lake Superior enabled the rapid growth of local steel industries. Local enterprises such as the manufacture of agricultural implements (McCormick Reaper Co.) and railroad-related products (Pullman Car Works) flourished as a result of the local steel industries. After World War II, mills in Indiana and Illinois accounted for about 20 percent of total US production capacity, and at this time the United States was making almost half the world's steel.[2] By the end of the nineteenth century, Chicago was a vital supplier of grain, meat and meat products, dairy products, vegetables, building materials, and high-grade steel for the rest of the county.

Farmland in northern Illinois, between the early city and the Mississippi River, had been acquired by the US government from the local Native American populations in a treaty of 1835. The land was then divided into "townships" of thirty-six square miles, each containing thirty-six plats of 640 acres each. Originally (1830s), the 640-acre sections were sold off at a minimum size of 80 acres, but most incoming settlers purchased larger tracts and established cattle pastures and grain fields.[3] Initial settlers came from the East Coast, but after the revolutions of the 1840s, increasing numbers came from Europe, especially from Germany.

Thus, Chicago's burgeoning economy was a unique compound of agriculture, industry, and manufacturing. As such, it was a preeminent destination for the flood of immigration from Europe to the United States that began in the 1820s. After the Great Chicago Fire of 1871, with new waves of immigration, the city became a kind of perpetual building site, a place where great entrepreneurs made their fortunes building new factories, but also one where the expansion of industry and manufacturing accommodated the ever-increasing flow of immigrants into the work force, and where its expanding population required ever greater numbers of dwellings. Chicago's working class was very large, and rather sharply divided between industrial workers and workers in the crafts and trades, especially the building trades. Chicago neighborhoods tended to be divided by class barriers; they were also strongly defined by ethnicity. As the "great migration" of African Americans from the South began during World War I, Chicago neighborhoods came to be sharply divided by race, as well as by ethnicity.

Chicago's central role in American architectural innovation has long been understood by historians writing about Frank Lloyd Wright and the Prairie School. Its contribution to the development of the American skyscraper is also widely acknowledged. Underpinning these architectural developments, though, were deeper currents in economy, geography, and patterns of work. Accessible timber, paired with an inventive spirit and a need for rapidity in construction, produced Chicago's "balloon frame" construction in the 1830s, the foundation for all later American "stick-built" structures.[4] The availability of high-grade iron ore to Chicago's efficient transportation network laid the basis for the evolution of steel and concrete industries, and these in turn permitted experimentation with the steel-framed, high-rise structures after the Great Chicago Fire. (This kind of experimentation was also a background to Wright's use of steel and concrete.) The fire itself, which produced a need for vast numbers of new buildings and at the same time attracted a new influx of builders and other construction personnel, led to new building codes and standards. Masonry walls were now required in almost all new buildings. During the last third of the century, innovation was wedded to high standards in construction, and masonry (more fireproof) was wedded to wood. The city attracted masons and carpenters from all over the United States and from Europe.

The vast growth of Chicago, together with the exceptionally rapid development of working class enclaves, also produced innovation and leadership in urban planning. Riverside, Illinois, nine miles to the west of the center city and laid out on a curvilinear pattern by Frederick Law Olmstead in 1869, served as a prototype for the subdivisions occupied by many generations of affluent house buyers, fleeing the dirt and dangers of working-class areas. Railroad magnate George Pullman's "company town," built in the 1880s on the South Side of Chicago and populated by Pullman workers, convinced Chicagoans of the possibility of producing good design for the "lower classes." Riverside and Pullman City were among America's first nineteenth-century "new towns." Daniel Burnham's "White City" at the Chicago World Columbian Exposition of 1893 and his visionary Plan for Chicago of 1909 helped to launch the City Beautiful movement in the United States and to attract new groups of planners, architects, engineers, and construction workers to the Chicago area. In the twentieth century, Chicago had a reputation as one of the nation's most important centers for urban design. It is probably not surprising that the first ambitious plan for a new town in the early years after World War II was for Park Forest, Illinois (1946–ca. 1954); this was one of the most sophisticated plans of the postwar period.[5]

Meanwhile, the mundane realities of urban expansion that underlay these plans offered some innovations of their own. While upper-class suburbs proliferated along the North Shore and acres of crowded tenements packed the Near West and South Sides, attracting the energies of great reformers like Lincoln Steffens, Edith Abbott, Jane Addams, and Upton Sinclair, new types of working-class housing began to dominate the newer areas to the west, south, and far north. These were the Chicago bungalows, built in the period 1900 to the 1920s, and composing what is now known as "the bungalow belt."[6] Chicago's bungalows came in many shapes and sizes, but they generally shared certain characteristics: they were free-standing single-family dwellings, built of masonry (usually brick) and wood; they were one to one and a half stories, and they were very small (perhaps 20 × 50 feet) and tightly planned. (For example, one entered directly into the living room, and circulation was from room to room, with no hallway [see figs. 149 and 150].) Standing close together on narrow lots (25–30 feet), they were relatively inexpensive. At the same time, they represented a far lower density than that of older inner-city neighborhoods.[7] Typically, Chicago's bungalow districts were built up piecemeal (a few houses at a time) by small builders, on subdivisions platted and improved by fairly large developers.[8]

In the nineteenth and early twentieth centuries, Chicago housing areas grew around its street railways and its longer distance railways. The city's straight, broad streets generally extended the grid laid down by the Land Ordinance of

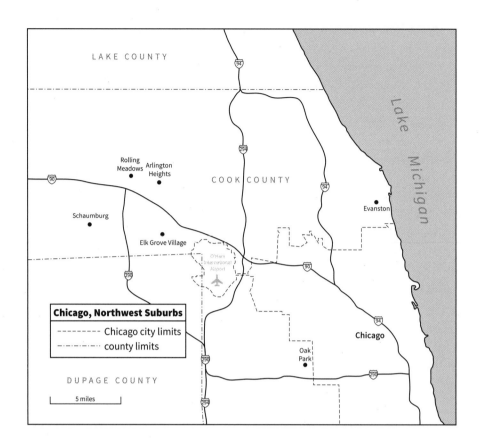

LAKE COUNTY

COOK COUNTY

Rolling
Meadows   Arlington
•   Heights
            •

Schaumburg
    •

Elk Grove Village
        •

O'Hare
International
Airport

Evanston
   •

Chicago, Northwest Suburbs

- - - - - - - Chicago city limits
- · - · - · - county limits

Chicago

Oak
Park
 •

DUPAGE COUNTY

Lake Michigan

|_____|
   5 miles

144. Chicago map, with suburban and highway locations. Nathanael Roesch.

1785, though many areas were punctuated by periodic efforts of builders and developers to introduce curvilinear patterns.[9] In the first decades of the twentieth century, streets began to be paved, and, inspired by the City Beautiful movement, some subdividers laid out a few blocks in which a central green strip created a boulevard-like effect. Then, with the beginning of automobile traffic in the 1910s and 1920s, city and county began to construct a few major highways.[10] After World War II, in collaboration with Illinois state agencies, city and county began to construct long-distance tollways, to the north, northwest, west, and south. (Planning preceded the establishment of the federal Interstate Highway System in 1956, but construction speeded up enormously with the help of federal funding after 1956.) It was these tollways, and the further development of communities and facilities along them, including the rapidly mushrooming O'Hare Airport, that dominated urban expansion in the postwar period (fig. 144, map).[11]

The most rapidly developing area in this period was the so-called Golden Corridor, which reached along Interstate 90, or Northwest Tollway, begun in 1956, extended westward in 1958–60, linked to central Chicago 1959–60 by the "Kennedy Expressway" and in 1971 to the new O'Hare Airport.[12] Local roads led to O'Hare Airport as soon as it opened in 1955, so that it served as a major engine of development in the area. Along the Golden Corridor, existing urban areas like Arlington Heights mushroomed in size and population from the mid-fifties, while new communities like Rolling Meadows, Elk Grove Village, and Schaumburg sprang up upon the surrounding bean and grain fields.[13] The economic base for these new towns was provided by the migration of technological and service industries to the Interstate 90 corridor. My last four examples of builders and their developments are drawn from these communities.

Stoltzner Builders in Arlington Heights: Split-Levels Evolve Out of the Bungalow Tradition

Of the four Chicago builders I discuss, the Stoltzner family, had the oldest roots in Chicago's building trades. They were active longer than any of the other builders in this book, and built the smallest developments; they exemplify the ways in which the country's older trades and crafts sometimes adapted successfully to building circumstances after World War II.[14]

John (Johann) Stoltzner, the patriarch, was a cigar manufacturer of modest means who left his native Denmark for political reasons in 1902 and came to the United States.[15] In 1904, he brought over his wife Sofie and their seven children (fig. 145).[16] Initially the family farmed in Michigan, but soon the eldest boys

145. Stoltzner family portrait, ca. 1905: Back row, left to right: Orla, Charles, Kai; middle row, left to right: Johann Heinrich Stoltzner, Frode, Sofia Olson Stoltzner, Helje; front row, left to right: Alfrieda, Roy. Roberta Stoltzner Burckle. Lent by Tara Stoltzner Blum.

146. 4701 West Wrightwood
Avenue, Chicago, ca. 1927,
corner view, architect Josef
Klafter. Photo by Mark
Bourne.

147. Stoltzner Builders,
Wrightwood Bungalows,
1923ff. Photo by Amanda
Robbins-Butcher.

found work in the building trades in Chicago. The Stoltzners brought with them the Danish passion for brick: of the six boys, five became skilled brick masons (Charles, Orla, Kai, Roy, and Frode); the sixth, Helje, became a master carpenter.[17] Such were the demands of their apprenticeships that none of the boys was schooled beyond the elementary grades. Several of the next generation carried on the family membership in the building trades: Harold (Orla's son, 1919–99), Jim (Roy's son, b. 1930), John (Helje's son, b. 1924), and Richard (Frode's son, 1930–2008).[18] From the late teens or early twenties onward, the Stoltzners entered into the business of housing construction: sometimes on a very modest customized basis ("we will build to your specifications on your lot," said an early advertisement), sometimes on a somewhat larger scale, buying up groups of lots in the "bungalow belt" of recently platted subdivisions and constructing series of look-alike single-family dwellings.[19]

Unlike the Campanellis, who insisted on unity and consensus within the family, the Stoltzner brothers and their sons tended toward individualism: they differed on policy issues, such as whether their main purpose was to build or to acquire land, and they sometimes formed separate companies, with slightly differing names.[20] Nevertheless, they always used the Stoltzner name, and advertised their houses as "Stoltzner-built." The work of the companies was in fact always closely intertwined, with family members moving often and easily from one to another. For simplicity's sake, I therefore refer to the group of firms and family members as "Stoltzner Builders," except when it is necessary to distinguish a particular firm during one period of its activity.[21]

Stoltzner Builders constructed their first sizeable group of houses at Wrightwood Bungalows, beginning in 1922 or 1923. Two long blocks of West Wrightwood Avenue (on the Near North Side, at the eastern edge of the Belmont Cragin neighborhood) were laid out as a boulevard around 1910 with two sides of the avenue separated by a long strip of trees and grass. Beginning in 1916, a variety of small builders built up the 4700 block; one of the houses, at 4701 West

Wrightwood, was a very elaborate showpiece built in 1925 (fig. 146).[22] From 1923 on, the Stoltzners alone built up the 4600 block; the two blocks together now constitute a historic district (fig. 147). The Stoltzners also constructed all the houses on a couple of nearby blocks at the same time (fig. 148).

The Stoltzners' Wrightwood Bungalows resembled many of the Chicago bungalows of the 1920s: they were squarish hip-roofed brick structures, with the basement partially raised above the ground. A half flight of stairs rose to the entry and main floor. A gabled attic contained one or two bedrooms (in addition to one or two on the main floor) (figs. 149, 150). Living space was about 1,000 square feet; lots were very small (about a tenth of an acre); lot widths were about 35 feet, depths about 145 feet; a detached garage or shed in the rear was accessed by a back alley and by a narrow walkway from the street. The houses were set well back from the street, with a deep strip of grass and trees between sidewalks and street. No fences divided the houses, so there was visual continuity along the street.[23] Living rooms were at the front, kitchens at the rear. With a bathroom on the first floor, a fully equipped kitchen, a dining room or dining area, a living room, two to four bedrooms, central heating, a full basement, and a garage, these houses were substantial and extremely desirable among the smaller dwellings of their era; they sold for about $6,000 in the mid-twenties ($75,800 in 2010 dollars).[24]

The Stoltzners continued building houses very similar to the Wrightwood Bungalows throughout the 1920s and early 1930s, in varied locations in the nearer suburbs, mostly in the near northwest, in groups of twenty to fifty (seventy on

148. Stoltzner Builders, 4600 block of West Deming Place, ca. 1923. Photo by Amanda Robbins-Butcher.

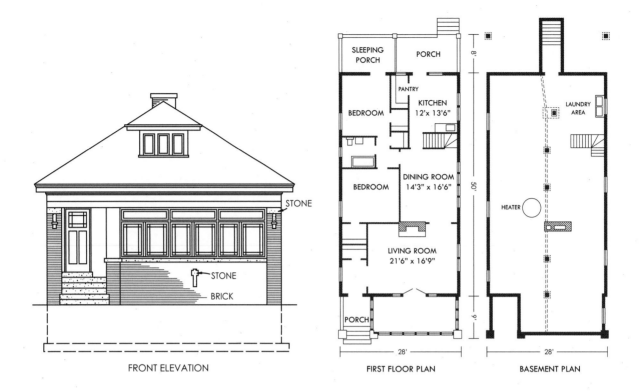

FRONT ELEVATION · STONE · STONE · BRICK

FIRST FLOOR PLAN · SLEEPING PORCH · PORCH · BEDROOM · PANTRY · KITCHEN 12'x 13'6" · BEDROOM · DINING ROOM 14'3" x 16'6" · LIVING ROOM 21'6" x 16'9" · PORCH · 28' · 8' · 50' · 9'

BASEMENT PLAN · LAUNDRY AREA · HEATER · 28'

149. Nathanael Roesch, typical bungalow, exterior, restored from *American Builder*.

150. Nathanael Roesch, typical bungalow, plan, restored from *American Builder*.

one occasion).[25] Always built of masonry, with elegant-looking tan face brick, these bungalows had hip roofs, a raised basement, a porch, a large band of living room windows facing the street, and a very small second story, often little more than a partial attic. In the late 1930s and early 1940s, Stoltzner Builders shifted to a somewhat different exterior and attic layout, with a steeply gabled roof, an asymmetrically placed dormer, and a high-pitched cross gable on the front, suggesting Tudor references and creating somewhat more space on the upper floor.[26] But the ground floor layout continued virtually the same, and the construction continued to be of brick, with plaster finishing on the interior.[27]

Beginning in the late twenties and continuing on into the late thirties and the early forties, the Stoltzners also expanded their custom building operations, usually on lots provided by the prospective owner. An advertisement for a Stoltzner bungalow "built on your lot" in 1929 promised a cost of $5,650 ($72,000 in 2010 dollars).[28] Increasingly they now built in the more distant suburbs of Park Ridge, Niles, Mount Prospect, La Grange, and Highland Park. These later dwellings were larger, sometimes had two stories, and frequently sported Tudor or other "period" detailing. Some (figs. 151, 152), including 6600 North Tower Circle Drive in Lincolnwood, Illinois, were very large and elaborate. In the more distant suburbs, the Stoltzners were able to build on larger, and especially wider, lots.[29] And during the same time period, the firm also constructed a number of two- and three-level apartment buildings. These buildings, too, were built of brick.[30] Most of the family building operations had halted by 1942, when building materials became unavailable; some family members went to work in the shipyards in Seneca, Illinois; members of the younger generation joined the armed forces. But Orla continued building—mostly war housing—and began to use concrete as a structural material at this point.[31] In these wartime houses (fig. 153), the porch was less emphasized, and the overall profile was radically simplified. Orla was also well placed, after the war, to be in close touch with the development of new subdivisions near projected highways in the Northwest.[32] Here, in a series of "houses for veterans," he was again able to build on wider lots, so that the older house form was stretched out further along the street and laid the basis for the ranch houses that the Stoltzners would later build in Arlington Heights.

After the war, all the Stoltzners returned to building: Orla expanded his firm, while a parallel firm was created by Frode, Roy, and Kai. Younger family members, former superintendents and former subcontractors, returning from service, joined both firms as workmen, foremen, and new partners. At this point, the Stoltzners constructed the largest housing developments of their careers, in Arlington Heights.[33] The Village of Arlington Heights had expanded hugely through a series of annexations in the period between 1945 and 1970, adding

151. Lincolnwood "Norman House" exterior. *Homes by Stoltzner*, sales brochure, ca. 1950.

152. Lincolnwood "Norman House" plan. *Homes by Stoltzner*, sales brochure, ca. 1950.

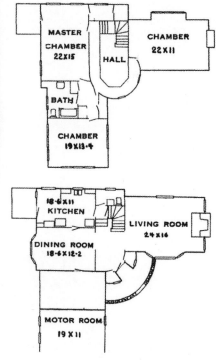

surrounding farms along the routes, or the anticipated routes, of new high-ways.[34] The village planned the layout of streets and platted subdivisions in anticipation of development.[35] Here, aided by Attorney Vernon Loucks, the family firms obtained options on three parcels of land, which then became, in rather quick succession, Greenview Estates (1955–ca. 1970, about 200 houses), Arlington Estates (late 1950s to mid-1960s, about 70 houses), and Arlington North (mid- to late 1960s, about 180 houses).[36] I focus on Greenview Estates, the largest of these developments.[37]

153. Stoltzner Builders, house on Karlov Avenue, Chicago, ca. 1942. Nathanael Roesch from modern view.

154. Stoltzner Builders, Greenview Estates, map. Nathanael Roesch.

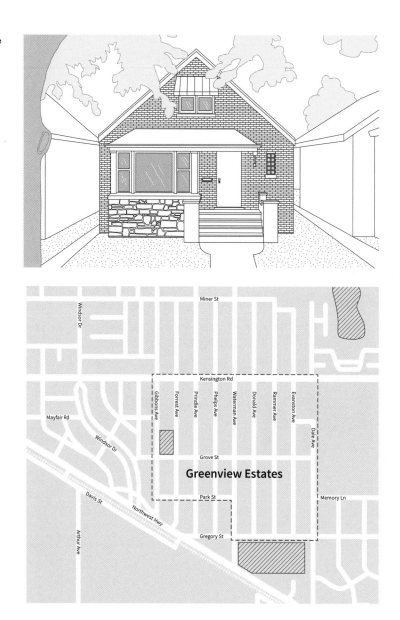

155. Stoltzner Builders, ranch
with raised entry, Greenview.
Photo by Amanda Robbins-
Butcher.

At Greenview (fig. 154), the Stoltzners acquired 43 acres early in 1955 for 145 lots; later they added smaller sections to this parcel. Arlington Heights Village's platting prescribed lots of about 0.25 acres each, with a frontage of about 67 feet and a depth of about 160 feet; the Stoltzners, like other builders in Arlington Heights, put up money in escrow for sewers, lighting, paving, and other "public improvements."[38] The Village prescribed wide streets with curbs, wide side-walks and tree-lined grass strips, and a small park. Setbacks were 26 to 36 feet for each house.[39] The Stoltzners introduced some amenities of their own, including pedestrian crosswalks in the middle of some blocks.[40]

The Stoltzners built slowly, as had been their practice in earlier decades. (In the first few years at Greenview, they sometimes built only a block—thirty-six to thirty-eight houses—per year.)[41] They did not advertise extensively: an occasional ad in the Chicago newspapers and three small sales brochures were the extent of their self-promotion.[42] As before, they worked with a small group of favored subcontractors, many of whom were also from Scandinavian immigrant families. Job foremen came almost always from their own family.[43] From the earliest blocks at Greenview, they developed a series of three house models: a small ranch (fig. 155), a "side-by-side" split-level (a type very familiar on the East Coast, and comparable to those by Ralph Bodek at Lawrence Park in suburban Philadelphia, discussed in the section on Ralph Bodek in chapter 3), and an unusual "front-to-back" split-level, in which the upper level is at the rear, almost invisible from the street (figs. 156, 157). They tended to alternate these models, and varied each in a number of ways, so that street views were quite distinctive. In combination with the wide streets and sidewalks and deep yards prescribed

156. Stoltzner Builders, side-to-side split, Greenview. Photo by Amanda Robbins-Butcher.

157. Stoltzner Builders, front-to-back split, Greenview. Photo by Amanda Robbins-Butcher.

by Arlington Heights Village ordinances, these designs produced streetscapes of great charm and urbanity (fig. 14).

The ranch houses at Greenview (and also at Arlington Estates) evolved clearly out of the bungalow type in general and, more specifically, out of the houses built by the Stoltzners from the later twenties through the early forties. Some even retained the raised entryway and visible basement windows so typical of the earlier bungalows (fig. 155). The ranches had varied rooflines: a simple gable with long axis parallel to the street, a low-pitched hip roof with a cross gable over the entrance, and a low-pitched hip roof with an additional layer of hip at the front defining the entry. Each had a full basement (partially finished floor over gravel [or later a concrete slab], laundry, heater); most had detached garages. Ground floor living space (that is, exclusive of the basement) was about

1,128 square feet (fig. 158). Like all the Stoltzner houses of this era, they were of wood frame construction, clad in handsome face brick similar to that of the bungalow era; inside they had oak floors and (initially) plastered walls.[44] Their sweeping roofs and asymmetrically placed windows also anchored them firmly in bungalow traditions.[45]

Of the other Greenview house types, the side-by-side split-level was the most conventional-looking, as mentioned above (figs. 156, 159). The Stoltzners were, though, among the earlier Chicago-area builders to construct split-level houses of any type.[46] Sometimes these split-levels were clad in the Stoltzners' traditional red/brown face brick; increasingly, however, the builders used horizontal siding on the upper story (fig. 159, the Wilshire, Arlington North). The front-to-back split-level, on the other hand, was extremely unusual. Often sited on a gentle double grade (upward from the street and then down again in the rear), the basement level was hidden at the front but visually open to the back, and the upper story was frequently not clearly visible from the street (figs. 157, 160, 161, 162). Thus, in the front view, these Stoltzner split-levels tended to appear low and horizontally oriented along the street. The front elevation had a large picture window or windows, centrally located or at the corners of the living room, which,

158. Stoltzner Builders, ranch house, Greenview, plan. Nathanael Roesch from sales brochure.

159. Stoltzner Builders, side-to-side split, Greenview. *Stoltzner Construction Co. Presents Arlington Estates in Arlington Heights*, sales brochure.

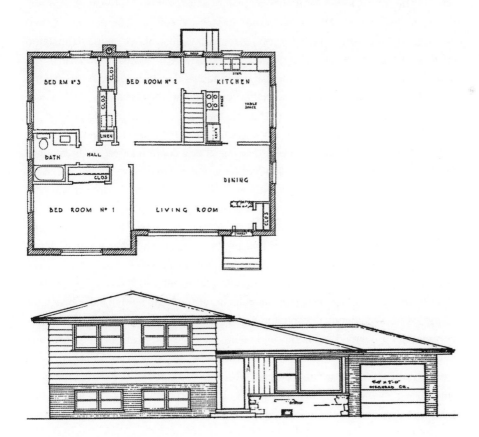

160. Stoltzner Builders,
front-to-back split, Greenview,
street side, modern view.
Photo by the author.

because of the openness of the plan, permitted some view from the front yard
through to the basement windows toward the backyard.[47] A two-car attached
garage completed the horizontal emphasis of these exteriors. Like the ranch
houses, the front-to-back splits had a strong visual connection to the Stoltzners'
earlier houses and to their roots in the bungalow tradition. The partially raised
basement of the bungalow, with its high windows just above grade, translated
easily in the imaginations of both builders and buyers into the lowest level of the
split, housing a recreation room with its windows almost level with the ground
level of the backyard. From the attic of the bungalow, the site of one or two bedrooms, the upper bedroom level of the split was also a logical progression.

The front-to-back split typically had three bedrooms on the upper level, one
and a half to two baths, an L-shaped living-dining room located at the front, a
kitchen with eating area at the side and rear, and a sizeable recreation room (21
× 16 feet in blueprint of 1961) on the lowest level, under the bedroom wing. (A
second bath or half bath, heater, hot water heater, and laundry were also on the
lower level.) These split-level houses were larger and more expensive than any
of the tract houses the Stoltzners had built before: With living areas of about
1,500 square feet,[48] they sold for about $20,000 in 1958 ($151,000 in 2010 dollars) and $23,900 and up in 1961 ($174,298 in 2010 dollars).[49] As in the ranches,
interior detailing involved plastered walls up until about 1960; a sales brochure
of the 1960s also specified "wooden windows, birch cabinets with formica tops,
ceramic tile walls in kitchen and bathroom, garbage disposal, colored plumbing
fixtures, thermopane picture windows" among other amenities. Polished wood
was an important feature of Stoltzner interiors—oak floors, stairs, and window-
sills were prominent. With their unusually large and undivided living spaces and
generous windows, these houses seemed exceptionally spacious on the interior.

Over the course of the early sixties, the Stoltzners slowly introduced a few more innovations in construction: radiant heating in the basement floors, more use of steel to support larger upper spans.

The house designs and building methods established at Greenview Estates continued to be followed at Arlington Estates, although ranch houses were proportionally much more numerous there. At Arlington North, John Stoltzner gave great emphasis to larger split-levels with horizontal siding and shutters on the upper stories. John Stoltzner retired in 1968; thereafter only Richard, the son of Frode, continued to build "Stoltzner" houses singly and in very small groups until his own retirement in 1986.[50]

Who designed the Stoltzner houses? This is a hard question to answer for all the builders considered here. The Stoltzners could not themselves draw up detail drawings, so they did not "design" in that sense. They always used an architect for the sets of working drawings required by the Arlington Heights building department (elevation, plans, sections, construction details, some isometrics).[51] But this person was not the "designer" either. The Stoltzners "designed" in the sense of choosing images, exterior and interior, that they liked and believed from experience that they could build. In the early years, pattern books such as those published by the American Face Brick Association in Chicago, or the Garlinghouse Company in Topeka, Kansas, probably provided some of these images. In the postwar period, the Stoltzners remained in close touch with plan vendors like Garlinghouse and could well have been partially inspired by their ranch house models.[52] On the other hand, as we have seen, their early ranch houses evolved rather straightforwardly out of their earlier work. When they created a truly innovative design, such as the front-to-back splits in Greenview, John Stoltzner says that they sometimes worked with an architect or draftsman to

161. Stoltzner Builders, front-to-back split, Greenview, rear, modern view. Photo by the author.

162. Stoltzner Builders, plan of front-to-back split, Greenview. Nathanael Roesch and Jonathan Lane.

realize their own visualization, which was sometimes, in turn, partially derived from newspaper, magazine, or journal illustrations.[53] Jim Stoltzner stresses that the designs were group efforts: for each change in earlier houses, all partners and foremen would confer and give their views; "the elders" would then decide. In the case of street and lot layouts, especially in the larger subdivisions, they would also consult lawyer Vernon Loucks.[54] In general, like many other builders, the Stoltzners visualized very clearly what it was they wanted to build, and realized their conceptions directly through the buildings themselves, with the help of their foremen, subcontractors, and the occasional architect.

The Stoltzners survived successfully two of the greatest upheavals of their time, the Great Depression and World War II, and then went on to greater successes in the demanding and rapidly changing climate of postwar building. The family and firms proved to be resilient, versatile, and adaptable while still maintaining their roots in older building traditions. Their beginnings in the "bungalow belt" trained them in repetitive building techniques, economical planning and construction, and in the use of patterns. Concurrent and later individual commissions (including their custom work for buyer-owned properties) taught them to tailor their buildings to individual needs, and to experiment with different plan types. In building small apartment buildings over a long span of time,[55] they gained additional experience with minimal dwelling requirements and solid construction; their involvement in war housing refined these lessons. Devotion to high standards of craft and construction became a family tradition, yet they gradually adapted their practices to new building technologies in the war and postwar periods. In its long duration and in many of its details, their story is unique in this book. Yet it is important to remember that other builders of the postwar period discussed here, especially Ralph Bodek and the Campanellis, shared the Stoltzners' insistence on high standards in construction.

Kimball Hill and Rolling Meadows: Ranch Houses Inspired by Prefabrication

Like the Stoltzners, Kimball Hill was a native Chicagoan, but in most other respects he was their antithesis. Hill came from a well-to-do family; he was never an architect and had little knowledge of building construction except what he taught himself. He favored innovative building techniques above all others, and he developed and built the largest Chicago housing tract of its era. This was Rolling Meadows, begun in 1953 on 537 acres of farmland adjacent to the northwest edge of Arlington Heights (fig. 163, map). Here he erected 1,700 single-family low-cost ranch houses initially, adding over the next few years another 663 acres and another 2,300 dwellings, for a total of 4,000 in eleven years.[56] Rolling Meadows

Northwest Suburban Map
© 1978 by Creative Sales Corporation.
Reprinted by permission.

Rolling Meadows, 1978
= Earliest Section

1978

was soon surpassed in size by Elk Grove Village, and equaled by Weathersfield in Schaumburg, but it was the giant of the mid-1950s.[57] Hill attained great prominence in Chicago building and on the national scene as well: he was president of the Home Builders' Association of the greater Chicago area in 1949, and later occupied leading positions in the NAHB. His firm, Kimball Hill Homes, grew to be one of the largest privately owned building firms in the country. During Hill's lifetime (or at least until he retired in 1969), the firm's building operations were concentrated in the Chicago metropolitan area, but Hill's son David took over as CEO after his death and branched out to other markets (Texas from 1989). This successor firm failed during the housing crisis of 2008.[58] At Rolling Meadows and elsewhere, Hill's building methods involved large-scale production methods. For most of their lives, Kimball Hill and his son built low-cost one-story ranch houses, of new materials and with rapid construction techniques.[59]

163. Rolling Meadows, map (shaded area is earliest section). Nathanael Roesch.

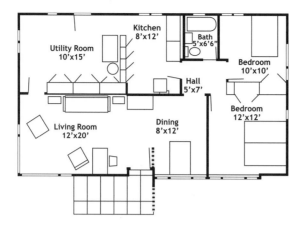

Kimball Hill (David Kimball Hill, 1910–93) grew up in an affluent neighborhood in Evanston, Illinois. On his father's side, he came from an old and
relatively socially prominent New England family. Hill attended Northwestern
University as an undergraduate (bachelor's, 1932) and Northwestern School of
Law, receiving his law degree in 1935.[60] One of his biographers asserts that there
were few attractive jobs in the legal profession in 1935 (in the middle of the Great
Depression); whatever the reason, Hill soon went to work for a mortgage company that was involved in buying and developing land throughout the Chicago
area.[61] He had no architectural or building experience, and little contact with
real estate or land speculation at this point in his life (although his grandfather had been a real estate broker in Maine, and his father had dabbled in land
speculation in Columbia), but he emerged within the mortgage company as the
person in charge of the development of new housing tracts.[62] From this early
date Hill displayed a fascination with new building technologies, and a desire to
develop inexpensive house plans. (One of his earliest enterprises, carried out in
collaboration with architect Glenn Q. Johnson, was a group of inexpensive five-
room houses built on slabs, with concrete aggregate walls and with the heating
mechanisms stowed in the tiny attic.)[63] At about this time (probably 1939), the
young lawyer-turned-builder founded his own building and development firm.
Shortly after the war, after a stint in the navy, Hill entered into partnership
with Ed Smith, another young member of the mortgage company.[64] Smith and
Hill, as the new firm was called, hired the similarly youthful architectural firm
of Perkins and Will to help them develop new inexpensive houses for returning
veterans. (Perkins and Will had worked with Eero Saarinen in the pathbreaking
Crow Island School of 1940, and thereafter became very eminent in American
modern design; the firm is still in business.)[65]

In the first postwar years, Smith and Hill attempted to develop two subdivisions in the Oak Lawn area of southwest Chicago (south of Midway Airport).

Here in 1946 Hill set up an operation to fabricate component building sections on-site for minimal-size ranch houses. Precut wall panels were made of plywood "veneered with brick or wood siding," with the wall sections moved into position by a conveyor system.[66] Oak Meadows (vicinity of Ninety-Ninth and Cicero, between Ninety-Ninth and One Hundred Second), the larger of two subdivisions in Oak Lawn, was planned for twelve hundred single-family houses. Another similar plan involved fabricating the walls entirely of plywood, omitting the veneers to achieve a lower cost, but Hill was unable to persuade Chicago's building code officials to accept this idea.[67] The Oak Meadows houses were efficiently planned and built: they were erected on slabs and had two bedrooms and an "open plan" (continuous living room and dining area); there was also a "utility room" for storage and heating that contained a large (ca. 10 feet) storage wall and used more space than the minimal kitchen; they contained about 880 square feet and averaged about $11,000 in cost (fig. 164).[68]

The original Oak Meadows/Oak Lawn houses proved to be hard to build and hard to sell, however. Soon Hill radically simplified the plans, shrank the living area to about 600 square feet (for a two-bedroom model), developed new modes of standardization for the parts of the house, and marketed the smaller version as a "Lockweld engineered" house (figs. 165, 166).[69] In constructing these houses, Hill obtained the cooperation of the local building trades, which had been dragging their heels in connection with his earlier buildings. The Oak Meadows house plans and construction methods earned Hill a great deal of attention among Chicago builders (and newspapers), and help to account for much of his later fame. But the subdivision itself was a financial disaster for Smith and Hill,

165. Kimball Hill, Lockweld engineered house, plan, *Chicago Construction News,* December 30, 1948. UCLA Library Special Collections.

166. Kimball Hill, Lockweld engineered house, exterior. *Chicago Construction News,* December 30, 1948. UCLA Library Special Collections.

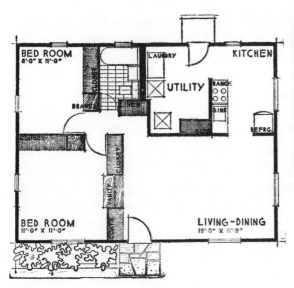

which declared bankruptcy in 1949.[70] Hill later claimed that "Chicago was not yet ready for prefabrication."[71]

For the next two years, Hill restructured his firm (which became Kimball Hill & Associates, now based in Des Plaines) and developed small and scattered sites, using a version of the Lockweld house, now produced and marketed by Pawling & Harnischfeger, a prefabricated homes manufacturer based in Port Washington, Wisconsin. He began to equip these minimal houses with unprecedented numbers and varieties of appliances: "self-storing" storm windows, dishwashers, waste disposers, gas ranges, refrigerators, washing machines, and clothes dryers, all of which, the ads promised, would guarantee "A [mere] 40 Hour Work Week for the Wife."[72] At the same time he looked for larger parcels to develop, preferably outside the boundaries of the city of Chicago's stringent building codes.[73] He found what seemed to be the ideal site in 1951: 537 acres of farmland abutting the south and west of the Arlington Park Racetrack, one of the nation's most famous tracks. The land, most of which was in Palatine Township, had been bought by California businessman Curly Brown to be developed into a golf course adjacent to the racetrack; subsequently it had been leased back to local farmers; then in 1952 the racecourse owners offered it for sale. The first sections to be developed (fig. 163) abutted, to the west, Route 53 (which soon became Interstate 290); to the south lay the future site of the Northwest Tollway, then in the planning stages. The property consisted of gently rolling farms and meadows, bisected from north to south by a stream and forested area, and from southeast to northwest by Kirchoff Road.

The property had not yet been incorporated into Arlington Heights Township but township developers hoped to buy the land for luxury housing. Hill moved too fast for them and quickly took up options on it. With his legal training, he assumed that he would be able to get it rezoned quickly from agricultural uses to lot sizes of 7,500 square feet.[74] Planning to build an entire new community for relatively low-income first-home buyers,[75] with houses based on his Oak Meadow and Lockweld houses, Hill built a model house in Des Plaines and began to market it. A protracted zoning battle with Arlington Heights political leaders ensued.[76] Armed with 150 down payments that he had placed in escrow, Hill won the battle, but had to compromise on 10,000-square-foot lots in the first section of development, above Kirchoff Road. Working with Fletcher Engineering, Hill laid out the first section of Rolling Meadows with gently curving streets, and proceeded to build 1,800 houses over a period of three years.[77]

In 1955, Hill mobilized the residents to seek incorporation as a city; when the incorporation took place, Rolling Meadows secured its independence from Palatine Township (and from the influence of Arlington Heights) and was able to develop its own building code and zoning ordinances.[78] Ultimately, Rolling Meadows doubled in size, with extensions to the west, north, and south containing more expensive housing and industrial and commercial strips along Northwest Highway and the Northwest Tollway. Most of these later areas were also owned by Hill, who sold them off to other builders. In 1964, when Hill stopped building single-family dwellings in Rolling Meadows (he built some apartment buildings after that), his original tracts contained 3,500 to 4,000 houses, with a population of about 14,000. Most of these original residents were people of modest means: they were often described at the time as "blue-collar workers," although precisely what was meant by this label is quite unclear.[79] Over time, as the Golden Corridor began to explode with development to the north, south, and west, the social composition of Rolling Meadows changed considerably; by 2000, its total population was about 25,000. It has remained, however, an unusually tightly knit community, with strong affections—for Kimball Hill and for the early history of the city. Many children and grandchildren of the original residents have returned and now live in the city.[80] In 2002, a historic house museum, which replicates one of the original Hill houses, was established (fig. 168); the museum has been extremely successful, and serves as the focus of the active Rolling Meadows Historical Society.[81]

Local historians ascribe the success of Rolling Meadows as a community in part to the homeowners' association that Hill insisted on at the start, and to the rapid incorporation as a city that followed soon thereafter.[82] At an early date, Hill also encouraged the city's leaders to separate both their park system and their school system from that of surrounding Palatine Township;[83] he himself built and donated the first elementary school (1954), and the land for a shopping center, in the middle of the original development on Kirchoff Road (1955). (Land for an industrial park was also set aside from the start; building began in 1958.) Later schools arose on property that he sold to the city at cost. The first elementary school, now remembered with great affection by original owners, was located in a historic barn on one of the earliest parcels that Hill bought. Hill also sponsored an interfaith center in the barn before local churches began to be built: Mrs. KM and her husband appreciated this greatly, because they were leaving the Catholic faith, yet needed a religious center. Also warmly remembered were the Saturday night outdoor movies held at the barn: "Saturdays we'd have potluck supper and sit in our cars watching the movie. That was a lot of fun," said Mrs. BG. Hill was always eager to encourage community endeavor: he involved the homeowners' association in naming streets (named after birds in the early sections), and instituted landscaping competitions with free trees and bushes for the winners. In the early days, he also offered to new owners classes in how to use and care for their houses—how to take care of the tile floors, for example, and how to use their automatic washing machines and dryers.[84] Not surprisingly, Hill had a reputation as an especially benevolent builder.

The houses that Hill built above and below Kirchoff Road beginning in 1952 were all one-story houses, and were closely based on the Lockweld designs he

167. Kimball Hill, Rolling Meadows house, exterior, ca. 1952, modern view. Photo by Amanda Robbins-Butcher.

168. Kimball Hill, Rolling Meadows house, exterior, ca. 1952, modern view. Photo by Amanda Robbins-Butcher.

had developed in Oak Meadow and while working with Pawling & Harnischfeger, the producer of prefabricated houses (figs. 167, 168, 169, 170). The two-bedroom plan was almost identical to the Lockweld plan of 1948 (fig. 165), except that the kitchens were much larger and more fully elaborated at Rolling Meadows. Unlike the earlier houses, however, those at Rolling Meadows were stick-built (with the exception of a few features like the gables, which were prefabricated) and were erected on a conventional floor over a crawl space and concrete foundations.[85] At about 850 square feet, the two-bedroom was substantially larger than that at Oak Lawn, and instead of a dining area each contained a large (ca. 12 × 13 feet) kitchen with room for a dining table. Buyers were especially enthusiastic about the large kitchens at Rolling Meadows. As one original buyer whom I interviewed described her new kitchen, "It was so *big*: it reminded us of the old days" (Mrs.

KM) (figs. 169, 170). National surveys of buyer desires at the time showed that the eat-in kitchen was a high priority for new owners: Hill's houses responded to this desire at an earlier date than those of other builders considered here.[86]

In the earliest section of Rolling Meadows, Hill built a combination of two-bedroom and three-bedroom houses, with the three-bedroom more numerous. The two-bedroom house (which was framed for the addition of another bedroom) was rectangular, with either a hip or gable roof; the three bedroom was L-shaped and usually had a gabled porch over the central entry (figs. 167, 168). Exterior walls were made of plywood, with a veneer of horizontal siding, shingles, or masonry.[87] All the houses had carports, rather than garages. Bedrooms ranged from about twelve and a half by ten and a half feet to about nine by nine and a half feet (three bedrooms); each contained a storage wall and several built-in features (bunk beds were common in the smaller bedrooms). Living rooms were eighteen by eleven and a half feet, a rather shallow space, but the oversized picture window and further windows on both sides opened them up and produced an impression of spaciousness; a side entrance to the drive also helped to open up the space visually (figs. 171, 172). (The side windows had already been present in Hill's earliest plans, but the kitchen entrance at the side was new.) Closets were far more generous than at Oak Lawn; and the kitchens contained a washer, dryer, and range, with a space for a refrigerator, which the early inhabitants were expected to provide for themselves. Initial prices ranged from $11,000 to $13,000 ($89,800 to $106,000 in 2010 dollars).[88]

Rolling Meadows interiors were finished in drywall, with asphalt tile floors throughout. Colors on interior and exterior walls were somewhat idiosyncratic, resulting from Hill's choices among shipments of paint that he was able to acquire inexpensively; residents often changed them. Hill devised an unusual heating system: a gas-powered furnace located outside the bathroom pumped warm air

169. Kimball Hill, Rolling Meadows house, two-bedroom plan, ca. 1952. Restored by Nathanael Roesch from a newspaper clipping of 1952 lent by Martha Roberts.

170. Kimball Hill, Rolling Meadows house, three-bedroom plan, ca. 1952. Restored by Nathanael Roesch from a newspaper clipping of 1952, lent by Martha Roberts.

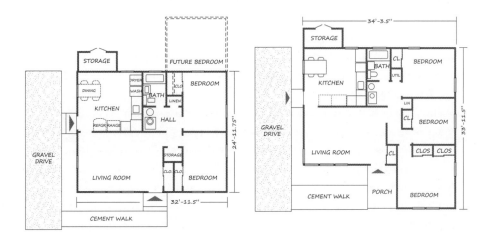

171. Kimball Hill, Rolling Meadows house, interior of living room showing windows, ca. 1952. Alexander Brey from a modern view.

172. Kimball Hill, Rolling Meadows house, interior of kitchen showing kitchen entrance, ca. 1952. Alexander Brey from a modern view.

into the heavily insulated crawl space under the house, from which it rose to rooms throughout the house—a technique that mimicked the effects of radiant heating without necessitating burying heating pipes in a floor slab.[89] In this, as in other aspects of his building, Hill employed recommendations published by the University of Illinois Small Homes Council, an influential organization devoted to research in building technology for small single-family dwellings.[90]

The Rolling Meadows houses were produced by a kind of assembly-line process not unlike that at Westchester, the Levittowns, or Panorama City: land was graded, crawl spaces excavated, and foundations laid down, block by block;[91] teams of construction workers then went from site to site on the block to erect walls and windows, install fixtures, add roofs, and provide interior finishes. These procedures were also similar to those used at Oak Meadow, but on a larger scale: Hill claimed that he and his teams could now build 20 homes a week at times of peak productivity.[92] Hill built about 600 houses per year in the first three years, and about 200 per year over the next ten.

Like other builders of his time, Hill wanted to respond to buyers' wishes. Aside from Bodek, who commissioned his own market research, most builders relied on buyers' choices among their model houses to arrive at their assessment of "the market." In 1958, however, when Kimball Hill believed that sales were dropping, he decided to establish a "research laboratory" because, he said, his knowledge of the "precise needs" of prospective buyers was inadequate. Over the next year and a half, Hill built twenty experimental model houses at Rolling Meadows, and asked visitors to complete a questionnaire prepared by the Chicago-based Real Estate Research Corporation.[93] This "Ideas, U.S.A., Research Show" a "unique demonstration of the latest ideas in new-home design and modern living" sponsored by the ISHC, included thirteen one-story houses, five one-and-a-half to two-story houses, and two split-levels.[94] The houses varied not only in external style, but also in plan, materials, construction, and equipment: one was all-aluminum; several had central air conditioning; one had a

U-shaped kitchen and multiple skylights; another had four bedrooms and two baths; one, a five-bedroom model, had hot water heat. One had a full basement. One, a "western style" house, had a built-in fireplace and barbecue pit.[95] The project represented a huge outlay of funds for Hill, who recouped some of it through the sale in 1959–60 of most of the houses. Overall, it reflected the commitment to research and experimentation that had characterized Hill's building career from the start.

This large research effort did not lead to a published report, but Erie Jones, co-coordinator of the Housing Research Laboratory and an associate in Hill's firm, summarized the results provisionally to the University of Illinois Small Homes Council in January 1959, and contemporary newspaper reports noted many of the reactions of potential customers. The visitor to each house completed a questionnaire about the features of that particular building, noting what he or she liked and the reverse. Afterward, the Research Corporation mailed out questionnaires, designed to elicit information about income, personal backgrounds, and buying preferences, to all visitors about the show as a whole.

In all, 25,000 visitors were surveyed; about 40 percent responded (according to Jones). The Real Estate Research Corporation found that 62 percent of the respondents had an income of $7,500 or less ($56,200 in 2010 dollars). A majority were looking for a new house within the year; a majority also currently lived in a single-family house, which they owned. These prospective buyers came predominantly from the environs of Chicago, from Cook County, but not from within the city limits. Almost 50 percent favored a 60-foot lot; a third wanted one and a half baths, while another third wanted two baths. About a quarter wanted a separate dining room, while another quarter wanted a dining alcove opening off another room. When asked whether they wanted to live in a neighborhood with varied modern and traditional architecture, two-thirds didn't care. A third expected to spend $17,500 to $19,999 ($130,000 to $149,000 in 2010 dollars); another third were willing to spend up to $22,499 ($168,600 in 2010 dollars).[96]

A favorite among the houses was the Whitcomb, a one-story house with three bedrooms, a dining area off the living room, a large living room, drywall construction, gas heat, and oak parquet floors.[97] Other preferences noted in newspaper reports included a strong demand for family rooms, fireplaces, and "cathedral beamed ceilings."[98] A high proportion of the questions related to materials and construction issues; responses showed that those questioned were happy with Hill's methods in these areas. The Housing Research Laboratory led Hill to introduce some new house types, and to shift some aspects of his site planning. Stemming from the exhibition were the California Contemporary, and a new four-bedroom model (figs. 173, 174, 175). Hill's later site planning also laid greater emphasis on varying the roof lines and turning the houses within a single block, so that street scenes in Rolling Meadows became more varied.

173. Kimball Hill, "California Contemporary." Restored by Nathanael Roesch from a newspaper advertisement of November 1958.

174. Kimball Hill, four-bedroom model, exterior, 1958, modern view. Photo by Amanda Robbins-Butcher.

175. Kimball Hill, four-bedroom model, plan, 1958. Nathanael Roesch from plans lent by owner.

There is a great deal of evidence that Hill saw himself as a "city-builder."[99] But was Hill a designer of houses? Contemporary newspaper reports almost unanimously ascribed the design of the Rolling Meadows houses to a prolific Chicago architect named A. J. Del Bianco (1911–82). Del Bianco came to be well known in the late 1940s and early 1950s for ranch houses built on slabs with radiant heat, and for the minimal "budget house" he built for the Greater Chicago Home Show at Navy Pier in April 1950 (ca. 795 square feet, storage walls, no interior bearing walls, drywall construction, and roof trusses). This and others of his early designs merged the dining area into the living room, and contained an enlarged kitchen with room for dining (fig. 176). Del Bianco was also affiliated as architect with a number of award-winning neighborhood plans. Having himself been a scholarship student in the School of Architecture of the University of Illinois, Del Bianco established a similar scholarship for Chicago high school students in 1953.[100] In 1954 he became director of the Chicago Metropolitan Home Builders' Association. His stamp appears on some of the Stoltzner blueprints, and he is credited in newspaper accounts with the design of houses at Elk Grove Village and Schaumburg, as well as at Rolling Meadows. Yet none of the materials published by Hill or Rolling Meadows mention him, the Stoltzner family has no recollection of him, and, as we will see, Centex and the Campanellis brought their house designs with them from Dallas and Boston. It is possible that, as Victoria Granacki writes, "his name [was] often attached to residential designs as a selling point,"[101] or that, as architect Stanley Tigerman recalls, Del Bianco was not so much a designer, but the producer on a huge scale of working drawings suited to Chicago area building codes. Tigerman remembers working in Del Bianco's office in those days: "In 1954, when I got out of the Navy, I think 10,000 houses were built with his registration stamp on them! . . . I, myself, was one of two that did all of the working drawings for Elk Grove Village, for Rolling Meadows. . . . I did all the drawings for the single-family houses. I was very fast."[102] Del Bianco was thus more of a facilitator for Golden Corridor builders than a designer of their houses.[103]

But Kimball Hill did work with architects on many occasions. The designs at Rolling Meadows were influenced by the early plans that Hill had developed with Perkins and Will, although he soon departed from those plans to develop

176. A. J. Del Bianco, "Budget House," plan. Restored by Nathanael Roesch from a newspaper advertisement of April 1950.

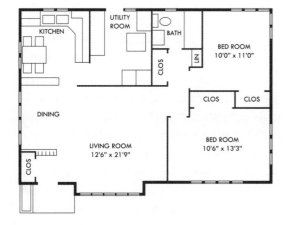

the more minimal Lockweld house. The emphasis on the eat-in kitchen, together with some aspects of the fenestration, may have been reinforced by Del Bianco. And it seems clear that Hill respected Del Bianco's expertise, since Hill allowed Del Bianco to design the first Rolling Meadows school, and the new shopping center.[104] The school was a flat-roofed one-story structure looking rather like a ranch house itself, the shopping center was a one-story strip mall.[105] Yet, when Hill established his Housing Research Laboratory in 1958 in Rolling Meadows, Del Bianco's firm was only one of the twenty-one builders of model houses.[106] It seems safe to say that the design of the Rolling Meadows houses was Hill's, in the sense that he had adapted his plans and elevations over a long period of time: first on the basis of the plans that Perkins and Will had designed to his specifications in Oak Lawn, and then on the basis of economic and technical improvements. Later, he introduced some other design features. Some of these may have been suggested by Del Bianco's work, some probably came from the houses exhibited in 1958 (as in the California Style house). Most important, his designs were *adaptations*, so that their uses, together with their execution, were Hill's. Thus, like many other builders, Hill used the ideas of architects and other designers when it suited him and when he believed that the buyers approved of them, just as he consistently applied new building technologies whenever they worked for him. On balance, Hill can be seen as an important innovator in both house design and building construction.

Centex and Elk Grove Village: House Forms Imported from Dallas

With the beginnings of the northwest toll roads, the explosive growth of the Golden Corridor began to be noticed outside Chicago; speculative builders from quite distant places began to build there. Among these were the Levitts, in Schaumburg; Father and Son builders from Tucson, in Hoffman Estates and in Naperville, due west of Chicago; the Dallas firm called Centex, in Elk Grove Village; and the Campanellis, in Schaumburg. I will be discussing the last two of these builders. Elk Grove Village was located to the south and west of Rolling Meadows, and immediately to the west of O'Hare Airport (fig. 144). With a population of 24,516 in 1970, Elk Grove Village began to surpass its neighbor to the north, and it continued to do so: its population was 32,745 in 2010 and its land area (including the Industrial Park) was 10.9 square miles. Centex Construction Company, the creators of Elk Grove Village, represented a new phenomenon in Chicago's expansion in the 1950s: the directors of the firm came in from outside the area with a lot of money and bought up a huge tract all at once.[107] They brought house plans, construction techniques, and a master plan with them from Dallas. On the basis of the building and planning of Elk Grove Village, Centex soon became one of the largest housing construction firms in the nation, and transformed itself into a long-lasting public corporation.

Centex was a Dallas firm, the creation of native Texans Tom Lively (1920–65) and Ira Rupley (1880–1960). In 1948, when the partnership was founded, Dallas had just doubled its prewar population of 300,000; it would grow to almost 700,000 by 1960.[108] Since the nineteenth century, Dallas had been the marketing, retail, and commercial center for local crops—cotton, wheat, and corn; with the discovery of oil in east Texas in 1930, Dallas began to grow as the headquarters of oil producers, investors, and corporations. From 1941, the war brought new industries, especially aircraft and instrument manufacture. Great new fortunes arose during the second quarter of the twentieth century; and great new waves of immigration—Hispanic, Asian, and African American—contributed to a fast-growing housing shortage. Before the war, Dallas had boasted many elegant upper-middle-class suburbs (the Cedars, Oak Cliff, Highland Park); after the war, the most urgent need seemed to be for middle- and low-income housing. In 1943 the city commissioned a new master plan, which laid the basis for the construction of about 100,000 housing units between 1945 and 1955 (many in newly annexed rural towns like Mesquite).[109] Lively and Rupley took advantage of this building boom: their first joint effort was city-sponsored housing for African Americans.

Tom Lively was the dominant partner in the new firm. Lively grew up in Whitewright, a tiny farming town sixty-five miles north of Dallas; his father was a dry goods salesman there.[110] Like many other rural Texans during the oil boom of the 1930s and the building boom of the war years, he left home at a young age to seek his fortune in Dallas, which became a financial center for the oil industry.[111] During the war, Dallas developed new war industries (especially aircraft); after 1945, it added many new technology industries. Initially Lively "sold clothing and hardware"; in the mid-forties he began selling real estate.[112] In 1946, he joined with two former members of the Army Corps of Engineers to create the "Standard Construction Company." Over the next two years, the company built a variety of apartments and rental units.[113] Soon (1948), he began to build custom houses of his own design for sale (fig. 177);[114] in the same year,[115] he formed a partnership with Ira Rupley, a Dallas land developer, to produce low-cost cottages for African Americans in a segregated housing area near Dallas.[116] By 1950, Lively and Rupley had enlarged their partnership and adopted the name "Centex Construction Company" ("Centex" was a combination of "central" and "Texas"); now they branched out into larger developments funded by FHA mortgages in Dallas's newer white suburbs (including Gaston Park, Indian Hills, Grand Prairie, and Country Club Park) (fig. 178). (These earliest Lively and Centex houses did not have attached garages.) In 1952, the company entered into a

177. Tom Lively, Northridge
Estates, Dallas, showing
sunrise. Restored by
Nathanael Roesch from a
newspaper advertisement
of May 1948.

178. Centex Construction Co.,
house, Gaston Park, Dallas,
Restored by Nathanael
Roesch from a newspaper
advertisement of April 1951.

series of housing contracts with US military bases, in collaboration with Tecon, a construction firm owned by the enormously wealthy Dallas Murchison family. According to the *Dallas Morning News*, by 1954 Centex had become known as the "second largest home builder in the nation, second only to William Levitt";[117] a year later the company was reported to have 7,000 houses under construction (and to "own, operate, or [have under construction] 6,200 apartments in the nation").[118] In 1955, Rupley and Lively were able to buy out their earlier partners with the help of Clint Murchison, Jr. (founder of the Dallas Cowboys) and his brother John, who then became shareholders in the firm. By 1959, Centex Construction Company was listed by the Dallas Chamber of Commerce as owning about $100 million worth of property outside Dallas, of which about a third was in Air Force bases in Indiana and Kansas; approximately another third was in Chicago.[119] Many writers have assumed that the Murchison brothers, heirs to the huge fortune amassed by their father Clinton Williams Murchison, Sr. from his investments in real estate and oil, immediately took control of Centex, but this was not the case.[120] When Ira Rupley died in 1960, Tom Lively became sole director, and firmly pursued his own policies. But there is no doubt that the Murchisons' bottomless pockets made a great difference to the young firm. And when Lively died in a boating accident in 1965, the Murchison stake in Centex was expanded. The company went public in 1969, and thereafter broadened and diversified its activities.

In 1954, Lively and Rupley secretly began to buy up land next to what would become O'Hare Airport, and just to the south of the planned Northwest Tollway. They were looking for "at least 1500 acres of land to implement a new planned Community . . . including [both] residential and industrial sections."[121] They were aided in assembling the land by a local realtor from Des Plaines, Charles Hodlmair. Over the next two years, the company was able to put most of the pieces together, and, together with Hodlmair and a small group of local residents, moved to incorporate the whole as Elk Grove Village, with Hodlmair as village president.[122] Only then was their far-reaching plan made fully public: six thousand dwellings were to be constructed on the western portion of the land, while an eastern portion would be an industrial sector stretching toward O'Hare. As an incorporated Village, Elk Grove proceeded to enact new zoning ordinances that made the Centex plan possible, especially by permitting industrial buildings and residences to be constructed in close proximity to one another.[123] As at Rolling Meadows, the inclusion of a large industrial section within town limits helped to keep residential taxes low for a long time.

Local Elk Grove Village lore holds that the plan for the village was "sketched by Hodlmair on a napkin." In reality, when Centex began to build Elk Grove Village, Lively and Rupley brought their house plans and their street planning with them. The houses, for the first four years at least, were designed by the Dallas firm of Milam and Roper, which had designed most of Lively and Rupley's Dallas houses (figs. 179, 180).[124] The master plan for Elk Grove Village, made public in 1956, was designed by a young Dallas firm of land planners, Phillips, Proctor and Bowers (Sid Bowers, Edward W. Proctor, Monty Bowers) (figs. 144, 181, 182).[125] From at least 1952, Rupley and Lively had depended on this firm to lay out the

179. Milam and Roper, "The Dallas," exterior. National Association of Home Builders *Correlator.*

180. Milam and Roper, "The Dallas," plan. National Association of Home Builders *Correlator.*

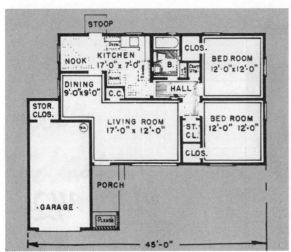

Centex master plan: 1956

O'Hare Field

BUSSE RD.

Centex Industrial Park

Shopping

HIGGINS RD.

ELK GROVE VILLAGE

Residential

DEVON AVE.

Elk Grove High School

Apartments

Shopping

ARLINGTON HEIGHTS RD.

181. Centex Master Plan for Elk Grove Village. *Chicago Daily Herald,* 1956.

streets of their subdivisions in Dallas. Phillips, Proctor and Bowers favored curvilinear street plans in which "facilities [are] tied together as a spider web with a network of streets and walks . . . [and] curving streets . . . provide ever changing vistas . . . [offering] the best climatic orientation and the best views."[126] The new master plan illustrates this "spider web" idea very clearly, with different "webs" focusing on parks, schools and a variety of community facilities. Streets were wider in Elk Grove Village than in the Dallas subdivisions, and lots were larger, but the pattern was similar. By the time Centex began building in Chicago, the firm had its own large staff (seventy-five in 1958), and the work of this staff was to a great extent dictated by the patterns of design and construction already developed in Dallas.[127]

The master plan of 1956 governed development up through the mid-1960s. At that time (1962–66), Centex purchased additional tracts to the west, totaling 2,000 acres, for residential purposes; street layouts in these new areas were very different in character from the original plan. But up to about 1965, development followed the 1956 plan almost exactly. A central spine along Salt Creek, lined with parkland, cut through the original area from north to south. (Centex elaborated further parks within this area.) Development proceeded from east to west: by July 1962 it had reached the eastern edge of the Salt Creek area.[128] Eleven further parks dotted the area to the east of Salt Creek.[129] By 1957, the first elementary school, named for Ira Rupley, was completed; by 1959, another had followed. A small shopping center was also soon built though the larger one shown on the 1956 plan was completed only in later years.

To the east, the Industrial Park area shown on the master plan (about 750 acres) mushroomed in size as Centex acquired new parcels adjoining the original purchase. By 1962, the Industrial Park contained 1800 acres. Further additions followed throughout the 1960s and 1970s.[130]

As was the case at Rolling Meadows, local newspapers ascribed the housing design at Elk Grove Village to A. J. Del Bianco, and perhaps he played some part in producing the plans.[131] But the houses themselves were clearly designed by Lively and his architects Milam and Roper. In Dallas and its suburbs, Lively and Rupley had developed a typical two- to three-bedroom house plan and exterior. These were ranch houses said to have a "traditional" look (according to contemporary Dallas advertisements): they were rectangular, parallel to the street, with a hip or gable roof (figs. 178, 179, 180). Many had an additional cross gable over the entrance. Some had a one-car garage or carport, but often there was no garage (a detached garage was usually added later). A picture window with multiple panes sometimes opened up the living room wall, but more often a pair or group of conventional double-hung windows served this purpose. Many had no separate dining room; instead there was a breakfast nook in the kitchen. Most had two bedrooms and, with about 880 square feet, were quite inexpensive.[132] (A two-bedroom house in Indian Hills, Dallas, cost $7,550 in 1952, or $62,000 in 2010 dollars.)[133] Circulation depended on an awkwardly arranged hallway that used up a disproportionate amount of living space.

Though they were often described as masonry, the Dallas houses were of conventional stud construction on a concrete slab. On the exterior, there was masonry veneer on the base and cladding above that looked like wood,

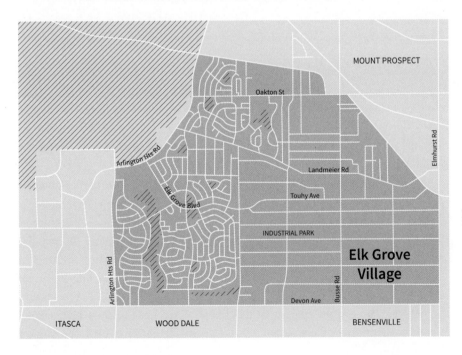

182. Elk Grove Village in 1956, map. Nathanael Roesch.

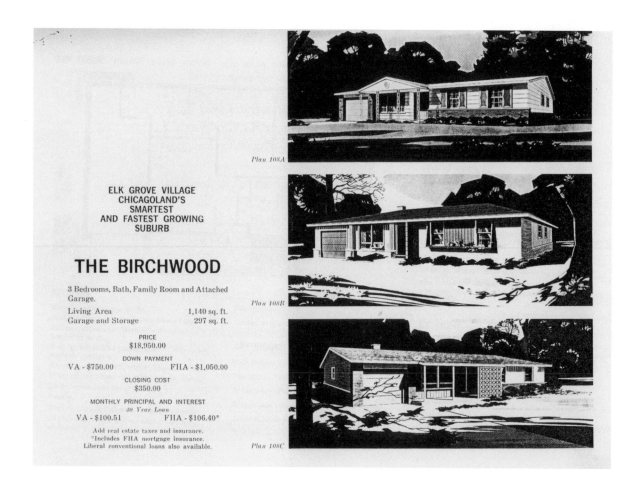

ELK GROVE VILLAGE
CHICAGOLAND'S
SMARTEST
AND FASTEST GROWING
SUBURB

THE BIRCHWOOD

3 Bedrooms, Bath, Family Room and Attached Garage.

Living Area .... 1,140 sq. ft.
Garage and Storage .... 297 sq. ft.

PRICE
$18,950.00

DOWN PAYMENT
VA - $750.00   FHA - $1,050.00

CLOSING COST
$350.00

MONTHLY PRINCIPAL AND INTEREST
30 Year Loan
VA - $100.51   FHA - $106.40*

Add real estate taxes and insurance.
*Includes FHA mortgage insurance.
Liberal conventional loans also available.

Plan 108A

Plan 108B

Plan 108C

183. Centex, "Birchwood" models, exteriors. Elk Grove Village sales brochure lent by Elk Grove Village library.

manufactured by Masonite. Interiors were finished with drywall. Lively and Rupley learned to build them very fast, first laying down the concrete slabs, and then bringing in materials and kitchen and bathroom equipment that they bought in bulk lots.[134] This was not "prefabrication," or even quite "mass production," although it was so described in contemporary news articles, but it did permit the rapid construction of multiple houses.

At Elk Grove, though, construction got a slow start. The earliest houses were begun in November 1956, but by the summer of 1958 the village had only about 400 resident families (or a population of about 1,400). By the summer of 1959, Centex had its construction procedures well under way, and the population had swelled to 5,000; by 1962 it had doubled. Population grew to 11,999 in 1962 and almost 17,000 in 1967. The 1970 census recorded 6,248 housing units and a total population of 24,516; some of these units, however, were located in the two- and three-story apartment buildings located near the new high school. When the last Centex house was built in Elk Grove Village in 1989, the total of

Centex-built single-family dwellings was 6,829, a little above the 6,000 projected in 1958. These figures suggest that Centex construction of single-family houses was substantially slower than what Hill achieved at Rolling Meadows.

The Elk Grove houses in the originally planned sections of Elk Grove Village (i.e., those built from 1956 to about 1964; figs. 183, 184) were strikingly similar in appearance to those that had been built by Centex in Dallas. Masonite siding topped a brick veneer base, and the house was erected on a slab foundation. Some models had a picture window, but many, like the top version of the Birchwood in figure 183, continued to use traditional double-hung windows to open up the living room. A central entrance (usually gabled on the exterior) led into the living room. There was rarely a space designated as a dining room or dining area, but the kitchen with breakfast nook expanded, at Elk Grove Village, to include a family room. In contrast to Dallas, most of the houses were three bedrooms (despite their small square footage) (1,152–1,326 square feet of living area, plus enclosed garages and storage), and somewhat better equipped and finished: living rooms had fireplaces, kitchen and family room had vinyl floors, bathrooms were tiled, heat was provided by gas-powered hot air furnaces (Birchwood model specifications).[135] House plans were rather conservative as compared with Rolling Meadows and Greenview: some houses had the continuous family room–kitchen used by Hill at Rolling Meadows, but their living rooms were neither especially large nor especially open (fig. 184). Interior hallways took up some of the ungenerous amount of interior space. Despite the existence of varied models and the ingenious curvilinear planning, street views appeared (and appear) repetitious and monotonous (fig. 185). This had also been true of Centex developments in Dallas, and had a great deal to do with the firm's practice of repeating many copies of a single model at a time on a particular block. The "spider web" plan was part of the problem too: elegant-looking on paper, the streets stretched at considerable length without cross streets, increasing the repetitive character

184. Centex, "Birchwood," basic plan. Elk Grove Village sales brochure lent by Elk Grove Village library.

185. Elk Grove Village, modern street view. Photo by Amanda Robbins-Butcher.

of the view. Prices were higher than in Dallas: a three-bedroom version, with 1,140 square feet of living space and an attached one-car garage, sold for about $128,000 to $134,443 in 2010 dollars, compared to $90,000 to $106,000 at Rolling Meadows and $78,000 to $81,000 in Dallas.

Elk Grove Village proved to be very attractive to new settlers in the 1960s. To an even greater extent than in Rolling Meadows, the presence of a large industrial district improved the tax base, so that property taxes remained relatively low. Elk Grove Village advertisements always claimed that prices and planning and production costs were aimed at income groups that were not affluent,[136] and this was true at first: In 1958, 90 percent of the inhabitants had annual incomes of close to $8,000 ($60,300 in 2010 dollars).[137] But over time the new subdivision attracted a population that was somewhat different from that of the earlier years. We have seen a similar process at Rolling Meadows: as housing types were elaborated and additional community facilities were provided, and as nearby O'Hare Airport ballooned, more affluent buyers moved in.

Meanwhile, as a public corporation, Centex greatly diversified its activities, investing in cement, oil, and gas. Revenues from these sources gave the firm a financial "cushion" so that it could continue to build single-family dwellings. Gradually the firm acquired a series of manufactured housing companies, and itself focused on the production of houses in many different states and regions. In 2009, it was absorbed by Pulte Homes, Inc.; the combined company then became the largest home builder in the nation, surpassing such giants as Lennar Homes, Kaufman and Broad, and Toll Brothers. Like its rivals, Centex as a public corporation (before and after incorporation into Pulte) built rather small groups of houses in particular places, but built a great many of them nationwide.[138] Centex and other late twentieth-century firms of this type (such as Lennar Homes or Kaufman and Broad) did not employ prefabrication in the fullest sense, but developed long-term relationships with suppliers of household equipment, such as kitchen appliances and plumbing fixtures, enabling them to short-circuit some of the slowdowns usually caused by local purveyors of these appliances and fixtures. House designs (with some regional and local variations) were created in the central office, but construction was (and is) carried out by local subcontractors.

Campanelli Brothers at Weathersfield in Schaumburg: New England House Forms Imported to Chicago

The development of planning and housing by the Campanellis in Schaumburg from 1957 to the early 1970s was rather different from the other Golden Corridor examples discussed here. Like Centex, the Campanelli firm was prospecting for large land parcels in the mid-fifties, looking all over the United States for opportunities. And like Centex, the Campanellis brought with them highly developed and well-oiled planning and construction practices that had already worked well at their home bases near Boston. But the Campanellis' capital was much smaller than that of Centex, and it is unlikely that they had aspirations to become a national firm. Their work in the "Weathersfield" section of Schaumburg was the largest house building effort they ever undertook, and it was very successful, both financially and in design terms. Yet it lacked either the planning coherence of Elk Grove Village or the roots in Chicago traditions of Rolling Meadows and Greenview. And for the Campanellis, unlike Kimball Hill or Centex, it marked both the high point of their housing and planning efforts and their departure from housing in favor of commercial and industrial construction.[139]

Schaumburg, a township thirty miles northwest of the center of Chicago, was settled in the 1830s by German immigrants, mostly from the tiny state of Schaumburg-Lippe in northwestern Germany. Most of its inhabitants were dairy farmers, though some grew grain.[140] By the early twentieth century, many of the farms had been repeatedly subdivided; by the 1930s and 1940s, some were in decline, while the proprietors of others had become substantial businessmen in addition to their farming activities. In 1954–55, the leaders among these farmers and businessmen began to be alarmed by the development, nearby, of Hoffman Estates, an enterprise of an Arizona firm called Father and Son Builders (Sam and Jack Hoffman were the father and son), who were also developing the town of Naperville, to the south.[141] Hoffman Estates began buying up land near Schaumburg Center in 1954, offering half-acre lots (21,780 square feet) with houses that appeared to the Schaumburg leadership to be substandard. A movement toward incorporation ensued in Schaumburg Center, in which the local leaders were joined by a relatively new resident, the dynamic Bob Atcher, famous at the time as a country singer on the radio program *National Barn Dance*, broadcast by the midwestern station WLS, and the man who popularized the song "You Are My Sunshine."[142]

As at Rolling Meadows and Elk Grove Village, the process of incorporation involved some odd political and legal maneuvers.[143] Late in 1955, after some false starts, Schaumburg Center was incorporated as a village consisting of two square miles and a population of 100 residents; in February 1956 the first Village Board was sworn in, with Louis Redeker as the first village president, and Bob Atcher as head of the new Village Planning Commission.[144] In 1959, Atcher replaced Redeker as president, and continued in that office until 1974. A "border war" with F & S Construction continued until 1959, when Hoffman Estates was incorporated. As a result of this border war, the map of Schaumburg Village was eccentric from its inception: there were (and are) large protrusions of Hoffman Estates properties at various points in the earliest part of the village core (fig. 186).[145] Atcher and the Planning Commission vowed to confine new development to parcels of no less than one-fourth to one-half acre.

At some point in 1956, Atcher and the Campanellis became friends and allies. Evidently, Atcher saw the Campanellis as the best available alternative to developers like F & S Construction. "We had a beautiful relationship with him" remembers Ray Celia, the Campanelli construction supervisor.[146] Thus, probably from the moment of their first land purchase of 400 acres in 1956, and continuing during Atcher's fifteen years as village president, the Campanellis had Atcher's full support. Together, they worked out the road layout for the new village.[147] The first zoning ordinance of 1959 enshrined their plans. By 1970, the village had expanded to 18,730 residents; its map was dominated by the 1,500 acres that Campanelli Brothers had put together in stages since 1956 (see the outlined areas in fig. 186).[148] The Campanellis named their section of Schaumburg "Weathersfield," after the Natick, Massachusetts, subdivision of that name (which had been misspelled in Massachusetts as "Wethersfield").[149]

In 1956, having scouted the area for at least a year, the Campanellis bought their first parcel, the Jennings Farm.[150] Further purchases and options followed, so that the firm was soon able to plan for three thousand single-family dwellings.[151] The Campanellis did not put together a master plan for their properties,

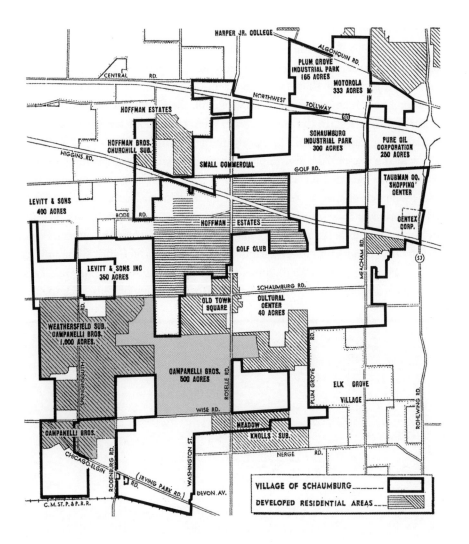

Map labels:
HARPER JR. COLLEGE
ALGONQUIN RD.
CENTRAL RD.
PLUM GROVE INDUSTRIAL PARK 165 ACRES
MOTOROLA 333 ACRES
NORTHWEST TOLLWAY
90
HOFFMAN ESTATES
SCHAUMBURG INDUSTRIAL PARK 300 ACRES
PURE OIL CORPORATION 250 ACRES
HOFFMAN BROS. CHURCHILL SUB.
HIGGINS RD.
SMALL COMMERCIAL
GOLF RD.
TAUBMAN CO. SHOPPING CENTER
LEVITT & SONS 400 ACRES
BODE RD.
HOFFMAN ESTATES
CENTEX CORP.
GOLF CLUB
MEACHAM RD.
53
LEVITT & SONS INC 350 ACRES
SCHAUMBURG RD.
OLD TOWN SQUARE
CULTURAL CENTER 40 ACRES
WEATHERSFIELD SUB. CAMPANELLI BROS. 1,000 ACRES
SPRINGINSGUTH RD.
CAMPANELLI BROS. 500 ACRES
ROSELLE RD.
PLUM GROVE RD.
ELK GROVE VILLAGE
ROHLWING RD.
WISE RD.
CAMPANELLI BROS.
MEADOW KNOLLS SUB.
WASHINGTON ST.
CHICAGO-ELGIN
ROSENBURG RD.
(IRVING PARK RD.)
NERGE RD.
DEVON AV.
C. M. ST. P. & P. R. R.
VILLAGE OF SCHAUMBURG
DEVELOPED RESIDENTIAL AREAS

186. Schaumburg Development in 1968, map. Nathanael Roesch from a newspaper advertisement of September 1968.

however; rather, their development proceeded piecemeal. Saivetz and Alfred Campanelli persuaded the local land planner and engineer, Charles W. Greengard Associates, to make the streets in the initial section curvilinear, as they had been in the Campanellis Boston developments. (Both Saivetz and the Campanellis thought that they were introducing New England curvilinear design to overwhelm the Chicago grid.) Streets in this first area to be built up, in the northwest segment of Weathersfield, were an amazing hodgepodge of curlicues (fig. 187); further sections, however, displayed the gentle curves that had been characteristic of most of the Campanellis' and Saivetz's work around Boston. This shift toward relatively greater coherence in street layout may reflect the growing influence of Alfred Campanelli on overall design issues: the Campanelli brothers continued to make "all important decisions" together, but Alfred, the youngest brother, took over the leadership of the new developments in Chicago, and, together with Ray Celia, the construction supervisor he had brought with him from Braintree, achieved a certain amount of independence from the parent firm.[152] Or, it is possible that the earliest section was laid out in a much greater hurry than subsequent sections. But above all, the Campanelli tracts in Schaumburg, unlike those in the Boston area, were contiguous, so it was possible, ultimately, to lay them out in a relatively uniform pattern.

From the outset, Alfred Campanelli and Bob Atcher had planned a series of community facilities for Weathersfield. The Campanellis built at their own expense the first elementary school (named after Francis Campanelli, the father of the brothers); they helped plan and contributed a community center containing recreation facilities and a village hall with administrative offices (West Schaumburg Road and North Braintree Drive, north of South Schaumburg Road), a shopping center (Weathersfield Commons, West Schaumburg Road and Springinsguth, south of West Schaumburg Road),[153] a major park (Campanelli

187. Weathersfield, map of first "W" section. Restored by Nathanael Roesch from a contemporary map.

NEW ENGLAND'S NO. 1 HOME BUILDER

INVADES

CHICAGOLAND

MODEL HOME #34

"THE BRADFORD"—Attractive 3 bedroom, brick front rambler with living room, dining room, G. E. kitchen with: dishwasher, disposal, hanging wall refrigerator, eye-level oven, counter top range, washer-dryer combination, plus ceramic tile back splash. The Bradford has 2 full ceramic tile baths (both walls and floor), brick fireplace, extra large playroom area and garage . . . V. A. $1,500, F.H.A. $2,000 down.

188. "New England's No. 1 Home Builder Invades Chicagoland," detail. Restored by Nathanael Roesch from a newspaper advertisement of September 1960. Subtitle reads "in Weathersfield . . . , Campanelli Bros have brought New England Values to the Midwest."

Park, north of West Weathersfield Way), and an industrial park (in the northeast section of fig. 186). These facilities had all opened by mid-1964; later, Campanelli Brothers donated and/or sold land at cost to the township for further schools (three additional elementary schools, three junior high schools, and a high school) and parks ("over 100 acres of park area").[154]

When the Campanelli brothers began to build in Schaumburg, they represented themselves as bringing New England architecture and planning to the Midwest. "New England's No. 1 Home Builder Invades Chicagoland" trumpeted an early advertisement (fig. 188). The ad shows "model home #34, The Bradford," a three-bedroom, L-shaped, gabled house with a one-car garage, wood siding, and some brick trim, virtually identical to the L-shaped Campanelli houses near Boston. An image of three eighteenth-century drummers and fifers introduce the house, while a Paul Revere–like figure shines his lantern on the appliances featured in the General Electric Colorama Kitchen. "Paul Revere" appeared again and again in the Campanelli ads and sales brochures, introducing house models with names like the Braintree, the Webster, the Bostonian, the Somerset, the Newport, the Sagamore, and the Essex. Similarly, street names in the Campanelli housing areas invoked New England models: gone were the names of family and friends from Massachusetts (except for Bradford, perhaps for Bradford Saivetz, perhaps for the town of the same name, or perhaps for William Bradford, governor of the Plymouth Colony in the sixteenth century); instead, streets were named for historic towns of the Boston area: Wayland, Waban (from the first section, all Ws), Brockton, Concord, Kingston, Duxbury, Dedham, Hingham, Plymouth, Salem, Cambridge, Woonsocket, Danvers, Yarmouth, Arlington, Lowell, Norwell. Warwick (after Warwick, Rhode Island, where the Campanellis built some of their earliest developments) also makes an appearance.

When Alfred Campanelli arrived in Schaumburg to conduct building operations there, the Campanellis in Boston had just begun to introduce more variety in their house models. In Schaumburg, the Campanellis continued to build their favorite ranches—L-shaped as in the Bradford in figure 188; slab-like as in the Salem, 1960 (fig. 189); cross-gabled as in figure 190; hip-roofed as in figure 191; and a giant-gabled series that closely resembled Brockton's Californian (fig. 130), but which was now marketed as the Fantasia.[155] The lowest-cost model, resembling the simpler of the Brockton houses, was the Essex, with three bedrooms and two bathrooms, a protruding garage, and a continuous kitchen, eating area,

189. Campanelli Brothers, Salem, ca. 1965, exterior. Restored by Nathanael Roesch from "Welcome to Colonial Weathersfield in Schaumburg, where the living is wonderful." Campanelli Brothers sales brochure, ca. 1967, lent by Schaumburg Library.

190 Campanelli Brothers, cross-gabled house, Weathersfield, ca. 1960, modern view. Photo by Amanda Robbins-Butcher.

191. Campanelli Brothers, hip-roofed house, Weathersfield, ca. 1965, modern view. Photo by Amanda Robbins-Butcher.

THE ESSEX

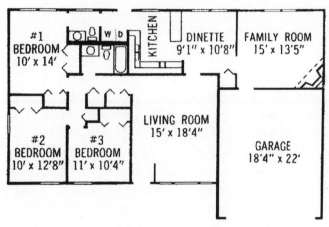

and family room (figs. 192, 193). Initially these ranches were set upon concrete slabs, but Alfred soon determined that Chicago buyers wanted a basement.[156] The ranch houses now appeared much longer than those in Massachusetts: fifty-five to sixty feet long was not uncommon.[157] But now, ranches were joined by split-levels: by conventional splits (fig. 194, the Fairview) and by the variant that the firm had been developing in the Boston suburbs, the midlevel-entry split (fig. 195). Alfred Campanelli also built a split-level with a giant gable with gingerbread (fig. 196), reminiscent of Cinderella Homes: a roof type that the brothers were trying out in Brockton at the same time (fig. 130). In Schaumburg, the firm marketed each of these types in several different versions: usually at least one had a good deal of "colonial" detailing. None of the houses was altogether new in its exterior design or plan: all or almost all were derived from earlier Boston area models, or were developed concurrently with the Boston designs. As in Massachusetts, marketing and advertising placed strong emphasis on both construction and interior equipment. Many of the firm's favorite kitchen appliances, such as the GE wall-mounted refrigerator (fig. 128) were used in both places.

192. "The Essex," exterior. Restored by Nathanael Roesch from "Welcome to Colonial Weathersfield."

193. "The Essex," plan. Restored by Nathanael Roesch from "Welcome to Colonial Weathersfield."

There were shifts in emphasis, however; splits were proportionally more numerous in Schaumburg than in the East Coast Campanelli developments. Two-car garages soon predominated. Exterior finishes were much more frequently brick veneer than had been the case in Massachusetts (fig. 191); horizontal or vertical "wooden" siding was also very frequent (figs. 195, 196), while the shingles so favored in Massachusetts and Rhode Island were relatively rare. Nearly all houses had fireplaces. Bow windows like those at Governor Francis Farms were often substituted for the multipaned picture windows that had been prevalent in the Boston area (fig. 189). In plan, too, some emphases shifted: all or nearly all of the houses had a dining ell (omitted in the lower-cost Campanelli houses near Boston—in Brockton, for example), and most had the continuous family room and kitchen the firm had begun to introduce near Boston around 1955 (fig. 197). Now, however, this innovative space was described as an "old-fashioned New England style kitchen and family room."[158] The midlevel splits offered larger and more elaborate family rooms than they had in the Boston area (Newport family room, fig. 198: note that this is the lower level and contains the *second* kitchen). Some refinements in design occurred first in Schaumburg and later near Boston: an elaborated master suite, for example, with partitions separating toilet and basins in the bathroom.[159] As the Weathersfield houses grew in size in the sixties, Alfred also introduced a two-kitchen model in which the basement offered an alternative living space for teens or in-laws (see the Newport [fig. 198] and the Seville: this, according to Ray Celia, was Alfred's idea).[160]

For the first few years, the Campanellis built both two- and three-bedroom models, ranging in price from $15,500 to $21,000.[161] Prices rose with inflation, of course, but continued, in the 1960s, in a low to middle range.[162] In the early 1970s, however, the character, size, and price of the houses changed. Two-bedroom versions virtually disappeared; four- and five-bedroom houses replaced them, and increasingly the Campanellis experimented with "garden apartments" and other types of multifamily dwellings, such as duplexes and quadroplexes.[163] Prices for single-family dwellings rose dramatically at the same time. From the 1970s, the Campanellis, led by Alfred, began to experience conflicts with Schaumburg planning and zoning officials about the size of planned houses on land that the Campanellis had newly acquired.[164]

195. Campanelli Brothers, midlevel entry split, Weathersfield, ca. 1965, modern view. Photo by Amanda Robbins-Butcher.

196. Campanelli Brothers, split-level with giant gingerbread gable, Weathersfield, ca. 1965, modern view. Photo by Amanda Robbins-Butcher.

197. "Salem," plan, ca. 1965. Restored by Nathanael Roesch from "Welcome to Colonial Weathersfield."

By 1976, the Campanellis had built 4,294 single-family dwellings in the Weathersfield subdivision and its extensions.[165] Construction numbers varied from year to year, but rarely exceeded 300 single-family dwellings per year, and sometimes were closer to 200. This was not a very rapid rate of production, but it was comparable to the way the firm had built in the Boston metropolitan area. At Weathersfield, after the firm had assembled a new construction team under the leadership of Ray Celia, they proceeded with much the same methods they had used, and were using, in Massachusetts: one crew cleared the land, another put down concrete slabs or dug basements. Alfred Campanelli ordered materials and equipment in relatively large numbers or amounts, so that successive crews could erect wood frames and roofs sequentially in 30 to 60 houses at a time. Installation of equipment and finishing of interiors and exteriors then also proceeded sequentially.[166] To a greater extent than any other builders in the Golden Corridor, the Campanelli team in Schaumburg offered extended consultation, advice, and minor repairs to new homeowners; this was also their practice in their Massachusetts developments.[167]

Nevertheless, Weathersfield in Schaumburg looked very different from its New England siblings. This was partly a result of the mixing of styles and models along the streets: to a much greater extent than in Massachusetts, ranches of various profiles alternated with split-level types (fig. 199). But above all, the look of Weathersfield as compared, for example, to Wethersfield in Natick, was the result of siting and street design. Schaumburg lot sizes were considerably more generous than those of the south shore Massachusetts developments and larger too than those at Elk Grove Village and Rolling Meadows: most Weathersfield lots were about 10,000 square feet (0.23 acres), as opposed to 7,500 in Elk Grove Village and in the second part of Rolling Meadows (after incorporation

198. "The Newport," 1963, view of family room. Restored by Nathanael Roesch from "Welcome to Colonial Weathersfield."

HERE'S A REAL FAMILY ROOM

24'9"x22'5"

at Weathersfield IN SCHAUMBURG

199. Modern view of cul-de-sac, Weathersfield. Photo by Amanda Robbins-Butcher.

permitted Rolling Meadows City to establish its own minimums). Setbacks were relatively deep, and above all, streets were wide and framed by concrete sidewalks and curbs, with wide grass strips lined with trees (fig. 199). Concrete was used for driveways. As in all the Chicago suburbs discussed here, electric lines were buried. Most of these features were mandated by Cook County building codes and then adapted by the local political entities. Schaumburg's version was particularly generous; when Schaumburg's broad streets, sidewalks, setbacks, and plantings are viewed together with the varied house profiles provided by the Campanellis, the result was an exceptionally pleasant streetscape.

At Weathersfield, Alfred Campanelli had the opportunity to put into practice some progressive ideas about community planning, an opportunity that the firm had not had in Massachusetts. But community identity in Weathersfield was to a great extent swallowed up by the later explosive growth of Schaumburg as a whole. Motorola established its World Headquarters in Schaumburg in 1967, other industrial and business complexes, manufacturing, commercial, and retail centers, and large hotels followed. The Woodfield Mall (one of the largest malls in the United States) soon dwarfed Weathersfield's shopping center; village government shifted to a new location in the east of Schaumburg, along with shopping and industry. The population tripled between 1968 and 1974 (reaching 36,000 in 1974, 53,305 in 1980). With this extraordinary growth, the social composition of the inhabitants also changed, with a concomitant demand for less expensive apartments at one end of the scale and high-end single-family dwellings at the other.[168] The Campanellis struggled with these changes in the 1970s, developing new kinds of multifamily dwellings on the one hand, and luxury single-family dwellings in new areas outside their original holdings in Weathersfield, on the other. But they also sought to return to their earlier, less expensive models, and in this they were unsuccessful.

By 1990, Schaumburg contained about 32,000 dwelling units, of which only a third were single-family houses; of these single-family dwellings, only about half were Campanelli-built and located in Weathersfield. Thus Weathersfield came to be less and less identifiable to the inhabitants of Schaumburg, and to outside observers. Now, however, as at Rolling Meadows, local attention in Schaumburg is returning to the history of the "early" Weathersfield; thus a new sense of identity is arising that is focused on the development of the town in its first postwar years.[169]

At the Weathersfield ranch houses in Schaumburg, Campanelli advertising lost all references to "western" themes, while split-levels were also divorced from local bungalow traditions. Instead, both were heralded as "New England" types. Certainly, the houses built by the Campanellis in Weathersfield had a decade-long New England tradition behind them, but they were, as we have seen, radically different from most historical models, and from all traditions of the polite plan. Asserting a connection of the new kitchen–family room–eating spaces to an "old fashioned New England style kitchen" was somewhat more plausible, if by "New England style kitchen" one meant the primitive kitchens of the earliest settlers, or farmhouse kitchens. Clearly Bradford Saivetz, and hence probably Alfred Campanelli as well, believed that the firm was bringing New England house types and New England street patterns to the Midwest, but the references to New England were also to a certain extent advertising hyperbole. The Campanellis must have believed that Illinois buyers would find such themes appealing. The mixture of house types, plans, and materials employed by the Campanellis in Weathersfield, on the other hand, served to de-emphasize any sense of regional origins or connections. This was also true of other builders' houses of the sixties discussed here—those of Cortese, for example, or the later Bodek. By the early and mid-sixties, suburbs were changing, and beginning to appeal to new kinds of buyers; their desirability was already well established and their newness well understood. At the same time, new land was less available, prices were beginning to rise, and financing was beginning to shrink. Appeals to the earliest American historical traditions may have seemed to be the only possible new emphasis for advertising to adopt.

CHAPTER 5

The Buyers, Their Backgrounds, and Their Preferences

According to the Campanellis, buyers were the builder's "best architects." But who were the early buyers of postwar tract houses, the people who shaped the new houses through their choices? Where were they from, and how did they acquire their preferences about house design? These questions not only were important to the builders; they preoccupied a great many other contemporaries too. In 1945 and for a few years thereafter, a huge number of surveys investigated the question "what do people want?" in a new dwelling. Later, the issue of what people actually were choosing in the new suburbs loomed large in newspaper accounts of the developing new communities. The builders themselves did market research of various kinds, building "research houses" like Fritz Burns in Los Angeles in 1946, or, like the Campanellis, analyzing buyers' choices among several model houses; sometimes, as with Bodek and Hill, they entered into more formal, questionnaire-oriented studies. Much later, from the 1990s onward, retrospective studies—of the formation of by then well-established communities—began to appear, in popular magazines and local newspapers. And recently, during the past decade, local historians have begun to write the histories of their communities, relying to a great extent on interviews with their elder residents. These kinds of investigation offer some answers about the identity and attitudes of the buyers.

In order to get an idea of the answers to these questions today, there are therefore many sources. The contemporary research based on questionnaires and interviews is particularly useful; I begin by examining its implications. It would be extremely valuable to be able to return to the interviews on a more individual basis, but so much time has passed that this is rarely possible now. I have been able to interview a few original owners from several of the developments among my case studies; I turn to this next, and attempt to interpret what I learned. I proceed to discuss the choices people made among house forms and review the possible influences upon these choices from popular culture—television, movies, magazines, and newspapers. Finally, I turn to the backgrounds of the buyers (as I understand them through my interviews): their dwelling experiences during the Depression and during the war. I suggest that experience of the war was formative for most of them, in shaping their design preferences.

Questionnaires and Market Research in the 1950s

Of the earliest studies, the most useful is Edward T. Paxton's *What People Want When They Buy a House: A Guide for Architects and Builders*, published by the US Department of Commerce in 1955, and based primarily on two large surveys of 1949 and 1950 conducted by the Small Homes Council of the University of Illinois and the Institute for Social Research at the University of Michigan. The Michigan group sampled a total of one thousand home buyers in 1949–50, including buyers of old houses as well as buyers of new ones. The Small Homes Council summarized the results of statistical surveys of housing likes and dislikes carried on by forty-one agencies and publications from 1938 to 1952 dealing with new housing of 1949–50.[1] To these results, Paxton added slightly later reports by the Housing and Home Finance Agency and the Bureau of Labor Statistics.[2] The Paxton publication has the great virtue of telling us about attitudes in the very earliest years of the formation of new house types; and it is also suggestive as to the social composition of a large group of new owners.

The Paxton surveys broke down questions and responses into several headings, including "Who were the buyers?" "What were the buyers looking for?" (with ten subheadings), price, financing, furnishing and alterations, and buyer satisfaction. The surveys found that 36 percent of new home buyers were first owners; of the others, 64 percent had owned housing before. They were predominantly low-income buyers: 44 percent had family incomes in 1950 under $3,000 and 53 percent under $5,000 ($27,000–45,000 in 2010 dollars).[3] They were young: 36 percent were under 34 and 54 percent under 39. Of the families, 59 percent had children. Occupations of the main breadwinner were mixed: 37 percent were skilled and unskilled workers, a quarter were managerial and self-employed; 15

percent were employed in clerical work and sales; 10 percent were professional people. Of the heads of household, 47 percent were veterans of World War II. The Paxton surveys did not ask specifically about women's work.

As to what they were looking for, the Paxton surveys found that the all-important consideration was location within commuting distance of work. (Of the families surveyed, 85 percent owned a car, so most people's definition of "commuting distance" was already automobile-based at the time of the surveys.) Size, siting, and price of the house were also highly valued. Interestingly, 79 percent of the respondents wanted a one-story house, although only 60 percent succeeded in purchasing one. Stylistic preferences varied regionally, with "modern" most favored in the West and Midwest, "traditional" (Cape Cod or colonial) most desired in the Northeast. (As a reminder, neither the ranch house nor the split-level was widely available at the time of these surveys.) Overall, 42 percent preferred "modern" (though this quality was not clearly defined). Most wanted a larger lot than they were able to obtain. Nearly all buyers were very concerned with the quality of construction; as to building materials, they preferred brick, or wood.[4] Many reported an intellectual or emotional attachment to the ideal of home ownership; many also saw their new houses as a good investment for the future.

Nearly all buyers were looking for six rooms or more, though many bought houses that were smaller than that. (Of new houses begun in 1949, 33 percent in 1949 and 36 percent in 1950 contained 800 to 1,000 square feet.)[5] Their priorities in rooms tended toward large multipurpose living rooms and kitchens. Almost half (in 1949) wanted a separate dining room as well as dining space in the kitchen. "There is strong demand for the provision of some types of eating facility in the kitchen, either in addition to or in place of eating facilities elsewhere in the house," wrote Paxton.[6] A majority wanted at least one full bathroom (with shower or bathtub). More buyers wanted basements than were able to find houses equipped with them. Nearly all wanted a fireplace, and a majority wanted central heating. A very high percentage of buyers in 1949–50 wanted an attached garage, but very few of these wanted to use the garage only for the car. Other planned uses for the garage included storage and laundry.

Prices paid for the house varied according to buyers' age and pre-tax income, and also according to area, with higher prices, not surprisingly, in the major metropolitan regions. Of all buyers, 48 percent of those surveyed paid under $10,000 in 1949–50 ($90,000 in 2010 dollars); another 28 percent paid from $10,000 to $15,000 ($90,000 to $136,000 in 2010 dollars); the median was $9,500 ($86,000 in 2010 dollars).[7] Of the new houses, 44 percent were financed at least in part by the VA, FHA, or a combination of the two.

These are immensely valuable data; Paxton also offered a great deal of detail and analysis that I have not included here. We can assume that builders familiarized themselves with these data even before the 1955 publication date of Paxton's work, by consulting the published versions of the reports on which the book was based.[8] But it is also clear that the studies of buyer preferences for 1949–50 do little to explain buyers' preferences at a later date, and among my examples of builders, only Burns, Hill, Facciolo, and the Campanellis were active at the time the surveys were conducted. Nor does Paxton help us with the views of those that bought split-level houses—these have no role in the surveys considered by Paxton. Paxton's surveys also do not give us much sense of the buyers as people, as individuals making momentous life choices.

Voices from the Fifties

The interviews with buyers that occurred in contemporary newspapers and magazines, together with the interviews with elderly original buyers on videos recorded by Lakewood in 2004 and by Schaumburg in 2006 are more helpful in giving us a sense of individual buyers, and I have used them when I could. Historians of the Levittowns have also published some interviews at various dates. But most of these groups of interviews are not specific to the particular communities dealt with here. Accordingly, I have sought out and interviewed a few original buyers (and their children) from within the settlements that constitute my case studies. I tried to make contact with "ordinary" people in the hope of finding reminiscences that approach the "typical." (Obviously, my judgment as to what is "ordinary" and what is "typical" is arbitrary and to a certain extent intuitive.)[9] Obviously, too, a full and careful study of each community would contain many more interviews, but because of the aging of the original inhabitants, this is no longer possible. Furthermore, most of the individuals I interviewed were original owners *who are still in residence*: this bespeaks a strong and long-term commitment to their houses and their communities.

I have selected twelve of these interviews to discuss here—they are reproduced in full in appendix 3, along with the questions that I asked. In each case where I talked to either the husband or wife, I heard a good deal about the attitudes of the other partner too. (When the spouse was still living, they consulted one another before and during the interview.) Sometimes, when neither parent was living, I talked to a son or daughter: each of these children seemed to have vivid recollections of their parents' attitudes. Thus, in effect, I have information from twenty-four individuals, distributed across the four metropolitan areas discussed in earlier chapters. In addition, each of the individuals, couples, or children whom I interviewed supplied their own impressions of their neighbors and friends as they remember them from the early years of their housing developments. I conducted the interviews in person and by telephone, letter, and email (often in combination). I asked open-ended questions, and let people talk more about what interested them most, so the results are very far from being standardized. Thus, the information I have from each varies somewhat as to emphasis and subject matter. On the basis of this material, and using Paxton and the Bodek and Hill surveys, together with other contemporary and modern interpretations, I have tried to construct some general hypotheses about who the early buyers were, what their housing preferences were, how their tastes were formed, and what their housing experiences were before they joined the ranks of tract house dwellers. It goes without saying, I hope, that such hypotheses are very tentative: to really understand the ways of life and the pattern of building choices in the early postwar suburbs, much more detailed study is needed, for many more communities.

Each of the people I interviewed was a strong, independent, and opinionated individual; the lives of many were quite dramatic. Let us listen to three of their voices, to get a sense of their stories. Mrs. KD of Lawrence Park, the daughter of original purchasers, reminds us of the devotion to property ownership felt by working-class people, and illustrates the loyalty of second-generation suburban people to their childhood communities. Mrs. BG of Rolling Meadows is somewhat atypical of the group because she was the main breadwinner, and because she and her husband had only one child. In other respects, however, her life is quite representative, full of adventure, risk, hard times, and resilience. Mrs. and Mr. HN describe the extreme crowding of the childhood homes of the new settlers, and demonstrate the willingness of both partners to work at almost any job in order to secure their house and their place in the community. Dates refer to the year the new house was purchased.

Mrs. KD, school bus driver, daughter of lace-maker and distillery worker, Lawrence Park, PA, 1955

> My parents were second-generation Italian and Irish. They grew up in row houses in Philadelphia. My Irish grandfather was a bricklayer. My father worked at Publicker Distillery in south Philadelphia, my mother operated a lace-making machine in a factory in north Philadelphia. My father was in the Army 1943–45, in Europe; when he got back we bought a second row house right next to the one we lived in, in North Philadelphia. We lived in that, and rented the other. Then my mother heard about the "houses in the country" that were being built outside Philadelphia and wanted to see what they were like. They found our Lawrence Park house in a newspaper ad (they didn't know anybody there), and came out there in 1955 to look. There wasn't much around at the time—not many other houses, no shops, no Catholic schools, but the salesman who showed them the models explained that the place would get to be over 1,000 houses, and that a new Roman Catholic parish had just started up. It was a new kind of house, a split-level, with three

bedrooms and one bath, a lot of house for the money. They decided the house would be roomier for the family (me and my four sisters and brothers) and that it looked like a good investment. (The row house had three bedrooms too, but these in the new house were bigger. Three kids slept in the master bedroom, two in the small bedroom, Mom and Dad in the medium-size bedroom.) So they sold the row houses in the city, paid off part of the mortgage, and we moved in. We lived there the whole time I was growing up, and when I got married, my husband and I bought a house just a couple of blocks away. Then after my parents died, I bought their house.

It was funny to hear birds instead of the clack-clack of the trolleys. (I liked the trolley noises too, though.) After a while, it didn't seem like "country" so much: a shopping center opened up near us and my mother worked there (as a cashier at Pantry Pride and then at the Pathmark), streets got paved, and the place grew. But we always had a big vegetable garden in the back yard. My dad had hoped to keep some sheep, but in Marple Township you had to have a one acre lot to do that. My dad continued to work at the distillery and drove to work. We had two cars.

It was a great place to be a kid, there were so many of us. We didn't all go to the same schools; lots of the kids went to the new public schools that opened up; we went to the nearest parochial schools. But we all played together all the time, and were in and out of each other's houses. Our families didn't socialize much, but they were always there for each other in emergencies, like snowstorms, power outages, or if a kid was hurt. After I took over the house, I fixed it up: replaced the old asbestos siding, converted the old garage to a den, moved the television there, opened up the dining room to the kitchen to make one big room; I also built a deck out back. Some of our family work in construction trades and they helped me. Now it's very nice: just how I like it.

Mrs. BG, machine operator, Rolling Meadows, 1955

I was a machine operator at Transo Envelope.[10] (Later I was a proofreader, and then the production manager.) We lived with our young son in a one-bedroom basement apartment in Albany Park (Chicago) and then on the ground floor of a two-story house in Richmond; these were all we could find that worked for my husband, who'd had polio in 1943 and was in a wheelchair. We kept watching the newspapers for a better place. One Sunday we were looking at the *Chicago Tribune* and saw an ad for ranch houses in Rolling Meadows. We visited the models, fell in love with the three-bedroom house, put down our last $10 to hold one. We were just barely able to swing the mortgage on my salary of $5,000/year.[11] My boss came out and guaranteed my employment. We paid the down payment with Rob's profits from the lamps he made at home and sold. At first, I carried him into the house on my back, but then we got a ramp for the wheelchair. I drove into Chicago to work, but later on some other people from Transo came to Rolling Meadows, and we carpooled.

We watched the house being built: we went out every Sunday. It was perfect for us: all on one floor, roomy, and the big kitchen! The washer and dryer—we'd never had anything like that. And we were so happy to have a place of our own. We didn't change too much. We had a choice of tile colors in the bathroom, and we also put wallpaper there. I liked light-colored walls and the wall color in the living room was an ugly green, so we had them change that to beige. We had to widen the bathroom door for Rob's wheelchair, and we built a garage out back. When people said there was a tornado coming, we'd all go down to the crawl space and wait it out. You couldn't stand up there, but you could sit well enough.

The neighbors were nice, they were all about the same age as us, in their early thirties. We didn't socialize a lot—just once in a while, at the street parties. The neighbors came from different backgrounds, German, Irish, Polish, English. We were Episcopalian, not great churchgoers (our neighbors weren't either), but we liked going to the nondenominational community church that Kimball Hill set up in the old barn. And then, on Saturdays we'd have a pot-luck supper and sit in our cars at the barn, watching outdoor movies. That was a lot of fun. The first school was in that building too. Our son went to school in the barn, and later to the public schools that replaced it. The schools were very good.

My dad was a foreman in a factory in upstate New York that made machine parts [Dodge Sales & Engineering Company, Oneida, NY]; we lived in a tiny town nearby in a two-story house where we had a garden, a cow, and chickens. The factory closed, so my dad drove us out to Sterling, Colorado, where two of his sisters lived.

Unfortunately when we moved, we had to auction off my mom's collection of first editions: all the best authors, Shakespeare of course, and all the best English and American novels. She'd only gone through eighth grade, but she loved books. Later, she built a new smaller collection, but in the new place we also used the public library a lot—all us kids were great readers. We kept the original house, though; my brother has it now.

So we went out west about 1925, and it was an adventure. They were building the roads as we went, and there weren't any good places to stay; we camped in the car at night. [There were two adults and four children.] In Sterling, we bought a hotel and restaurant. We lived in the hotel. Rob was a traveling salesman who came to the hotel; he and I met then. His father was a miner; growing up, Rob and the other kids lived with their grandmother in a beautiful big three-story brick house in Provo, Utah. It's gone now, of course.

Our house in Schaumburg was the twentieth house to be built in Weathersfield. It was "our great adventure." Weathersfield wasn't really there yet, it was still country. Cows would escape onto the roads. At first, the well wasn't approved, so the Campanellis arranged to have water delivered to the houses—that lasted about six months. We loved the house, the design, the spaces, the way it was built. It was a castle to us. We found the house through a friend of Laura's who married a civil engineer working in Massachusetts. They lived in a Campanelli house in Peabody. When they moved to Chicago and learned that the Campanellis were building in Schaumburg, they told us that this was the house we had to have. "The Campanellis are the best home builders in the world," he said. They moved in on the same block, three weeks ahead of us, but later they moved back to Massachusetts. We had a VA mortgage, paid no money down.

We had both grown up in bungalows, mine a three bedroom one-bath house in Cicero, Laura's a five-bedroom house with one bath (there were ten kids) in Oak Park. I had three brothers and two sisters—there were six kids. We were both used to doubling up (my brothers and I had our beds in the second parlor). When we got married and started our family we couldn't find the right apartment in Chicago; we moved into Mom's house in Cicero. (My grandparents owned the whole block.) So when the salesman at Schaumburg told us the three-bedroom ranch would be too small for us and our four kids, we laughed. We did add two bedrooms later, though, because we eventually had seven kids. We remodeled the garage into a bedroom and added another at the back, we also added a laundry room and another bathroom, so we added a total of 900 square feet. We used the same radiant heating system in the floor of the new areas as in the rest of the house, and it still works well. Some of Campanelli's subcontractors did the work for us.

The neighbors worked at a lot of different things: one was a cookie salesman, another drove a truck, one installed heating systems, one was a pilot for United, several worked in airplane maintenance at O'Hare. They all became our good friends. Some were Irish Catholic, like us; others were Italian and Polish. At first we had to go to the church in Hoffman Estates, but St. Marcelline's opened soon and that was good for us. A black family moved in in 1972; the pastors and priests lectured everybody about tolerance, and it worked out. Laura took care of their baby while the parents worked.

We had bonfires, lots of informal parties. At Halloween, and when we wanted to have block parties, the police would close off two of the streets for us. The kids played in the streets; there wasn't much traffic then. Our kids went to the Catholic schools from the third grade on (St. Hubert's, in Hoffman Estates), but before that they went to the Campanelli school, which was terrific. When our oldest was in school, Laura went to work for the Village school system. Earlier, she babysat for other people's kids and also helped to show the model houses on weekends. I started out in Schaumburg as a milkman; then I took over milk distribution for the area. I also drove the school bus.

It was a wonderful era.

The occupations of the people I interviewed varied in ways similar to those suggested in the Paxton surveys, from working class (like Mr. HN, the milkman, and Mrs. KD's father, the brewery worker, quoted above) to professionals (like Mr. OC, the engineer). The other male wage earners included an airlines clerk, a horticulturalist, two pharmacists, two researchers in a government laboratory in Massachusetts, a factory foreman, and an insurance salesman. Among her family's neighbors in Torrance, California, Mrs. FC noted great variety: "construction people, tradesmen . . . insurance salesmen, factory workers . . . a few elementary school teachers, and people who worked at the airplane companies." In addition to his neighbors who worked at Natick Labs, Mr. LT remembers others who "worked in management with private companies. Some ran their own small businesses: a grocery store, auto parts store, a fabric store." Mr. KC, a pharmacist in Brockton, describes his neighbors as "lower middle class": "one neighbor was an accountant, another a cab driver, another a salesman." Clearly the inhabitants of Rossmoor were more affluent than the other communities I have discussed, but if it is possible to generalize on the basis of these reports, these other communities held a mixture of lesser professionals, artisans, factory workers, white-collar workers, and small businessmen. In this, again, they were rather similar to the Paxton surveys.

I spoke more often to women than to men, and therefore learned a great deal about women's work (missing from the Paxton surveys, perhaps because it was often a later development in families' lives). The story of Mrs. OC, resident of the most affluent community studied here, was the only one that conformed to older stereotypes about stay-at-home suburban wives. The experience of the other wives I talked to or that were described to me was quite different. Mrs. MH worked full-time as a township officer near Facciolo's Rose Tree Woods. Mrs. KD's mother operated a lace-making machine in a factory and then, after they moved to Lawrence Park, became a full-time cashier at a local supermarket, as described above. Mrs. FC's mother worked first for a catering company part-time and then "as a [full-time] clerk in the local junior high school." Mr. LT's mother worked as a sales clerk in the local department store, "mostly evenings at first, but then for longer hours"; Mr. IN's wife worked "in a handbag factory." Mrs. BG, quoted above, was a machine operator in Chicago and commuted by car from their home in Rolling Meadows to her workplace in the city. Mrs. KM, also of Rolling Meadows, "went to work part time when the youngest [child] was six months old, and then when they were all in school I went to full-time, first in a department store, then as an accountant, then as the business manager for an oncologist. I had had two years of college, and then I went to Harper College [near] Rolling Meadows for some accounting courses; I'd always had a head for numbers." While her seven children were very young, Mrs. HN, of Weathersfield (Schaumburg), quoted above, worked at home as a babysitter for the children of other couples. On weekends, she demonstrated model homes for the builder.[12] When all the children were in school, she worked full-time as a grade school assistant. Mrs. MQ (also of Weathersfield), with four children, described herself to me initially as a "homemaker," but then added "after the youngest was in school, I taught at the local elementary schools, first as a substitute, and then later, after I went back to junior college for more education credits, I taught first grade on a regular basis." After her three children were all in school, Mrs. TU went to work for a travel agency; she also worked as a census interviewer. These women needed to work; but they also wanted to. Their jobs were in occupations such as sales, which they could manage part-time initially and without much training, in factory work in which many were already experienced, or in white-collar jobs and education, for which they sometimes obtained additional training. In all cases except that of Mrs. BG, they worked close to home. For them, their first concern seems to have been the security and well being of the children, but this did not preclude their membership in the work force. Many of the jobs held by suburban women were new jobs, created by the new suburbs and by the housing boom: jobs in schools, in real estate, and in shopping centers.

Family size as reported in my interviews also varied dramatically. Mr. IN and his wife had no children; Mrs. HN and her husband had seven; Mrs. BG and her husband, one; Mrs. MQ and her husband, four; Mr. TU and his wife, three. Mrs. MH and her husband had two of their own, and raised two others. In Mrs. KD's family there were five children; in Mrs. FC's and Mr. and Mrs. HN's, three each. Only the families of Mr. LT, Mrs. OC, Mr. TU, and Mr. KC contained the two children that are usually described as typical of the period. These households did not include elderly relatives: indeed, among the people that I interviewed, their parents, aunts and uncles, and grandparents were reasonably well established and independent in their own urban dwellings. The nature of the postwar suburban family is often described as inward-turning and assertively "nuclear." But I observed many contacts with nearby extended families, and at a later stage, some families expanded their houses to accommodate the visits, sometimes quite lengthy, of their own married children. After she married, Mrs. KD (quoted above) bought a house within blocks of her parents (who were original owners in Lawrence Park) and later took over the parents' house; her brother also lives nearby. Mrs. KM bought additional houses in Rolling Meadows for her children and grandchildren. Although many commentators have argued that the prevalence of the nuclear family in the early postwar suburbs was unusual, historians have shown that some version of the nuclear family has been quite common throughout Western history.[13] Probably the nuclear family seemed unusual at the time because so many of the buyers of new houses had emerged from very crowded multigenerational households during a period of housing scarcity.

Although occupation and income varied considerably among these people, they all thought of the journey to work as one of the most important considerations in deciding where to buy their houses, another similarity to the Paxton and Bodek surveys. Proximity to the husband's work, or at least to a reasonable commute by automobile, was almost always decisive in the choice of an area in which to buy. A "reasonable commute" could be long, though: Mr. MQ took the train for almost an hour to his job in the Loop; Mr. KM had a long drive to his job in Skokie. Proximity to the wife's work was also regarded as important. Every household had a car; some had a pickup truck, van or second car too. When they could, the men in the family carpooled, leaving the car with their wives for the rest of the week. Once these buyers were established in their new environment, they tended to stay there: of the three families that moved after buying their first house, only one moved away in order to follow the main breadwinner's job; the others moved close by within the same community, in order to occupy a larger house.

The interviews also show great variations within each community in ethnicity or nationality, and religion. The majority of the people I talked to were second- or third-generation immigrants of European origin, from such diverse places as Armenia, Poland, Italy, Ireland, Germany, Norway, Lithuania, and the Netherlands. The others came from families that had been here longer, and this included the two Jewish couples that I talked to. All were white, although there were a few examples of Mexican Americans reported in one of the communities, and a lone African American in another. (That is, they were "white" as it has now come to be understood, although prior to the war, in many places in the United States, Jews would not have been considered really "white," nor would Italians, or, in fact, most Catholics.)[14] Five families were Catholic, two Jewish; one belonged to the Armenian Apostolic Church; the others attended a variety of Protestant churches, including Lutheran, Presbyterian, and Episcopalian. Generally speaking, they grew up in places *without* much ethnic and religious variety: on farms, in very small towns, in Protestant areas of single-family dwellings in medium-size cities, or in ethnic enclaves within the larger cities. The "diversity" of their new communities was a source of considerable pride to them.[15] I will return to this point shortly.

Like incomes and occupations, educational levels also varied within each community. Both of Mrs. FC's parents had college educations, but this was unusual among their neighbors. Mrs. KM had some college, but her husband had not finished high school. Three individuals had finished high school but had no college. Several had post–high school certifications of various types: pharmacy, education, horticulture; several went back to school, sometimes aided by the GI Bill, to obtain this further training. At Rossmoor, though, the most affluent of the new settlements I have studied, educational levels were quite high: as Mrs. OC remembers, "Most of the neighbors were well educated. . . . The men were mostly professional people, doctors, engineers in the aerospace industry." The two men in Natick who worked at the government laboratory had advanced degrees.

Despite these variations in ethnicity, religion, income, occupation, education and place of origin, the refrain that I heard most often was "but we were all alike." "The neighbors were pretty much like my parents: mostly younger couples with small children" (Mr. LT). "The neighbors were all young and struggling, like us" (Mrs. KM). "They were all like us: young and struggling financially" (Mr. KC). Several added to this refrain, "The best thing [about the new place] was the neighbors" (Mrs. OC, Mrs. KM), and "the neighbors became our good friends" (Mr. and Mrs. HN, Mrs. OC). This willingness, even eagerness, to "live with strangers," to have them as "our good friends," and this retrospective pride about it, deserve special emphasis. "Living with strangers" has always been an element in urbanization, of in-migration by new settlers into existing cities.[16] In the past, however, the impact of strangers on one's way of life had been softened by the existence of family and/or ethnic and religious networks within the new urban environment. The new tract house developments were very different: usually they did not have such networks nearby (although many kept in touch with their extended families), everyone else was also new, "everyone was from somewhere else."[17] Like the physical environment, the social environment was also new.

There were other commonalities too. The people to whom I spoke often referred to the "freedom" of the new communities, by which they seem to have meant freedom of movement for themselves and their children, freedom from the proximity of neighbors and extended family, and freedom from the constrictions of landlords and municipal regulations. They also seem to have meant "freedom" to move around inside, without the constrictions of small rooms. One of the new owners interviewed by Creighton and Ford around 1960 praised the "free movement" from one room to another; another said, "The open aspect of the house . . . gave me a glorious feeling of freedom."[18]

But here again, the people I talked to stressed the needs of the children. The new owners were not simply escaping from crowding, but also looking for houses designed in such a way as to give their kids a particular kind of good life. Nearly all referred to opportunities for children to move around freely. In ranch houses, the fact that all rooms were on a single level facilitated movement to the outdoors, and while the adults appreciated this for themselves, the greatest benefit they perceived was for the children and other children from the neighborhood, who moved in and out and around "like flocks of birds."[19] The ease of moving in and out (also a feature to a somewhat lesser extent in split-levels) was undoubtedly a major factor in what they describe as the "freedom" of the new houses and their neighborhoods. So was the absence of fences and hedges. Looking back, the three children of original owners that I talked to all agreed that "it was a great place to be a kid . . . we all played together all the time, and were in and out of each other's houses" (Mrs. KD). "We all played together, in the back yards, on the sidewalks, in the streets, and on the building sites where new houses were in construction. We rode our bikes on the sidewalks and around the block" (Mrs. FC). "As kids, we ran free. . . . There were no fences then" (Mr. LT). It is no accident that one of the most popular songs of the early fifties was Cole Porter's "Don't Fence Me In." In this song, as performed by Gene Autry, Roy Rogers, and Bing Crosby (or by Bob Atcher, mayor of Schaumburg), the cowboy-singer plumbs the land hunger of the era: "Oh give me land, lots of land, under starry skies . . . don't fence me in." The song had a lot to do with all the restless and rebellious instincts of its audience, and therefore resonated with their views of "freedom" too.[20]

Although "freedom" for the children (and the new homeowners) was a dominant issue, nearly all the people I talked to were emphatic about the importance of new schools and good education for their kids. All commented on the excellence of their local educational systems, and many of the wives worked in the schools. The local PTAs were often mentioned. Among Catholics, the availability of Catholic schools had great importance. "This was the Sputnik era," Mrs. OC said. "It was absolutely necessary to build up the education of our kids." She thought, in other words, that the continuation of peace depended upon American technological supremacy, which in turn depended upon the American educational system. This was a logical view for people who had experienced American victory in World War II as a victory for American technology. Education was also seen as a means for "going forward," that is, to achieving better status in the future than one's family had experienced in the past.

The commitment to the education of their children was part of a broader commitment to building up a new community. Many speakers said that they (or their parents) had wanted a house "in the country"; recollections of rural sounds and sights from the early days of the new developments were common (birdsongs for Mrs. KD; the view of "cows in the streets" for Mr. and Mrs. HN and Mr. TU). I would argue that buyers of this era often felt nostalgia for the farmsteads of their parents, grandparents, or other extended family. (See, for example, Mr. IN's comments about his wife's wishes for a new house.) But at the same time, all of the new settlers understood that their new houses were *not* rural, and the birth of a new community attracted them, as buyers. They were delighted by the task of building up new schools and churches in their new communities. The women, with some free time while their children were very young, were particularly active in the new community and church organizations. In the early days of these settlements, people seem to have thought of themselves somewhat as colonists building new utopias for a new era.

Were the founders of the tract house communities also the creators of an era of feverish buying, of a "consumers' republic," as Lizabeth Cohen and others have argued?[21] And were their house purchases a manifestation of their lust for ever-newer commodities? I don't think so. The people I talked with remembered being enchanted with their new appliances, and fascinated by the new materials and methods used to construct their new dwellings, but this was at least partially because they had never experienced such amenities and technologies before. Nor was the new house seen merely as a commodity: for nearly all, the house was the investment of a lifetime, to be treasured and made to last for generations into the future. It is possible—even likely—that their children, or the later suburbanites of the period after 1965, had different views about consumption, but the original owners in the earliest postwar settlements were frugal and modest in their material aspirations. As Don Waldie, who grew up in Lakewood, remembers his parents, "They were grateful for the comforts of their not-quite-middle-class life. Their aspiration wasn't for more but only for enough, despite the claims of critics then and now who assume that suburban places are about excess."[22]

There were other common patterns among the people I talked to. Although not all the men were veterans, the war had been a profound experience for both them and their wives. They looked forward to, or hoped for, an era of peace and prosperity. They shared, too, a willingness to take risks, and a particular kind of work ethic. For most of them, the mortgage was a heavy burden, even with a GI loan. Both men and women worked very hard, first to pay off the mortgage, and then to pay for improvements. The purchase of a new house, and especially a new kind of house, was risky for them, even with cheap loans. Many had had some experience with property ownership within their families, but some also remembered a family member who did not want the risk or responsibility of owning a home. Mrs. KM, for example, says of her parents, "My father was born on a farm and when we were growing up, he did insulation work in a factory; we always rented a house; he didn't want to own any property." As a result, Mrs. KM says, "We moved a lot—my mother was always looking for something better." Mrs. KM's mother was the one in the family who cared most about the family's housing, and I found that this was often the case among the parents of the buyers I talked to. On the other hand, family stories of great mobility were quite common, including stories of immigration to the United States and of following employment across vast distances, as did Mrs. BG's family (quoted above). There was a desire among them for social mobility—not so much upward, as *forward*. (When asked whether he couldn't have looked for a better apartment for his new family within his old neighborhood, Mr. KC was astonished: "Oh, no," he said, "*that* would have meant going *backward*. We couldn't do that.")[23] So they were highly individualistic; they wanted new roles in society; they wanted new choices and risked a lot to achieve them; they also settled down and valued their new communities and their new houses.

The new inhabitants were firmly democratic in nearly all respects, and felt a high degree of social solidarity. But, as Gary Gerstl has remarked, the war had heightened racial divisions within American society: African American servicemen were segregated within the armed forces, war housing was segregated, Asian Americans were interned. So the kinds of perceived solidarity that builders and buyers felt, and that buyers felt among themselves across class and ethnic lines, did not extend to "people of color." Much has been written about racism among the new suburbanites, and about "white flight" from the urban core as a fundamental cause of the proliferation of the new tract house settlements. But I did not find that racist motives in buying a new house were obvious among the people I interviewed. Two of the families who bought houses in the early sixties described the decline in property values in their older neighborhoods (and the increase in crime because of racial strife) as a result of an influx of African American owners and renters. Another, from California, remembers being troubled by the proximity of Mexican American, "lower-class" areas near Rossmoor. These comments seem to have more to do with protecting property values than with racism per se. If we remember that five million African Americans migrated to northern and western cities between 1940 and 1970, where they lived mainly at first in the poorer neighborhoods, such attitudes become more intelligible, if still reprehensible. Andrew Wiese and others have shown that African Americans and Mexican Americans shared the prevalent enthusiasm for a suburban way of life. Separate African American suburbs existed in the United States from the 1920s, and separate Mexican American suburbs grew up around Los Angeles in the 1950s.[24] Builders, and probably buyers too, accepted the "separate but equal" idea so prevalent in the forties and fifties as a rationale for segregation in the armed forces and in schools. The NAHB *Correlator* ran a series on "Housing Minority Groups" in the May 1955 issue, where it documented the building of new housing tracts (mostly in the South) of substantial-looking ranch houses, for "minority" buyers who were said to be eligible for FHA and VA mortgages.[25] Among the builders discussed here, both Centex and the Campanellis built similar housing for African Americans. It is clear that all racial and ethnic groups subscribed to similar suburban aspirations in the 1940s and 1950s.[26]

Buyers' Choices of House Forms

None of the original owners seems to have known much about architecture as an art or a profession, an observation confirmed in the studies by Paxton, Bodek, and Hill. A few knew engineers, and many were familiar with the construction trades. But they did display a great deal of visual sophistication, and had rather highly developed perceptions about the formal aspects of their houses. Two couples spoke of the "newness" of their houses as symbolic: As Mr. TU put it, he and his wife waited more than a year for their Campanelli ranch because "it was a whole new kind of house; it seemed right for a whole new time." They saw their houses as spacious and roomy, while appreciating efficient planning: "[It] didn't seem small . . . the rooms were big. . . . We liked the design very much and the spaciousness of it—for example, the kitchen had a wall-mounted refrigerator, which gave us a lot more counter space than we were used to. The living room was open to the dining room, and the dining room was open to the kitchen: that was very nice" (Mr. KC). They were predictably enthusiastic about all the new appliances, but above all they praised the generous size of the kitchen: "It was so *big*: it reminded us of the old days" (Mrs. KM).

They saw the variations among the houses as extremely significant; they also modified their houses almost from the start: by changing colors on the inside or outside, and by adding rooms in the garage or at the back at a later date. They had great respect for sound building methods, but they also admired new building materials and technologies. They were handy and practical: they expected, from the first, to modify and expand their new dwellings. (In many cases, the builders had designed their houses for easy expansion, usually through the garage.)

It is instructive to see what they added or changed. Most began very quickly to change the exterior colors and siding, and many added one or more bedrooms, either by remodeling the garage, or by adding a wing at the rear. As yet, however, additional bedrooms did not reflect the idea that each child must have his or her own room. Most children's bedrooms continued to have bunk beds, but they were segregated by sex (a requirement of VA mortgages according to Mrs. KM). The other most popular modification was the addition of a den or family room, again either by cannibalizing the garage, or in a new wing at the rear. This was a relatively darker space than the others, and contained the television after the early buyers became television enthusiasts. When a family felt the need for more eating space, they enlarged the kitchen (by absorbing space from the garage or living room) rather than by carving out a separate dining area within the living room. Only one (Mrs. MQ) regretted not having a separate, formal dining room. Entertaining people for dinner was rare, and seen as best done outside, or in a restaurant. Many also added a rear patio, for eating and entertaining outdoors: "There wasn't really room inside to have people over, but we all did a lot of grilling outside, on the old Weber grills with the round domes" (Mrs. KM, from Rolling Meadows). We should remember that these new homeowners had had little or no experience of formal "entertaining" during the Depression and war. When these families wished to entertain indoors, it was

usual to have people over for drinks and snacks and then go out, rather than to give a formal dinner (fig. 200).[27]

Other additions, again pieced together out of the garage, included a workshop, a laundry room, and some extra closets. Where a new wing was created, it was added at the rear. Only one of the buyers I talked to (Mrs. KM) added a modest second story, at a much later date. All were proud of their yards, front and back, and planted trees and bushes in them, often obtaining the help of the builder in purchasing new plantings. Just as they did not erect fences, they did not plant hedges, which would have impeded movement from house to house and front to rear.[28] Their planting schemes within each neighborhood were far from uniform.[29] Thus, these buyers individualized their houses, suiting them more closely to their needs, family size, and tastes. But they did not greatly change their plans and layouts, or their overall form as seen from the street.[30] They were especially careful to retain the look of the facades. The new spaces they added were practical, utilitarian, informal, and unpretentious, geared toward enhancing family life. The new owners did some of the work themselves, using the new tools that accompanied the postwar "do-it-yourself" movement; friends, family, and local contractors did the rest.[31]

How did these buyers form their ideas about what was desirable in a new house? When they speak of "a new kind of house" for "a new time," does this indicate any knowledge of modernist architectural ideas? Almost certainly not. These buyers were even less likely than the builders to know much about Frank Lloyd Wright's Usonian houses, or about the work of William Wurster, Cliff May or Royal Barry Wills. Like Mrs. BG, quoted above, some buyers had read a good deal, but they do not seem to have read much about architects. As for houses that resembled the "International Style," these were certainly present and regarded as newsworthy in most of the metropolitan areas I am discussing, but they rarely appeared in low-cost versions; nearly all the people to whom I talked were unaware of them. As we have seen in chapter 1, public discussion of the housing boom had often centered around the theme of "the house of the future"; buyers must have been excited by such ideas, but they do not seem to have connected them to issues of architectural style. Many buyers seem to have viewed new kitchen and bathroom appliances as the essence of "the house of the future."[32]

Influences from Mass Media

A series of writers have ascribed postwar house preferences to imagery conveyed by mass media: by popular magazines, television and movies. Magazines such as *Life* and *Popular Science* devoted frequent articles to new kinds of housing, but many of the buyers of the early and mid-1950s would not have been able to afford these heavily illustrated magazines.[33] The magazine most often remembered by those I talked to was *Reader's Digest*. Popular because it offered condensed versions of current essays and novels, *Reader's Digest* rarely offered illustrations. The circulation of the glossy "home" magazines skyrocketed during the fifties, but it is probably safe to say that their popularity was the *result* of the housing boom, rather than a source of its forms.[34]

The sitcom television shows of the fifties have been described as important molders of opinion,[35] but first-time buyers in the early fifties rarely had television before they bought their houses. More importantly, the house types discussed in the previous chapters were developed and widely sold *well before* most of the popular sitcoms were aired.[36] And in any case, the sitcoms themselves did not represent dwellings that resembled the tract houses. In *Leave It to Beaver* (1957–63), for example, both of the Cleavers' houses were two-stories, elaborate, and formal, with a foyer and a large and well-equipped separate dining room. The second Cleaver house, at Pine Street, had expanded to include two and a half baths, a den, and two guest rooms. The setting was small-town America, not the suburbs.[37] Over time, as the suburbs and their house types became more and more attractive to new buyers, more and more new householders would have been television watchers, but by then, the basic forms of the new dwelling types were already well established. The television sitcoms may have reflected enthusiasm for a suburban way of life, but they did not inspire it, nor did they describe the reality.[38]

On the other hand, the earliest postwar house buyers had been inveterate moviegoers since childhood: for their generation, the impact of movies was far greater than television was.[39] Wealth and high living had been frequent movie themes during the 1920s and especially during the depression years. Movies of the 1930s depicted an America, in Frederick Lewis Allen's words, "in which almost everybody was rich or about to be rich, and in which the possession of a huge house and a British-accented butler and a private swimming pool . . . was accepted as the normal lot of mankind. . . . The . . . movie-goer . . . was unlikely to be surprised to find a couple of stenographers pictured as occupying an apartment with the newest built-in kitchen equipment and a living-room 35 feet long and 20 feet wide."[40] Allen suggests, though, that these movies were understood to be "escape entertainment," not far removed from the immensely popular Disney's *Snow White and the Seven Dwarfs* of 1937. The broad enthusiasm for westerns (including the *Ramona* romance) from the thirties onward reflected a longing for simpler and more primitive times, and easier moral choices.[41]

But social consciousness was not lacking in the 1930s: this is suggested by the leap of Steinbeck's *Grapes of Wrath* to the top of the best-seller list in 1939 and its transformation by John Ford into a box-office hit movie in 1940.[42] Social consciousness found its way into motion pictures increasingly in the 1940s and early 1950s. *Mildred Pierce* (1945), who in her lust for social climbing turns her back on the little house where she grew up in favor of a pretentious Pasadena mansion, comes to a bad end.[43] In *All That Heaven Allows* (1955), the happy ending results from the reverse process: Cary Scott (Jane Wyman) forsakes her upper-class house, filled with expensive kitsch, and finds happiness with her landscape gardener (Rock Hudson) in his simple rustic dwelling.[44]

The top box-office hit of 1946 was *The Best Years of Our Lives*, the story of four veterans and the great difficulties, social and psychological, that they experienced on returning home after the war. Their prewar dwellings seem alien to them, as do their prewar occupations. Al, a banker before the war, finds his redemption in making loans to veterans to build new houses or to start new farms. Fred, the outstanding war hero of the group, ultimately finds work with a company that is dismantling wartime bombers, turning them into parts for prefabricated houses. With two other films of the years 1945–47, *The Best Years of Our Lives* offers a kind of metaphor for the concerns of new tract house dwellers: in *Living in a Big Way* (1947), a group of veterans gut a huge old-fashioned house, transforming it into apartments for themselves and their families. And in *It's a Wonderful Life* (1946), George Bailey, head of the Bailey Bros. Building and Loan Association, 4F during the war, battles the evil plans of slumlord Henry F. Potter, and succeeds in building Bailey Park, a new community of small houses for low-income buyers (fig. 201).[45] Much more clearly than contemporary television programs, such films *expressed* people's thoughts and concerns about housing. But it is not at all clear that they *influenced* them.[46]

Newspapers provide another, much more obvious, source of ideas about houses for new tract dwellers. Newspaper articles dealt often with housing

themes, while manufacturers' ads in newspapers emphasized the attractions of new appliances, and frequently published pictures of the "modern" houses that used them. Realtors certainly also played a role: in many cases, they wrote the ad copy for new houses, and once a prospective buyer arrived at the site, realtors made their sales pitch. But the reminiscences that I have quoted and summarized make clear that the first specific knowledge of new houses was often obtained from a friend, work colleague, or army buddy, and above all from a visit to the community itself. Like the builders, the buyers learned from what they actually saw, in the flesh, so to speak.

Buyers' Childhood Dwellings

I think that the most important factor in forming the buyers' preferences must have been their own backgrounds and housing experiences. They came from dwelling traditions that are unfamiliar to most architectural historians (and to most writers about suburbs in general).[47] They grew up in the modest houses and apartments of America's working-class and lower-middle-class neighborhoods: row houses, apartments in low-rise buildings, and especially very modest single-family dwellings of one, one and a half, or (rarely) two stories. Let us look, first, at a few of their childhood homes, and then at their housing experiences during and after the war.[48]

Mrs. OC, of Rossmoor in Orange County, grew up in a free-standing one-story house in west Minneapolis; with its living room, dining room, kitchen, and two bedrooms, it was originally about 1,100 square feet (figs. 202, 203). Built not long after World War I, it was sited in the middle of a rather generous lot of about 5,500 square feet, with ample lawns in front and rear. Entrances at front and rear opened directly into living room and kitchen respectively. There were six children; for a while the dining room (thirteen by ten feet) was used as an additional bedroom. Over time, with increasing affluence, Mrs. OC's parents were able to sandwich two more bedrooms into the minimal attic space.[49]

Mrs. FC's father, of Torrance, grew up in the outskirts of Santa Barbara, in a house of about 600 square feet (figs. 204, 205). It was close to the street, but the back yard stretched through an unbuilt area (perhaps 500 feet) all the way to a mesa in the rear. The house had only one full bedroom, occupied by Mrs. FC's grandparents; a further sleeping area was formed by partitioning the back porch; Mrs. FC's father and his brother usually slept here, although some sheds in the backyard provided additional sleeping facilities in the mild Santa Barbara weather. There was a dining "nook" in the kitchen but no dining room; larger family meals, and entertaining of all sorts, took place outdoors. (Mrs. FC's grandmother had supported her family during the Depression by domestic service. "She was a fantastic cook, and insisted that anyone who came to her door had to be fed.") The house remained to a considerable extent the center of family life even in Mrs. FC's generation: it was here that her parents lived in a trailer after World War II; after they moved to Torrance they often returned; Mrs. FC's uncle moved just down the street. "My grandmother's house was the true center

202. Small house of the type described by Mrs. OC, exterior. Jones, *Authentic Small Houses.*

203. Small house of the type described by Mrs. OC, plan. Jones, *Authentic Small Houses.*

of my family's life: [it] gives me the template of home that I carry in my head," says Mrs. FC.

These were minimal houses for their time. LM of Rolling Meadows (Mrs. KM's husband) also grew up in a minimal free-standing single-family dwelling, but his memories were far less idyllic. LM "grew up poor" in Polish Town, an immigrant community in west Chicago (in what is now called Bucktown). His childhood home was a one-story, two-bedroom wood laborer's cottage located behind an apartment building; the house was rented by his mother, the family breadwinner. Eight people lived there ("his mother, his two brothers, his sister, her husband and her two kids"). "It was a two-bedroom house, so some of them slept in the dining room, and some in the living room on a hide-a-bed. Only the dining room was heated. Fuel and food were hard to come by: they ate bacon grease instead of butter and sometimes the kids had to go to the railroad yards, to get coal that had been dropped from the coal cars, for their stove." Such wooden cottages dated back to the mid-nineteenth century in Chicago, where they appear in some photographs and drawings as lone survivors of the Great Fire among the more numerous later brick tenements (fig. 206).[50] Their plans are not well-documented, but they probably resembled the Oakland, California, workers' cottages that have been carefully studied by historian and urban geographer Paul Groth and his research teams (figs. 207, 208).[51]

Several other residents of the Golden Corridor developments spent their early years in bungalows, the typical working-class and lower-middle-class dwelling of the early twentieth century in Chicago. These came in many versions; at their most modest, they clearly owed a good deal in form and layout to the laborer's cottage type of Mr. LM's childhood (see figs. 206, 207, 208, and

204. Small house of the type described by Mrs. FC, exterior. Jones, *Authentic Small Houses.*

205. Mrs. FC's Grandmother's House, plan. Nathanael Roesch from plan drawn by Leonardo Chalupowicz and lent by Mrs. FC.

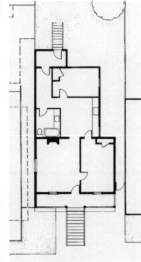

bungalow plan, fig. 150).[52] According to Mr. HN, quoted above, of Weathersfield in Schaumburg, he and his wife had both grown up in bungalows, with twelve people in one five-bedroom house, and eight in a three-bedroom house.

In the Philadelphia area (as in Baltimore),[53] row houses served some of the same purposes for the less affluent as the Chicago workers' cottages and the later Chicago bungalows. Mrs. KD's parents, second-generation Italians and Irish, grew up in Philadelphia row houses (figs. 209, 210); after they were married, they bought two adjoining row houses and began to raise their five children in one of them, renting out the other. Row houses were sited on exceptionally narrow lots, sometimes as narrow as sixteen or seventeen feet, sometimes as wide as thirty feet. Widths of houses built around 1900 varied from fifteen feet to about twenty-five feet; depths from thirty to forty feet, so that the total interior space might be as large as 1,500 square feet distributed on two floors. Since the staircase used up about a quarter of this space, however, the actual living space was rarely much in excess of 1,000 square feet. Some owners rented out one floor, and lived on the other. With five children distributed between two bedrooms (with the parents in the third), Mrs. KD's family was a tight fit, even though they used both floors of one of the houses.[54]

206. Laborer's cottage, Chicago, nineteenth century. Abbott, *Tenements of Chicago.*

207. Laborer's cottage, Oakland, CA, early twentieth century, exterior. Photo by Paul Groth.

208. Laborer's cottage, Oakland, CA, early twentieth century, plan. Paul Groth, Benjamin Chuaqui, and Sibel Zandi-Sayek.

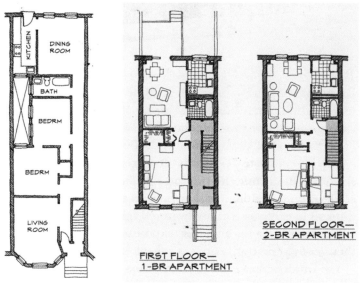

209. Philadelphia row houses, exteriors, ca. 1909. Hunter, *Ranches, Rowhouses, and Railroad Flats*.

210. Row houses, plans: two-level house and single level apartment. Hunter, *Ranches, Rowhouses, and Railroad Flats*.

In the northeastern United States, frequent alternatives to the row house were the "three-decker" and "two-decker": two- or three-level houses with a raised basement and separate apartments on each floor (figs. 211, 212). Some of these, like Mr. KC's family house in Dorchester, had one apartment per floor; others, like that of Mr. IN, were wider, with two apartments per floor, each the mirror image of the other. The two-decker, more common in Connecticut and upstate New York, contained two stories with a substantial attic. Triple-decker apartment buildings were more spacious than comparable row houses, offering sometimes as much as 1,100 square feet in a single apartment. Lot sizes were correspondingly larger than those of row houses or other apartment buildings, and the single-loaded version of the two- and three-decker had windows on all four sides. Porches and balconies frequently adorned both front and rear. Mr. KC's family owned the whole building and lived on the ground floor while renting out the upper floors. But it was not uncommon for an extended family to occupy two or more floors.[55] Like row houses, though, these houses varied greatly in size and elaboration: Mr. KC's three-decker in Dorchester was relatively large and elaborate, while Mr. IN's in the industrial working-class district of Lowell was much narrower, smaller and plainer. Chicago had its own version of the two-decker, the "two flat," common in the first decades of the twentieth century. Mrs. MQ's family rented the ground floor of one of these, in West Chicago, in a working-class area of Austin. Many of her relatives owned houses nearby. The Chicago two flat resembled New England two-deckers in plan but not in exterior appearance.

Before her family drove across the country to Sterling, Colorado, in 1925 in search of new work, Mrs. BG, her father, mother, sister, and two brothers lived in a tiny hamlet near her father's factory in Oneida, New York. This was "a two-story house where we had a garden, a cow, and chickens." Mrs. BG does not remember much more than that about the house, since she was quite small when her family trekked across the country. The houses that were built in hamlets and small towns in the early twentieth century to serve either farm workers or

211. New England triple-decker, exterior. Hunter, *Ranches, Rowhouses, and Railroad Flats.*

212. New England double-decker, 1922, plan. Marissa Vigneault.

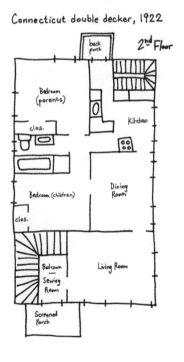

Connecticut double decker, 1922

2nd Floor

back porch

Bedroom (parents)

clos.

Kitchen

Bedroom (children)

Dining Room

clos.

Living Room

Bedroom — Sewing Room

Screened Porch

industrial workers are hard to document. Alan Gowans shows a row of two-story detached houses in Oswego, New York (fig. 213), inhabited originally by industrial workers, and rather closely spaced. But considering the garden, cow, and chickens owned by Mrs. BG's parents, the house was probably larger than these and was certainly on a larger lot. It may have resembled the house in Milford Center, New York, southeast of Oneida, shown in figure 214.[56]

Mrs. IN had lived as a child on a farm, and wanted to live "in the country" after she and Mr. IN were married. A farm childhood was rare among the people that I talked to, but many remembered a relative who had lived on a farm. An agricultural way of life was certainly experienced by many who moved to new tract house developments. (This was also true of several of the builders I have discussed: Ross Cortese, Jean Vandruff, and some of the Stoltzners. Frank Facciolo's family too had been active in farming before moving to the Philadelphia area.) As we have seen in discussing the land available to builders after the war, the dramatic decline in farms and farm population that began in the early twentieth century became ever more rapid in the 1930s and 1940s.[57] We can therefore assume that a significant proportion of the migrants to tract house developments came originally from farms.

We know a good deal about the various "types" of American farmhouses now, thanks to the work of historians of vernacular architecture and of American landscape.[58] Farmhouses came in almost every size and shape, large and small, two-story and one-story, single-family dwellings standing alone, or with several attached wings, or in a complex of barns and outbuildings. We do not know as much about their plans, or about how people lived in them. A few certainly had the elaborated polite plan (discussed in chapter 1) that was then common in towns, with foyer or entrance hall, parlor or sitting room, and separate dining room. But a great many were one story, with spaces that focused on sleeping and

215. Ozarks Farmhouse, early twentieth century, exterior. Marianne Ezell.

216. Ozarks Farmhouse, early twentieth century, plan. Marianne Ezell.

eating; their plans lacked all or most of the more elaborate and specific spatial arrangements of houses in towns and cities. Normally, farmhouse plans recognized the kitchen as the hub of household living, so that the auxiliary rooms on the first floor were bedrooms. (A toilet, if present, was also located on the first floor.) Foyers were normally absent, as were separate dining rooms. Hallways could be used for sleeping or as living quarters.[59] Often there was a front room labeled "living room," but this too was often turned into a bedroom (figs. 215, 216).[60] As Sally McMurry has shown, American farm dwellers of the later nineteenth century explicitly rejected the notion of a parlor or formal living space as citified and effete, preferring either the kitchen or an informal "living room" or "family room" as gathering spaces.[61] When the US Department of Agriculture set out to study farmhouses in 1934, in order to propose new, low-cost models, it was this kind of flexible plan that they featured (fig. 217).[62] Depending on family size, such dwellings could be densely populated too, of course, but flexibility of use was built into the plan. Farmhouses on working farms were also much more oriented to the outside than were other early twentieth-century American house types.

Thus, the interior spaces of the childhood dwellings that are remembered by "my" speakers were very small, even by prewar standards. Rarely did the living space in any of these dwellings exceed 1,200 square feet, some were as small as 600 square feet. For the origins of some of them, we need to look to long-standing American traditions of the minimal dwelling: one or two rooms used in a flexible manner, of which the kitchen was the primary space for family gathering, one or two bedrooms, and, at least in some cases, a relatively close relationship to the outdoors. This type of plan was introduced by the early settlers and perpetuated in the early frontier cottage; it had, therefore, a hint of romanticized adventurousness about it—at least in people's memories.[63] (The reality, of course, was not so nice.) During the industrial era, though, minimal dwellings came to be the

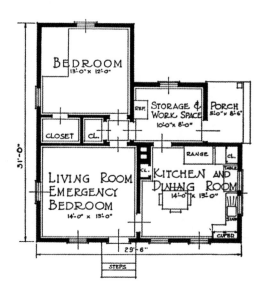

home-places of the working class: rural industrial workers, small farmers, and immigrants in the poor districts of large cities. The one-room tenement dwelling, so often the target of late nineteenth-century housing reformers, can also be thought of as part of this tradition, although none of my speakers seems to have grown up in an apartment of this type. If my case studies had included New York City (Manhattan and the boroughs), I would have heard from some people who had grown up in four- to six-story tenement buildings.[64]

The majority of the childhood dwellings that were described to me, however, can be seen as part of the polite tradition of house building and planning described in chapter 1. This plan, with its emphasis on formal reception spaces at the front, domestic quarters at the rear or in the upstairs, and a high degree of specialization of spaces, goes back at least to the Italian Renaissance of the fifteenth century—to the palaces of wealthy and powerful urban oligarchs. Thereafter, it was imitated first in France and England; then in the rest of Continental Europe. Beginning in the eighteenth century, the polite plan, with a number of variations, evolved in this country primarily through the efforts of well-to-do buyers and their builders to emulate the dwelling styles of the English aristocracy and merchant classes. Such plans implied the presence of household servants.

It is possible to argue that this kind of plan was stimulated by early nineteenth century ideas of landscape design: by the admiration among intellectuals for the "country cottage" popularized by J. C. Loudon, Andrew Jackson Downing, and other landscape romanticizers.[65] Most such "cottages" were nothing of the kind, but they displayed a full-fledged polite plan, and, in addition, gave prominence to a landscaped lot, with a closely mowed lawn. A further stimulus to the notion that a multiplicity of highly specialized spaces (and attendant landscaped grounds) were worth imitating because they were inherently "aristo-cratic" was provided in the later nineteenth century by the publication of Robert Kerr's *The Gentleman's House (Or, How to Plan English Residences)* of 1864 and 1871.[66] The polite plan was repeated over and over again in this country in small towns and urban neighborhoods, and in dwellings of almost every income level: we can see it in most of the early twentieth century offerings of Sears, Aladdin, or Garlinghouse house catalogs, and in numerous publications of the twenties that show examples of small houses.[67] It appears, in modified form, in bungalows and row houses. It also had a strong presence in apartment buildings, even in those built for the poor, partly because of the efforts of late nineteenth-century housing reformers to introduce some privacy into working-class life, and partly because of the desire of builders to appeal to the upwardly mobile aspirations of nineteenth-century middle-class buyers.[68]

In the case of the families I have been discussing, however, because of the economic circumstances of their childhoods (during the Depression), or because of the size of their families, the way that these spaces were used violated the preexisting plans in an almost revolutionary fashion. All or nearly all of the new buyers to whom I spoke grew up in what we would regard today as very crowded circumstances. Children slept in the living room or parlor, and in the dining room, parents slept in halls. A great deal of family life was concentrated in the kitchen—and outside, in yards, on stoops and porches, on streets. These families used their dwellings in a fashion similar to the dwelling situations of the poorest people: the laborers' cottages, the simpler farms. Thus the future buyers of tract houses had early learned to use both interior and exterior spaces in a flexible way, and had no particular fondness for the more formal spatial arrangements of the past.

Would this first generation of tract house buyers have understood the traditions behind the Renaissance palazzo, the English "cottage," or the "gentlemen's house"? I think this is extremely unlikely. They were, after all, the children of working-class parents, and, in a great many instances, of immigrants from poor districts of European countries. Growing up in this country, they would not have had the opportunity to see many grand mansions or even many elaborate houses. The second-generation immigrants might have heard from their parents and grandparents reminiscences of the Shtetl or the Italian hill town, but not of the great houses of England or Continental Europe (unless, of course, their parents or grandparents had been domestic servants). Nor would the new tract house settlers have been likely to read Loudon, Downing, or Kerr, or the popular writers on Victorian domesticity: they were too young, and though most of them had finished high school, and about half had some college, with the exception of Mrs. BG and her family, they were not great readers. Their intellectual interests were quite practical and task-oriented.[69] They could have been familiar with rustic themes in American park buildings and camps of the early twentieth century, and these may have had some relation to English picturesque styles and writings.

I think that their understanding of "the country" would have had American, rather than English, roots. They would have known something of the romance of the American frontier as it was then understood—its adventure and individualism, the heroism of pioneers who defended their new settlements against the Native Americans. Closely related to the imagery of the frontier was that of homesteading, the land grant system whereby new settlers established ownership of land parcels in the Midwest and Far West by using it, by establishing farms or larger settlements.[70] They would have learned about these traditions in school, or in novels like those of James Fenimore Cooper, Mary Ingalls Wilder, Willa Cather, and Zane Grey, or from movies and games. (Mrs. BG and her siblings had read such novels, with the encouragement of their working-class mother.) Their parents and grandparents would have known about these traditions too: the notion that America was full of plentiful free land in the wilderness was widespread in Europe, where it had been disseminated by popular novels and travelers' reports. Even when immigrants did not come to this country to farm, the image of the frontier cabin in the wild, surrounded by fresh-cleared pasture or crops, was familiar to them. The same imagery inspired those Americans who had lived here longer. Attitudes to "country" living derived from these popular traditions and imageries rather than from more elevated intellectual traditions. And in most people's imaginations, "living in the country" was synonymous with property ownership: property ownership, that is, by ordinary people, not by wealthy people or by aristocrats.

Buyers' Wartime Experiences

Most of the couples I interviewed had not yet been married during the war, so for this and other reasons I do not have a great deal of specific information about

218. Fort Brady, exterior under construction, Sault Ste. Marie, MI, 1942. Clarke Historical Library.

219. Camp Edwards, Western Barnstable County, MA, 1941, interior.

their wartime living conditions. But it is possible to develop some hypotheses about their war experiences and that of others of their generation of tract dwellers. Among the veterans, those who were or remained enlisted men, and all those on active service in distant places, lived in military barracks of various kinds (fig. 218, 219). So did all servicemen during their training in boot camps. Such barracks housed many millions of soldiers all over the world during the war. They necessarily involved new kinds of (highly regimented) crowding, and also a kind of minimalist but very functional and well-organized arrangement of spaces for sleeping and storage. Those veterans who spent significant periods of service on ships and submarines experienced extremely constricted, but also extremely functional, living spaces. Often, they lived in close proximity to sophisticated machinery (fig. 220).[71] These servicemen had spent time in "machines for living" (to twist Le Corbusier's phrase a little), and while they certainly did not idealize them, they understood their efficiency.

Officers, and specialized military personnel such as doctors and nurses, lived and worked in somewhat more spacious circumstances, even at the front lines. On base, married officers sometimes had access to various kinds of basic war housing such as the nearly full-fledged ranch houses built by Fritz Burns at Westchester in Los Angeles, or the Levitt's one-story houses at Norfolk (figs. 54, 62, 63).

220. Submarine interior, 1942. Ralph Morse/ LIFE Picture Collection/ Getty Images.

Workers at every level of war industries—and this included hundreds of thousands of civilian men and women—lived in a variety of kinds of temporary housing; some of this was altogether makeshift—lean-tos, shacks—and worse than the slum housing of the era; most of it was also racially segregated.[72] Other war housing resembled military barracks (fig. 221); some again resembled Fritz Burns's early Westchester housing; some took the form of multistory apartment dwellings planned around rather elaborate public facilities, such as Henry Kaiser's at Vanport, Oregon, adjacent to the Kaiser shipyards. In all of these but the first, war workers experienced minimalist but highly functional planning, and new kinds of household equipment.[73] Often, war housing was remodeled after the war to serve the needs of returning veterans (fig. 222).

One kind of temporary war housing deserves special emphasis: the trailer. Trailers began to be manufactured in this country in the 1930s as equipment that could be hooked up to an automobile and used for dwelling space during a camping expedition or a long car trip. Initially, when the number of cars owned by individuals or families was relatively small, trailers were a luxury. During the war, trailers were pressed into service at some sites for war workers (for example, in Oakland and in Ypsilanti, Michigan), where they offered a toilet, refrigerator, sink, cook stove—and sleeping facilities that were even more cramped than those in military barracks (figs. 223, 224).[74] This wartime use, and the innovations in materials and construction that accompanied their mass production, greatly stimulated the production of trailers and the development of their design in this country. For example, trailers were made with molded plywood and cloth impregnated with plastic, put together with staple guns, and mounted on wheels.[75] By the later 1940s, the "ten wide," that is, the ten-feet wide trailer, had come into general use as both temporary housing and as low-cost housing (fig. 224). Relabeled the "mobile home," the new version of the trailer represented a minor miracle of functional planning, low cost, and low land cost.[76]

221. Richmond, CA, *Maritime Commission Housing for Shipyard Workers*, ca. 1944. Photo by Dorothea Lange.

222. Pilgrim Terrace. Santa Barbara, CA, war housing remodeled for veterans, 1953. Mrs. FC.

223. Trailer interior, 1941.
Defense worker's family in a
trailer home near Ypsilanti,
MI, 1941.

224. Peerless "ten-wide"
trailer, cutaway and exterior
view, ca. 1950.

As my interviews demonstrate, veterans and their new wives and families sometimes lived in these dwellings on land owned by their families while searching for
a new home. It is not unlikely that some builders of tract houses were inspired
by the design of trailers; certainly the later versions, relabeled as "manufactured
homes" in the mid-1950s and afterward, paralleled very closely the plans and
exterior appearance of ranch houses in the new tracts.[77]

Among the dwelling experiences of soldiers, workers in war industries, and
their families during the war was another that is important for postwar thinking

about house design. Barracks, war housing, temporary dwellings of every sort near bases and war industries, were built very swiftly, on farmland or otherwise unoccupied sites, as were the new military bases themselves. Land was cleared for new bases or other groups of buildings with new kinds of heavy equipment, pavement laid down in what seemed like an instant, electricity and some kind of water supply and sewage system introduced in a trice. Hundreds of thousands, even millions, of Americans experienced almost instant settlements on a very large scale. When they later confronted model houses in the midst of orange groves, cornfields or cow pastures, they had little difficulty in believing in developers' promises that houses would be serviceable, equipment and infrastructure would work, and that large new communities would soon follow.

* * * * *

The inhabitants of the early postwar tract house communities, like most of their contemporaries, had experienced profound social and cultural transformations. Raised in the Depression, with its social consciousness and ambivalence toward class differences, young adults during the war, with its experience of solidarity against a common enemy, had also experienced vast technological changes, and extraordinary conquests of time and space. In the armed forces, or in war work, they served with strangers, with people from new places, from diverse ethnic backgrounds and from many walks of life. In order to perform their army service or their war work, they were uprooted (or uprooted themselves) from long-established patterns of dwelling and living. They had seen, and often participated in, airplane travel over huge distances, and had observed the use of new weapons from the skies (in movies on the home front; in action in Europe and the Pacific theaters of war). Travel to outer space, even to the moon, Mars, or Venus, a theme in popular literature since the later nineteenth century,[78] began to seem possible in the 1950s and 1960s.[79] After the war, their earlier homes often seemed to them "too small"; they felt that they could not "go back," even though these earlier homes aroused for them intense nostalgia. After the war, too, a huge boom in prosperity led them to believe that the time had come to realize successfully their aspirations (and those of their earlier families) to increased prosperity, social mobility, and personal autonomy—through education, self-improvement, and investment in property. In later years, these "grand expectations"[80] were often disappointed, and shown to contain, or cloak, inherent flaws (racism, property and its limitations, the necessary frustrations of land hunger, lack of planning and faith in technology, with their unfortunate consequences for ecology). But the experiences of the early tract house buyers allowed them to help create new dwelling forms and new community forms in the early postwar years, forms that defined the suburbs of the later twentieth century.

CHAPTER 6

Conclusion
Houses and Suburbs
Transformed

Between 1945 and 1965, the landscape and character of American dwellings were dramatically transformed: millions of Americans now lived in ranch houses or split-levels, in a new suburban ring outside older cities. The ranch houses and split-levels had little resemblance to typical American dwellings of the past: they were both sleek and unpretentious, wholly unlike earlier upper- and middle-class houses. In their flexible-use interior spaces, they had some kinship to earlier working-class dwellings and to some rural dwellings. But their open rooms, efficient workspaces, many windows, plain walls, and shiny appliances set them apart from all, or nearly all, earlier prototypes. They represent the American version of "modern architecture" in the first postwar years: not the "modern architecture" of the European International Style, but rather a hybrid of comfort and function, affordable by the majority of buyers and highly prized by them. Also unlike the European housing, American tract houses were not imposed by government; instead, they were the product of private builders and their customers. They were "grassroots" phenomena.

The design of these houses had, as we have seen, a number of native origins. They had a certain rustic flavor deriving from American nostalgia for the farmstead, the homestead, and the frontier. Prominent in their plans was the hearth and fireplace, so long a symbol of home in the American tradition. They had some roots in the "small house movement" of the 1920s and 1930s, and to some traditions of self-building (if we think of postwar "do it yourself" as part of these traditions). But their sleek surfaces and efficient planning bore the imprint of wartime experiences with airplanes, submarines, warships and trailers, while their up-to-date appliances were marvels of the American admiration for the newest in technology. Their windows looked out on the new landscapes that formed around them, and also enhanced the perception of spaciousness so much desired by this generation.[1] At the start of the period discussed here, the houses were affected in their exterior appearance by local and regional traditions, but over a period of about twenty years, most regional distinctions disappeared.

These houses were unique not only in themselves, but also in their setting. Their wide lots, manicured lawns and wide, curving tree-lined streets, set them apart not only from all European housing, but also from most of the urban traditions of North America. So too did their visual relationship to the public spaces of their new communities. The new developments of which they were a part therefore also represented a revolutionary break with the past. These house types and these settlements laid the basis for American suburban development in the following decades.

This book has attempted to show how some of the houses and their settings came to be during their formative years. The cases of nine builders and the places they created, together with interviews with a dozen families of early buyers, cannot explain all aspects of the new dwellings and the new communities. Much more research is needed before we can be certain about the tastes of the buyers, the authorship of the builders, and the overall social and cultural inspirations for both. But I think that these few cases are suggestive. I would argue that the principal authors of new postwar house forms were the builders and the buyers, interacting with one another by means of market forces. This was a close and almost intimate interaction: the builders (at least those considered here) cared far more about the wishes of the buyers—and went to great lengths to find out what those wishes were—than they did about earlier standards of taste or earlier forms of suburban communities. While some of the builders may have consulted concurrent work by leading architects—especially Wright, Wurster, and Wills—they were more influenced by plan books, government regulations and publications, and by their own assessments of what the buyers wanted. They arrived at these assessments through building and selling model houses, through market research, and in many cases through personal interactions with the buyers themselves. The buyers, meanwhile, had quite clear ideas of what they wanted: a well-planned "modern" house (preferably one story), on as large a lot as possible, "in the country," far from their old neighborhoods and families, in new communities of their own creation. The builders themselves often lived in houses that were larger-size versions of their tract houses. Builders and buyers had a great deal in common: many builders shared the buyers' immigrant backgrounds and poor and/or rural origins. Most builders were self-made men. So were the buyers, in the sense that they were creating new identities and a new way of life for themselves.

"Who built the new houses and how?" was one of the questions I started with. The answer is not a simple one. The builders, of course, built them, but did they design them? As we have seen, none of the builders discussed here (with the likely exception of Jean Vandruff, who had some training in architecture) could produce a measured drawing of a plan, elevation, or section. They therefore turned to young or lesser architects, or "illustrators," to produce such drawings, in greater or lesser complexity depending on the requirements of local building officials, and on the needs of foremen and subcontractors. To design their houses, they may sometimes have turned to a process of "ripping, building and ripping again," as the Levitts were said to have done, and as Ralph Bodek claimed to do. But this begs the question of design: a builder had to have a rather detailed mental map of the new structure for "ripping and building" to make sense at all. In their various ways, all of the builders discussed here had such a mental conception; most of them probably were able to sketch these designs freehand, as well. Where did these conceptions come from, and how did they evolve? There were many potential sources, as we've seen: FHA publications, earlier pattern books, popular writings such as Cliff May's, various types of magazines and technical publications, and a long development of modest small houses in this country. Last but not least, a barrage of reporting, in newspapers and a few popular magazines, constantly emphasized the newness and the importance of the new dwellings.

Yet the specific origins of the ranch house and the split-level remain a little mysterious. What thought occurred to a builder that enabled him to take an older "Cape Cod" or "bungalow" form and turn it into, for example, a long low house with an open plan, with a new kind of relationship to the street, and a new kind of relationship to its site? In a sense, this only needed to happen once, and other builders could have been inspired by it. But we are no closer to knowing what that one-time event was, or if it happened at all.

The role of the buyers in all this is a good deal clearer. The builders built their models, the buyers chose their preferred selections, and then the builders built again, according to the buyers' choices. The process provided an engine of design development: new houses quickly adapted to the preferences for use held by the buyers, which they had demonstrated in their purchases. Two bathrooms needed? They were soon provided. A liking for a patio? The same. A preference for a picture window, a fireplace, a large kitchen, a lot of windows, a garden— these, too, help to explain the evolving forms of ranches and splits in the two decades after the war. We have seen how some of these preferences developed among a generation deeply marked by the war. Central to this evolution, in my opinion, were the values that the builders and buyers shared. This sharing of values has usually been the case in the history of "vernacular" building types, as Henry Glassie has often maintained: I would suggest that tract houses of the postwar period developed similarly. For a wave of innovation to occur in traditional vernacular building, Glassie argues, only one builder had to build something a little different; imitations would then multiply.[2] This process would have been far more rapid—even almost instantaneous—in postwar America with its highly sophisticated communications.

Perhaps the most important precondition of the close communication between builders and buyers, and among the members of the new suburban communities, was the common experience of World War II. The war produced powerful new kinds of perceived solidarity, welding people together across class, ethnic, and geographical lines, through patriotism and common effort against the enemy. As Andy Rooney put it, "The War . . . was the ultimate experience for anyone in it. If you weren't killed or seriously wounded, it was an exhilarating time of life. . . . Life is real at war, concentrated and intense . . . lived at full speed. . . . "At no time do people work so well together to achieve the same goal as in wartime."[3] People at home, working in war industries, or supporting the war effort in other ways—conserving vital materials, accepting rationing, deferring consumption— also participated in this new sense of profound solidarity. Returning soldiers demonstrated plenty of those signs of trauma that have since been understood to characterize the experience of modern warfare: psychic disturbance and a sense of alienation from society.[4] But the memory of wartime comradeship in the face of aggression was widespread in the first postwar years.

Of course, builders' and buyers' shared experiences and values were not the only sources of the new American house. Without the huge government commitment to new roads and cheap mortgages, the early suburbs could not have happened. Without the economic transformations that brought vast new prosperity to working class and lower middle class Americans, the early suburbs could not have happened. Without the migration of jobs from the old cities, and without new technologies of construction and new building materials, they also could not have happened. And above all, without the availability of large tracts of buildable farmland, freed up by the rapid mechanization of agriculture in the war and postwar periods, and now accessible to the great numbers of people who possessed an automobile, the tract house would never have existed. Local government policies (zoning and building codes)—at the state, regional county, and municipal levels—also helped to shape the new houses and their communities.

Not all the new settlements that resulted were successes. In Panorama City for example, the closing of the General Motors plant in 1992, and the lack of easy access to other job centers led to the rapid decline of the community.[5] But most of the tract house settlements of the late forties, the fifties, and the early sixties were magnets for industry, new service enterprises, a great wave of new jobs, and new building nearby in consequence.[6]

Under these conditions, the new tracts were amazingly successful as mass housing; probably more successful than any other effort at large-scale housing anywhere in the world during the postwar period. Insofar as the wishes of buyers prevailed in shaping the new houses, it is probably also accurate to say that tract houses represented a triumph of participatory design, a goal that later (and more politically radical) planners and designers of the next half century found to be, at best, elusive.[7]

Some writers have also described the new tract house suburbs as a success for the traditions of the Garden City movement in planning and as part of a postwar "new towns" movement. The Garden City movement in Europe derived from the work of Ebenezer Howard in England (*Garden Cities of Tomorrow*, 1899). Howard saw new towns as a means toward urban decentralization, and proposed that these new entities would be self sufficient, though connected by new transportation networks. They would have their own urban centers and their own economic base (usually manufacturing). Welwyn Garden City and Letchworth were the earliest successes of the English Garden City movement, but new towns in Germany and the Scandinavian countries founded in the 1920s and 1930s carried on Howard's ideas, as did Radburn, New Jersey in 1929, in this country. Garden City planners also believed that each new town must be surrounded by an agricultural "green belt," to provide food supplies and insulate the community's design identity. After World War II, Scandinavian and British governments enacted sweeping legislation to create New Towns based on Garden City ideals. Harlow, Hemel Hempstead, and Stevenage in England, Vällingby in Sweden, Tapiola in Finland were the first of these new planned settlements.

Marc Weiss sees the new tract house developments of the 1950s as deriving from many of similar garden city principles. For Weiss, the early postwar suburbs are best described as collectively creating "the garden metropolis, which . . . meant better houses, lower densities, more green space and other natural features of the landscape available for a much larger share of the urban population than at any time since the beginnings of large-scale industrialization in the 19th century."[8] But Weiss is referring to entire new rings of suburbs around the older cities. As we've seen, the communities studied here were usually not large enough to form whole cities, or even small ones. Most of them were dependent for jobs and many services on older cities and older suburbs. Nor were they surrounded by "greenbelts." Among American planned communities of the first two decades after the war, Lakewood, California, Park Forest, Illinois, and Levittown, Pennsylvania were the only places large enough, and separate enough, to conform in many respects to Howard's Garden City ideal. On the other hand, the communities built by Burns and Kaiser (at Panorama City), Ross Cortese (at Rossmoor), Ralph Bodek (at Lawrence Park), the Campanellis (at Weathersfield/Schaumburg), Kimball Hill (at Rolling Meadows), and Centex (at Elk Grove Village) had town centers, schools, churches, parks, and shopping centers; some also had master plans. Some of these communities also included manufacturing enterprise or an "industrial park" (Panorama City, Lawrence Park, Rolling Meadows, Elk Grove Village). Clearly their builder/developers had some notion of new towns or garden city planning. Yet these builder/developers were not encouraged in town planning by any far-reaching government action or legislation (only by the FHA publications on "neighborhood" planning): no lasting planning institutions or overall government policies were created to aid any type of "new towns" planning. Nor were the merchant builders of the fifties and sixties wealthy enough to assemble the huge tracts that later housed James W. Rouse's Columbia, Maryland (1967) or the Irvine Company's Irvine, California (1971). In general, private enterprise has not proved to be a sufficient foundation for town planning in this country.

These communities were never static either: they were prey to changing economic circumstances, as well as to changing patterns of taste. From the mid-sixties, land became scarcer and more expensive, financing was tighter; house prices rose accordingly. At the same time, the popularity of the suburbs grew enormously, with new populations moving in, groups with somewhat different age compositions, different attitudes to social status, and higher incomes. New kinds of builders created small tracts of more expensive "infill" housing for these buyers, most of whom wanted larger and more expensive houses. In the absence of significant planning controls outside the local community, any protection to the original visual identity of the tract house communities of the fifties that had been offered by surrounding open land was lost. Planning remained highly localized, the perquisite of local zoning boards, which more and more focused on property values, and encouraged more expensive houses in order to increase local taxes. At the same time, the economic base of the earlier suburbs sometimes dwindled or disappeared (as at Panorama City). Often, earlier manufacturing was replaced by service sector employment, consisting of relatively prestigious white-collar jobs. We can see the implications especially clearly in the Golden Corridor suburbs west of Chicago, where the older industrial enterprises remained, but newer service industries were added: great office buildings and office "parks" containing the corporate headquarters of Motorola, IBM, IKEA, and other national firms. Rolling Meadows, Elk Grove Village, and Schaumburg today consist of older cores with small, relatively inexpensive houses, surrounded by larger houses on smaller properties, with less attention paid to public amenities than was true in the early postwar era. The nature of the building business changed to keep pace with these changes. Small- and medium-size building enterprises that were also land developers gave way to large, often "public" nationally-based firms that could afford to buy up small properties in many different places. Ultimately, there came to exist a strong division between developer and small builder (of the type described by Rybczynski), with concomitant implications for design and construction quality, and community planning.

While private enterprise, individual initiative, and a steadfast belief in private property may be seen to have contributed mightily to the new house forms and their new communities, in the longer run these same qualities contributed to some obvious failures. One issue had to do with *scale*, as we have just seen: a new subdivision was usually too small to permit constructive town planning, or to prevent the encroachments of new builders and new suburban populations at the peripheries of the older ones. The community leaders in the larger of the new developments discussed here, often savvy lawyers and businessmen, understood this problem, and moved quickly toward incorporation as a self-governing town, city, or village. Incorporations at Rolling Meadows and Elk Grove Village enabled the inhabitants to control their own futures as communities to a much greater degree than other suburban places of the early period. They could, for example, pass their own zoning ordinances, building regulations, and open space plans. Homeowners' associations of various sorts lobbied with local, county, and state governments for similar controls, and sometimes were successful. But they did not, and could not, control the builders and buildings that moved in around their peripheries, and this peripheral building was one of the great contributors to "sprawl." The long-term consequence of this infill and/or surrounding growth was that many developments, especially those without their own political organization, lost some of their early sense of identity.

A deeper problem for the future was the early settlers' need to protect their investments—understandable because, after all, the new house was the largest investment of their lives. The first generation of postwar suburbanites had often had to battle restrictive covenants that excluded Jews, Italians, and all other "nonwhite" people, together with all working-class people, from buying into areas within earlier settlements. The new settlers and their builders also had to do battle with older zoning ordinances that restricted lot sizes to those prescribed for farms, or with those that had been designed for well-to-do early suburban communities. But soon the new homeowners sought ordinances for themselves that would prevent the building of less expensive dwellings near their own neighborhoods, fearing the decline of the value of their own investments. Both Frank Facciolo and Alfred Campanelli complained about this growing pattern that it made it difficult to build inexpensive housing for less affluent buyers. (Campanelli, we remember, tried to solve this problem by building row houses and low-rise apartment dwellings, but this effort was not very successful.) Thus the very people, formerly working class or lower middle class, and coming from ethnic groups previously discriminated against, the people who initially benefited from the new suburbs, now helped to make it impossible for other less affluent people to move into their communities. A huge wave of new zoning ordinances arose in the 1970s, both in the self-governing new communities and as a result of homeowner actions in unincorporated areas. In his survey of this new legislation, economist William Fischel emphasizes that the American passion for the detached single-family dwelling placed "the detached and (typically) owner-occupied home . . . at the top of the zoning pyramid" in zoning laws.[9] The same wave of zoning regulation produced new restrictions on the use of yards—no livestock, no gardens in the front yard, the use of particular forms of planting, for example—that had not been universal in the earliest tract house communities.[10]

It seems clear that there was something of a generational shift in the new suburbs, such that the newcomers, more affluent and probably more status conscious, had different attitudes to their new communities than the original buyers had had. Some of the people I interviewed (mostly those from the Golden Corridor) remarked on this shift; it is also described, quite melodramatically (and from a later period), in W. D. Wetherell's well-known story "The Man Who Loved Levittown."[11] Here the aging World War II veteran who is the protagonist (Tommy DiMaria, a retired Grumman aircraft worker, widower with grown children) laments the influx of new neighbors who do not share his values (they don't mess around in their workshops, help each other build additions, or enjoy fooling the electric company with self-installed electric gadgets). He says of them, "They're sad more than anything. . . . You know what these kids know? Shopping centers, that's it. If it's not in a mall they don't know nothing. And talk about dreams, they don't have any. A new stereo? A new Datsun? Call those dreams? Those aren't dreams, those are pacifiers. Popsicles. . . . You find your own dream, pal, you're walking on mine. My generation survived the Depression, won the war, got Armstrong to the moon and back."[12] Tommy's older neighbors move away, seduced by the high prices they're getting for their properties to buy land and homes in Florida for a sunny retirement. The new and more affluent middle-class neighbors see Tommy and his house as bringing down their newly-acquired property values. They pressure him to leave, forcing new assessments leading to higher taxes; reporting him to the electric company so that he is faced with a huge fine; spilling his garbage; arranging an "accident" to his dog, which he refuses to keep on a leash. Eventually, he burns down his beloved house rather than sell out.

A commitment to the new house as an investment co-existed among the first postwar inhabitants with the view that the house was the building block of a new way of life and a new community. The notion of the house as an investment, though, changed and grew, so that by the 1980s many buyers were purchasing new dwellings as "starter houses." Moving ever on and up to more and more expensive houses came to be an established basis for wealth accumulation, to the point where it came to seem normal to young couples to borrow huge amounts in order to acquire a dwelling that was too expensive for them. This pattern is still widespread today, despite the recent recession and collapse of the housing bubble.

Economists suggest that many of the changes that took place in suburbs in the 1960s and 1970s were inevitable. Economic history shows that rapid increases in size and density of urban (or suburban, in this case) population almost always result in increasing prices—in increasing rents, or increasing purchase prices. Typically, in the past, this fundamental law of supply and demand has been violated only in cases of new settlements on cheap and plentiful land. Pioneer settlers of the East Coast and of the American West benefited from such conditions, and so did the new suburbanites of the fifties—for a little while. But soon the pressure of demand for land, together with its increasing scarcity, and the increasing costs of infrastructure (including the maintenance of the new highways), led inevitably to higher prices and increasing taxes. This was the situation that made it difficult, if not impossible, for builders to continue to provide "affordable" housing.[13]

Broadly speaking, the decades after this study ends, between 1965 and 1990, brought land scarcity and rising prices to the suburbs. New owners now looked for more and more space *inside* their houses, unable to find lots of the size they desired. Between 1945 and 1990, the average square footage of floor area in new single-family houses doubled (from ca. 1,000 to 2,080; 2,392 in 2010). Family life turned inward at some point in these years, with ever more hours spent around the television set and the kitchen table. This was an era in which two-career families became a necessity, rather than an option. A recent anthropological study of the lives and material possessions of thirty-two middle-class Los Angeles families in 2000 shows that outdoor yards are almost never used.[14] (That all the parents in the study had full-time jobs may help to account for the absence of adults in these outdoor spaces, but not for the absence of children.) American attitudes to public space more generally have changed during the same period: uncontrolled, unpoliced public spaces have come to be regarded as unsafe—for children above all, but also for adults. In the 1970s, suburban shopping malls (complete with security guards) took over many of the functions of earlier shopping streets.[15] And, as Tommy DiMaria observed, rampant consumerism came to be widespread. Consumption of household goods and cars may have had its roots in the enthusiasm of the 1950s buyers for their kitchen appliances, but I think that the lust to consume vast quantities of clothing, toys, ever-newer kitchen and electronic equipment, and cars, came a little later.

The development of suburban tract housing after the war, and the history of the new communities that were founded then, was a dynamic process. Major changes in costs and social composition occurred in the sixties and seventies, and new ones again in the eighties and nineties, and again in the early twenty-first century. Because of rising real prices, increasingly scarce land, and new kinds of zoning, it became ever harder to build low-cost housing. Ultimately, the early twenty-first century has brought dramatic changes in social structure and ethnic representation, while the physical character of the older suburbs has, in most cases, remained. Lakewood, for example, is now multicultural in population, as are Panorama City and Willingboro, New Jersey, the third of the "Levittowns." Much of what has been written about "the suburbs" conflates the different phases of this history, and often buttresses (or revives) the negative views of the 1950s and 1960s critics. I have tried to sort out and characterize the earliest—and formative—phase of this long and complicated process. The makers of the earliest postwar suburbs were the parents and grandparents of today's Americans. We need to know a great deal more about the physical environment and the way of life that they created. It shapes our lives even now.

We also need to know a great deal more about the development of the suburbs in succeeding decades.[16] Above all, future researchers in the history of all phases of the postwar suburbs will need to understand why, for so long, commentators in so many fields of endeavor condemned the early suburbs: their builders, buyers, and building style. There may be many reasons for the almost universal condemnation of the suburbs that dominated critical writing about them for so long, but clearly, I think, one was disappointment of the "grand expectations" people had felt at war's end. People who hoped for, or expected, the founding of "new towns" on the basis of new systems of planning were disappointed, as were those who expected the comprehensive victory of modernist architecture. Prefabrication did not succeed, a disappointment to many architects, builders, and engineers. Social justice appeared to be absent in the new suburbs, to social reformers who favored government-sponsored public housing for the poor. Women may have expected dramatically new roles in the new communities of the postwar world. Beyond this series of disappointments, there was another factor, often overlooked. We often forget the enormous visual impact that the new postwar developments had upon the American landscape. Where once the green spaces of farms or large estates surrounded older towns and cities, now those spaces were filled with streets upon streets of millions of little houses. A pleasurable Sunday excursion into the country now had to negotiate the views of these places. The constantly published new aerial views taken by low-flying aircraft reinforced the widespread impression that an older American landscape had disappeared. The impact of this change might be characterized as "loss of landscape," or, as poet and essayist Deborah Tall describes it, the "loss of a sense of place." Tall suggests that we depend upon familiar landscapes for our sense of roots and identity.[17] Thus the addition of vast tracts of new houses may have appeared to be not an addition but a subtraction—a subtraction of fundamental evidence of our roots. It seems to me that some criticism of suburban growth stemmed from grief or anger at this loss of familiar landscape.

Once we understand the roots of the long-term disaffection with postwar tract houses among American intellectuals—writers, academics, newspaper editors, film and television creators—we will be better able to appreciate the actual contributions of the early builders and buyers in their own terms. I hope that my research on builders and buyers will suggest hypotheses that can guide further work. The choices, plans, and practices considered here show the eagerness of postwar builders to create something very new for veterans and other less affluent people, and the enthusiasm of their buyers for the new way of life that these houses seemed to embody. The changing character of builders and buyers in American suburbs after the early nineteen sixties is part of a different story, or a succession of different stories. But the patterns that were established in the first two decades after the war—the new house types designed around a new lifestyle—continued to prevail for a long time and still influence the forms of our metropolitan regions in the twenty-first century.

APPENDIX 1

Chronological List of Campanelli Developments, Massachusetts and Rhode Island

In the absence of the records of the Campanelli firm (destroyed by fire in 1977), these dates and names are derived primarily from newspaper advertisements. The dates on the left are usually the dates of the first advertisement. The numbers are estimates, probably conservative, based mainly on searches in Google Maps, but also on reports in newspapers, and on the testimony of contemporaries (especially Bradford Saivetz and Ronald Cerel). A more accurate picture might have been derived from a comprehensive study of deeds, but this would have been very difficult and extremely time-consuming. The local records that would have shown subdivision plans would have helped, but these are almost always missing. A great many of the subdivisions in Massachusetts from Natick onward are ascribed in the newspapers to Cerel; my reassignment of these places to the Campanellis is based on painstaking analysis of newspaper reports, as well as on occasional use of local deeds and plans. An asterisk marks those instances where I have been able to consult original deeds or subdivision plans.

1947ff. Warwick, RI 250+
Governor Francis Farms, 1948–56
"Behind Aldrich High School," 1948–55
Sheridan Park, 1955–

1948ff. Braintree 250
Braintree Dam, 1948–ca. 1953
Fairfield-at-Braintree, 1954–
Highlands of Braintree, 1955–

1949 Barrington, RI, according to Mr. TU, "centrally located" (I have not been able to find it)

1949 Natick 800–1,500 (1,500 according to R. Cerel clipping)
Beaconsfield 130, 1949–51
Westfield (Westminster Gardens)* 175, 1953–
Wethersfield* 500, 1950–55

1953 Framingham 2,600
Elmfield 100, 1953–

Fairfield 500, 1953– (several sections)
Pinefield* 750–1,000, 1954–
Cherryfield 300, 1955–
Ridgefield 100, 1957–
Longfield 500, 1958–
Woodfield 75, 1959–
Deerfield-at-Framingham-Centre 100, 1960–
Greenwich 50, 1965–66

1953 Newton 100: Albemarle-at-West Newton, 1953–54

1954 Needham 50: Albemarle-at-Needham, 1954–

1954 Wayland 100: Fairfield-at-Wayland, 1954 or earlier

1954 Beverly 100: Raymond Farms, 1954, 1956

1954 Holbrook 200
Brookfield-at-Holbrook, 1954–
Fairfield-at-Holbrook, 1955–

1956 Brockton 2,000
Indian Heights, 1956–
Brookfield*, 1957–61 (names vary: Brookfield, Brookfield Estates, Brookfield Heights)
Courtfield*, 1960–
Southfield*, 1961–
Field Park Estates, 1962–
Eastfield, 1964–65

1956 Peabody 300
Jordan Acres, 1956–
Centrefield, 1957–
Westfield, 1960–
Pinefield-at-Peabody, 1961–65

1957 Hingham 200: Country Club Estates, 1957–

1958 Danvers (I could not locate the subdivisions) 200

APPENDIX 2

Stoltzner Business History

Woodvale, 1958–61
Northfield, 1963–65

1959 Chelmsford (I could not locate the subdivisions) 200
Chelmsford Farms Estates, 1959–63
Olde Stage Estates, 1964–69

1960 Bellingham 300: Wethersfield-at-Bellingham, 1960–66

1961 Raynham 200
Pleasantfield, 1961
Raynham Farms, 1966

1962 Hudson 200: Phillips Hill Farms, 1962–66

1963 Ipswich 100
Cherryfield, 1963–64
Pinefield, 1964–66

1968 Sudbury 100, 1968–69

1968 Westford 100: Tar-kiln Meadows, 1968–70

Stoltzner business history is characterized by an almost bewildering complexity. The family firm began as Stoltzner Construction Company (1918–ca. 1935), with all the brothers and their father active at the start. (They also, originally, had a partner named Ralph Hanson.) After Charles, injured in a construction accident, dropped out of the company in 1928, Orla, Kai, Roy, and Frode formed the Stoltzner Building Company (ca. 1929–45). Kai, Roy, and Frode diverged in 1945, reviving the Stoltzner Construction Company name; this branch was responsible for Arlington Estates, and continued building through the early 1960s. Richard and Jim (Jim was a mason, Richard a carpenter) entered this firm as apprentices in the early 1960s; Richard then served as foreman at Greenview as well. In the early 1940s, Orla, his son Harold, and his sister Myrtle and her husband Erik Erikson (together with Carl Carlson) reconfigured the Stoltzner Building Company as the Stoltzner Building Organization; then, when Orla died in 1949, this branch was led by Harold and Carl Carlson, and soon by John Stoltzner and a mason named Fred Fisher. This branch was responsible for Greenview Estates. Around 1959, Harold Stoltzner and Carl Carlson retired; the firm continued as Stoltzner and Fisher Building Corporation, and completed Greenview Estates. Subsequently, John alone took over leadership of this firm, and built at Arlington North. Some of these changes in name may have been for legal purposes, and some were related to the need for new partners resulting from deaths and retirements. But there were also differences in leadership style. While each of the partnerships obviously involved equal rights and responsibilities, I have the impression from family members that some personalities were more dominant than others. Charles appears to have been more adventurous and entrepreneurial than his partners until his retirement; the same may be said of Orla until his death in 1949.

APPENDIX 3

Interviews with Original Buyers or Their Children

Interviews are arranged in roughly chronological order, according to the dates of the construction or purchase of the houses. Interviews were not recorded and are not quoted verbatim. I made extensive notes, and have attempted to retain the individual voices. Initials have been changed to conceal the identity of participants. I have checked the factual content with the speakers, but they have not reviewed or endorsed the specific texts as they appear below. The list of questions asked appears at the end.

Mr. TU, clerk, American Airlines, later manager, Governor Francis Farms, Warwick, RI, 1950–52

I was in the Army in WWII, served in Germany, ended up in Leipzig. In the army, I worked in surveying and mapmaking. I didn't go on with that after the war, though; I went to work as a clerk for American Airlines at the new airport in Providence RI, and lived at home nearby with my family. When I got married and started my own family, we lived for a while in a trailer in my mom's backyard. We needed a house, but there weren't any then that were near work. By 1949, a lot of houses began to be built in Warwick, right next to the airport; a friend of ours bought one that was built by the Campanelli Brothers from Brockton, a ranch. We loved it, it was a whole new kind of house; it seemed right for a whole new time. We waited until we could find one like it, and when the Campanellis built at Governor Francis Farms, we bought the first model. With a VA/FHA mortgage, of course. We liked Governor Francis Farms—it was said to be a very exclusive neighborhood, and it was in a beautiful location, near the ocean. There were hardly any other houses there like ours when we moved; five years later, though, there were quite a few. We raised our three children there and still live there. We fixed up the house a little as time went by: we put front and back patios in, turned the one-car garage into a two-car garage, replaced the exterior siding. It used to be white and yellow "clapboards"; now it's dark wood shingles. We still love the house, and the heating pipes in the floor slab still work!

Mrs. MH, township officer, wife of pharmacist, Rose Tree Woods, Broomall, PA, 1953

I grew up in the Philadelphia suburbs, went to college, and married a veteran who was studying to be a pharmacist on the GI Bill. He was from Jersey. We needed a house and were looking around; my husband's sergeant was a friend and turned out to be living in a new development in Rose Tree Woods. This was about 1953. Some of the neighborhood was already built up with unusual-looking modern houses; people called them "flat tops." We liked the houses pretty well, but we especially liked the neighborhood because everything was wooded; we really bought our house because of the lot (one-third of an acre). Our street was still a mud hole when we moved in, but we got to know Frank Facciolo and liked and respected him. He planted evergreens, rhodos, hollies on the properties and helped us find ornamental shrubs for our yard.

We still live in the house; I went to work for the township after a couple of years, and still work there. We raised our two kids in the house, and two relatives' kids. We've made changes. A lot of the work was done by Frank, or by his cousins. Frank added a powder room at our request (and at our expense). We added closets, replaced the roof, took down a kitchen wall, converted the garage, combined two of the bedrooms. We put in a new heating system in 1972 because the radiant heat had failed in a lot of the houses, and we didn't want to go through that. Eventually, we replaced the siding. It still looks pretty similar to the original from the front, though. The neighbors, when we moved in, were a mix of professional people and working-class people. Many were Jewish (like us) or Catholic, some were other Christian denominations. The Presbyterian Church was old; a new Temple was built about 1956, and St. Pius parish and church began in 1955.

Mrs. KD, school bus driver, daughter of lace-maker and distillery worker, Lawrence Park, Broomall, PA, 1955

My parents were second-generation Italian and Irish. They grew up in row houses in Philadelphia. My Irish grandfather was a bricklayer. My father worked at Publicker Distillery in south Philadelphia, my mother operated a lace-making machine in a factory in north Philadelphia. My father was in the Army 1943–45, in Europe; when he got back we bought a second row house right next to the one we lived in, in North Philadelphia. We lived in that, and rented the other. Then my mother heard about the "houses in the country" that were being built outside Philadelphia and wanted to see what they were like. They found our Lawrence Park house in a newspaper ad (they didn't know anybody there), and came out there in 1955 to look. There wasn't much around at the time—not many other houses, no shops, no Catholic schools, but the salesman who showed them the models explained that the place would get to be over 1,000 houses, and that a new Roman Catholic parish had just started up. It was a new kind of house, a split-level, with three bedrooms and one bath, a lot of house for the money. They decided the house would be roomier for the family (me and my four sisters and brothers) and that it looked like a good investment. (The row house had three bedrooms too, but these in the new house were bigger. Three kids slept in the master bedroom, two in the small bedroom, Mom and Dad in the medium-size bedroom.) So they sold the row houses in the city, paid off part of the mortgage, and we moved in. We lived there the whole time I was growing up, and when I got married, my husband and I bought a house just a couple of blocks away. Then after my parents died, I bought their house.

It was funny to hear birds instead of the clack-clack of the trolleys. (I liked the trolley noises too, though.) After a while, it didn't seem like "country" so much: a shopping center opened up near us and my mother worked there (as a cashier at Pantry Pride and then at the Pathmark), streets got paved, and the place grew. But we always had a big vegetable garden in the back yard. My dad had hoped to keep some sheep, but in Marple Township you had to have a one acre lot to do that. My dad continued to work at the distillery and drove to work. We had two cars.

It was a great place to be a kid, there were so many of us. We didn't all go to the same schools; lots of the kids went to the new public schools that opened up; we went to the nearest parochial schools. But we all played together all the time, and were in and out of each other's houses. Our families didn't socialize much, but they were always there for each other in emergencies, like snowstorms, power outages, or if a kid was hurt. After I took over the house, I fixed it up: replaced the old asbestos siding, converted the old garage to a den, moved the television there, opened up the dining room to the kitchen to make one big room; I also built a deck out back. Some of our

family work in construction trades and they helped me. Now it's very nice: just how I like it.

Mrs. FC, writer, daughter of horticulturalist, Torrance, CA,[1] 1954

We moved to the ranch house in Torrance in 1954, when I was five. My dad was a horticulturalist, the son of German/Norwegian immigrants who had come to LA in 1918. My mom was from New England, from a well-educated family; when I was growing up, she worked for a catering company part time, and then later as a clerk in the local junior high school. My dad was in the army and then after the war he got training through the GI Bill in ornamental horticulture at Cal Poly in San Luis Obispo. When they were first married, my mom and dad lived in former war housing that had been built by remodeling army barracks, but for most of the time until we moved to Torrance, they lived in a trailer in my grandmother's backyard in Santa Barbara. Then he got a job with a big nursery (Japanese-owned) near Torrance and they bought the house. I don't know how they found it—probably through newspaper ads. It had two and a half bedrooms and one bath. They loved the house, because it was their first time to be independent and to have their own place. My grandmother helped with the down payment, but the mortgage was through the GI Bill. A few years later, in 1959, the nursery moved a short distance, and we moved to another ranch house in Torrance, a little bigger, a little roomier for us three kids, and they liked this one even better. It had more space and more amenities: three bedrooms, one and a half baths, a two-car garage, living room in the back with sliding glass doors onto the patio, a dining area, a fireplace, central heating. It was a step up in a lot of ways. And then eventually, in 1964 when the nursery moved again, we moved to a two-story house in Santa Barbara; it seemed quite posh to us, since most of the lower-middle-class suburbs in Southern California at that time were one-story ranches.

At the houses in Torrance, my father did a lot of landscaping in the front- and backyards; we were always considered the best-landscaped house on the block. Other people had big vegetable gardens and kept chickens, though we didn't. There were dairy farms nearby. There was quite a bit of socializing for the grownups in both neighborhoods: block parties, barbecues, indoor entertaining. The first neighborhood had lots of construction people, tradesmen (my father often bartered for services in exchange for landscaping other people's houses), insurance salesmen, factory workers, and the like. I think there were a few elementary school teachers, and people who worked at the airplane companies (Northrop). I may be wrong, but I get the feeling my parents were unusual in both having college education. In the first neighborhood in Torrance there were quite a few Mexican families, some our close friends: one family had six kids and we would *all* go to their house to eat the *stacks* of tortillas and beans that she made every day. But the next neighborhood was "all white," that is, no Mexican families. Of course, there were never any black families in any of these neighborhoods.

There were lots of kids in Torrance. We all played together, in the back yards, on the sidewalks, in the streets, and on the building sites where new houses were in construction. We rode our bikes on the sidewalks and around the block. There weren't any parks or playgrounds near us. When I got older, I went to the beach every day in the summer. My mother or my father would drive a whole bunch of us, with surfboards, in my dad's pickup truck.

But in a way, my grandmother's house was the true center of my family's life. We went over there a lot of weekends. My grandmother had supported her family during the Depression by working as a cook. She was a fantastic cook, and insisted that anyone who came to her door had to be fed. There always seemed to be a lot of people at the outdoor tables where we ate. Her house gives me the template of home that I carry in my head.

Mr. LT, carpenter and later senior project manager for construction, pharmaceutical company; builder; son of army officer and researcher employed by Natick Labs, Natick, MA, 1954

My dad joined the Army Quartermaster Corps during World War II, in 1942, and worked for their research section, testing clothing materials for soldiers' uniforms and equipment. After the war he stayed in the reserves, and went back to college to finish his BA on the GI Bill; then he rejoined the Quartermaster Corps research group, living in a rented house in Maryland near Washington, DC. The research group moved to Natick in 1952,[2] and soon came to be called Natick Labs. My parents followed the Labs to Natick with my sister and me in 1954 (I was three); several of my dad's coworkers moved to Natick at the same time. (They went to work together and carpooled.) The Campanellis had three models that you could choose from, three styles, and then you could choose different numbers of rooms, room sizes, floor finishings, appliances, wallpapers, and materials. Ours was three bedrooms, one and a half baths, with a fireplace in the living room; my parents paid $13,500 for it. The house felt very modern and luxurious; it was my parents' pride and joy. And mine as well.

They loved the location too. My school was only a couple blocks away, so I could come home for lunch every day (there

were no school cafeterias in those days), and the new shopping center, Shoppers World, was exciting to look at and to shop in. Since my dad carpooled to work, my mom had the car four days a week.

We are Catholic. My grandparents and my wife's came from Lithuania and Poland; my grandfather was a coal miner in Pottsville, PA. My dad was born in Pottsville, but moved to Cleveland, where he met my mother. Both of my parents were born here, and grew up in very crowded circumstances. My father and his four brothers lived with his married sister and her family in their small house in the outskirts of Cleveland, in a Polish and Slovak neighborhood. There were three bedrooms and a bath on the second floor; foyer, living room, dining room and kitchen on the ground floor. And a basement and attic. Maybe about 1,500 square feet in all. My mother and her six brothers and sisters grew up in a very similar house in Cleveland, somewhat smaller, in an Irish Catholic and Italian neighborhood. Mom and Dad met in high school. During the war, my mom and dad lived in army housing. They had a GI loan for the house in Natick, but my mother still worked; she worked at Jordan Marsh as a sales clerk for twenty years or so, mostly evenings at first, but then for longer hours.

The neighbors were pretty much like my parents: mostly younger couples with small children. As I said, some worked at Natick Labs; others worked in management with private companies. Some ran their own small businesses: a grocery store, auto parts store, a fabric store. Because there was a Temple and Catholic Church nearby, most were Jewish and Christian denominations. People were very sociable. They had frequent open houses, especially at Christmastime, when as kids we would go from house to house all night long. Even neighbors of the Jewish faith would have open houses during Christmas. As kids, we ran free in the block. There were no fences then.

My parents didn't make many changes to the house, but after I took it over I replaced the shingles with vinyl siding, added two bedrooms, a family room, a patio, and replaced the windows. The windows were Andersen windows, very good quality, so I was able to replace them with windows from the same company. We also had to replace the radiant heat with baseboard electric heat in the '70s; we really missed those warm floors! Over the years, we've added 1,000 square feet to the original 1,300 square feet.

Mr. IN, Chemist, employee of Natick Labs, Natick, MA, 1954

I had a graduate degree from the University of Massachusetts in Lowell; I specialized in insecticides and rodenticides. During the war, I was an instructor for the army in chemical warfare. After the war, I worked for a government agency in Philadelphia for four to five years, on mothproofing. Then, many government labs were consolidated into Natick Labs in Natick, MA; I worked for Natick Labs for 35 years.

My wife and I moved to Natick in 1954 so that I could work in Natick Labs. We bought one of the new Campanelli houses. Ours was three bedrooms and one and a half baths. Our families were both Armenian; our parents came over and settled in Massachusetts, mine to an industrial district in Lowell, hers to a farm in Methuen. I grew up in a three-floor house with six apartments, my wife grew up on a farm (and then later worked in a textile mill in Lawrence, after she graduated high school). I wanted to get away from the crowding; she wanted a place in the country. So we both wanted a house of our own, not in the city.

The new house was just right for us. We didn't have children; we both worked hard, I at the Labs, my wife in a handbag factory until the mortgage was paid. We liked the neighbors, the yard, and the location convenient to work. The car pool was very useful. We worked on the house, but didn't change it much. We took part of the garage to enlarge the kitchen (we doubled the size of the kitchen), and replaced the shingles with vinyl siding. I remodeled the rest of the garage as a workshop; I do some research there and also work on maintaining and restoring the original fixtures of the house.

Mrs. BG, machine operator, Rolling Meadows, IL, 1955

I was a machine operator at Transo Envelope.[3] (Later I was a proofreader, and then the production manager.) We lived with our young son in a one-bedroom basement apartment in Albany Park (Chicago) and then on the ground floor of a two-story house in Richmond; these were all we could find that worked for my husband, who'd had polio in 1943 and was in a wheelchair. We kept watching the newspapers for a better place. One Sunday we were looking at the *Chicago Tribune* and saw an ad for ranch houses in Rolling Meadows. We visited the models, fell in love with the three-bedroom house, put down our last $10 to hold one. We were just barely able to swing the mortgage on my salary of $5,000/year.[4] My boss came out and guaranteed my employment. We paid the down payment with Rob's profits from the lamps he made at home and sold. At first, I carried him into the house on my back, but then we got a ramp for the wheelchair. I drove into Chicago to work, but later on some other people from Transo came to Rolling Meadows, and we carpooled.

We watched the house being built: we went out every Sunday. It was perfect for us: all on one floor, roomy, and the big kitchen! The washer and dryer—we'd never had anything like that. And we were so happy to have a place of our own. We didn't change too much. We had a choice of tile colors in the bathroom, and we also put wallpaper there. I liked light-colored walls and the wall color in the living room was an ugly green, so we had them change that to beige. We had to widen the bathroom door for Rob's wheelchair, and we built a garage out back. When people said there was a tornado coming, we'd all go down to the crawl space and wait it out. You couldn't stand up there, but you could sit well enough.

The neighbors were nice, they were all about the same age as us, in their early thirties. We didn't socialize a lot—just once in a while, at the street parties. The neighbors came from different backgrounds, German, Irish, Polish, English. We were Episcopalian, not great churchgoers (our neighbors weren't either), but we liked going to the non-denominational community church that Kimball Hill set up in the old barn. And then, on Saturdays we'd have a pot-luck supper and sit in our cars at the barn, watching outdoor movies. That was a lot of fun. The first school was in that building too. Our son went to school in the barn, and later to the public schools that replaced it. The schools were very good.

My dad was a foreman in a factory in upstate New York that made machine parts [Dodge Sales & Engineering Company, Oneida, NY]; we lived in a tiny town nearby in a two-story house where we had a garden, a cow, and chickens. The factory closed, so my dad drove us out to Sterling, Colorado, where two of his sisters lived.

Unfortunately when we moved, we had to auction off my mom's collection of first editions: all the best authors, Shakespeare of course, and all the best English and American novels. She'd only gone through eighth grade, but she loved books. Later, she built a new smaller collection, but in the new place we also used the public library a lot—all us kids were great readers. We kept the original house, though; my brother has it now.

So we went out west about 1925, and it was an adventure. They were building the roads as we went, and there weren't any good places to stay; we camped in the car at night. [There were two adults and four children.] In Sterling, we bought a hotel and restaurant. We lived in the hotel. Rob was a traveling salesman who came to the hotel; he and I met then. His father was a miner; growing up, Rob and the other kids lived with their grandmother in a beautiful big three-story brick house in Provo, Utah. It's gone now, of course.

Mrs. KM, homemaker, later clerical worker, ultimately business manager for a doctor's office; wife of factory worker, Rolling Meadows, IL, 1956

In 1956, we were living in Chicago in a one-bedroom apartment with our two small children. Apartments were very hard to find: my father got it for us, through his contacts in the insulation business. My husband Lou was in charge of metal stocks at Powers Regulator [a maker of heating and ventilating controls]; it moved to Skokie in 1955. The apartment was too small (Lou and I had to sleep in the dining room), and the trip to Skokie was long, even though Lou got a car. And we expected more children; we had to move. We thought we might build somewhere up north, and bought a lot at Fox Lake [a village about twenty-five miles northwest of Skokie], but it didn't work out. A work friend from the Powers factory had bought a house at Rolling Meadows and invited us out; we fell in love with the area and the houses. We bought a two-bedroom model, pretty crowded but all we could afford (we paid $13,250). It was fabulous—it was *ours*! No landlords, no neighbors on the other side of the walls. And the kitchen! It was so *big*—it reminded us of the old days.

We liked almost everything about the house—the appliances, the white walls—but we didn't like the big windows, they were cold in the winter and hot in the summer (they didn't open all the way). So we replaced the floor-to-ceiling windows with shorter ones. We added a garage as soon as we could, then another bedroom and bath; then we added to the garage and pretty soon a utility room and a family room out back. Actually, I guess most of the ideas about the additions were mine: I scribbled them down for different contractors on a paper and told them to build them, but we did all the dry wall and finishing touches ourselves. Later (1983) we put on a second story with three more bedrooms—places for kids and grandkids to stay. And we added a front porch, to make it look better with the second story. A friend of Lou's framed the upstairs for us, and my son Frank, who works in heating and ventilating, put in the new furnace. The house is now nine rooms and three baths.

The best thing about Rolling Meadows was the neighbors, the friendliness, and the kids: there were fifteen kids on our block alone. The neighbors were all young and struggling, like us. Nobody had the money to go out anywhere, but the women with young children had coffee at each other's houses and there were block parties. There wasn't really room inside to have people over, but we all did a lot of grilling outside, on the old Weber grills with the round domes. There were a lot of different religions. My husband and I were Catholic, but

we gave it up (we didn't like the local Catholic churches, they always wanted money for something) and went to the nondenominational church in the old barn. We liked that a lot. And the schools were wonderful. I could walk to the grocery store, or ride my bike.

After our last child, our third, was born, I learned to drive. I went to work part time when the youngest was six months old, and then when they were all in school I went to full time, first in a department store, then as an accountant, then as the business manager for an oncologist. I had had two years of college, and then I went to Harper College [near] Rolling Meadows for some accounting courses; I'd always had a head for numbers. My father was born on a farm and when we were growing up, he did insulation work in a factory; we always rented a house; he didn't want to own any property. We moved a lot—my mother was always looking for something better. She came over from Germany as a child, did welding work at Zenith during the war. Mostly my brother and I slept in the same bedroom and my parents (or my mother, after they divorced) had the other. Lou grew up poor in Polish Town [Bucktown]; his parents came from Poland. His father died early, his mother worked in a clothing factory. Eight of them (his mother, his two brothers, his sister, her husband and her two kids) rented a one-story hundred-year-old house in back of an apartment building. It was a two-bedroom house, so some of them slept in the dining room, and some in the living room on a hide-a-bed. Only the dining room was heated. Fuel and food were hard to come by: they ate bacon grease instead of butter and sometimes the kids had to go to the railroad yards, to get coal that had been dropped from the coal cars, for their stove. Lou never graduated from grade school; he enlisted as soon as he could, and then re-enlisted.

Our daughter and older son still live in Rolling Meadows, and I've bought houses for two of our grandchildren's families, who rent from me. They'll inherit their houses when I die.

Mrs. OC, homemaker, volunteer, wife of corporation executive, Rossmoor, Orange County, CA, 1957

My husband and I met at the University of Minnesota and were married in 1951. Chet was a petroleum engineer; I was working on an education degree that would let me teach school, but I didn't finish because I wanted to follow him. He went to work in a managerial position for National Tank Company (later Combustion Engineering, then ABB), which got to be a big national company and sent us all over the country. First we went to Odessa and then Abilene, in Texas, and then in 1957 to the LA area where the company had set up a new headquarters. After that, we were moved to Oklahoma, then Connecticut, and then back to Texas. LA was our longest stay—five years—and we liked it best.

We had one child by then and needed a house, but we had no money and no knowledge of LA. A man from the company took us around to look at houses, and we found one in Rossmoor that we liked. It was a ranch house with three bedrooms, two full baths, living room, dining area, and a two-car garage—it seemed very big and luxurious and cost a lot, $19,000 [about 1,600 square feet]. But it was in a good location for Chet's work and, since he'd been in the army, we had a very generous mortgage. Our second child was born there. The house was beautiful: there was lots of nice dark wood and wonderful new kinds of appliances—a washer-dryer, and a dishwasher. We could choose pink, avocado green, or yellow for the colors of the appliances. The house was yellow wood siding on the outside and the walls inside were nicely plastered. There was a patio in back, with sliding glass doors leading to it. After a couple of years, we added a den at the back.

The best thing about that house was the neighbors and the neighborhood. There were a lot of children, company for our two, and a lot of nice places to go: the beach, Knots Berry Farm, Disney World. And for longer trips, Big Bear Mountain, Lake Tahoe, Mammoth Mountain. The children played on the sidewalks and in the tiny backyards (and in and out of each others' houses). None of us had known each other before, of course—everybody was from somewhere else. But we socialized a lot: at block parties and barbecues; we even took vacations together, and became very close friends. (I'm still in touch with some of these neighbors after fifty years. A group of them still has annual reunions.) We were among the first owners in Rossmoor, which later grew very big, to 4,000 houses. Being new, maybe we were especially close to our nearest neighbors.

Most of the neighbors were well educated, and active in the community, especially in the PTA: they took education really seriously. (And, of course, it *was* very important, since we were just getting the school system going. This was the Sputnik era: it was absolutely necessary to build up the education of our kids.) The men were mostly professional people, doctors, engineers in the aerospace industry. There were some retired couples, though, and a few ran small businesses. Most of the women were well educated, and had worked as secretaries or teachers, but after their kids were born they didn't work, except as volunteers in the schools, scouts, community organizations of different kinds. We were Lutheran and the neighbors we knew well were either Protestant or Jewish.

As I said, the house seemed very big and luxurious to us. I had grown up in a little one-and-a-half-story stucco house on the outskirts of Minneapolis. To begin with, there were two bedrooms; then my father finished the attic, adding two more kids' bedrooms (we were six kids). At that time, we were not at all well off. Initially my dad, who had an accounting degree, worked for the IRS; later he became a bank officer and we did better. My mother had no college and never worked. One side of her family was originally from England and the British Isles, but way, way back. My husband's grandparents came over from Germany, and settled in Wisconsin. His father was a plumber, his mother a schoolteacher, so his mother had a college education, but his father did not. My father grew up in a modest house; my mother's family rented.

Mr. KC, pharmacist, purchased a Campanelli ranch in Brockton in 1962

We were not the original owners of the house in Brookfield Heights, Brockton. The first owners, who'd bought it in 1957, went through a divorce and had to sell, so we were able to buy it in 1962. We needed a place: we lived in an apartment in the Dorchester section of Boston, up three flights of stairs, and we'd just had twins. It was too hard to drag those strollers up and downstairs all the time. I had finished my pharmacists' training (got my license in 1959) and was switching jobs to one at a more professional level. I found the right one in Brockton, so we were looking around there. We wanted a one-story house, in the country. And we wanted to move out of Dorchester, even though I had grown up there: staying there would have felt like going backwards, and we didn't want that. Also, blacks were moving into Dorchester, whites were moving out, and property values were falling; staying there wasn't a good investment. The house in Brookfield Heights seemed just right. We brought both sets of parents to look at it, and they liked it. We paid $15,000, with a thirty-year FHA mortgage, and scraped together the down payment somehow (it took all our savings).[5]

The new house didn't seem small to us. We had both grown up in "three-decker-houses." My parents, and my wife's mother, were born in Poland, and then came over here. My family owned the whole house and rented out the second and third floors, so we had the ground floor (three bedrooms and one bath for four people). Three bedrooms and one and a half bathrooms in the new house seemed about right for us, and the rooms were big. We thought we would have more kids eventually, but we didn't. It was a good lot, near the end of a dead-end street, and it backed up on a big field. The neighborhood kids could play there, but there was also a lot of privacy. We liked the design very much and the spaciousness of it—for example, the kitchen had a wall-mounted refrigerator, which gave us a lot more counter space than we were used to. The living room was open to the dining room, and the dining room was open to the kitchen: that was very nice. Of course, over the years we had to fix a few things: we put on a new roof, replaced all the windows, replaced the heating system, replaced the original shingles with aluminum siding, put on a patio and a deck, and made the garage into an extra room. We also added central air and a central vacuum system.

We had one car: I drove it to work. We could walk to Angelo's Supermarket for groceries.

We got along with the neighbors fine. All the kids played together, in the yards, in the streets, in the field. It was good for the kids and the schools were excellent. People didn't socialize much, but they were friendly. They were all like us: young and struggling financially. We are Jewish, and there weren't many other Jewish families nearby, so that seemed a little uncomfortable at first. But it worked out. It was very diverse: there were Protestants and Catholics, Irish and Italians. There are black families now too, but that's very recent. One neighbor was an accountant, another a cab driver, another a salesman. Economically, I guess you'd call it lower middle class.

Mr. and Mrs. HN, Weathersfield, Schaumburg, 1960

Our house in Schaumburg was the twentieth house to be built in Weathersfield. It was "our great adventure." Weathersfield wasn't really there yet, it was still country. Cows would escape onto the roads. At first, the well wasn't approved, so the Campanellis arranged to have water delivered to the houses—that lasted about six months. We loved the house, the design, the spaces, the way it was built. It was a castle to us. We found the house through a friend of Laura's who married a civil engineer working in Massachusetts. They lived in a Campanelli house in Peabody. When they moved to Chicago and learned that the Campanellis were building in Schaumburg, they told us that this was the house we had to have. "The Campanellis are the best home builders in the world," he said. They moved in on the same block, three weeks ahead of us, but later they moved back to Massachusetts. We had a VA mortgage, paid no money down.

We had both grown up in bungalows, mine a three bed-room one-bath house in Cicero, Laura's a five-bedroom house with one bath (there were ten kids) in Oak Park. I had three brothers and two sisters—there were six kids. We were both

used to doubling up (my brothers and I had our beds in the second parlor). When we got married and started our family we couldn't find the right apartment in Chicago; we moved into Mom's house in Cicero. (My grandparents owned the whole block.) So when the salesman at Schaumburg told us the three-bedroom ranch would be too small for us and our four kids, we laughed. We did add two bedrooms later, though, because we eventually had seven kids. We remodeled the garage into a bedroom and added another at the back, we also added a laundry room and another bathroom, so we added a total of 900 square feet. We used the same radiant heating system in the floor of the new areas as in the rest of the house, and it still works well. Some of Campanelli's subcontractors did the work for us.

The neighbors worked at a lot of different things: one was a cookie salesman, another drove a truck, one installed heating systems, one was a pilot for United, several worked in airplane maintenance at O'Hare. They all became our good friends. Some were Irish Catholic, like us; others were Italian and Polish. At first we had to go to the church in Hoffman Estates, but St. Marcelline's opened soon and that was good for us. A black family moved in in 1972; the pastors and priests lectured everybody about tolerance, and it worked out. Laura took care of their baby while the parents worked.

We had bonfires, lots of informal parties. At Halloween, and when we wanted to have block parties, the police would close off two of the streets for us. The kids played in the streets; there wasn't much traffic then. Our kids went to the Catholic schools from the third grade on (St. Hubert's, in Hoffman Estates), but before that they went to the Campanelli school, which was terrific. When our oldest was in school, Laura went to work for the Village school system. Earlier, she babysat for other people's kids and also helped to show the model houses on weekends. I started out in Schaumburg as a milkman; then I took over milk distribution for the area. I also drove the school bus.

It was a wonderful era.

Mrs. MQ, retired elementary school teacher, wife of insurance salesman, Weathersfield, Schaumburg, IL, 1961, 1968

Ken and I met in Milwaukee when we were college students. Ken had grown up in a single-family house in east Milwaukee; my parents and we three kids had rented in a brick "two-flat" in the Austin district of west Chicago (three bedrooms, one bath), across the street from the rest of my mother's family. After we were married we settled in Chicago and lived in a one-bedroom apartment. Ken worked in the Loop, first as a salesman for AT&T

and then as an accounts manager for Illinois Bell, so we had to be near public transportation. We had very little money. By 1961, we had two babies and had to have more room. We decided we would need a house. We started looking around and saw that we might be able to afford the houses in Schaumburg. We moved to the "W" section, where we bought a three-bedroom ranch, the most basic model, for about $17,000. We weren't eligible for a GI loan, but we scraped together the down payment and Ken's aunt gave us another $1,000, so we were able to reduce the mortgage to a point where we could afford the payments. From Schaumburg, Ken carpooled to the Roselle Station four miles away; from there he was able to take the train to the Loop. It took an hour each way.

We loved the house: it was a beautiful lot, on a hill; we looked out over open farmland. I was thrilled with the laundry area and equipment, a full-size refrigerator, an attached garage, a quarter of an acre of our own with young couples and families for our children to play with. The elementary school, with several classrooms, a gym and offices, already built and donated by Campanelli Brothers, was just half a block away. The house was a little cramped, though: the dining area was an extension of the kitchen, so if we had people in, we had to set up tables in the living room. There was no dishwasher. We got hot air heating, not the heating in the floor. I would have liked a warm floor for when the children were crawling around, but Ken said it made his feet feel funny. He really wanted a basement.

By 1968 we had two more children and needed a bigger house. We sold the first house and moved a few blocks away to another new house, a raised ranch [i.e., a midlevel split]. That was much roomier and better equipped, with three bedrooms, living room, dining room, and kitchen on the main floor and a very large room on the lower floor next to the big garage. We had the Campanellis divide the big room into two, so we ended up with four bedrooms, two and a half baths, a recreation room, and a two-car garage. It cost about $21,200, and we had got $18,000 for the first house, so we were able to swing it with the help of some AT&T stock that we sold. We put in central air, which we really needed since there weren't many trees yet. We couldn't do this in the first house, because there was no crawl space under the slab.

Ken and I had always gone to Catholic schools, but when we moved to Schaumburg there weren't any Catholic schools nearer than Hoffman Estates, and we didn't think we could afford to send our kids anyway. So they all went to the public schools, and these were very good. After the youngest was in school, I taught at the local elementary schools, first as a substi-

tute, and then later, after I went back to junior college for more education credits, I taught first grade on a regular basis.

Our closest friends were Catholic, and we saw them a lot because we were active in building up the new parish. Many were Italian; I am Dutch, Irish, and Scots; my father came to this country as boy, from Holland. My husband's family came over from Germany a long time ago, to Milwaukee, where they built up a chain of bakeries. We were friendly with all the neighbors, and socialized with them often, because of the kids. There were block parties and parties for holidays. There were masses of kids playing together, in the backyards, the front yards, the streets, and in nearby parks. They'd leave the house in the morning and come back when they felt like it, maybe when they were hungry. There were no fences then, so they moved back and forth in and out of each other's yards and houses. They'd have lunch in whatever house they were at, at mealtime.

The neighbors worked at different jobs—there were skilled laborers, printers, electricians, schoolteachers. Over the years, though, quite a few have moved away: as they've improved their incomes they've moved to better neighborhoods. Or they've been transferred by their companies. We've stayed; it's home to us and our family.

Interview Questions for Original Owners/Residents

I tried to start with factual questions about the house, and to slide into personal questions casually, after there was rapport. I also wanted to permit the person to talk about what interested him or her, so the interviews sometimes have quite different emphases.

When did you buy your house? Was it new then? Why did you buy it?

How did you know about it? Ads, friends?

Did you have friends/family also buying, or already there?

What did you like about it? (kitchen, equipment, furnishings, windows, lighting, yard?) Try to be specific.

Did it seem small? How did it compare with the size of the place you lived in before?

Was the house already built when you bought it, or did you have a choice among models? What other choices did you have—carpet, wall coverings, appliance colors, furniture?

How big was your family when you moved in? How big eventually?

Where did you come from, and what kind of work did you do? What about your family? Immigrants? When and from where? Where did you live while growing up? If in the city, was it an apartment, single-family house, or something else? Was it crowded? Why didn't you want to return to the family neighborhood (if this applies)? Did your family own or rent in your previous neighborhood?

What did you think about the new neighborhood? Who were the neighbors and where were they from? Did they go to your church, or another one? What work did they do—same as yours, or different? (Here I'm trying to discover, without quite asking, about the mix of ethnicities and classes in the original development—or at least about people's perceptions of this mix.)

Were there good places for the kids to play? Were there fences or hedges between yards?

Did you have a garden? Flowers? Vegetables?

Did your kids go to the public schools? (Or to religious schools?) Were the schools good? Did you take an active part in PTA or other school-related activities?

Did you have friends among the neighbors? Were there neighborhood entertainments? Block parties? Barbecues (sometimes called "fire pits")?

Did the woman of the family work? Where? Where did the man of the family work? Did that job continue?

Where did you shop?

Did you have a TV when you moved in? When did you get it?

What magazines or books did you like to read?

What movies did you like? Did you go often?

Did you have a washer and a dryer at the start? If not, where did you do the laundry (if neither), or where did you hang out the wash (if washer but no dryer)?

Did you have a car at the start? More than one? When did you get a car or cars? Did you car pool to work?

What alterations have been made to the house? When and why?

Do you have photographs of the house and the family in it (or yard, or street) from the early years? Would you be willing to lend them to me for a short while?

ABBREVIATIONS

BH Boston Herald
CT Chicago Tribune
DMN Dallas Morning News
LAT Los Angeles Times
NYT New York Times

NOTES

Prologue

1. For full texts of the interviews, see appendix 3. The interviews are discussed in detail in chapter 5.

Chapter 1: New Houses and New Communities

1. "American Dream": Phrase coined and defined by James Truslow Adams in *Epic of America*; see also Jim Cullen, *American Dream*. Homeownership is usually described as the dominant part of the American Dream, but many writers point also to the expectation that hard work inevitably buys economic improvement. In the early postwar years, these attitudes were also almost invariably associated with patriotism—with pride at winning the war.

2. Thirteen million is my own estimate, based on tables in *Historical Statistics of the United States* and US Bureau of the Census, *Housing Construction Statistics 1889 to 1964*. Other writers offer other estimates: "Between the end of World War II and 1965, the building industry constructed over 26 million nonfarm houses, most of them in the suburbs." See Nicolaides and Wiese, *Suburb Reader*, 257–58.

3. "Tract house" refers to houses built by a builder on a number of lots at once, lots that were part of a new land subdivision or "tract." It is usually applied to postwar houses.

4. The "baby boom," 1943–64. The birth rate had been 19.4/year (total live births per 1,000 population); it rose to 26.6 in 1947, then remained at 24.0 or higher until 1959, falling to 21.0 in 1964. See Patterson, *Grand Expectations*, 77.

5. Interviews with Greg Feroli, Jack Conway, Evelyn Rosen.

6. Federal-Aid Highway Acts of 1938, 1944, 1952, and 1954, http://www.fhwa.dot.gov/programadmin/interstate.cfm (accessed December 6, 2012).

7. On "liminal" space, see Beckham, "American Front Porch."

8. For the term "polite plan," see Cromley, *Food Axis*; Groth, "Workers'-Cottage and Minimal-Bungalow Districts."

9. Proportionally much larger than in earlier houses such as "the Kingston."

10. Except in Southern California: ranch house developments in LA had fenced backyards.

11. Not always there, since they were a function of local subdivision ordinances.

12. In contrast, patios displayed in advertisements and in model houses were far more elaborate. See figs. 48 and 129.

13. The house had a footprint of 25 × 30 feet, according to Kelly, *Expanding the American Dream*, 196n17. The Levitt "ranch" was 800 square feet.

14. "The Builder's House," 86. The Levitts "do not [draw] lines on tissue paper. It is their custom to build by building and ripping, building and ripping again." The Levitt builders were Abraham Levitt and his sons William (Bill) and Alfred. Bill functioned as the principal designer, and is the best known of the three.

15. I have translated prices into 2010 dollars, using the Consumer Price Index. I chose 2010 as the most recent census year, so that readers can, if they wish, supplement price information with further census information about the buying power of the dollar in 2010. These equivalences based on the CPI do not tell the whole story, of course: people use their money differently in different time periods. But at least the equivalences provide a common standard over the various time periods discussed in my text.

16. See, for example, *LAT* articles on Biltmore Homes and Aetna Construction, 1948 and 1949.

17. See also Garlinghouse split-level models 6252 and 6318, in Garlinghouse, *Split Level Homes*.

18. Split-level construction involved more excavation, and heavier framing, than a ranch house built on a slab.

19. See, for example, advertisements for New Jersey split-level houses in *NYT*, October 21, 1951.

20. Note, though, that Panorama City houses could expand into the two-car garage, and the recreation room or family room was a common addition.

21. The walls were painted in bright colors at Ramona Ranch. And according to Mr. LT, buyers in Natick, MA, soon put up wallpaper. There was also wallpaper in the kitchens at Lawrence Park.

22. Description of the "Webster," Campanelli Brothers, "Welcome to Colonial Weathersfield in Schaumburg, Where the Living Is Wonderful," sales brochure, ca. 1965; Schaumburg sales brochure, ca. 1960.

23. Jean Vandruff at Cinderella Homes; occasional mention in other *LAT* ads.

24. Interview with leading Massachusetts realtor Jack Conway, Norwell, MA, May 5, 2008; also mentioned in many Boston and Los Angeles ads.

25. In split-levels, the lowest-level walls were usually concrete block. See Bodek drawing section, fig. 113.

26. Harris, "Talk of the Town."

27. Keats, *Crack in the Picture Window*. Later writers have also summed up suburban history by referring to the picture window; see, for example, Baxandall and Ewen, "Picture Windows." In his important analysis of ideas of "spaciousness" in the modern American house (*Modern American House*), Sandy Isenstadt traces the evolution of the window from the "landscape window" of the late eighteenth and nineteenth centuries, and sees the placement of the window at the front of the house in the postwar period as a betrayal of this tradition. The Levitts had used these windows extensively in their upscale houses at Strathmore, LI, either at the rear of the house or on the side. In such houses, the living room was also at the rear or on the side.

28. Beckham, "American Front Porch."

29. See Dobriner, *Class in Suburbia*, 9, on this: "The *visibility principle* is a characteristic suburban feature: suburbanites can observe each other's behavior and general life style far more easily than the central city dweller."

30. As the modern photo in fig. 36 shows, this is still true today. Italian journalist Beppe Severgnini writes, "American windows have [a] feature that generates anxiety in Europeans. There are no blinds or shutters worthy of the name. Curtains, if any, are there only as decoration. After a while, you get used to it but for the first few days, you feel as if you are living in the middle of the street. . . . As you sit in front of the television, you wonder if you should wave at people going past" (*An Italian in America*, 25).

31. See also Isenstadt, *Modern American House*, 212.

32. Irene Cieraad, "Dutch Windows," in Cieraad, ed., *At Home*, 31–32.

33. Isenstadt points this out in his "Four Views, Three of Them through Glass," 213–40.

34. Kodak's Brownie was a small and very inexpensive box camera that took number 127 rolled film. On home movies, see especially Ishizuka and Zimmermann, *Mining the Home Movie*.

35. Song composed by folk singer Malvina Reynolds in 1962 (describing Daly City, CA) and made hugely popular by Pete Seeger from 1964 on; part of his repertoire throughout his career (he died in January 2014).

36. Popular literature condemning the new places ranged from highly colored denunciations such as Price and Hytes,

Trick or Treat and Split Level Sin, to Keats's wildly popular *Crack in the Picture Window*. At a somewhat more elevated level, amateur and not-so-amateur social scientists produced a number of studies of social relations in tract house settlements, some of which are still in use today. See, for example, Packard, *Status Seekers*; Whyte, *Organization Man*. Sloan Wilson took up similar themes in his novel *The Man in the Gray Flannel Suit*. So did Betty Friedan, seen by many today as the founder of modern feminism, in her *Feminine Mystique*. Of the social analyses published in the fifties and sixties, only a few have stood the test of time. See especially Gans, *Levittowners* and *Urban Villagers,* and his writings on Park Forest in *Commentary*.

37. On the sense of community in LA suburbs, see the recent work of Becky Nicolaides: "Suburbia and Community," "Exploring Social and Civic Transformations," and "Exploring Social and Civic Engagement."

38. Hayden and others. For correctives, see Bruegmann, *Sprawl*; Hise, *Magnetic Los Angeles*. On the continuity between "suburban" and "urban," see Findlay, *Magic Lands*; Starr, *Golden Dreams*.

39. Nicolaides, "Suburban Landscapes of Los Angeles," 126–35.

40. Archer, *Architecture and Suburbia*; Isenstadt, *Modern American House*. Archer traces an American attitude toward home ownership back to English ideas of self-expression and identity; Isenstadt looks at attitudes toward space within the modern American middle class.

41. Rybczynski, *Home* and *Last Harvest*.

42. Andrzejewski's "Building Privacy and Community" is extremely important in its analysis of the decision-making processes of builders and buyers within a single small development. Also noteworthy is Jacobs's book *Detached America* on the marketing of builders' houses, especially in the 1960s.

43. Keane, *Fritz B. Burns*; Hise, *Magnetic Los Angeles*; Cuff, *Provisional City*.

44. See Weiss, *Rise of the Community Builders*; Checkoway, "Large Builders"; Maisel, *Housebuilding in Transition*.

45. Kelly, *Expanding the American Dream*; Harris, *Second Suburb*; Longstreth, "Levitts, Mass-Produced Houses."

46. *LAT*, 1957.

47. Building began in March 1950, the population rose above 70,000 in 1953 and the city was incorporated in 1954. For Newville's retrospective defense of the plan, see "Lakewood Grid Made Good," *LAT*, June 20, 1965.

48. Waldie, *Holy Land* and *Where We Are Now*. See also Waldie, "Falling in Love."

49. Whyte, *Organization Man*, about Park Forest; Gans,

"Park Forest: Birth of a Jewish Community"; Gans, "Progress of a Suburban Jewish Community."

50. Randall, *America's Original GI Town*. See also Teaford, *Metropolitan Revolution*; Schnay, *Park Forest*.

51. Teaford, *Metropolitan Revolution*.

52. Two men led Centex originally.

53. Kit builders, selling do-it-yourself kits nationally, included Sears, the largest, 1893–; Aladdin Homes, Bay City, MI, second largest; Montgomery Ward; Gordon Van Tine of Davenport, IA; Lewis Manufacturing; Harris Brothers; Sterling Homes. Of the regionally based companies, Pacific Ready-Cut Homes (originally Pacific Portable Construction Company, based in Southern California, 1908–40), was probably the largest. These kit builders shipped packaged kits of precut lumber, plans, elevations, and construction instructions, largely to individuals, though some small builders and carpenters also bought them and built houses with them. Also important, both for individual purchasers and for small builders, were the nationally published pattern books, offering photographs and plans in a single volume, and selling the plans on order. Of these latter publishers, the most important was Garlinghouse Company, Inc., established by Lewis F. Garlinghouse in ca. 1910 and based in Topeka, KS. Garlinghouse began publication around 1910 and is still in business today. Garlinghouse publications are useful to the scholar in many ways, not least because the illustrations are photographs of actual buildings captured by one of the editors in a variety of midwestern, eastern, and southern locations. See Harris, "Talk of the Town"; Reiff, *Houses from Books*.

54. Federal Housing Administration, *Technical Bulletin No. 2: Modern Design*. In this important booklet, "modern" or "functional" is contrasted with "modernistic," meaning buildings that affectedly use strange and unlikely forms.

55. See, for example, Federal Housing Administration, *Land Planning Bulletin, No. 1: Successful Subdivisions*; *Land Planning Bulletin, No. 3: Neighborhood Standards*.

56. Clarence Perry, 1872–1944, planner and influential proponent of the neighborhood unit, often credited with inspiring the plan of Radburn, NJ (Fairlawn, NJ, 1929). On Radburn, and American garden city ideas more generally, see Weiss, *Rise of the Community Builders* and "Developing and Financing." For other perspectives, see Silver, "Neighborhood Planning in Historical Perspective"; Orvell, *Death and Life of Main Street*. In *Paradise Planned*, Robert Stern, David Fishman, and Jacob Tilove present an encyclopedic series of vignettes illustrating "garden suburbs" built during the past 200 years. The inclusiveness of the book contradicts most well-known definitions of "garden suburb," but the volume is beautifully illustrated, and useful as a reference work.

57. Federal Housing Administration, *Land Planning Bulletin, No. 1: Successful Subdivisions*, 9–11.

58. Many are listed in Paxton, *What People Want*. *Better Homes and Gardens* and *Architectural Forum* published several similar studies.

59. Summarized in Beyer, *Cornell Kitchen*. Reported in "Revolution in the Kitchen," *CT*, March 22, 1953, and "Scientists Develop a Kitchen to Suit Needs and Comfort of All," *CT*, March 23, 1953. Cornell also had a housing research laboratory within its Department of Housing and Design; its Agricultural Experiment Station did research on rural housing and the journey to work. See National Research Council, *Survey of Housing Research*.

60. Ludwig Mies van der Rohe, 1886–1969, German architect, director of the Bauhaus. Emigrated to the United States in 1937, head of the Department of Architecture at Illinois Institute of Technology, 1938–58.

61. Marcel Breuer, 1902–81, emigrated from Germany 1937, joined fellow émigré Walter Gropius (1883–1969, German architect and director of the Bauhaus, dean of the Graduate School of Design at Harvard 1937–52) in his practice in Cambridge, MA, and on the faculty at Harvard, jointly designed with Gropius the Gropius House in Lincoln, MA, and severed his connection with Gropius in 1941.

62. Postal, in his dissertation of 1998, "Toward a Democratic Esthetic?," offers a thorough and persuasive analysis of the role of Elizabeth Mock at the Museum of Modern Art. See also Mock, "Tomorrow's Small House" and *If You Want to Build a House*. On the role of mass housing in European Modernism, see Lane, *Architecture and Politics*, chapter 4.

63. A Google Books N-gram search for the term "house of the future" from 1900 to 2010 showed a high and dramatic peak in 1942. Another search for "house of tomorrow" produced a very similar pattern, with a peak slightly earlier—in 1941. A Google Books N-gram search tracks the uses of a phrase or word over a selected period of years (within the corpus of books and magazines digitized by Google Books) and produces a graph of the frequency of use. Because of the limited database, such searches are not truly authoritative, but they are suggestive of the rise and fall of various usages.

64. Nye, *Electrifying America*, 265–67.

65. "Future Home Pictured," *LAT*, June 30, 1929; "House without Wood Exhibited," *LAT*, April 19, 1931; "Visions Homes Costing $4,000 in Near Future," *CT*, May 29, 1931; "Sees Future Homes Bought Like Autos," *NYT*, May 25, 1932.

66. On Europe, see "The House of the Future as Science Now Visions It" (on Le Corbusier), *NYT*, June 7, 1931; "Visions of the House of the Future" (on garden apartments in Kassel, Germany, by Otto Haesler), *NYT*, July 9, 1932.

67. A reporter in the *CT* found the 1933 fair's "House of Tomorrow" "freaky" (Burns Mantle, "Critic Finds Drama at a Century of Progress," *CT*, August 12, 1933).

68. *NYT*, March 14, 1939.

69. *NYT*, March 14, April 16, and May 28, 1939.

70. See also Bletter et al., *Remembering the Future*.

71. See, for example, "House Wonderful: A Glimpse of Things to Come," *LAT*, October 17, 1943; "Preview of Tomorrow's House," *LAT*, May 6, 1946; "Architect Views House of the Future," *NYT*, May 30, 1943.

72. Published in *House Beautiful*, May 1946, and in *Architectural Forum*, March 1947, and illustrated by the glossy images created by the leading architectural photographer Maynard Parker.

73. "Laboratory to Test Your New Housing Preferences," *CT*, September 13, 1958.

74. A scholarly study of the home shows is sadly lacking. In "Making the Modified Modern," David Smiley discusses the New York Modern Homes Exposition of 1946, and an important series of department store shows.

75. For example, Mennel, "Miracle House Hoop-La." For a useful overview of wartime debates about future architecture and planning, especially among manufacturers and leading architects, see Shanken, *194X*.

76. On the collaboration of builders and manufacturers, see Harris's excellent *Building a Market*.

77. *Better Homes and Gardens* was $0.25 per issue in 1949, a price that translates to $2.29 in 2010 dollars. See also chapter 5, on *Life* magazine.

78. Except, perhaps, for the possible influence of Disneyland and some Disney movies, discussed in later chapters.

79. Newspapers, of course, have their own problems as source material for the historian. Information in advertisements is often inflated and inaccurate. News stories are based on what someone tells the reporter just as often as they are based on actual observation or recorded data. As a result, all factual statements in newspapers have to be interpreted with a certain skepticism, and when possible confirmed from other sources. Nevertheless, if one is trying to assess what was actually built, or at what cost, or what the builders and buyers thought about it, newspaper accounts provide greater certainty than anything but original records—building permits, sales contracts, speeches, interviews, photographs—that were produced at the time. For postwar tract houses, these latter records are all too often absent.

80. See, inter alia, Walker, *Shaping Our Mothers' World*.

Chapter 2: West Coast Builders

1. Gottman, *Megalopolis*, introduced the term "megalopolis" into urban analysis. Gottman meant a conurbation formed out of older urban centers by the forces of modern transportation systems into a relatively cohesive urbanized whole. He applied the concept not only to the eastern seaboard but also to the Chicago area and to the California coast from San Francisco to San Diego. I am using it in a somewhat more restricted sense, to characterize the multiple and diverse settlements in and around Los Angeles in the later twentieth century.

2. Oil was discovered in 1892. By 1923 the region was producing one-quarter of the world's total supply.

3. Fishman, *Bourgeois Utopias*, 156.

4. Except for Reyner Banham's brilliant *Los Angeles*.

5. "History of National Association of Home Builders," appendix IV, 36–39.

6. Ibid., 22 and passim. See also the excellent biography by Keane, *Fritz B. Burns*, 93.

7. *American Builder and Building Age* (Chicago, Simmons-Boardman, 1930–48, later titled *American Builder and Marketing*, 1948–69) was strongly influenced by the NAHB leadership and by the NAHB's own publications.

8. "Toluca Wood" sales brochure in the Fritz Burns Papers at Loyola Marymount University says 1,300.

9. "Toluca Wood" sales brochure mentions some others: Riverside Ranchos, 500 homes; Torrance Terrace, 150 units in "double bungalows"; Burbank Gardens, 200 units in double houses; Alameda Gardens, double bungalows (no number); Parkside Gardens, 150 units in four-family buildings; "in the new Westchester district, 600 homes to date"; and in "Westchester Project over 1000 homes to date." So the sales brochure was probably published in 1945 or 1946.

10. Panorama City 1947–52; first houses 1948; total 800 acres. Total houses, 2,999; total built by Burns/Kaiser, 2,175. Total houses in tracts Welton Becket designed, 1,246.

11. According to the Marlow memoir described by Keane, *Fritz B. Burns*, Fred Marlow bought a house at Windsor Hills.

12. In 1943. See Keane, *Fritz B. Burns*, 104.

13. J. Paul Campbell, associate builder; Howard Hunter Clayton, "designer." Clayton was an artist.

14. Advertisements, sales brochures, clippings on Toluca Wood, Fritz Burns Papers.

15. Hise, *Magnetic Los Angeles*, 140.

16. Californian, Cape Cod, American farmhouse, suburban, colonial, and modern at Westside; Toluca added a "rancho" model, as did Westchester I.

17. The two-bedroom plan contained 888 square feet of living space and a two-car garage that Burns's market research had indicated was a priority to buyers. Hise, *Magnetic Los Angeles*; Cuff, *Provisional City*; and Keane, *Fritz B. Burns*, think that the Westside Village plan was permanent, but at least half of the houses in Panorama City used a different plan. See n. 10 above.

18. Burns, *Livable Homes*, 3.

19. Ibid.; pamphlets and sales brochures in Burns Papers.

20. Keane, *Fritz B. Burns*.

21. This was 1941. Douglas Aircraft, next to Long Beach Municipal Airport, employed 43,000 (half women) by 1942. The company laid off "all but 1200" in late 1946. But it still built airplanes. See Hise, *Magnetic Los Angeles*; Keane, *Fritz B. Burns*. Cuff, *Provisional City*, 249, mentions other aircraft factories: Douglas, Hughes, Northrup, and North American.

22. The ads show grass strips too, but they do not appear in contemporary photographs. City planning agencies were growing in power and influence at this time; this may have played a part in shaping new streetscapes. See Keane, *Fritz B. Burns*; Hise, *Magnetic Los Angeles*.

23. Burns owned about one-fourth of the total of Westchester, and was one of four developers. Westchester had an overall plan by Frank Ayers, with a central business district, but no overall plan for community services, including schools. Cuff, *Provisional City*, says that the total of all developments was 3,000 acres.

24. Including Westchester I. It is clear that they subcontracted out much of the building on their land. On aircraft manufacturing, see Cuff, *Provisional City*, 249; Hise, *Magnetic Los Angeles*. Keane, *Fritz B. Burns*, 131, seems to suggest that KCH may have produced 3,000 units at Westchester II, but actually documents only 1,295 in this section of Westchester. My total of 2,500 dwellings is an estimate.

25. Foster, *Henry J. Kaiser*, 5, says that Kaiser was a serious possibility as FDR's running mate in 1944.

26. Ibid., 9: "Kaiser's war-time housing projects in Portland and Richmond drew complaints which might be expected for temporary facilities. However, by building several hospitals and day-care centers, and by offering prepaid health insurance, Kaiser demonstrated more than the usual commitment to the communities he served and to his workers as individuals."

27. Crawford, "Daily Life," 90–143.

28. Keane, *Fritz B. Burns*, 18.

29. "Kaiser to Build Homes at Low Cost," *NYT*, May 10, 1945. Press conference at San Francisco describes Kaiser's Westchester plans in partnership with Fritz B. Burns, "permanent honorary president of the NAHB." Kaiser planned, it was said, a total of 10,000 homes at a cost of under $5,000, partially prefabricated, with solar heating "where adaptable." See also December 8, 1944, "Kaiser aims to cut costs of housing." Speech at National Committee on Housing in NY.

30. Westchester, of course, had an overall plan, by Frank Ayers, and a CBD, but Burns hadn't been involved in the planning, and his houses (in both sections) were only part of the whole.

31. Hise and Keane say 1950, but it was probably earlier, since development was already going on below Roscoe by Diller & Weber early in 1949. The Kaiser-Burns work below Roscoe started February 11, 1950. Richard S. Diller and Arthur B. Weber specialized in "building and community development" according to *LAT*, September 28, 1947. They were active in the area for fifteen years, having built about 6,000 houses "in the Los Angeles region" by 1947. Burns was friendly with them.

32. Keane, *Fritz B. Burns*, 147.

33. Ibid., 158–59; Kaiser, *Panorama City Shopping Center*. "Virtual downtown" confirmed by Mrs. Jerry Pollack, interview, April 15, 2006.

34. Keane, *Fritz B. Burns*, 250n31. Several of the early residents interviewed by newsman David Colker contradicted this assertion, however: David Colker, "Building a 'Future' in 1948: A Riddle and a Single House Launched 'American Way of Life' in Panorama City," *LAT*, September 4, 1999.

35. Hise, *Magnetic Los Angeles*, 197–200.

36. My plan differs from the one published by the LCPC because it is based on the tract maps created by local planning officials, which show the full development of the settlement. These tract maps, used in Los Angeles and Orange Counties, are legal documents, signed by local officials and by the builder and surveyor at the time that permission is given for building. They differ from subdivision plans in the rest of the United States because they are of a more or less standard size, and do not cover all of a new community. Tract maps are not, in other words, "master plans." Within Panorama City, there were eleven tract maps north of Roscoe and seven south of Roscoe. All the Panorama City tract maps are dated 1948–50, except for one in the extreme northwest, developed by Western Products Corporation, 1953–54.

37. "Construction of Kaiser Foundation Hospital Begins," *LAT*, November 14, 1959.

38. Continuous street arrangements above and below Roscoe are clear evidence of a preexisting plan.

39. The Engineering Service Corporation also planned Lakewood, with J. R. Newville as engineer.

40. Keane, *Fritz B. Burns*, 149–50.

41. See chapter 1.

42. Frank Sharp, for example, and David Bohannon.

43. *LAT*, January 23, 1949.

44. For solving a riddle, see David Colker, "Building a Future"; Keane, *Fritz B. Burns*, 152–54, for details.

45. *LAT*, May 14, 1949, April 10, 1949. Welton Becket was a member of Wurdeman and Becket, the firm that had designed Burns's "Research House" in 1946.

46. *LAT*, March 3, 1946, and discussion above in chapter 1.

47. Ads always said KCH "in collaboration with" Wurdeman and Becket. Becket did other models too, such as the "New Englander," with two baths and elaborate built-in elements, including a radio and sound system, which may have inspired the Levitts' version at Levittown, PA.

48. Original drawings lent by Welton Macdonald Becket.

49. *LAT*, June 5, 1949.

50. The successful proposal made to the National Register of Historic Places in 2002 states that the foundations of the houses were sunk into the ground, but I do not see any evidence of that in the Welton Becket drawings. See California Department of Parks and Recreation, Historic Resources Group, "Panorama City Historic District"; Welton Macdonald Becket correspondence.

51. "Fritz Burns' 500 New Homes," 84–85, remarks on the long, low look. Ceiling height goes from seven to nine feet at the peak. See also for plan, construction.

52. *LAT*, December 8, 1948.

53. Keane, *Fritz B. Burns*. Also Hise, *Magnetic Los Angeles*; Cuff, *Provisional City*. But note that Hise sees Westside Village ca. 1939 as the beginning of "mass building" techniques (140–41).

54. *NYT*, January 26, 1941: Texas Ranch House style on LI, Flower Hill Estates for George Bangs Sr. from plans by Moore & Hutchins, architects. Two bedrooms, laundry room, dining room, maid's room; U-shaped; *NYT*, July 5, 1942, rambling ranch house style, Walter Uhl builder, Flower Hill Estates. Chicago: *CT*, October 27, 1944, display ad: "Your Post-war, one-floor, colonial ranch house"; Timken ad, October 29, 1944, "Modern Ranch House for Postwar Planners"; January 28, 1945, same title and illustration, but with radiant heat; June 24, 1945, lumber ad for "Rambling Ranch House"; November 2, 1947, big ranch style development in Deerfield (colonial exterior, rambling).

55. At Toluca Wood, ca. 1941, and Westchester, ca. 1942. See Cuff, *Provisional City*, book and letter to author, June 20, 2009. Also Keane, *Fritz B. Burns*. Westside Village ca. 1939 introduced the plan that Burns continued with at Toluca Wood and Westchester, and also introduced the form of large-scale production that he continued. See Hise, *Magnetic Los Angeles*, 140–41.

56. Midwestern investors were especially active in buying up all or parts of the old ranchos. See *CT*, November 21, 2009, October 21, 2006, and "Chicagoans Buy Bartlett Ranch, World's Finest," *CT*, May 21, 1922. (The Bartlett Ranch was in New Mexico, a cattle ranch but equipped for "sportsmen" from 1901.)

57. "Dude Ranches Preparing for a Busy Season," *CT*, October 22, 1944.

58. See, for example, "Homes for Vets Built on Acres Near La Grange," *CT*, April 21, 1946, reinforced concrete houses; "Modern Ranch House for Postwar Planners" (Timken heating ad for radiant heat; see also other Timken ads), *CT*, January 28, 1945; lumber company ad, "Plan Your Home Now: 4 Room Rambling Ranch House," June 24, 1945.

59. January 27, 1946.

60. Connally, "Cape Cod House."

61. On Adobe traditions, see among others Spears, *American Adobes*; Stewart, *Arizona Ranch Houses*. Bungalows were initially a low-cost form of dwelling, but over time, as they were elaborated by designers inspired by the Arts and Crafts movement, they came to be attractive to the affluent as well, and to inspire prominent architects like Greene and Greene. Now, bungalows are beginning to find a place in some studies of American "high architecture." See, for example, Winter, *California Bungalow*.

62. See chapter 5, figs. 206, 207, 208.

63. Sexton, "Small House in Warm Climates." See also the *Life* house 1938, Ramsey House, by Richard Koch, with combination kitchen/dining room, and attached garage.

64. Hutchison, "Building for Babbitt."

65. See, for example, "Rurban Homes Project" and Architectural Forum, *The 1938 Book of Small Houses*, 186–87 (Jersey Homesteads, Hightstown, NJ) and 174–75 (Gardendale Homesteads, AL); these are tract house look-alikes on concrete slabs, built of cinderblock at Hightstown and rammed earth at Gardendale. The El Monte group of houses was not a cooperative venture, but the group on the East Coast was. The settlement at Hightstown was populated by Jewish garment workers and centered around a clothing factory. The planning was related to that of Greenbelt, MD. Both the factory and the cooperative

farm failed, but the town became an artists' resort in the forties and fifties. It has now been renamed Roosevelt, NJ, and has gained Historic Register placement. Not all the Resettlement Administration houses were one-story—quite a few two-story houses are shown in *The 1938 Book of Small Houses*.

66. Garlinghouse, *New American House*, nos. 84, 1754. Not yet described as ranch.

67. Aladdin catalogs are online: Clarke Historical Library and Central Michigan University, Aladdin Company Annual Sales Catalogs, http://clarke.cmich.edu/resource_tab/aladdin _company_of_bay_city/annual_sales_catalogs/annual_sales _catalogs_index.html (accessed September 13, 2012) (1939 and 1941 had more one-and-a-half-story houses than 1940; 1939 had quite a few two-story houses also).

68. Oak Ridge, with its many temporary dwelling units, "victory cottages," and especially the Cemesto House of 1941, provided some prototypes of concrete slab construction with new materials, but there has been no thorough general study of defense housing.

69. See Longstreth, "Levitts, Mass-Produced Houses," nn31–32. See also Rodney, "Oakdale Farms"; Mason, "Levitt and Sons of Virginia"; Schlegel, *Conscripted City*.

70. The Levittown, PA, models were developed and displayed in December 1951. See also the houses published in *American Builder*, March 1949, 78–81, but not yet executed then.

71. 1927, Gregory Farm House; 1931, Voss House; 1935, Butler House; 1936, George Pope House.

72. Royal Barry Wills, 1895–1962. See Leon Keach, "Architect and the House." In collaboration with the young Hugh Stubbins, Wills also built some assertively "modernist" houses near Boston (ibid., 73, 79).

73. For example, Wills, *Houses for Good Living* and *Better Houses for Budgeteers*.

74. For examples through 1945, see Henry Russell Hitchcock, *Frank Lloyd Wright*, and *In the Nature of Materials*; Frank Lloyd Wright, *Modern Architecture* (1931), *Autobiography* (1932), "Broadacre City" (1932), *Taliesin Fellowship* (1934), *Broadacre City* (1935), *Organic Architecture* (1939), *When Democracy Builds* (1945); "Usonian Architect," *Time*, January 17, 1938 (Frank Lloyd Wright on cover); Lewis Mumford, *Reflections on Modern Architecture*. Wright's early house designs were published already in the *Ladies Home Journal* in 1901 and 1907.

75. As opposed to its earlier volumes on small houses, which had included many examples of the type, but not the name.

76. Interestingly, though, there is no mention of the ranch in Koues, *Encyclopedia of Decorating*, and a section titled "Built in California" (891–92) has no resemblance to ranches.

77. On the Philadelphia project, see "Avondale Knowles," broadsheet filed under Miscellaneous, 1947–48, box 77, Office of the Dean Records, School of Design, UPB 8.4, University Archives and Records Center, University of Pennsylvania, and lent to the author by J. M. Duffin.

78. *Washington Post*, June 23, 1949.

79. Editorial staff of *Sunset* magazine in collaboration with May, *Sunset Western Ranch Houses*. On initial sales, see Penick, "Pace Setter Houses," chapter 3, note 14.

80. See among others Bricker, "Built for Sale"; Gallegos, "Cliff May"; Gregory, *Cliff May*. The recent exhibition on May at the Art, Design & Architecture Museum of UC Santa Barbara, February–June 2012, has sorted out many unanswered questions. See Gibbs et al., *Carefree California*. I wish to thank Jocelyn Gibbs and Caitlin Lempres Brostrom for helping me to identify which of May's illustrations are houses by Wurster. See also Brostrom and Peters, *Houses of William Wurster*.

81. Note that the 1958 *Western Ranch Houses by Cliff May* was not a "second edition" of the first, as the publishers of a facsimile have claimed. It was devoted almost exclusively to Cliff May's buildings *after* 1946. It was only after the publication of the first book that May began to win major commissions.

82. Gallegos, "Cliff May." He must have obtained a building contractor's license. See also Gregory, *Cliff May*. The Cliff May Home registry lists about a dozen custom houses in the thirties: http://www.cliffmayregistry.com/results.php.

83. An advertisement of December 1953 in *House and Home* magazine shows distributors of the system, located in thirteen western and southwestern states. Illustrated in Papineau, "Carefree Californian," 187. The prefabrication system was sometimes called "the magic money house," and sometimes "Quick Delivery Systems." The May-Choate partnership dissolved in 1957 (ibid., 190). According to Papineau, ibid., the May-Choate ranch house kits sold between eighteen and twenty thousand dwellings. Choate was the principal designer of this prefabrication system: see Papineau to the author, January 16, 2014, and the section on Ross Cortese and Rossmoor in chapter 2.

84. Note that *Sunset Western Ranch Houses* does not specifically identify either Wurster or May houses; I am depending on the acknowledgments section at the end, which gives people as sources, and on the advice of Wurster scholars. Other designers (besides May and Wurster) appear in the acknowledgments too, but none have many images.

85. May, *Sunset Western Ranch Houses*, 27, 51, 24.

86. On May's more elaborate houses of the fifties and later, see Gibbs et al., *Carefree California*; Gregory, *Cliff May*; and Penick, "The Pace Setter Houses." In the fifties, *House and Home*, *House Beautiful*, *House and Garden*, *Architectural Record*, and *Architectural Forum* often published his designs. From the forties on, May's work was often photographed by the brilliant architectural photographer Maynard Parker (the Ezra Stoller of the Southwest), who was also affiliated with *House Beautiful*. The Huntington Library in San Marino possesses the Maynard Parker collection of negatives, most of which can be accessed online.

87. In contemporary advertisements in *LAT*, all the Kaiser/Burns houses were marketed as "Homes for the Thrifty," with a price of $9,195 in 1948 and $9,950 in 1949.

88. "Kaiser Home Draws Crowds," *LAT*, June 12, 1949; "Panorama City Plans Display," *LAT*, August 28, 1949.

89. [John Normile,] "October Five Star Home," *Better Homes and Gardens* 28, no. 2 (October 1949): 37–41, 238–40.

90. The Levitts, in particular, would have known Burns's work. Their lumber mill and nail factory was established at Blue Lake, CA, prior to 1948 (according to Matarese), and Bill Levitt got to know Fritz Burns briefly when working for the NAHB. For their familiarity, see also Longstreth, "Levitts, Mass-Produced Houses," note 26, which shows it by 1950. At some point, they also knew Cliff May's books and/or work: see Harris, *Second Suburb*, note 51, quoting William Levitt letter of March 18, 1957, to Cliff May, in the tone of a familiar.

91. *LAT*, June 5, 1949, reports exposed heavy beams and grooved wood ceiling planks, tongue-and-groove planks of Douglas fir on ceiling throughout. *LAT*, December 8, 1948, says hardwood floors, inlaid linoleum in kitchen and bath, "floor-to-ceiling storage walls." Formica or stainless steel countertops, built-in vanities with plate glass mirrors, double sinks with chromium fixtures, closet space galore. *Better Homes and Gardens* had a circulation of about 2.5 million in 1949. This is rather small in comparison to the prevalence of popular home decorating magazines later in the century (ca. 8 million in 2010), but it would still have been visible to many people at newsstands and libraries. On the importance of popular magazines for buyers' tastes, see chapter 5.

92. All these features of the exhibition house were relatively expensive. In the present day, it is impossible to be sure how many of the houses in Panorama City were built according to this model, since so many of the houses have been remodeled since their original construction.

93. Prices vary a lot in the ads. *Better Homes and Gardens* says about $8,000, as does *LAT*, September 10, 1949, but

August 14, 1949, says an average price of $9,950, and 1948, though not for this model, a range from $8,950 to $9,295 ($82,000–85,160 in 2010 dollars).

94. It is amusing, if confusing, to note that the building usually believed to be "Ramona's Marriage Place" was the home of one of Cliff May's grandparents. This was the Casa Estudillo, an adobe structure of 1827. By 1910 the Casa Estudillo had been turned into a museum for Ramona tourists, according to DeLyser, *Ramona Memories*, 102–7. May illustrated the Casa Estudillo in *Sunset Western Ranch Houses* of 1946, 12, but made no reference to the Ramona myth. In contrast, the brief historical introduction to *Western Ranch Houses by Cliff May* of 1958 includes long quotations from Helen Hunt Jackson's *Ramona*. By 1958, then, May was building on the popularity of Fritz Burns's house at Panorama City.

95. DeLyser, *Ramona Memories*, 165–67: 1910 (D. W. Griffith with Mary Pickford), 1916 (Clune Studios), 1927–28 (with Dolores Del Rio), 1936 (in Technicolor, with Loretta Young and Don Ameche), 1946 (Spanish-language version).

96. Or maybe not. According to Keane, *Fritz B. Burns*, it was precisely at Panorama City that Burns began to relax his earlier discriminatory policies.

97. Opened 1940, many new attractions 1950. The Orange County–Los Angeles County boundary was created in 1889.

98. From 216,000 in 1950 to 704,000 in 1960 and to 1,420,000 in 1970 (1,932,000 in 1980).

99. *LAT* ads and OC tract maps. Ivan Wells and Sons, Ed Krist, Charles Godbey, A. L. Gindling, William Malat, and William L. Lyon appeared on the Orange County tract maps at this time.

100. Rancho La Palma, 1954, $10,350–11,900; Lucky Western Ranchos, 1955, $12,000; Circle Arrow, 1956, $13,875.

101. Findlay, "Disneyland: The Happiest Place on Earth," in *Magic Lands*, 56–116.

102. Most of the biographical information below is derived from interviews with Jean Vandruff and letters from him. But see also his online autobiography: "An Eventful Autobiography," http://jean.vandruff.com/autobiography.html (accessed August 1, 2008, and March 19, 2012).

103. Vandruff's father was a tenant farmer near Hominy, OK, earlier a "cattle-man" in Kansas and New Mexico (letter of March 21, 2012, and autobiography). His mother taught in a one-room schoolhouse in Pawnee County, OK. As far as he knows, his father and mother were native to the Southwest, but their families were originally from Scotland, Ireland, and the Netherlands.

104. The first tract, of 168 houses, stretched from West Ball Road to West Stonybrook Drive and from South Beach Boulevard to South Dale Avenue. The second tract, of 435 houses, stretched from Western Avenue almost to Knott Avenue and from "a couple of blocks" below Cerritos Avenue almost to Orange Avenue. The third tract, of 266 houses, ran from West Orange Avenue through West Stonybrook Drive and from South Magnolia Avenue to South Brenwyn Drive. I have verified the boundaries of the first tract in Orange County tract maps; the descriptions of the other two are from correspondence with Jean Vandruff.

105. "Modified" in the sense that most of the interior streets were cul-de-sacs.

106. Vandruff, letter to the author.

107. Begun in 1945, by 1956 the home show had become a very important event locally: in 1956 it was days long, and was visited by 200,000 people (*LAT*, June 24, 1956). Two model homes and a huge amount of household equipment were displayed.

108. "Color Psychologists Consulted," *LAT*, May 13, 1956: "Color combinations good results shown." See also Vandruff, Cinderella Estates sales brochure (fig. 80).

109. *LAT*, May 6, 1956.

110. See also the study for the dwarf cottage in *Snow White* (1937), published in *Once upon a Time*, 227.

111. Compare the "theme song" of the movie: "A dream is a wish your heart makes / When you're fast asleep / In dreams you will lose your heartaches / Whatever you wish for you keep / [Have faith] in your dreams and someday / Your rainbow will come smiling through." Quoted from http://www.lyricstop.com/albums/disneymania4/adreamisawishyourheartmakes-disneychannelstars.html (accessed April 22, 2010).

112. Mason, *History of Housing*. Mason was an architect and builder, and thus a participant in the events he described, and an admirer of the ranch house as built by Cliff May and David Bohannon. But despite its age and biases, Mason's book remains the most complete account of housing in the fifties and sixties.

113. Other Cinderella "look-alikes" included Sun Ray houses at South Hills Heights (*LAT*, July 24, 1960), Skylark Homes by Tietz Construction Company (*LAT*, April 20, 1958 [with a gable almost to the ground], and August 31, 1958), and South Hills Heights (not in Anaheim) by Sun Ray (*LAT*, July 24, 1960), with a gable down to the ground.

114. Los Alamitos History Project, timeline, http://www.localsports.biz/history/timeline1950s. Accessed May 12, 2010, and *LAT*, May 12, 1957. Much of the material in the website also appears in a book by the website founder; see Strawther, *Los Alamitos & Rossmoor*.

115. Rossmoor Way was the original main thoroughfare; it contained a mix of styles.

116. Findlay, *Magic Lands*, 51–55.

117. Cortese had close relationships with the Disney design studios through his wife and brother-in-law. See below, note 142.

118. Heidi Cortese documents, sales brochure with a color version of Salem on outside. Other quite bizarre roof shapes in the first section appear in the sales brochure lent by Granger Riach, real estate agent and long-term resident of Rossmoor. See especially the "Georgetown" and the "Pennsylvania."

119. The "Golden Estate" received a design merit award from the NAHB in 1959.

120. Images from the builder's sales brochures, courtesy Granger Riach, Granger Group Realty, Long Beach, CA. There are ten basic models and thirty exteriors among Riach's copies of sales brochures.

121. See dimensions on Orange County tract map 3189-TR005400. At 12181 Ballantine Drive, for example, side yards were about 7.5 feet, giving 15 feet between houses. Front and back yards totaled about 47 feet; the result was a backyard of about 24 feet and front yard of about 12 feet (including the grass strip and sidewalk). House sizes varied: the "Cornell," for example, was 1,440–1,568 square feet.

122. Exceptions: the Farm House, Hamilton, Bostonian, and Princeton models have a continuous family room and kitchen but no dining room; the Georgetown, Providence, and Wardlow have no family room. In some models, the family room was convertible to an additional bedroom.

123. *LAT*, March 16, 1958.

124. Only one model, the Williamsburg, had two stories. It did not sell well, according to Granger Riach, who is a long-term resident.

125. Betty Furness, 1916–94, actress and television personality, affiliated with Westinghouse 1948–60 as "Miss Westinghouse," demonstrated appliances on TV, was famous for, among other things, singing the advertising jingle "You can be sure, sure, sure if it's Westinghouse," and was later a television commentator on consumer issues. Furness was featured in the ads for Frematic Houses a little earlier.

126. One could also choose a wall-mounted refrigerator (optional, "available for the first time anywhere" according to *LAT*, January 6, 1957). On the colors, see my interview with Mrs. OC.

127. Los Alamitos History Project, Rossmoor: Timeline January 22, 1959—Enterprise, 3.

128. Information about construction is very scarce. It is possible that some of the houses employed the prefabricated wall systems developed by Chris Choate and Cliff May and used by them and Cortese at Lakewood Rancho Estates. Cortese probably used such a panel system at Leisure World: see *Mindextra*, supplement to *Minifax*, a quarterly published by the Marketing Information Network, New York, ca. 1964 (copy lent by Heidi Cortese), 3.

129. Engineers were Boyle Engineers of Santa Ana. The later hospital was not built. The Mitchell plan ("Proposed Development Plan for Rossmoor Subdivision, County of Orange—California") is very close to the actual street plan as it shows up on Google Maps. There are a few more almost through roads on the latter, but not many. The Mitchell plan appears on page 5 of the "Rossmoor Shopping Center" booklet in the HC papers, which includes a layout for the shopping center dated January 13, 1959, and an aerial view of development July 31, 1958. See also plan shown in *LAT*, June 26, 1960, which, however, does not have most of the eventual bottom third.

130. Heidi Cortese interview, May 10, 2010.

131. Kendrick, HC interview.

132. Los Alamitos History Project, Rossmoor: Timeline says 1951, but this may have been when he acquired land, not when he was associated with May and Choate.

133. Sales brochure of 1954, which lists participants as follows: architect, Chris Choate; designer, Cliff May; subdivider and builder, Ross W. Cortese; sales agents, Walker and Lee, Inc. (7). "Built for You, a Modern Western Family" (sales brochure). "Over 36 different elevations." Two basic floor plans: 1,112 square feet and 1,341 square feet, three and four bedrooms, each with two baths. Advertising played on the proximity to Lakewood, but the subdivision was not part of Lakewood.

134. Papineau, "Carefree Californian," 181–91. Papineau has found documents in the Cliff May Papers (Architecture and Design Collection, Art, Design & Architecture Museum, University of California, Santa Barbara) that show that Choate was the designer. See especially a letter of Al DeWeese to Leon Brown: "Chris Choate developed the structural system and designed the houses, while Cliff May promoted the system and sold the houses." DeWeese was an officer of the Ranch House Supply Corporation, which marketed the houses. My thanks to Katherine Papineau for furnishing me with a copy of DeWeese's words, and for helping me interpret them. Choate's career is not yet very fully understood. I have supplemented Papineau's essay with interviews with Peter Choate, Chris's son (August 10, 2010), and with his granddaughter Courtney Moritz (August 31, 2010), with notations in the sales brochure on Rossmoor (which link Choate and Frematic) lent to me by Granger Riach, and with scattered references in the Los Angeles newspapers.

For the appearance of the panel system, see the rendering in Gibbs et al., *Carefree California*, 191. Some of the vertical members (battens) seem to indicate the joints of the panels.

135. See especially *LAT*, March 11, 1956, August 19, 1956.

136. *LAT*, February 19, 1956. Working with Jones was Benjamin P. Urmston.

137. The Irvine Company had bought the property from the estate of the Fred Bixby Ranch Company in 1947. Sales agents were Walker and Lee; financing was by John D. Engle, Edward Mushfield (Insurance Funds Mortgage Co.), and Emmert H. Sink (California Bank) (*LAT*, September 16, 1956).

138. Originally conceived as a "second Rossmoor," but then Cortese changed his mind and decided to build retirement communities. See the proposal for Memorial Hospital, HC documents. For the Leisure Worlds, see Lasner, *High Life*, and for his comments on Cortese, 274–77.

139. For the panel system at Leisure World, see the circular on Cortese panel systems ca. 1960, HC documents: *Mindextra*, supplement to *Minifax*, 3.

140. Most of the models in the Rossmoor sales brochure identify Frematic Homes, Inc., as the copyright holder. Several of those identified with Frematic in this way also say "designed by Chris Choate architect and Robert G. Jones" (Brittany Gardens, Canterbury House, El Camino, and El Dorado). See Rossmoor plans, Riach copies of sales brochures. Bob Jones was described to me by Peter Choate as an assistant in Chris Choate's office, and as a participant in the building of Leisure World.

141. Choate had been deeply involved in low-cost workers' housing before the war; this concern continued in his designs for the May-Choate panel system. He was well known as an illustrator, and at some point taught at UCLA. During the Depression, he designed sets for MGM, including that for *Gone with the Wind* (1939) (see *Spokesman Review*, May 13, 1956, http://news.google.com/newspapers?nid=1314&dat=19560513&id=H2spAAAAI-BAJ&sjid=wuYDAAAAIBAJ&pg=3756,1165715).

142. Heidi Cortese interview. Alona's brother, Armor Goetten, became a set director for Disney. Alona and her other siblings performed in a number of Hollywood films.

143. The area around E. Palestine, OH, contains many barns with elaborate and striking designs.

Chapter 3: East Coast Builders

1. Philadelphia suburbs dated back to the 1850s; the development of the Main Line began in the 1880s.

2. The city and county of Philadelphia were made coterminous in 1854. The MSA population in 1950, 2,071,605, was second only to those of New York and Chicago. Delaware County grew in population from about 300,000 in 1940 to about 600,000 in 1960. See Espie, Findley, and Walden, "Pennsylvania Suburbs Population," "extrapolations," 7. The Marple Township population was 1,553 in 1930, 2,170 in 1940, 4,770 in 1950, 19,722 in 1960.

3. See Baltzell, *Philadelphia Gentlemen*.

4. There were exceptions: some of the old Main Line suburbs were developed by builders, with local financing. Wayne is a principal example. On growth patterns in the Philadelphia area between 1940 and 1970, see Leigh and Lee, "Philadelphia's Space in Between," 16, referring to the Neighborhood Change Data Base produced by GeoLytics: http://www.geolytics.com/USCensus,Neighborhood-Change-Database-1970-2000,Products.asp.

5. Construction of Interstate 95 began in 1958, but was agonizingly slow, not finishing until the 1980s.

6. Warner, *Private City*, 209.

7. Leigh and Lee, "Philadelphia's Space in Between"; Mathis, *Marple and Newtown Townships*.

8. Interviews with Lee Gershenfeld, township zoning officer, and Don Urbano, a cousin.

9. Lee Gershenfeld, Marple zoning officer, multiple interviews; family stories. Of course, there were important modernist houses in Los Angeles, built on hillsides, that could have provided inspiration for the split-level type. The most obvious of these is Richard Neutra's Lovell House of 1927–29. But it seems unlikely that Bodek would have liked the very austere design of such houses.

10. Bowden, "Suburbia at 50," a six-part series on Marple Township, February 9–14, 1997. This is a particularly useful series, based on local interviews. Bowden also interviewed Facciolo himself several times.

11. It was called the Trent Construction Co. and was succeeded by the Saxony Construction Co. William F. Barrett was formerly with Sclufer Construction. See *Philadelphia Evening Bulletin*, July 3, 1960 (Temple Urban Archives), and *Chester Times*, May 27, 1953 (first mention), which refer to the firm and link it with Saxony Construction Co.

12. Bowden: total was 400 acres (according to Lee Gershenfeld, Facciolo and Barrett owned it all, but assembled it over time), most of which were in the Broomall area of Marple Township, about eight miles northwest of Clifton Heights (and not far from Villanova University). The local township officer says that financing was aided by Facciolo's family contacts, through their construction businesses.

13. *Delaware County Daily Times*, October 2, 1949: Atwater Kent Properties Auction ad; 1,200 acres in parcels of a half acre or more; auction was October 25–27, 1949. Foxcroft and Woodcroft: 600 acres in the southern Bryn Mawr area, 450 acres on Sproul Road south of West Chester Pike, 145 acres in Edgmont and Radnor Hunt country.

14. The name may have been borrowed from the slang term often used for World War II aircraft carriers.

15. This may have been the dairy farm established by Allen McClullough, a Scottish immigrant, in the 1870s. Damon Engineers has a survey (Allen McClullough, Springfield Road, August 13, 1925). Media courthouse has a proposed subdivision for Springfield Road and Coopertown Road, which abuts a park (24-153-52, Allendale Farms #1, Robert C. Fallon), and a Rose Tree Woods plan of lots dated 1954 (24-656-55, Allendale Farms #3, South of Highland Avenue, West of Sproul Road).

16. *Chester Times*, June 16, 1954; the third section of Allendale Farms was south of Highland and west of Sproul, according to *Chester Times*, March 16, 1955. On Barrett and Facciolo's splits, see also Daniel F. O'Leary, "Community at Broomall Continues to Grow," *Philadelphia Evening Bulletin*, July 3, 1960—clipping from Temple Urban Archives.

17. According to Bowden, Facciolo sold his last house in 1960, but it is not clear if this pertains only to Rose Tree Woods.

18. Setbacks varied from 30 to 50 feet; lot depth was from 150 to 190 feet. Lot sizes also varied a good deal. A typical lot from the Rose Tree Woods plan of lots in 1951 was 188 by 72 feet.

19. Interview, Mrs. MH.

20. *Chester Times*, April 22, 1950, 8, which says fifty houses in the development would be finished by July.

21. Ibid. But $14,000, *Philadelphia Inquirer*, October 8, 1950, and $14,750, *Philadelphia Inquirer*, May 6, 1951. One-story ranch houses were already being built in the Philadelphia area: see *Philadelphia Inquirer*, Lawrence Hill Corp. ads, September 17, 1950, and October 8, 1950.

22. I have not been able to find out anything about David Scott.

23. Burns and Becket used it in the "research house" of 1946, but only in the patio. Some of the Eichler tract houses used it in the fifties, but for the most part it was restricted to expensive, custom-designed houses.

24. Only one unit in the first cluster of the four planned cluster units was built. The project was surrounded by public controversy, widely reported, over a period of several years. Facciolo must have known about it.

25. Bowden, "Suburbia at 50."

26. Ibid.

27. Interview with Don Urbano.

28. Quoted in "Economic Discrimination, Obsolete Zoning, Old Building Techniques Contribute to Housing Mess," editorial, *Delaware County Daily Times*, November 28, 1969. The original Marple zoning ordinance of 1938 went through many modifications, beginning in 1959.

29. Gordon Bodek, 1920–2010, class of 1942, donor and member of Board of Overseers.

30. Olympia (Olympic Homes), Richland Park, Windsor Village, Llanwellyn Gardens (Folcroft, garden apartments), Overbrook Park, Saxony Village.

31. Interiors had some "colonial" detailing too: relatively complex moldings, chair rails, and the like. Dave Damon's wife remembers them as having a much more retrograde aesthetic than the Lawrence Park houses.

32. Bill Lawrence, William W. Lawrence, and Adele Mocerino, "The History of Marple and Newtown," *Broomall and Newtown Square (PA) County Leader*, February 21, 1957.

33. *Broomall and Newtown Square (PA) County Leader*, February 21, 1957, sec. 3, 1ff.

34. The architect was Joseph L. Bannett, who prepared "basic" plans of models to be repeated. There is practically no later information on Bannett: one record in PAB (Philadelphia Architects and Buildings, part of the American Architects and Buildings database) for 1959 shows some row houses on Packer Avenue in Philadelphia.

35. Formica work tops, cabinets were finished birch. Heating was gas-fired forced-air heat.

36. Guesstimate, based on price in Brookwood Park, advertised without air conditioning in *Philadelphia Inquirer*, May 2, 1954. Cost was ca. $8.70/square foot, one of the lowest prices in the Philadelphia area at the time. Facciolo's three-bedroom, in contrast, was about $14.32/square foot.

37. Lee Gershenfeld describes earlier examples in the vicinity. Advertisements in the *Philadelphia Inquirer* show split-levels in Langford Hills, Wayne, and Strafford—which, however, looked very different from the Bodek splits.

38. See Rouillard, *Building the Slope*. According to the NAHB *Correlator* article of 1955, 184, Bodek or his helpers visited both New Jersey and Texas. Frank Lloyd Wright had employed intermediate levels at the Baker House and the Isabel Roberts House, both of 1908.

39. For example, the houses by Royal Barry Wills and Maurice Dunlavy at 49 and 50 Blake Road (1930, 1931) and the houses by Ralph I. Williams and Simon S. Black at 61 and 77 Welland Road (1941, 1940, fig. 100), all at Blake Park

(also called Muddy River), an enclave in Brookline, MA, built between 1920 and 1941. See http://muddyriver.us/75blake .html (accessed October 12, 2009). Williams was an early collaborator of the Campanellis. See also Wills, *Life*, "traditional house of the Blackbourns of Minneapolis": on a hill, two stories in front, three in back, attached garage on the middle level (level of the kitchen). A similar arrangement appears at Burns and Marlowe's Windsor Hills, 1938–41.

40. *Architectural Record* 46 (March 1940); *Architectural Record* 86 (July 1939): 45; Reed, "Why Not a Split-Level Plan?"; "On the Level, 3 Ways!" Many more articles from 1952 on. Split on several levels appears in *Architectural Forum*'s *1938 Book of Small Houses*.

41. *NYT*, October 23, 1949, May 28, 1950, October 1, 1951, November 25, 1951, June 8, 1952.

42. *NYT*, October 21, 1951.

43. Garlinghouse, *Split Level Homes*, design 6252.

44. See *LAT*, September 1, 1946, for a multilevel small house by Frederick Emmons, flat roof, not called a split.

45. It was slower and more expensive to build than the ranch because it required excavation of at least a partial basement, and because the structure had to be stronger, to support the upper levels. It usually required a more elaborate heating system as well.

46. Curt Miner to the author, December 18, 2013; Dianne Harris to the author, December 19, 2013. The Gottscho-Schleisner Collection shows some split-level houses at Levittown, NY, from the 1960s. On the Levitts' attitude, see Gans, *Levittowners*, 11. One would like to know about Willingboro, and about some of the Levitts' later developments.

47. Its more compact footprint made it easier to heat, too.

48. Springer, "Split-Level Houses," calls this the "ranch-style split" in contrast to the "side-to-side split." Today, real estate agents refer to this version as a "raised ranch." Bodek sometimes dug a full two stories into a steep hill. The result was a conventional two-story house, in which the top-floor living quarters resembled a ranch. This was probably the case in fig. 112.

49. Interviews with Claude De Botton and Joseph Bodek. Note that according to an NAHB *Correlator* September 1955 article, 150 houses had permits and were "already started" (184).

50. See De Botton below and interviews with Joe Bodek, Ralph Bodek's son.

51. Interviews with Dave Damon and Joe Bodek; see also Bodek's specifications for a new shopping center, Lane Collection.

52. Interviews with Mrs. KD, and documents furnished by her.

53. The shopping center was "preplanned" by Bodek according to Claude De Botton. Bodek submitted a preliminary plan to township supervisors in either 1954 or 1955. He had no role in planning the industrial park. The shopping center ground breaking was in June 1956; the first section opened February 21–23, 1957—*Philadelphia Inquirer*, September 18, 1957. The prominent Philadelphia architect George W. Neff (1908–90) was hired to design the shopping center.

54. $16,990, *Philadelphia Inquirer*, September 14, 1958. *Philadelphia Inquirer*, October 6, 1957, "The Executive," $17,990, three bedrooms, two baths.

55. Interview with Evelyn Rosen (Bodek's daughter) and "A Planned Community: Homes, Schools, Parks, Shopping Center, Industrial Area," NAHB *Correlator*, September 1955, 182–85.

56. By June 1956, there were "nearly 800 families": *Philadelphia Inquirer*, June 28, 1956. Thirty-six acres of proposed Lawrence Park Shopping Center and 153 acres of adjacent land zoned for light industrial use had been sold by Lawrence Park Shopping Center, including numbers 1–5, and Marple Land Development Corporation, of which Ralph Bodek was president; the purchasing group is listed as Food Fair Stores, Inc. Work on construction of the first stores in the center was already under way (ibid.).

57. St. Pius X Parish History doc. 1955ff., 9.5 acres. Cardinal O'Hara High School, 1701 Sproul Road, Springfield, was opened in 1962 according to Mrs. KD, about a mile from her home. Elementary and middle schools opened a little later.

58. On McClatchy, see especially DiFilipo, *History and Development*, 94–97.

59. See Philadelphia Tri-State District, Regional Planning Federation, *Regional Plan* for Temple holdings and description. See also http://discover.hsp.org/Record/hsp.opac .v01-136350 for a digital copy.

60. Interview with Claude De Botton, June 9, 2009. De Botton received an engineering degree from Penn in 1954, and pursued an architecture degree at Drexel at night. He designed the asymmetrical A-line roof, though it was drawn up by a young local architect. See also *County Press* online, July 4, 2007.

61. Bodek, *How and Why*, 35. Here, one should remember that Bodek's previous effort in tract house building had been Colonial Park in Springfield, entirely composed of two-story colonial-looking houses (see fig. 106).

62. Cohen, in *Consumers' Republic* (208–9), uses the Bodek book to buttress her argument that consumption goods were coded according to class in the 1950s. Bodek's text certainly sounds like this, but I would note that it is also full of the author's own social condescension to the people being interviewed. (For example, Bodek reproduces extensively the poor grammar of interviewees in their printed interviews.) Bodek himself was very class-conscious, but it is not at all clear that his buyers were.

63. Suggested by Bowden, "Suburbia at 50"; confirmed by my interviews with residents of both Lawrence Park and Rose Tree Woods, especially interviews with Mrs. MH and Mrs. KD.

64. Materials were in strong contrast too: wood instead of stone or stone and stucco.

65. Popular in the "small homes movement" too. Used by local Boston-area builders like Sumner Hersey. Popularized in the thirties and forties by Royal Barry Wills (see chapter 1). Arguably, the minimal house in FHA publications was a Cape.

66. Note that the Campanellis built one Cape at Governor Francis Farms, but apparently (judging from later sales brochures) did not repeat it.

67. "Not Just Another Campi: My Life in a 1950s Slab Ranch," blog (accessed August 20, 2013), later at http://www.feedblitz .com/f/f.fbz?Sub=357283 (accessed December 11, 2013).

68. The twenty-one different locations contained some fifty subdivisions (see appendix 1 and map). Campanelli research is challenging. Local municipal and county records are dispersed, sometimes absent. A 1977 office fire destroyed the firm's early records. Additional problems for research include the following: multiple names for the firm were used in legal transactions; newspaper ads, especially early ones, often only mentioned Martin Cerel, the firm's broker and salesman. I believe that I have successfully sorted out questions of authorship in appendix 1.

69. Most dates are from Josephine DeFlavis at Campanelli Companies, letter to the author of September 22, 2010. Robert P. DeMarco provided information about the Italian background of the family: interview of November 24, 2008, and correspondence thereafter.

70. Jon Campanelli/BL, December 7, 2012, email, plus Alfred obituary.

71. According to Ronald Campanelli, son of Michael: interview of April 19, 2008, correspondence, and several later interviews.

72. Ronald Campanelli.

73. Saivetz. For a list of all the Campanelli housing developments in the Boston metropolitan area (including Warwick, RI), see appendix 1.

74. The first houses at Governor Francis Farms (GFF) all have a 1950 date in the Warwick Assessor's records. Presumably, this would have been the date of completion.

75. According to Henry A. L. Brown, correspondence.

76. Interviews with Mr. TU.

77. According to Gross, "Governor Francis Farms," the western end of the settlement was first platted in 1931 and represented a response to increasing taxes on the farm, as well as other plans at the state level for its use. See also *Providence Journal*, December 10, 2006, http://mygfna.com/History.html and "Henry Brown Named City Historian," *Warwick Beacon*, February 19, 2013, http://warwickonline.com/stories/A-story -to-tell-Henry-Brown-named-City-Historian-73160 (accessed February 20, 2013).

78. Gross, "Governor Francis Farms," 29.

79. Henry A. L. Brown, sales brochure 1b, lent to the author by the Warwick Historical Society.

80. Ibid.

81. Henry A. L. Brown to the author, July 27, 2011.

82. According to a GFF broadside and sales brochure published by Liscomb's office ("Governor Francis Farms in Gaspee, Warwick, R. I." signed by Roswell B. Liscomb and "Governor Francis Farms at Gaspee in Warwick, R. I., 1682–1954" [five-page sales brochure] signed by Liscomb—both from the Henry A. L. Brown Papers, and lent to the author by the Warwick Historical Society), all included venetian blinds and screens. All are "forced hot water radiant heat." From broadside: "Most models furnished with the following General Electric equipment, and included in the price quoted:—Washing machine, Dish washer, Kitchen wall cabinets, Texolite counter tops, Electric clock and kitchen ventilating fan."

83. Compare (not shown) Warwick 1954. It is possible that Liscomb inspired the bow window, which he is said to have favored.

84. Sometimes twelve or more panes: See GFF sales brochure 54.

85. *BH*, October 8, 1950, 7; see also 4 Beaconsfield Drive, 1949, and GFF pictures and descriptions. The nine-paned version of the "picture window" was used later at Levittown, PA. The Campanellis often placed this window at the corner of the living room on the front facade; they also employed a bow-window version at Westfield and Wethersfield (August 31, 1952, Natick sales brochure ca. 1954).

86. Sales brochure.

87. Interview with Mr. TU, July 28, 2011.

88. *BH*, October 8, 1950.

89. For Olde Towne Realty Co., see *BH* ads and plot plans obtained by Kathleen Kelly Broomer from local archives.

90. The name of the Massachusetts development called "Wethersfield" was the result of a mistake. According to Bradford Saivetz and Robert P. De Marco, a sign painter misspelled the intended name "Weathersfield," turning it into Wethersfield, and the mistaken name stuck. The Campanellis used the originally intended form, "Weathersfield," in Schaumburg. See Saivetz interviews, February 2, 2010, and January 28, 2010, and Robert P. De Marco interview.

91. A kitchen continuous with the family room was first advertised by the Campanellis for Ridgefield at Framingham, 1955.

92. Farina kitchens. Furniture by Windsor, Mayflower, Holbrook, Paine (the largest Boston furniture house, very famous at the time in the area).

93. The Campanellis first advertised the use of the wall-mounted refrigerator at Braintree Highlands in May 1955. A very similar refrigerator was advertised by Frematic Homes in Anaheim, CA, in the summer 1955 ("Preview of New Tract Scheduled for Today," *LAT*, August 28, 1955).

94. See, for example, "Buying for 1500 Homes," *BH*, March 3, 1957, 73. Photo shows Nicholas C., Joseph C., their wives, and Harry W. Sundberg, "head of GE Appliances Co. contract sales."

95. Nicholas Campanelli interview, November 24, 2008, and Robert P. De Marco interview, November 24, 2008, and telephone conversations.

96. Mid-level split: Centrefield-at-Peabody 1957–; Deerfield-at-Framingham-Centre, May 1, 1960; Southfield, Brockton, Campanellis 1961–; Pinefield-at-Peabody, 1961; Chelmsford Farms, Chelmsford, 1962; Phillips Hill Farms, Hudson, 1962. Two-story from Chelmsford Farms, 1959–; Split, plain: Brookline, November 9, 1965, September 30, 1967; Pinefield-at-Peabody, 1961–; Field Park Estates, Brockton, 1962; many later. All these split and two-story versions were more frequent in the North Shore suburbs than in the South Shore and Brockton.

97. Saivetz to the author, October 21, 2009. According to Saivetz, during at least one public hearing in Natick, Cerel saw to it that a majority of the audience was composed of new or prospective buyers of Campanelli houses. In other words, he "packed" the meeting.

98. See Commonwealth of Massachusetts, "Subdivision Control: An Overview of the Subdivision Control Law [of 1953–54]," October 1996, revised August 1998. One of the purposes of the law of 1953–54 was to restrain "overzealous city planners

[who] have attempted to extend their authority to an extent greater than was intended by the framers of the [original law of 1936]" (1). The "purpose section" of the new law confined the powers of local planning boards to streets and sanitary measures. Further provisions mandated that local planning boards make public a set of "reasonable rules and regulations" before the process of subdivision began, so that "a prospective subdivider will know in advance what will be required of him" (2–5). These measures represented a significant victory for the developers of subdivisions, since they prevented a local community from changing the rules midstream.

99. Robert P. De Marco, Nicholas Campanelli, interviews and conversations. Interview with Jack Conway (May 5, 2008), leading Massachusetts realtor who sold Campanelli houses for Martin Cerel in the mid-fifties. According to Greg Feroli of the Brockton Engineering Department, they occasionally tried a Cape at several different locations (as at Governor Francis Farms), but did not repeat it.

100. See Gutheim, *One Hundred Years*; and "Carl Koch," Modern Homes Survey, National Trust for Historic Preservation, http://www.preservationnation.org/travel-and-sites /sites/northeast-region/new-canaan-ct/architects/carl-koch. html (accessed March 20, 2013).

101. On Wurster, see the section on Fritz Burns in chapter 2. By 1949, though, Wurster was better known for his Case Study House and his commitment to international modernism than for his earlier houses. It is also likely that discussions of the ranch house type were as frequent in the *Boston Post* and the *BH* as they were in *NYT* and *CT*. I have not been able to do this kind of search for Boston because the Boston newspapers are not available online.

102. Websites, Lexington; and Lilah Groisser, ed., *Five Fields—Five Decades: A Community in Progress*, lent by Jeffrey Cohen.

103. See references in chapter 4, on Schaumburg. Earlier, they could have seen ranch houses displayed at the New York Metropolitan Home Show, April 19–26, 1947 (*NYT*, March 30, 1947).

104. On Ralph Williams, interview with Bradford Saivetz, December 13, 2008, and letters of January 4, 2009, January 19, 2009, and February 1, 2009. In the thirties and forties, Williams was designing neocolonial and neo-Tudor suburban houses in the Brookline area (see fig. 110). The architects who later worked for the Campanellis were Edward Poskus and Amalio Giovaniello. Poskus is mentioned as the firm's architect in 1958 (*BH* June 29, 1958); later he became a building inspector. So perhaps one can assume that he was not especially

design-oriented. Giovaniello (or Giovanello) is remembered (from the sixties) by Jon Campanelli, son of Nicholas, as a flamboyant personality with considerable artistic flair; he was, in fact, credited with a design for a Campanelli entry in a *Parents Magazine* feature in 1967 (*BH*, June 18, 1967). This was a two-story "Garrison colonial" with a side wing containing a garage, built as a model home on Edgell Road in Framingham. By the later sixties, the Campanellis were building plenty of two-story houses.

105. Saivetz, letter of November 10, 2013.

106. *BH*, September 6, 1964.

107. Jon Campanelli, Nicholas's son, believes the house was built in 1958; real estate sites suggest a date of 1955. Currently the house sits on eight acres and has about 6,000 square feet in eight rooms.

108. Saivetz to the author, August 6, 2012.

109. Saivetz to the author, November 10, 2013, and passim.

110. Ca. 1949. The first plan is June 1950: this was a group of about 130 ranch houses on slabs with radiant heat, laid out in streets designed by the Campanellis and their engineer as modifications to an already-platted subdivision. Advertisements described the firm as "New England's largest builders of quality ranch homes," which indicates the brothers' aspirations in 1949–50, if not yet their actual accomplishment. *BH*, October 8, 1950, describing section 2. Plan for section 1 by Saivetz, June 24, shows lots on Bacon, Beacon, and Charles Streets. See also Saivetz to the author, January 20, 2009.

111. The Campanelli brothers formed a commercial division in the mid-sixties (soon headed by Robert P. De Marco, son of Salvatore De Marco and Ann Campanelli), and shifted entirely to commercial and industrial work (except in Florida) in the 1970s. Among their early executed projects were Westgate Mall in Brockton and Hanover Mall in Hanover, MA.

112. Saivetz, April 9, 2010. Several of the plans were obtained from local offices by Kathleen Kelly Broomer.

113. Kaufman and Broad, for example. Saivetz's firm also later worked for Kmart (along the eastern seaboard), Howard Johnson (nationally), and BJ's Wholesale Club (Saivetz, January 4, 2009).

114. Interview, December 13, 2008.

115. Bachelor's degrees conferred across all categories of engineering rose in 1949–50 to the extraordinary height of 52,246 (Tolliver and Armsby, *Engineering Enrollments*, table XXI). The training of civil engineers, the kind of engineers most involved in construction, is suggested by data on civil engineering degrees conferred by MIT between 1936 and 1970 (MIT, Office of the Registrar, table compiled for the author on

August 2, 2011): civil engineering degrees conferred by MIT rose from a total of 23 in 1936 to 49 in 1949 and to 55 in 1950. The total remained at that level until 1953, and sank back down again to 21 in 1963.

116. Saivetz, February 24, 2009. Ignorance, that is, on the part of local neighbors ("the Mrs. Nimbys") and of conservative municipal officials.

117. Obituary, *Boston Globe*, October 11, 1987; interviews with son Ronald Cerel, November 13–27, 2008, and later correspondence; correspondence with Martin's daughter Cynthia Cerel Sandler, September 2008; correspondence with grandson Brad Sandler, September 15 and 18, 2008, together with documentation provided by him; interview with Jack Conway, realtor, May 5, 2008; Saivetz interview and correspondence, passim; Robert P. De Marco interview, November 24, 2008, and telephone conversations.

118. Of course, like any real estate agent, Cerel was paid a percentage of the sales. He may have invested in Florida, and in some of Natick's commercial development. I have not been able to determine whether a portion of the 400-acre estate that he eventually used for his own Natick house was conveyed at any point to the Campanellis.

119. See "Cerel Expresses Views on Planning a New Development," *BH*, April 3, 1949, 5, which talks about community planning and describes the successful developer as "a combination of experienced broker, builder, engineer, architect, lawyer and philosopher."

120. Morley, *Hometown Natick*.

121. Ronald Cerel believes that Joseph Connelly, vice president of United Homes, had worked for the Levitts on Long Island and then left to establish his own business near Boston. Pelham Capes, like the Levitt prototypes, were built on slabs.

122. Especially Wellesley-at-Natick, Walnut Park, Park Hill, Walnut Acres. Cerel's own house was on Hunnewell property that he purchased, probably at the same time. See "440 Acres . . . a Gem of a Gentleman's Farm," *Boston Traveler*, August 18, 1959, lent by Ronald Cerel.

123. Ronald Cerel, interview; realtor Jack Conway, who worked for Cerel in the mid-fifties, made the same points to the author.

124. Carnivals and pony rides: Martin Cerel, obituary, *Boston Globe*, October 11, 1987.

125. *BH*, May 25, 1952.

126. Ronald Cerel says he also helped make the contacts for their financing.

127. Shoppers' World in Framingham, which opened in October 1951 with Jordan Marsh as the anchor store, "was only the second regional shopping center in the nation to be organized around a pedestrian mall." Broomer, "Shoppers World," 5.

128. *BH*, October 10, 1954. Ultimately, the industrial park included "General Electric, Bestpak, Sperry & Hutchinson, Johnson's Wax, and Alcoa" (Brad Sandler, unpublished paper on the industrial park, 20–21).

129. Especially those in Westfield. Interviews with Mr. LT and Mr. IN.

130. According to his grandson Brad Sandler, though, he was poverty-stricken when he died.

131. Ronald Cerel and Brad Sandler.

132. *BH* ads of April 16, 1949, April 17, 1949, September 11, 1949.

133. *BH*, October 10, 1950, advertisement for Wellesley-at-Natick. See also July 22, 1951, the Yorkshire, "a better, finer way of life."

134. *BH*, ads for Westfield-at-Natick and Fairfield-II-at-Framingham, July 12, 1953, August 23, 1953, October 4, 1953, October 18, 1953, November 29, 1953, April 4, 1954.

135. See Ronald Cerel, October 17, 2010, and his clipping from the *Boston Traveler* of August 18, 1959: Martin Cerel had 400 acres in S. Natick, fronting on Eliot Street (211), which he had planned to develop, but then used for his own house. According to the *Boston Traveler* clipping, the Cerels moved in from Medway "6 years ago." There were outbuildings, a caretaker, a variety of livestock, a built-in TV and hi-fi, a pine-paneled recreation room, eleven rooms, two phone lines, and a pool.

136. Including Frank Equi in the north, Dominic Gherin-Ghelli in the west, and Doucette and DeSantis in Brockton. Saivetz to the author, November 10, 2013.

137. See, inter alia, *NYT* display ad, September, 30, 1956, and "Huge Project Set in W. Palm Beach," September 22, 1957; also Saivetz to the author.

138. Saivetz, Robert P. De Marco.

139. Robert P. De Marco worked at Bellingham as a youth.

140. For example, Ray Celia, who became construction supervisor in Schaumburg, and Dominic Gulla (the man on the left in fig. 143), who oversaw the Campanellis' Florida building operations.

141. On the meetings: interviews and correspondence with Saivetz, De Marco, and Ronald Cerel. The role of Sully De Marco (Ann's husband) is not quite clear here. He was certainly present at the meetings, but I am not certain whether he had as much voice as the brothers.

142. Ibid.

143. The new family house outside Brockton was occupied by Lisa Marie Campanelli until her death; thereafter Nicholas, Doris, and their family took it over. The brothers had breakfast with their mother whenever they were in Brockton or nearby, and they took her out to dinner in Boston at frequent intervals, as in fig. 142.

144. Most of the builders of the early postwar years had to find ways of naming the hundreds or even thousands of new streets that they created, and sometimes they turned to the names of family members to do it. The Campanellis, though, were very consistent in this, in the Boston metropolitan area. At Schaumburg, in contrast, all street names were derived from Massachusetts towns and villages (see below). The Campanellis occasionally deviated from the "field" suffix, but not often (see appendix 1). Martin Cerel appears to have duplicated this process in naming streets of later, non-Campanelli-built areas in which he was involved: in Holliston, for example, streets are named for his grandchildren (Brad Sandler to the author, December 4, 2012).

145. "Highlights of Russian Housing Tour," NAHB *Correlator*, December 1955, 2–3. This visit was a prelude to the exhibition of a "typical" low-cost modern American house as part of the American National Exhibition in Moscow, July 1959. The kitchen of the exhibition house was the site of the famous "kitchen debate" between Khrushchev and Nixon. The exhibition placed great emphasis on US consumer goods and household appliances; it received huge exposure on TV. For the kitchen displayed in the American ranch house at the exhibition, see fig. 11. See also Marling, *As Seen on TV*.

146. Interview with Mr. and Mrs. HN. Mrs. HN had a friend who was a civil engineer working in Massachusetts, who lived in a Campanelli house in Peabody: "They told us that this was the house we had to have [because] the Campanellis are the best home builders in the world."

147. Rocky Marciano, professional boxer and world heavyweight champion 1952–56, was a friend of the Campanellis, and introduced them to several Hollywood stars. See Nicholas Campanelli Photo Archive.

148. Except for two years on the Stock Exchange and their continued activity in Florida.

Chapter 4: Chicago's Golden Corridor

1. See especially "Rails and Water," chapter 2 of William Cronon's *Nature's Metropolis*.

2. *Electronic Encyclopedia of Chicago* (Chicago Historical Society, 2005), http://www.encyclopedia.chicagohistory.org/.

3. Perica, *They Took the Challenge*, 14–18, citing, inter alia,

McManis, *Initial Evaluation*. Some big land purchasers (Arthur McIntosh, H. D. "Curly" Brown) began to move in by the 1920s. In the 1940s, many other farms broken up into smaller tracts were bought by gentlemen farmers; some larger tracts were rented to concerns like the Campbell Soup company, which grew tomatoes (39).

4. The "balloon frame" is usually ascribed to Chicago builders, though there is of course plenty of debate about it. See Joseph Bigott in the *Encyclopedia of Chicago*, who suggests that the balloon frame developed in many places and over a long period.

5. By Elbert Peets and Philip M. Klutznick. See, inter alia, Randall, *America's Original GI Town*.

6. Pacyga and Shanabruch, *Chicago Bungalow*; and many other titles.

7. See Sonoc, "Defining the Chicago Bungalow," 9–30: earlier (ca. 1900) densities were 28–40 units/acre, later 10–12 units/acre. Newer planning and architecture were in part a response to Jane Addams and other reformers (12).

8. Pacyga and others, especially Prosser, "Chicago and the Bungalow Boom." Many small builders erected houses singly, others in groups of three and four. Some buyers bought the land and then used kit houses. According to Prosser (92), "a handful of businessmen specialized in large tracts." Prosser gives the example of Westwood in Elmwood Park, built by Mills and Sons Company, 1927–29, with ca. 1,000 houses. Prosser emphasizes the influence of the Prairie School.

9. "Streets and Highways," in *Encyclopedia of Chicago*.

10. *Encyclopedia of Chicago*.

11. On the patterns of suburban development in the nineteenth and early twentieth centuries, see Keating, *Building Chicago*.

12. "Chicago-Area Expressways," in *Encyclopedia of Chicago*. Ultimately reached to Seattle and Boston. O'Hare opened (perhaps in a small way) in 1955. The Eisenhower and East-West Tollways, to the south of Interstate 90, began a little earlier (1954–58) and helped to shape other areas of explosive growth, such as at Naperville and vicinity.

13. Arlington Heights was a former train depot, an incorporated village; its biggest population explosion occurred in the 1950s and 1960s (population in 1900, ca. 1,400; 1970, 64,884, partly through annexations). Rolling Meadows, Elk Grove Village, and Schaumburg all grew up on farmland, almost entirely within Cook County. Each was eventually incorporated: Rolling Meadows as a city, Elk Grove Village as a village, Schaumburg as a township. See *Encyclopedia of Chicago*.

14. None of the Stoltzner subdivisions exceeded 250

single-family dwellings; most remained much smaller. Throughout the history of the Stoltzner firms, individual houses and small groups of houses accounted for a large part of their production. In the late 1940s, a Stoltzner sales brochure described the family as "Builders of over 3,000 homes in 28 years." In the mid- to late sixties, a similar sales brochure claimed 10,000 homes.

15. According to family recollections, he was "exiled" for anarchism or socialism.

16. Charles (Karl) (1887–ca. 1970), Orla (1893–1949), Kai (1895–1972), Helje (1897–1938), Alfrieda (1899–1964), Roy (1901–83), Frode (1903–72).

17. I think it is likely that Charles (Karl), the eldest, born 1887, and seventeen or eighteen years old when he arrived with his mother in 1904 (John [Johann] came in 1902), received all or most of his training as a brick mason in Copenhagen, one of Europe's most important centers of brick construction. (A Danish mason might complete his apprenticeship by the age of nineteen. Such apprenticeships typically lasted five or six years.) But some of his training was certainly here, in Chicago. Charles is said to have worked as a bricklayer on the famous Carl Schurz High School in Chicago, finished in 1910. He would have had to qualify with the bricklayers' union in Chicago to do this work. The younger brothers received their training in Chicago. On the "Danish passion for brick" in the later nineteenth century, see Lane, *National Romanticism*, 59–60.

18. My version of the Stoltzners' history is based on correspondence and interviews with Tara Blum (Richard's daughter), John Stoltzner, son of Helje, Roberta Stoltzner Burckle (daughter of Kai, b. 1930), Jim Stoltzner, son of Roy, and Jim's son Kirk. Jim and John have provided vivid reminiscences from a very early date; from Jim I also have genealogical records, and a series of notes written by Harold before he died. Tara has lent me blueprints and other materials, and Roberta lent sales brochures. I am exceedingly grateful to these far-flung family members. Emily Ramsey, formerly of the Historic Chicago Bungalow Association (January 30, 2009), has been helpful with the history of the Wrightwood bungalows. Newspaper sources for the Stoltzners, especially the *Chicago Daily Tribune*, were exhaustively searched by Carrie Robbins. The history of the "Greenview" development depends, in addition to these sources, on my own research (and that of my Chicago assistant Maude Baggetto) in the archives of the Arlington Heights Historical Museum. My special thanks for her help go to Mickey Horndasch at the Historical Museum.

19. On the "bungalow belt," see Pacyga and Shanabruch, *Chicago Bungalow*; Bigott, *From Cottage to Bungalow*.

According to Jim Stoltzner (telephone interview, September 12, 2008), the business was founded in 1918, the year "when my father was 18."

20. The Campanellis also used slightly different names for their business at different points, but the core leadership remained the same throughout, and management and leadership were consistent. Stoltzner business history, on the other hand, is characterized by an almost bewildering complexity. For a brief history of the Stoltzner firms, see appendix 2.

21. See appendix 2.

22. In the Wrightwood Historic District draft nomination form, kindly lent by preservation researcher Emily Ramsey, Josef Klafter is named as the collaborating architect for 4701 West Wrightwood. See also letter of Emily Ramsey to the author January 30, 2009, and Celeste Busk, "1910–1940 Building Booms Were Force behind Chicago's Classic Homes," *Chicago Sun-Times*, April 29, 2005.

23. Sonoc, "Defining the Chicago Bungalow," 16–17, makes a similar point.

24. According to Sonoc (ibid., 28–29), bathrooms were tiled and kitchens had a sink, icebox, and gas stove, sometimes designed as "Pullman kitchens." There was a door from the icebox to the outside for the iceman.

25. They were aided in assembling lots by Vernon Loucks, an attorney and family friend. They also built at least one large group of houses on the Near South Side, at Damen and Seventy-Sixth Streets.

26. See 7630 South Damen, 1937, and 7653 South Damen, 1940–45.

27. Brick, sometimes veneer over wood frame, but more often structural.

28. *Chicago Daily Tribune*, June 5, 1929: Stoltzner Construction Co., $5,650 bungalow ad, "we build on your lot" (lent by Emily Ramsey).

29. On Berry Parkway, for example—see ad, *Chicago Daily Tribune*, Park Ridge, June 16, 1929, lot 50 × 155 feet, full basements, one and a half stories.

30. *Chicago Daily Tribune*, May 29, 1925, article, lent by Emily Ramsey: "To Build 40 Bungalows." See also *Chicago Daily Tribune*, March 30, 1927, 28; *Chicago Daily Tribune*, May 11, 1929, 28.

31. Interviews with Jim Stoltzner, Roberta Burckle.

32. On war housing at Karlov and Sixty-Eighth, see *CT*, March 29, 1942, July 25, 1943. On new subdivisions in the northwest, *CT*, July 21, 1946 (from Emily Ramsey): application to rezone "110 acres of farm land" with lots that were planned for 60 feet wide, 7,500 square feet total. Loucks, representing Orla and Agnes, stated that "building would not be undertaken except in the south end until it was determined where the superhighway roads would be located."

33. Almost all of the family's house building enterprises ceased by the late 1960s.

34. The Arlington Heights population was 1,380 in 1900, 8,768 in 1950, 27,878 in 1960, 65,056 in 1970 (US Census Bureau). See also *Encyclopedia of Chicago*; Souter and Souter, *Arlington Heights Illinois*.

35. Illinois is divided into six kinds of political entities: counties, townships, precincts, cities, towns, and villages.

36. Greenview: first phase of forty-three acres (145 lots) was five blocks (Gibbons, Forrest, Pringle, Prindle, and Waterman) running north–south between Kensington and Grove. Donald and Rammer were added by 1961, Evergreen and Dale soon thereafter. The east–west blocks below Grove appear to have been developed by others; the Stoltzners may have done some building on them, however. "Arlington North" reached over two north–south blocks (Drury Lane and Wilshire Lane) between Oakton and Euclid, one mile west of Rand Road. Building began here in the late fifties, but peaked in the early and mid-sixties. "Arlington North" was built up in the sixties by John Stoltzner working alone, on land acquired earlier by Orla's successor firm; a parcel of about eighty acres (according to John Stoltzner, but I think he exaggerated the size) at the northeast corner of Thomas and Arlington Heights Road, west of Rand. It may have included as many as 180 houses. Orla's successor firm (Orla died in 1949), headed by his son and son-in-law, was responsible for the first and third of these developments; the second was developed by the branch of the business led by Frode, Roy, and Kai.

37. And the one with which I'm most familiar, since I visited my son and his family there often between 2000 and 2005.

38. *Arlington Heights Herald*, May 19, 1955, "Start Work on 2 New Subdivisions Means 300 More Homes for Heights," approval given May 17, 1955, at Arlington Heights Village Board Meeting for Greenview Estates, Stoltzner (Foundry Road and Waterman Avenue), forty acres (Stoltzner provided three acres), 145 lots, to be developed in three units; money was placed in escrow for public improvements (unit 1 = $73,987; unit 2 = $87,713; unit 3 = $34,245) (article from Susan Kazlo, Arlington Heights Memorial Library, sent to the author in July 2008).

39. Measured from the front of the house to the front property line, which is the same as the edge of the right-of-way. The lower number corresponded to properties on the west side of the street; the higher, to the east.

40. Greenview planning and building was executed by Orla's successor firm, headed by his son Harold (1919–99), his son-in-law Erik Erikson, and Carl Carlson, Orla's former superintendent. (Orla died in 1949.) This version of the family business also took on Orla's nephew John (Helje's son), a master carpenter; John then finished the Greenview operation, and was responsible, on his own, for Arlington North. Kai's side of the family built Arlington Estates. Richard Stoltzner acted as a supervisor in both Greenview and Arlington Estates. See appendix 2.

41. On the earliest blocks, the houses vary greatly in date, suggesting that the family held on to the lots here and waited to build until a buyer committed to buy.

42. Stoltzner Builders, sales brochures, lent by Jim Stoltzner, Roberta Burckle, and Tara Stoltzner Blum: *Stoltzner Construction Co. Presents Arlington Estates in Arlington Heights; Arlington Estates in Beautiful Arlington Heights; Homes by Stoltzner (Stoltzner Building Co.).*

43. Younger members of the family, like Richard and John, were foremen and later partners. Richard was a trained mason, John a master carpenter.

44. Drywall was used at Arlington Estates, and began to be used at Greenview about 1960 (according to Jim Stoltzner).

45. And linked them to the Prairie School of architecture too. But I think that the bungalow tradition was—at the very least—an intermediary.

46. Not uncommon in *CT* articles and ads from ca. 1954. The University of Illinois Small Homes Council had begun to recommend them already in 1951. But most builders rejected them for quite a while: see Rolling Meadows and Elk Grove Village.

47. Construction at Greenview was different from that used by Ralph Bodek at Lawrence Park. Bodek used a truss to support the upper level; Stoltzner used steel lally columns. Stoltzner spans were greater, and interiors were much more spacious in appearance as a result. Windows at Greenview were larger, views more comprehensive.

48. Figured from 1961 blueprint, exclusive of basement laundry and utility rooms. The ventilation schedule on the Stoltzner 1961 kitchen blueprint adds up to 1,495 square feet. Comparing Bodek and Stoltzner models from 1958: Bodek ca. $10+/square foot, Stoltzner ca. $13+/square foot.

49. 1958: "Red Carpet Houses," *CT*, September 7, 1958, referring to 335 South Waterman and Greenview Estates. 1961: Stoltzner & Fisher ad, 1961. Note that in ad of April 22, 1961, Greenview houses are described as having "class D" prices (i.e., seven rooms, $22,000–30,000), while Rolling Meadows has "class C" prices (seven to eight rooms, $19,000–22,000).

50. Richard Stoltzner died in 2008. My information about his life is derived from his obituary, and from my correspondence with his daughter, Tara Blum.

51. In Greenview, they used A. J. Del Bianco (see further discussion of his roles in the section on Rolling Meadows below). In Arlington North, they used a different architect. Interview with Jim Stoltzner, November 4, 2013.

52. It is intriguing that a calendar from 1956, which had been in Richard's possession and which has been lent to me by Tara Blum, appeared with advertising for Greenview, but displayed pictures and plans of Garlinghouse models. In other words, the Stoltzners marketed Garlinghouse plans ("Complete Plans, Blue Prints and Specifications of these and many other Modern Homes are available through our office," i.e., through the Stoltzner office at 5500 West Lawrence Avenue). The houses depicted in the calendar are all ranch houses; most of them are clad in siding, not masonry, but in other respects there are striking similarities between some of them and those actually erected by the Stoltzners. Of course, the possibility exists that the Stoltzners influenced Garlinghouse, rather than vice versa.

53. John Stoltzner, letter, in connection with the plan for 320 South Rammer and others like it that he advertised in 1961: "I saw something in a magazine that I thought would work, and I asked my friend architect Charles Banks to sketch it for me. Then it wasn't quite what I wanted, so he did it over until it seemed right."

54. Interview, November 4, 2013.

55. Jim Stoltzner has described these apartment buildings to me, and located some of them, but they have been torn down by now.

56. Three thousand dwellings by 1958, four thousand by 1964. See Perica, *They Took the Challenge*; and retrospective newspaper accounts, especially Mary Umberger, "They're Ready to Recreate the Nifty '50s," *CT*, June 3, 2001; and Lisa Black, "Revering the Ranch," *CT*, January 2, 2000.

57. Naperville's rapid growth, to about 12,000 people by 1960, began a little later. Park Forest was ultimately bigger, with 5,500 single-family dwellings in 1962, but it was slow to develop to this level.

58. David Hill obituaries, *CT*, January 16, 2008, January 18, 2008, and December 7, 2008.

59. Sharon Stangenes, "On the Level; Single-Story Living Growing in Popularity among Over-55 Home Buyers," *CT*, January 26, 2007.

60. Northwestern University Archives, letter to the author.

61. For an adulatory biography, see Perica, *They Took the*

Challenge. The job was with the Fort Dearborn Mortgage Company, subsidiary of Chicago Corporation, according to newspaper articles of the time. According to Hill interview in *CT*, May 13, 1989, the company was "involved with property bailouts and defunct buildings sold under bonds." In 1936, Hill was assigned to "build houses on 40 vacant lots in Elmwood Park that were not selling fast enough to satisfy the mortgage company." This experience led to his love of the house construction business.

62. On father and grandfather, see http://familytreemaker .genealogy.com/users/w/a/l/Katherine-T-Walter-VA/GENE9-0003.html (accessed January 31, 2014).

63. "Attics Do Basement Duty," *CT*, February 16, 1941.

64. "Early Residents, Founder's Son Discuss Our City's Past," *Rolling Meadows Review*, July 4, 2002: "Hill had been honorably discharged from the Navy although he hadn't actually served in World War II."

65. Lawrence B. Perkins, 1907–97. Bachelor's of architecture from Cornell, 1931. Phillip Will Jr. was his roommate. Firm (originally Perkins, Wheeler & Will) established 1935. See "Lawrence B. Perkins," *Life*, October 19, 1942 (part of a Revere Copper & Brass ad); obituary, *Chicago Sun-Times*, December 4, 1997; *NYT*, December 9, 1997; "Oral History of Lawrence Bradford Perkins," compiled under the auspices of the Chicago Architects Oral History Project, Art Institute of Chicago, 1986.

66. *CT*, February 23, 1947, and May 11, 1947, on Park Ridge Manor, which Smith & Hill were attempting to develop at the same time: "a method of semi-prefabrication on the job, an 'engineered construction' method developed by the firm for its . . . Oak Meadows veterans' housing project. . . . 'This method employs advanced on the job modular fabricating of materials, walls, trusses, roof sections, windows, doors, and built-in cabinets in standard multiples to minimize waste and to conserve site erection time,' said Hill. 'Precision union labor construction methods . . . have cut normal construction time in half. Because of large scale commitments suppliers have assured continuous, on-schedule deliveries of building materials, plumbing, heating, and electrical equipment.'"

67. *CT*, September 21, 1949.

68. *CT*, February 23, 1947, May 11, 1947.

69. "Lockweld engineered" seems to have been a new label for Hill's earlier construction methods. A marketing leaflet of December 1948 speaks of "Hill's Lockweld plant at Oak Lawn," and promises that at Oak Meadows, "specially trained crews of AFL building mechanics . . . [will] rotate between fabricating work in the plant and finish work at the home sites." See

"Lockweld Home News," *Chicago Construction News*, December 30, 1948. The two-bedroom version was advertised in *CT*, February 26, 1949, at Oak Meadows; the ad shows the same illustration as in figs. 165, 166.

70. Interview, *CT*, May 13, 1989.

71. Ibid. Smith went on to become a prominent Chicago realtor.

72. *CT*, January 27, 1951: three-bedroom model.

73. Pawling & Harnischfeger (P & H Homes) was an offshoot of the Harnischfeger Corporation, originally a manufacturer of mining equipment and then after World War II a manufacturer of diesel engines, heavy construction equipment, and manufactured homes, based in Port Washington, WI. P & H became quite prominent in the Chicago area for a decade or so after the war. For Hill's P & H homes, see display ads in the *CT*, inter alia: July 15, 1950, September 17, 1950, October 14, 1950, November 11, 1950, January 2, 1951, January 27, 1951, July 14, 1951. Chicago seems to have been a center for the marketing of manufactured homes during this period: see ads in NAHB *Correlator* 1955 for prefabricated houses.

74. *CT*, April 12, 1953, on zoning dispute; see also February 16, 1959.

75. *CT*, April 25, 1959: 62 percent of respondents had an income of $7,500 or less (ca. $56,200 in 2010 dollars).

76. Numerous Arlington Heights property owners and realtors attempted to influence Cook County zoning officials against Hill's plans.

77. On Fletcher, see Perica, *They Took the Challenge*, 44–45. Building superintendents were Gottlieb Hauser and Dick Scott; construction of sewer and water lines was by the D'Andrea Construction Company. Ibid. See also *CT*, February 10, 1956.

78. After incorporation in 1955, Rolling Meadows introduced its own zoning ordinances, allowing Hill to reduce lot sizes to the originally planned 7,500 square feet. Population at the beginning of 1955 was 5,162. Twelve hundred voted, approximately two-thirds of the votes were for incorporation. The new city included the Arlington Park Racetrack and a piece of Palatine Township. See Perica, *They Took the Challenge*, 57.

79. In November 1959, 62 percent of respondents to a survey had an income of $7,500 or less ($56,200 in 2010 dollars). A survey of total city population in 2003 (Decision Resources, *Executive Summary*) describes a median household income of $74,000 (about $88,000 in 2010 dollars), with 17 percent of households reporting incomes of over $100,000. In 2003, 35 percent were "white collar jobholders," "20% household heads were clerical-sales persons and fifteen percent were Blue Collar workers" (ibid.). The same survey reports that 25 percent of residents had lived in Rolling Meadows for more than thirty years, and describes "a very low transience rate." The survey concludes that "residents exhibit a very high level of confidence in the direction of their community in comparison with other Greater Metropolitan Area suburbs." According to two successive presidents of the Rolling Meadows Historical Society, Martha Roberts and Beverly Keagle, the "working class" label came partly from rivalry with Arlington Heights, whose newspapers coined pejorative terms like "Rolling Ghetto" for the new community. But the original residents were not affluent: Martha Roberts characterized them as "working class on the way up."

80. Martha Roberts interview, February 3, 2012; interview with Mrs. KM, and Kathy Kwandras interview in "Early Residents."

81. The museum is at 3100 Central Road. Martha Roberts, third president (2006–8), was particularly helpful to the author.

82. According to Martha Roberts, incorporation as a *city* conferred special tax benefits.

83. Park district. Hill set aside land along Salt Creek for the park district, arranged its legal separation from Palatine Rural Park District, and donated it (Perica, *They Took the Challenge,* 86–88).

84. Rolling Meadows Museum, *Guide*; see also appendix 3.

85. Perica, *They Took the Challenge*, 45, shows framing, prefabricated gable. The foundation and crawl space were poured concrete walls on concrete footings, tar paper over dirt floor, with gravel on top. Thanks to William Roberts, who was the original heating contractor, husband of Martha Roberts, former president of the Rolling Meadows Historical Society. On construction, see also Mrs. KM correspondence.

86. See also chapter 5, on Paxton, and the Campanelli Brothers sections of chapters 3 and 4 on Campanelli kitchens.

87. *CT*, September 23, 1953, featured as festival home: "gray cedar shingles and a front of cream clapboard and plywood paneling."

88. *CT*, May 24, 1953, classified advertisement.

89. My thanks for this description to William Roberts, an original owner and also an HVAC specialist.

90. See such University of Illinois Small Homes Council publications as *Contemporary Houses Developed from Room Units; A Report of an Architectural Investigation in House Design Making Use of Improved Building Techniques* (1951); *Heating the Home: Central Heating Systems* (1945); *Planning for Electricity in the Home* (1945); *Basementless House Construction* (1950);

Handbook of Kitchen Design (1950); *Designing the Home* (1945); *Homes from Pre-assembled Wall Panels* (1955). Note that Hill's 1958 Housing Research Laboratory was sponsored by this organization. Hill's relations with the Small Homes Council deserve further research.

91. According to Martha Roberts, "People moved in all at once," creating "instant neighborhoods." Letter of February 19, 2012.

92. *CT*, February 25, 1954.

93. "Their Finger Is on Your Pulse!," *CT*, October 4, 1958. Some accounts say there were twenty-one houses: see especially "Meadows Developer's Son Recalls Building Boom," *Arlington Heights Daily Herald*, June 7, 1996. The houses were erected on Wilke Road just north of Central Road, and on Fulle Street, an east–west cross street.

94. *CT*, November 22, 1958, ad for "California Contemporary," and picture page of questionnaire, p. 16 of download, included in http://archives.library.illinois.edu/archon/?p=collections/controlcard&id=1705. See also Hill, "I Built 20 Model Houses"; and *CT*, January 3, 1959.

95. All my information on the models comes from Erie Jones's report to the Small Homes Council.

96. These figures are derived from penciled amounts in the notes on the "Supplementary Information Sheet" accompanying Erie Jones's report to the Small Homes Council. This sheet was part 2 of the questionnaire devised by the Real Estate Research Corporation.

97. *CT*, May 3, 1959.

98. *CT*, March 7, 1959.

99. Interview, and *CT*, September 12, 1955.

100. Administered through the Chicago Metropolitan Home Builders' Association. See "Entry in Modern Living Design Contest," *CT*, February 15, 1953.

101. Granacki Historic Consultants, "Architectural Resources in Highland Park, Illinois: A Summary and Inventory," prepared for the City of Highland Park Historic Preservation Commission, 2006, 19.

102. Stanley Tigerman, 1930–, well-known modernist opponent of Mies van der Rohe and his followers; director of the School of Architecture, University of Illinois; principal with Stanley Tigerman and Associates Ltd., 1964–, interview (Art Institute, Chicago). For his remarks on Del Bianco, see Chicago Architects' Oral History Project, Art Institute of Chicago, http://digital-libraries.saic.edu/cdm/landingpage/collection/caohp.

103. In the cases of Elk Grove Village and Weathersfield, with their out-of-town builders, he probably also helped them adjust to local building codes and union labor organizations. Bradford Saivetz remembers him as a local person who was "politically useful." For Kimball Hill, he may have offered additional contacts with the University of Illinois housing research organizations.

104. Note that none of the Rolling Meadows schools were designed by Hill's former partners Perkins and Will. By the mid-fifties, this firm had become very successful, and famous for their school designs. Perkins and Will would have been too expensive for Hill at this point.

105. Perica, *They Took the Challenge*; *CT*, December 26, 1954, October 29, 1955.

106. Granacki. According to *CT*, September 13, 1958, the "lab" was to run for ninety days; 100,000 visitors were expected. *CT*, October 4, 1958: 8,000 had visited. Other articles remark on the "California Contemporary," with its vaulted ceilings and parquet oak floors.

107. A close parallel, and maybe a little earlier, was "Father and Son Construction Company" of Phoenix, Arizona. The head of this firm, Jack Hoffman, bought up 300 acres just to the northwest of Elk Grove Village in 1953, and named it "Hoffman Estates," which had 5,000 houses by the time of its incorporation as a village in 1959. Incorporation permitted annexations: ca. 2,000 acres annexed by 1962. See also http://articles .chicagotribune.com/1986-08-24/business/8603030287_1_ commercial-development-hoffman-estates-jack-hoffman, which says 160 acres in 1954. The *Encyclopedia of Chicago* confirms this figure. And see below, on Schaumburg.

108. Hazel, *Dallas*, 50.

109. Ibid., 46, 50.

110. *DMN*, April 11, 1956.

111. Whitewright had a population of 1,480 in 1936, 1,712 in 1990. Dallas's population was 260,000 in 1930, 295,000 in 1940, 400,000 in 1945, 861,000 in 1950, 996,000 in 1955. http://books .mongabay.com/population_estimates/1950/Dallas-USA.html.

112. *DMN*, September 28, 1958.

113. *DMN*, 1946, 1947, 1948.

114. "Live in a Lively Home," *DMN* ad 1948, Northridge Estates: two bedrooms, $15,750: "huge living room with large picture window over wood-burning fireplace."

115. *Newsweek*, March 26, 1956, says 1945; in 1949, "first big subdivision" of three hundred houses for $6,500 each. Houses "now" a little bigger and more expensive: some near Dallas, three bedrooms, with air conditioning, $11,000–12,000. Still selling to veterans, but says "families get bigger every year."

116. *DMN*, July 21, 1948, November 20, 1949, November 29, 1949, September 28, 1958.

117. *DMN*, February 7, 1954, quoting *House and Home* on the largest builders of 1953.

118. *DMN*, October 1, 1955.

119. *DMN*, February 1, 1959, "Out of Dallas Property Holdings," which describes the holdings as belonging to Lively as president of Centex. See also *DMN*, January 1, 1955.

120. According to *DMN*, February 1, 1959, the Murchisons are "said to have a substantial interest" in Centex. After Lively's death, the Murchison stake in Centex grew to about 65 percent: *DMN*, September 4, 1969. In 1977, Murchison interests shrank to about 50.4 percent; they began selling off their remaining interests in that year. On the vicissitudes of the Murchison fortune, see Wolfe, *Murchisons*.

121. McCarthy, *Elk Grove*, 63–64.

122. *CT*, July 17, 1956, October 9, 1956. Elk Grove Village at this point had a population of 123; a miniscule group of 60 gathered to vote on the incorporation issue.

123. The earliest residential portion stretched from Higgins Road in the north to Devon Road in the south, bounded by Arlington Heights Road in the west and Tonne Road in the east. This area was about 1,350 acres. Soon, the industrial section to the east was expanded all the way to the borders of O'Hare, while the residential and shopping areas to the west expanded to include the area around Biesterfield Road west of Arlington Heights Road, which contains the Elk Grove Town Center and the village's principal shopping district. Further expansion has brought the village boundaries beyond Interstate 290 to the west, right up to the boundaries of Schaumburg. In contrast to Rolling Meadows, the social and occupational character of the inhabitants does not appear to have changed very much: In 1958, a "survey of buyers showed most hail from north and northwest Chicago and northwest suburbs, 90% white collar workers with an average income of $8,000" (*CT*, February 15, 1958; = ca. $60,000 in 2010). In 2010, the median family income was $71,834. Currently, 81 percent of jobs are classified as white-collar and 19 percent as blue-collar. Approximately 40 percent are management and professional workers, and about 56 percent work in the sales, office, and service sector. See http://www.clrsearch.com /Elk_Grove_Village_Demographics/IL/60007/Employment -Occupation-and-Industry (accessed April 6, 2011).

124. C. Sidney Milam, d. 1961. Streets and a school in Dallas were named after him. The house illustrated in figs. 179, 180 closely resembles the Centex houses of Gaston Park, with a garage added, and also very closely resembles Centex models such as "the Birchwood" built in Elk Grove Village (fig. 183).

125. "Centex Operations Cover Vast Area," *DMN*, March 27,

1955; PP&B plans in University Park, FL, *DMN*, September 28, 1959; Master Plan for Elk Grove Village from *Chicago Daily Herald* 1956, no month or day, lent by Elk Grove Village librarian.

126. *DMN*, March 27, 1955; and see Google Maps street views of Gaston Park, Dallas.

127. *DMN*, September 28, 1958.

128. Aerial view in *CT*, July 14, 1962.

129. In 1966, the park district was established; Centex deeded land for eleven parks (McCarthy, *Elk Grove*, 86). Nine additional parks opened from 1966 to 1981.

130. *CT*, May 5, 1962. In 1996, Elk Grove Village had over 3,600 firms in the industrial park; more than one-fourth of its population was employed there. See the July "Happy Birthday" issue of the *Chicago Daily Herald*, lent by Elk Grove Village librarian; and *NYT*, July 25, 1957.

131. A street in Elk Grove Village was named for him.

132. Ads for Indian Hills Park and Country Club Park, *DMN*, October 8, 1952, November 28, 1954. A two-bedroom house with hardwood floors (linoleum in the kitchen and bath), wall heaters, kitchens with steel cabinets, and a "guaranteed roof" sold for $7,550 in 1952 (Indian Hills Park ad 1952; $62,125 in 2010 dollars). Extensive Google real estate searches have produced the following comparisons to the Elk Grove Village sales brochure containing model houses, lent by the Elk Grove Village library: The "Birchwood" model resembles 1714 Virginia Street, Grand Prairie, 1956. The "Meadowlark" resembles 10865 Cassandra Way, 1955. There are many other similarities.

133. *DMN*, October 8, 1952.

134. *DMN*, March 27, 1955.

135. By 1962, an L shape was adopted in some of the larger houses (*CT*, June 16, 1962; see also the Springmont model in the Elk Grove Village sales brochure).

136. *CT*, February 15, 1958: three bedrooms for $17,000 ("company hopes to [attract] families earning $6,500 to $7,200/yr" ($45,000 to $54,000 in 2010 dollars).

137. *CT*, February 15, 1958, June 7, 1958.

138. See Rybczynski on Toll Brothers builders in *Last Harvest*.

139. Except for Florida. After their experiences in West Palm Beach (see the Campanelli Brothers section of chapter 3), Campanelli Brothers continued for several decades to build some houses in Florida.

140. Armistead, *Schaumburg*.

141. Ibid.; Sibbet, "Suburbia, Farms Mingle," "Schaumburg Fights," "Schaumburg's Development," "Mayor Atcher."

142. Bob Atcher, 1914–93. He was famous and widely recorded before the war. After war service, he moved to Schaumburg. He performed on *National Barn Dance* from 1948 to the early sixties and was one of their biggest stars. Born in Kentucky, Atcher was described in Schaumburg publications as "the singing cowboy," a label usually reserved in the fifties for Gene Autry, Tex Ritter, John Wayne, and Roy Rogers.

143. A complicated series of actions by community leaders, involving moving the legal addresses of some inhabitants by changing boundaries. See the three DVDs issued by the Village of Schaumburg (Schaumburg Prairie Center for the Arts), marking the town's fiftieth anniversary in 2006: *Village of Schaumburg*, *Images of Schaumburg*, and *Schaumburg: An Oral History*.

144. Armistead, *Schaumburg*; Sibbet, "Schaumburg's Development," *CT*; DVDs issued by the Village of Schaumburg, 2006.

145. On Schaumburg's development, see Sibbet, "Schaumburg's Development"; on its final boundaries, see Village of Schaumburg, *Zoning Map*.

146. Ray Celia interview in the early sections of *Schaumburg: An Oral History*.

147. Schmocker and Eyrich, "Schaumburg 1956," 23.

148. Campanelli single-family dwellings totaled about four thousand; total Campanelli-built residential units may have reached six thousand.

149. On the name, see Saivetz, February 2, 2010, January 28, 2010; on other history, Sibbet, "Schaumburg's Development." The population was 800 in 1960, 6,500 in 1965, ca. 15,000 in 1968.

150. Sibbet, "Schaumburg's Development"; Schaumburg librarian Jane Rozek to the author, April 23, 2008.

151. Unidentified newspaper clipping of April 16, 1959, lent by Jane Rozek.

152. Ray Celia, interview, January 29, 2010.

153. Designed by Del Bianco, but described as following the model of "New England colonial design" used by the Campanellis in the East. Constructed by the Campanellis, as was the school.

154. *CT*, February 23, 1974. The park area included "a 10 acre lake stocked for fishing." Note that Francis Campanelli School and Weathersfield Commons were designed by Del Bianco, who was also described by Alfred Campanelli as "our architect."

155. Advertisement, *CT*, June 16, 1962.

156. Campanelli advertisements in *CT* make it clear that full basements and hot air heat were introduced by 1961, but both appeared much more often in the later sixties.

157. See fig. 192 and the house plans in "Welcome to Colonial

Weathersfield in Schaumburg, Where the Living Is Wonderful," Campanelli sales brochure, ca. 1967, lent by Schaumburg Library.

158. Ads, *CT*, September 20, 1959, July 15, 1966.

159. Ray Celia, interview.

160. The Seville was introduced in 1962, with a second version in 1965; it contained two kitchens, a basement family room continuous with the basement kitchen, two bedrooms on the lower floor. See *CT*, February 17, 1962, August 18, 1962.

161. This equates to $116,000–157,000 in 2010 dollars. See advertisement in *CT*, April 16, 1959, on model homes.

162. *CT*, October 24, 1964: $16,500–26,000 ($116,000–183,000 in 2010 dollars).

163. Campanelli sales brochure, "Welcome to Colonial Weathersfield in Schaumburg," ca. 1965, lent by library, and see, for example, *CT*, June 26, 1964, August 4, 1972, and January 17, 1976.

164. See the "downsizing" conflict reported in the *CT* in the late seventies and early eighties. For example, March 12, 1981, March 22, 1983.

165. Schaumburg Table of "Planned Unit Developments and Residential Developments," ca. 1990, lent by library. The Campanellis built 131 additional single-family dwellings at Weathersfield Lakes, 1972ff., and 390 at Weathersfield West, 1978–86, as well as a number of condos, duplexes, and "quadrominiums"—they built these multifamily units from 1971 on. Total multifamily units in tables is 21,008, so the Campanellis built 41 percent of these. Other single-family units were almost all in very small groups and by other builders, *except* for Levitt Brothers' Sheffield Park, 1969–78, which contained 1,890 single-family dwellings.

166. In Schaumburg, the Campanellis were working with union labor; according to Robert P. De Marco, this process went very smoothly (De Marco interview).

167. *CT*, July 9, 1966, which compares Centex, to the disadvantage of the latter.

168. The International Village apartment complex opened in 1967 (*Village of Schaumburg: 50th Anniversary 2006*).

169. See Village of Schaumburg DVD series, 2006.

Chapter 5: The Buyers, Their Backgrounds, and Their Preferences

1. Paxton, *What People Want*, appendix C, 125–26.

2. Ibid., 3nn2–3.

3. The US government-defined poverty level in 2010 was $22,050 for a family of four, so 44 percent of these families were just above what would now be considered the poverty level.

4. No masonry option other than brick was mentioned.

5. Paxton, *What People Want*, 24.

6. Ibid., 34.

7. Ibid., table 14-01.

8. Ibid., appendix C, and 3nn1–3.

9. Contacts with original owners or their children are not easy to come by, and the difficulties vary among the communities I've studied. Rolling Meadows, Natick, Brockton, and Lawrence Park have had much more stable populations over time than some of the other communities. Suburbs in Southern California (like those in New Jersey and most of the rest of the New York metropolitan area) experienced high mobility almost from the beginning. Panorama City, in addition to the general high mobility characteristic of the region, suffered a rapid economic decline after the General Motors plant moved away in 1992. As a result, I was unable to locate any original owners there. Here, I substituted an interview from Torrance, a rather similar Los Angeles community. See appendix 3, interview with Mrs. FC.

10. Transo Envelope Company, 1900 North Austin, in the "near northwest."

11. The purchase price was $13,000 or maybe a few dollars more ($105,773 in 2010 dollars).

12. Jack Conway, leading Massachusetts realtor who had worked for Cerel and the Campanellis in the mid-fifties, remarked to me that women began to move into real estate sales positions in the sixties (interview, May 5, 2008).

13. Ruggles provides a useful summary of the historiography, together with new data of his own, in "Living Arrangements and Well-Being." See also Ruggles, "Multigenerational Families."

14. See, for example, the restrictive covenants at Governor Francis Farms, discussed in the Campanelli Brothers section of chapter 3. Such covenants had excluded not only African Americans but also anyone from Southern or Eastern Europe or Latin America. This implicitly included Jews. Legal restrictions like this were breaking down everywhere in the country after World War II, but it took a long time for people to forget about the attitudes they embodied.

15. Even when they stressed church membership, they discussed it not as a source of division within their neighborhoods but as an additional path to socialization.

16. See Cromley, *Alone Together*.

17. See especially "Linked Lives: Personal Communities in the Suburbs," in Corcoran, Gray, and Peillon, *Suburban Affiliations*. Corcoran and coauthors also make clear that in most suburbs, family ties remain strong even at a distance. Bodek, on the other hand, claimed to have found feelings of considerable relief among his buyers at shedding their parents and relatives.

18. Creighton and Ford, *Contemporary Houses*. This book is mainly about clients' reactions to the houses they commissioned from architects, but some of the respondents had lived in builders' houses, and the houses are all small, so the remarks may have resonated among the occupants of builders' houses.

19. Jacqueline Rynerson interview, in *Lakewood Story*.

20. Karal Ann Marling writes about American enthusiasm for the West and for cowboys in the song "Don't Fence Me In," in Gibbs et al., *Carefree California*, 116–29. The song was by Cole Porter (1934) and widely performed from 1944 onward (Roy Rogers in the films *Hollywood Canteen* [1944] and *Don't Fence Me In* [1945]). The singer rides a horse, but the song works for riding around in cars or on bicycles, too.

21. Cohen, *Consumers' Republic*.

22. Waldie, "Falling in Love."

23. A later conversation; not recorded in appendix 3.

24. Wiese, *Places of Their Own*; Gonzales, "Place in the Sun"; Little, "Getting the American Dream."

25. NAHB *Correlator*, May 1955, 21–28. These and other government agencies were responsible elsewhere for massive credit rationing—for the "redlining" of African American and Mexican American areas of the cities to *prevent* the granting of mortgages in such districts.

26. African American efforts to move into older white suburbs are discussed for Levittown by Sugrue, "Jim Crow's Last Stand."

27. But Mrs. MQ in Schaumburg moved because she wanted a formal dining room.

28. Rossmoor had fences, though, as did some developments that I have learned about informally but that are not among my case studies.

29. This can still be observed today, although there are now plenty of fences and hedges. While the Levitts are well known for enforcing particular planting schemes, this does not seem to have been true of other builders (or buyers). Among my case studies, only Greenview had (and has) noticeably repetitive front yard plantings. In Torrance, Mrs. FC's father the horticulturalist was in demand as a planner of individualized planting arrangements for the neighbors.

30. See appendix 3; see also Kelly, *Expanding the American Dream*.

31. See Goldstein, *Do It Yourself*; Harris, *Building a Market*.

32. And so, perhaps, did their parents. Thomas Hubka argues that the acquisition of new kitchen and bathroom fixtures was an essential element in conferring status in the twenties and thirties. See Hubka, "From Working-Class to Middle-Class."

33. *Life* magazine cost $0.20 per issue in 1955 and $6.75 per year, or $1.63 and $54.92, respectively, in 2010 dollars. See also Mrs. KM, original interview notes. In 1949, *Life* had a circulation of about five million; this means that it reached only about 12 percent of all households (ca. 43 million), and these were the more affluent ones. One could have seen copies of most of these magazines in libraries, at bookstores and newsstands, or in office waiting rooms, however.

34. *Better Homes and Gardens*, for example, rose in circulation from around two million in 1946 to five million in 1960. See Farber, "General Periodicals." But, as I just observed about *Life* magazine, five million was a small percentage of all possible readers.

35. See especially Hayden, "Sitcom Suburbs," in *Building Suburbia*; Marling, *As Seen on TV*; Spigel, *Welcome to the Dreamhouse*; and other works by Spigel.

36. Dates of sitcoms, chronologically: *I Love Lucy* (mostly sited in an apartment), 1951–57; *The Honeymooners*, 1951–56, occasional revivals through 1978 (sited in Brooklyn apartment building); *Adventures of Ozzie and Harriet* (sited in Nelsons' actual home in LA, five bedrooms, five baths, built in 1916, two and a half stories, somewhat Victorian looking), 1952–66; *Make Room for Daddy*, 1953–64 (took place in apartments); *Father Knows Best*, radio 1949–54, television 1954–63 (midwestern middle-class family, two-story rather colonial-looking house, sort of a Cape, with gables, four bedrooms; nineteen million people watched it in 1955); *Leave It to Beaver*, 1957–63; *Family Affair*, 1966–71; *The Brady Bunch*, 1969–74. There were, however, instances in which movies and television were used for promotional purposes by builders working with publicity agents and manufacturers. For example, GE and RKO erected seventy-three replicas of "Mr. Blandings' Dream House" (1948) around the country in 1949, partly as publicity for the movie of the same name, and partly to advertise GE appliances. Mr. Blandings' house in its Natick, MA, version, was a two-story traditional New England saltbox (with a one-car garage), furnished in traditional prewar styles, that sold (furnished) for $45,000, it bore no resemblance to the model houses popular in the housing developments of the 1950s. See Carlton L. Smith, "What Ever Happened to Mr. Blandings' Dream House?," courtesy James Morley, president, Natick Historical Society.

37. See Bennett, *TV Sets*, and http://www.retroweb .com/universal_leave_it_to_beaver.html. Jim and Margaret

Anderson's house in *Father Knows Best* (1954–63) (Bennett, *TV Sets*, 9–12), a Dutch colonial two-story with about 4,000 square feet of living space, was even more formal and elaborate.

38. In contrast to the *content* of television programs, television *advertising* was important in forming buyers' ideas and aspirations. Builders like Fritz Burns and Ross Cortese used both radio and TV advertising very effectively in their sales campaigns.

39. In a Turner Classic Movies interview that aired June 10, 2012, Judy Garland said that already in 1939, 65 percent of Americans went to the movies at least once a week. Movies were often mentioned as entertainment by people I interviewed. One of the most vivid memories of residents of Rolling Meadows was of the free outdoor movies shown every weekend at the Town Center while it still resided in an old barn.

40. Allen, *Since Yesterday*, 223–34.

41. The version of *Ramona* shown in 1936, with Loretta Young and Don Ameche, was one of the first Technicolor movies. See also chapter 1 on "Western" enthusiasms.

42. John Steinbeck's *The Grapes of Wrath* (1939) won the National Book Award and the Pulitzer Prize; the movie version, directed by John Ford (1940), starring Henry Fonda, won two Academy Awards.

43. Directed by John Curtiz, with Joan Crawford in the title role, released September 1945.

44. *All That Heaven Allows*, directed by Douglas Sirk, 1955.

45. Affron and Affron, *Best Years*, 218–21.

46. After the mid-fifties, Disney movies (and the allure of Disney World) probably had some influence on buyers seeking a touch of fantasy in the exterior ornamentation of their houses. See chapter 2 on Vandruff's Cinderella Homes and on some of Cortese's inspiration at Rossmoor. See also chapters 3 and 5 on exaggerated gables in some Campanelli houses.

47. This is changing, though. See Bigott, *From Cottage to Bungalow*; Pacyga and Shanabruch, *Chicago Bungalow*; Hunter, *Ranches, Rowhouses, and Railroad Flats*; Ore, *Seattle Bungalow*. Gowans's *Comfortable House* was an early exception.

48. People described their childhood homes to me in great detail, and in many cases I was able to locate and view them on Google Maps street views. The illustrations I have offered are usually not the houses themselves but as similar as I could find among published and manuscript sources.

49. "Initially my dad, who had an accounting degree, worked for the IRS; later he became a bank officer and we did better. My mother had no college and never worked."

50. They could also have been built just after the Great Fire, before new building regulations were instituted.

51. Groth, "Workers'-Cottage and Minimal-Bungalow Districts"; Groth, "Les minimal bungalows"; Bigott, *From Cottage to Bungalow*. See also Hubka, "From Working-Class to Middle-Class" and *Houses without Names*, 28 and fig. 14.

52. Further examples of the bungalow type are discussed above in chapter 4 overall and the Stoltzner Builders section of chapter 4. See also Hubka, *Houses without Names*.

53. There was row housing also in Boston and New York City, but it was usually supplanted for the poor in the later nineteenth century by tenements and other forms of apartment dwellings.

54. See also Hayward, *Baltimore's Alley Houses*.

55. As in Marissa Vigneault's grandparents' house in fig. 212. On New England two- and three-deckers, see Heath, *Patina of Place*.

56. My family rented this house from 1938 to 1940. It is located in a tiny hamlet in upstate New York and sits on about two acres of land, with room for gardens and pasture. There is no barn.

57. "In 1900, 41% of the American workforce was employed in agriculture; 1930, 21.5%; 1945, 16%; 1970, 4%." This transformation was largely the result of the increasing mechanization of agriculture; "small diversified farms" came to be replaced by "a small number of large, specialized farms." See Dunlop and Galenson, *Labor*, 24.

58. Glassie, *Vernacular Architecture* and *Material Culture*; Upton, *Architecture in the United States*; Hubka, *Big House, Little House*. Cromley, *Food Axis*, is enlightening on the influence of the frontier house on American planning and on the role of the kitchen. See also the "Rural Memories and Desires: The Farm, the Suburb, the Wilderness Retreat" section of readings in Lane, *Housing and Dwelling*, 196–236. Note that the plan of Andrew Jackson Downing's "Bracketed Farm-House" (1850), fig. 32 in ibid., has no foyer or dining room.

59. See Earley, "Hallway"; this is fiction but confirmed by my own experiences of rural dwellings in upstate New York in the 1940s and 1950s.

60. Student papers in my "Housing and Dwelling" course at Bryn Mawr College, 2000–2005, investigated the student's grandparents' house; in several, the former living room was used as a bedroom. Or, according to Cromley, *Food Axis*, 142, it served as the eating place of the house, when the kitchen was too small. The origins of the term "living room" are unclear. Cromley suggests that it came from the late nineteenth-century efforts of housing reformers to diversify the spaces of working-class dwellings into rooms for specific purposes (127). But the label appears in Downing's plans of 1850 and in Ranlett's *Early Victorian House Designs*. See also Freeman, "Home and Work," 231–32.

61. McMurry, "City Parlor." Note her reference (176n57) to Vincent Scully on the Shingle Style "open plan" among professional architects as "nostalgia for a lost agrarian simplicity" and a "desire for informal living." See Scully, *Shingle Style*, 88, 73.

62. Ashby, *Farmhouse Plans*, 70. The publication was the result of a wide survey of farmhouse types in 1934 organized by the University of Illinois under the auspices of the Bureau of Agricultural Engineering within the Department of Agriculture. The plans it published were said to be based on this survey, but were intended as models for new farmhouses.

63. Wright, *Building the Dream*, esp. chapter 1; Cromley, *Food Axis*, on frontier cottages.

64. Among the students in my "Housing and Dwelling" course, two students had family members who had grown up in such an apartment. Adina Loeb's grandparents' apartment is published in Lane, *Housing and Dwelling*, 94–99, and fig. 12.

65. The most persuasive of interpretations along these lines is Archer, *Architecture and Suburbia*.

66. Excerpted in Lane, *Housing and Dwelling*, 155–63, illustrations showing Kerr's design for Bear Wood, Wokingham, Berkshire (1865–74), figs. 25, 26.

67. An especially useful example of the books on small houses is Jones, *Authentic Small Houses*.

68. Cromley, *Food Axis*.

69. Among the families I interviewed, seven of the husbands and five of the wives had some college-level education. The husbands' college training included pharmacy, horticulture, chemistry, and engineering; one had advanced degrees in chemistry. Three of the wives had college-level training in education; one studied accounting in junior college.

70. Homestead Acts, 1862–1916.

71. For example, bunk beds, already known to some Americans from railroad sleeping cars and rustic camps, came to be intimately familiar to all personnel on ships and submarines during the war.

72. See Crawford, "Daily Life," 114–16.

73. Photographs in the Library of Congress collections show the installation of electric stoves and refrigerators in some war workers' housing. See the Library of Congress online photo catalog picture descriptions, for example: "Each defense home is equipped with a gas operated refrigerator, gas range, and central heating plant"; "Complete with icebox for raiding. Workman peering into refrigerator in one of a group of trailers being used for purpose of temporary housing of defense workers. Note efficient utilization of interior space

for cabinets and work surfaces." Another description speaks of lots 25 feet wide, 50 feet deep, in trailer camps.

74. Crawford, "Daily Life," 90–143, illustrations of trailers on 105, 115.

75. See the many descriptions of construction in the Library of Congress collection.

76. Cheap land for mobile homes could be found in trailer parks, villages, empty rural areas, and backyards. See Wallis, *Wheel Estate*; Jackson, "The Mobile Home on the Range," in *Sense of Place*, 53–67. Both are excerpted in Lane, *Housing and Dwelling*.

77. By the end of the century, manufactured homes began to appear in two-story versions. The split-level form, however, has not been compatible with modular production in centralized factories.

78. Jules Verne, *From the Earth to the Moon* (1865). Later, H. G. Wells, *The First Men in the Moon* (1901); Edgar Rice Burroughs, Mars series and other science fiction, 1912–48; Isaac Asimov, "Trends," 1939, and other science fiction writings thereafter up to 1992. See Bennett, "Edgar Allan Poe."

79. Sputnik in orbit 1957.

80. This is the phrase with which James T. Patterson characterizes the early decades of postwar American history in *Grand Expectations*.

Chapter 6: Conclusion

1. The desire for a sense of spaciousness is a dominant theme in Isenstadt, *Modern American House*.

2. Glassie, *Folk Housing in Middle Virginia*, 66–111.

3. Rooney, *My War*, 5.

4. Childers, *Soldier from the War Returning*.

5. See Rifkind, "L.A. Story."

6. Glaser and Kahn, *Decentralized Employment*.

7. The label "participatory design" is normally used to refer to postwar movements to involve the user, especially the poor, in the design of mass housing. This idea has inspired such disparate figures as community activist John F. C. Turner and architect Ralph Erskine. But logically, all self-building, all "do-it-yourself" remodeling, and most "vernacular architecture" should belong under the same rubric. See the "Participatory Planning and Design" section in Lane, *Housing and Dwelling*, 310–49.

8. Weiss, "Developing and Financing," 309. See also Weiss, *Rise of the Community Builders*.

9. Fischel, "Economic History." See also his *Economics of Zoning Laws* and *Homevoter Hypothesis*.

10. The Levitts are said to have extensively regulated the appearance and use of lots, but I do not think this was the case in most of my examples. Joseph Campanelli, for example, was very fond of front-yard gardens. Of course, the regulation of the appearance and use of one's property had long-established precedents in the zoning regulations of earlier suburbs, where zoning and other regulations functioned to exclude "undesirable" neighbors. (For example, in front yards, the grass had to be kept mowed to a certain height.) The regulations against front-yard gardens are under attack now in many municipalities, partly as a result of the writings and actions of the "local food" (locavore) movement, and partly by environmentalists more generally—those who see mowed lawns as bad for the environment. See among others Schindler, "Backyard Chickens"; Bormann et al., *Redesigning the American Lawn*.

11. Wetherell, *Man Who Loved Levittown*.

12. "Armstrong to the moon and back": Neil Armstrong landed on the moon July 20, 1969, planted an American flag, and returned to Earth July 24, 1969.

13. Voith and Wachter, "Urban Growth."

14. Arnold et al., *Life at Home*, 70–79.

15. Warner, "Public Invasion of Private Space," 171–77.

16. On changing social and economic structures, see Schwartz, *Housing Policy in the United States: An Introduction*; Kneebone and Berube, *Confronting Suburban Poverty*.

17. Tall, "Dwelling," excerpted as "Where Is Home?" in Lane, *Housing and Dwelling*, 408–39.

Appendix

1. While my discussion of the builders is organized regionally, the interviews are presented chronologically. All the regional areas are represented in the interviews, but not all the specific developments on which I have focused are present there. Arlington Heights is absent, and so are Elk Grove Village, Cinderella Homes, and Panorama City. Since it seemed to be especially important to have additional testimony from the Los Angeles area, I introduced an interview from Torrance, Los Angeles County, just south of LA and due west of Lakewood, quite close to Redondo Beach. Postwar Torrance was rather similar in social composition to both Lakewood and Panorama City, and similar in house designs to Panorama City. It was founded in 1912 as a mixed industrial-residential community, with an original Y-shaped plan attributed to Frederick Law Olmsted, Jr. Incorporated in 1921, its growth was stimulated first by steel and electrical industries, small manufacturing, canneries, and then by the discovery of oil in 1921. Its most rapid growth took place, however, after World War II, when the city developed its own aircraft and aerospace industries. Postwar residential areas were developed from 1948 on, initially by Biltmore Builders, whose owner, Mark Taper, was also one of the developers of Lakewood. The period of most rapid development was 1953 to about 1963 (population: 7,271 in 1930; 9,950 in 1940; 22,241 in 1950; 100,991 in 1960; 145,438 in 2010). See Dalton, *Torrance*.

2. Authorized by Congress in 1949: called Natick Laboratories in the sixties; originally the Quartermaster R&D Center, and then the Quartermaster Research and Engineering Command.

3. Transo Envelope Company, 1900 N. Austin, in the "near northwest."

4. Purchase price was $13,000 or maybe a few dollars more. Equivalent to $105,773 in 2010 dollars.

5. The price of $15,000 in 1962 would be $108,306 in 2010 dollars.

BIBLIOGRAPHY

Archives

Arlington Heights, IL, Historical Museum

Welton McDonald Becket Architectural Archives, Dana Point, CA

Boston Public Library, Prints and Photograph Collection

Brockton, MA, Departments of Engineering and Planning

Henry A. L. Brown Archives, Warwick, RI

Fritz B. Burns Collection, Charles von der Ahe Library, Loyola Marymount University, Los Angeles, CA

Nicholas and Doris Campanelli Photo Archive, Brockton, MA

Ronald Cerel Photograph Collection, Brookline, MA

Heidi Cortese Papers, Corona del Mar, CA

Dallas Public Library, Department of Special Collections, Dallas, TX

Elk Grove Village, IL, Public Library

Getty Images Inc., Seattle, WA

Gottscho-Schleisner Photograph Collection, Library of Congress, Washington, DC

Huntington Library Photographic Collection, San Marino, CA

Barbara Miller Lane Document and Photograph Collection, Wayne, PA

Library of Congress, Division of Prints and Photographs, Washington, DC

Los Angeles County land records

Los Angeles Public Library, Visual Collections

Marple, PA, Zoning Office (Broomall, PA)

Marple Township Archives, Media, PA

Middlesex South, Registry of Deeds, Cambridge, MA

Orange County, CA, land records

Rolling Meadows, IL, Historical Society

Schaumburg, IL, Township District Library

Temple University, Urban Archives, Paley Library, Philadelphia, PA

Jean Valjean Vandruff Collected Papers and Drawings, Westminster, CA

Warwick, RI, Assessors' Records

Published Works

Abbott, Edith. *The Tenements of Chicago 1908–1935*. Chicago: University of Chicago Press, 1936.

Accomplishments. Los Angeles: City Planning Commission, 1946.

Accomplishments. Los Angeles: City Planning Commission, 1947.

Adams, Annemarie, and Sally McMurry, eds. *Exploring Everyday Landscapes*. Knoxville: University of Tennessee Press, 1997.

Adams, James Truslow. *Epic of America*. Boston: Little, Brown, 1931.

"The Adaptable Ranch House." *Sunset*, April 1945, 10–13.

Affron, Charles, and Mirella Jona Affron. *Best Years: Going to the Movies, 1945–1946*. New Brunswick, NJ: Rutgers University Press, 2009.

Agricultural Experiment Stations of [seven southern states] and the Housing and Household Equipment Division of the Bureau of Human Nutrition and Home Economics, US Department of Agriculture. *Farm Housing in the South: A Study of Household Activities, Facilities and Family Preferences in Selected Areas of the South as a Basis for Development of Functional Farmhouse Plans*. Athens: College Experiment Station, University of Georgia, 1951.

Ahern, Sheila. "Investing in the Community: Alfred Campanelli Helped Develop Town's YMCA." *Arlington Heights (IL) Daily Herald*, September 20, 2006.

Aladdin Company. *Aladdin "Built in a Day" House Catalog, 1917*. Bay City, MI: Aladdin, 1917. Reprint, New York: Dover, 1995.

Albrecht, Donald, ed. *World War II and the American Dream*. Washington, DC: National Building Museum, 1995.

Allen, Barbara. "The Ranch-Style House in America: A Cultural and Environmental Discourse." *Journal of Architectural Education* 49, no. 3 (February 1996): 156–65.

Allen, Frederick Lewis. *Since Yesterday: The 1930s in America*. New York: Harper & Row, 1939.

Allen, James Paul, and Eugene Turner. *The Ethnic Quilt: Population Diversity in Southern California.* Northridge, CA: Center for Geographical Studies, 1997.

American Builder. *Blueprint Plans from American Builder Magazine: 12 Complete Blueprints, 21 Homes, 7 Garages.* Chicago: Simmons-Boardman, 1946.

———. *Book of Modern Home Decoration.* New York: Simmons-Boardman, 1959.

———. *Book of Modern Kitchens.* New York: Simmons-Boardman, 1958.

———. *Defense Homes Hand Book: Portfolio of Low Cost Homes and Rental Housing Units; "Critical List" Materials and How to Get a Priority Rating.* Chicago: Simmons-Boardman, 1941.

———. *Home Ownership for Renters: Good Design Suggestions; Security Homes: Suggestions for Planning, Building, Financing.* Chicago: Simmons-Boardman, 1941.

———. *How to Remodel Your Home.* New York: Simmons-Boardman, 1958.

———. *Small Homes of Charm.* Chicago: American Builder and Building Age, 1931.

American Face Brick Association. *Five-Room Face Brick Bungalow and Small House Plans.* Chicago: American Face Brick Association, 1923.

———. *Industrial Buildings and Housing: Valuable Information for the Designer and Prospective Owner of Factories and Homes for Industrial Workers.* Chicago: American Face Brick Association, 1926.

———. *Six-Room Face Brick Bungalow and Small House Plans.* Chicago: American Face Brick Association, 1920s.

———. *Three and Four Room Face Brick Bungalow and Small House Plans.* Chicago: American Face Brick Association, 1923.

American Institute of Architects. *Your Future Home: A Selected Collection of Plans for Small Houses from Three to Six Rooms, for Which Complete Working Drawings May Be Secured at Nominal Cost.* Saint Paul, MN: Weyerhaeuser Forest Products, 1923.

The American Woman's Home of Tomorrow: A Report of the Home Contest. New York: McCall, June 1945.

Anderson, C. "Split Level: A Better Small House?" *Better Homes and Gardens* 33 (April 1955): 74–77.

Andrzejewski, Anna Vemer. *Building Power: Architecture and Surveillance in Victorian America.* Knoxville: University of Tennessee Press, 2008.

———. "Building Privacy and Community: Surveillance in a Postwar American Suburban Development in Madison,

Wisconsin." *Landscape Journal* 28, no. 1 (2009): 40–56.

Anton, Mike. "A Splendid Isolation Up Against the Wall; On Its 50th Anniversary Bricked-Off Rossmoor Ponders Its Fate." *Los Angeles Times*, February 4, 2007, B5.

Archer, John. *Architecture and Suburbia: From English Villa to American Dream House, 1690—2000.* Minneapolis: University of Minnesota Press, 2005.

Architects' Small House Service Bureau of the United States. *Better Homes in America: Plan Book of Small Homes (Three, Four, Five and Six Rooms).* Washington, DC: Better Homes, 1924.

Architectural Forum. *Building, U.S.A.: The Men and Methods That Influence Architecture in America Today.* New York: McGraw-Hill, 1957.

———. *The 1938 Book of Small Houses.* New York: Simon & Schuster, 1937.

———. *The 1936–40 Book(s) of Small Houses.* New York: Simon & Schuster, 1936–40.

Architectural Forum. *The Builders.* April 1949.

Architectural Forum. *The Small House.* April 1950.

Armistead, Betty. *Schaumburg.* Mount Pleasant, SC: Arcadia, 2004.

Arnold, Jeanne E., et al. *Life at Home in the Twenty-First Century.* Los Angeles: Center on Everyday Lives of Families, Cotsen Institute of Archaeology, 2013.

Ashby, Wallace. *Farmhouse Plans, Farmer's Bulletin no. 1738,* Washington, DC: US Department of Agriculture, 1935.

"Assembly-Line Living." *Newsweek*, October 5, 1953, 64–69.

Atcher, Bob. *Bob Atcher's Best Early American Folk Songs.* Columbia Records, 1965.

———. *The Dean of Cowboy Singers: The Western Side of Bob Atcher.* CBS, 1960s.

"Awards in Architecture." *House and Garden*, January 1946, 56–59.

"Awards in Architecture 1945." *House and Garden*, December 1945, 86–89.

Baker, Allison Leslie. *The Lakewood Story: Defending the Recreational Good Life in Postwar Southern California Suburbia, 1950–1999.* Ann Arbor: University of Michigan Dissertation Services, 1999.

Baldwin, Robert Morton. "Lewis F. Garlinghouse." In *Illustriana Kansas: Biographical Sketches of Kansas Men and Women of Achievement Who Have Been Awarded Life Membership in Kansas Illustriana Society*, 428. Hebron, NE: Illustriana, 1933.

Baltzell, E. Digby. *Philadelphia Gentlemen: The Making of a National Upper Class.* Philadelphia: University of

Pennsylvania, 1979.

Banham, Reyner. *Los Angeles: The Architecture of Four Ecologies.* New York: Harper & Row, 1971.

Bauer, Catherine K. *Modern Housing.* Boston: Houghton Mifflin, 1934.

Baumgartner, M. P. *The Moral Order of a Suburb.* Oxford: Oxford University Press, 1988.

Baxandall, Rosalyn, and Elizabeth Ewen. "Picture Windows: The Changing Role of Women in the Suburbs, 1945–2000." *Long Island Historical Journal* 3, no. 1 (1990): 89–108.

———. *Picture Windows: How the Suburbs Happened.* New York: Basic Books, 2000.

Beckham, Sue Bridwell. "The American Front Porch: Women's Liminal Space." In *Making the American Home: Middle-Class Women and Domestic Material Culture, 1840–1940*, edited by Marilyn Ferris Motz and Pat Browne, 69–89. Bowling Green, OH: Bowling Green State University Popular Press, 1988.

Ben-Joseph, Eran. *The Code of the City: Standards and the Hidden Language of Place Making.* Cambridge, MA: MIT Press, 2005.

Ben-Joseph, Eran, and Terry S. Szold, eds. *Regulating Place: Standards and the Shaping of Urban America.* London: Taylor & Francis, 2004.

Bennett, Mark. *TV Sets: Fantasy Blueprints of Classic TV Homes.* New York: Penguin, 1996.

Bennett, Maurice J. "Edgar Allan Poe and the Literary Tradition of Lunar Speculation." *Science Fiction Studies* 10, no. 2 (1983): 137–47.

Ben Weingart & Weingart Foundation. Los Angeles: Weingart Foundation, 2002.

Bergdoll, Barry, and Peter Christensen, eds. *Home Delivery: Fabricating the Modern Dwelling.* New York: Museum of Modern Art, 2008.

Berger, Bennett M. "The Myth of Suburbia." *Journal of Social Issues* 17, no. 1 (1961): 38–49.

———. *Working-Class Suburb: A Study of Auto Workers in Suburbia.* Berkeley: University of California Press, 1960.

Bernhardt, Arthur D. *Building Tomorrow: The Mobile/Manufactured Housing Industry.* Cambridge, MA: MIT Press, 1980.

Berry, Wendell. *The Unsettling of America: Culture and Agriculture.* New York: Avon Books, 1977.

Beuka, Robert. *SuburbiaNation: Reading Suburban Landscape in Twentieth Century American Fiction and Film.* New York: Palgrave Macmillan, 2004.

Beyer, Glenn H. *The Cornell Kitchen: Product Design through Research.* Ithaca: New York State College of Home Economics, 1953.

———. *Housing: A Factual Analysis.* New York: Macmillan, 1958.

Bigott, Joseph C. *From Cottage to Bungalow: Houses and the Working Class in Metropolitan Chicago, 1869–1929.* Chicago: University of Chicago Press, 2001.

Bingaman, Amy, Lise Sanders, and Rebecca Zorach, eds. *Embodied Utopias: Gender, Social Change, and the Modern Metropolis.* London: Taylor & Francis, 2002.

Black, Lisa. "Revering the Ranch: Rolling Meadows Plans to Honor Its Ranch-House Past. . . ." *Chicago Tribune,* January 2, 2000.

Bledstein, Burton J., and Robert D. Johnston, eds. *The Middling Sorts: Explorations in the History of the American Middle Class.* London: Taylor & Francis, 2001.

Bletter, Rosemarie Haag, et al. *Remembering the Future: The New York World's Fair from 1939–1964.* New York: Rizzoli, 1989.

Bloom, Nicholas D. *Suburban Alchemy: 1960s New Towns and the Transformation of the American Dream.* Columbus: Ohio State University Press, 2001.

Bodek, Ralph. *How and Why People Buy Houses: A Study of Subconscious Home Buying Motives.* Philadelphia: Municipal Publications, 1958.

Bormann, F. Herbert, et al., eds. *Redesigning the American Lawn: A Search for Environmental Harmony.* New Haven, CT: Yale University Press, 1993.

"Boston Women Design Their Dream Home." *Parents' Magazine and Better Homemaking* 42 (June 1967): 80–83.

Bowden, Mark. "Suburbia at 50: A Case Study." *Philadelphia Inquirer*, 1997. Six-part series on Marple Township, February 9 ("Classic Suburb Adjusts to New Set of Growing Pains"), 10 ("Child-Rearing on a Fast Track"), 11 ("Pioneers' New Frontier: Aging"), 12 ("The Once-Prized Schools Become a Battleground"), 13 ("Layoffs Land Unexpected Blows"), 14 ("New Arrivals; Traditional Hopes").

Bricker, David. "Cliff May." In *Toward a Simpler Way of Life: The Arts & Crafts Architects of California*, edited by Robert Winter, 283–90. Berkeley: University of California Press, 1997.

———. "Ranch Houses Are Not All the Same." National Parks Service Cultural Resources, n.d. http://www.cr.nps.gov/nr/publications/bulletins/suburbs/Bricker.pdf (accessed March 24, 2009). Based on master's thesis,

"Built for Sale: Cliff May and the Low Cost California Ranch" (University of California, Santa Barbara, 1983).

Brill, Alida. "Lakewood, California: 'Tomorrowland' at 40." In *Rethinking Los Angeles*, edited by Michael J. Dear, H. Eric Schockman, and Greg Hise, 97–112. Thousand Oaks, CA: Sage, 1996.

Brinckloe, William Draper. *The Small Home, How to Plan and Build It: With Sixty Practical Plans for Low Cost Bungalows, Cottages, Farmhouse Apartments, Garages and Barns*. New York: Robert M. McBride, 1924.

Bronner, Simon J. *Consuming Visions: Accumulation and Display of Goods in America 1880–1920*. New York: Norton, 1989.

Broomer, Kathleen Kelly. "Shoppers World and the Regional Shopping Center in Greater Boston." *Journal of the Society for Commercial Archaeology* 13, no. 1 (1994–95): 2–9.

Brostrom, Caitlin Lempres, and Richard C. Peters. *The Houses of William Wurster: Frames for Living*. New York: Princeton Architectural Press, 2011.

Brown, Henry A. L., and Richard J. Walton. *John Brown's Tract: Lost Adirondack Empire*. Canaan, NH: Phoenix, 1988.

Bruce, Alfred, and Harold Sandblank. *A History of Prefabrication*. New York: Arno Press, 1972. Reprint of the 1944 ed., which was issued as *Housing Research*, 3. Original ed. reprinted from a series of articles appearing in the *Architectural Forum* beginning in December 1942.

Bruegmann, Robert. *Sprawl: A Compact History*. Chicago: University of Chicago Press, 2005.

"Builder 100." *Builder*, May 1993, 172.

"The Builder's House." *Architectural Forum*, April 1949, 81–93.

Builders' Idea Kit: Home Owners' Catalogs. 4th ed. New York: F.W. Dodge, 1940.

Building Research Advisory Board, National Research Council, National Academy of Sciences. *A Survey of Housing Research in the United States*. Washington, DC: Housing and Home Finance Agency, November 1952.

Buisseret, David, and James A. Issel. *Elk Grove Village and Township*. Chicago: Newberry Library and Elk Grove Historical Society, 1996.

Burbank, Nelson Lincoln. *House Construction Details Based on Reproductions from American Builder and Building Age, and Other Sources*. Comp., 2nd printing with corrections. New York: Simmons-Boardman, 1940.

Burby, Raymond J. *Recreation and Leisure in New Communities*. Cambridge, MA: Ballinger, 1976.

Burnett, John. *A Social History of Housing 1815–1970*. London: Eyre Methuen, 1980.

"Burns, Fritz." *Life* 26 (January 31, 1949): 82–85.

Burns, Fritz. *Livable Homes for Those Who Love Living*. New York: Revere Copper and Brass, 1944.

———. "Toluca Wood." Sales brochure, ca. 1944.

Burns, Fritz, and Henry J. Kaiser. "Kaiser Community Homes." Sales brochure, ca. 1946.

Burns, Fritz, and Fred Marlowe. "Windsor Hills." Sales brochure, ca. 1938.

California Department of Parks and Recreation, Historic Resources Group. "Panorama City Historic District." Application for listing in the National Register of Historic Places. Approved 2002.

"A California Ranch House." *Architecture* 71 (January 1935): 17–18.

Callender, John Hancock. *Before You Buy a House*. New York: Crown, 1953.

Cammarota, Anne Marie. *Pavements in the Garden: The Suburbanization of Southern New Jersey, Adjacent to the City of Philadelphia, 1769 to the Present*. Madison, WI: Fairleigh Dickinson University Press, 2001.

Campanelli Brothers. "Governor Francis Farms in Gaspee, Warwick, R.I." Sales brochure, ca. 1954.

———. "Welcome to Colonial Weathersfield in Schaumburg, Where the Living Is Wonderful." Sales brochure, ca. 1960.

"Cape Cod, but Not a Cottage." *Architectural Record*, January 1945, 88–89.

Carlson, Allan C. *The Family in America: Searching for Social Harmony in the Industrial Age*. New Brunswick, NJ: Transaction, 2003.

Carrasquillo, Avian. "Housing a Rich History in Schaumburg." *Arlington Heights (IL) Daily Herald*, August 11, 2006.

Cassidy, Marsha F. *What Women Watched: Daytime Television in the 1950s*. Austin: University of Texas Press, 2005.

"Casual Ease for Family Life." *Architectural Record*, May 1957, 188–91.

"Centex Climbs in Chicago Market." *Professional Builder*, March 1999, 48.

"Centex Enters Manufactured Arena." *Builder*, January 1998, 15, 17.

Chapman, Tony, and Jenny Hockey, eds. *Ideal Homes? Social Change and Domestic Life*. London: Routledge, 1999.

"Charles H. Cress." *Chicago Tribune*, May 26, 1963, D7.

Charles, Robert. "Atlanta Women Design Their Dream Home." *Parents' Magazine and Better Homemaking* 42 (1967): 83–85.

———. "Boston Women Design Their Dream Home." *Parents' Magazine and Better Homemaking* 42 (1967): 80–83.

———. "Chicago Mothers Design Their Dream Home." *Parents' Magazine and Better Homemaking* 42 (1967): 53–56.

———. "Detroit Women Design Their Dream Home." *Parents' Magazine and Better Homemaking* 42 (1967): 68–70.

———. "Los Angeles Women Design Their Dream Home." *Parents' Magazine and Better Homemaking* 42 (1967): 88–90.

Checkoway, Barry. "Large Builders, Federal Housing Programs, and Postwar Suburbanization." *International Journal of Urban and Regional Research* 4, no. 1 (March 1980): 21–45.

Childers, Thomas. *Soldier from the War Returning: The Greatest Generation's Troubled Homecoming from World War II.* Boston: Houghton Mifflin Harcourt, 2009.

Chow, Renee Y. *Suburban Space: The Fabric of Dwelling.* Berkeley: University of California Press, 2002.

Christie, Robert A. *Empire in Wood: A History of the Carpenters' Union.* Ithaca, NY: Cornell University Press, 1956.

Cieraad, Irene, ed. *At Home: An Anthropology of Domestic Space.* Syracuse, NY: Syracuse University Press, 1999.

———. "Dutch Windows." In Cieraad, *At Home,* 31–32.

Clapson, Mark. *Suburban Century: Social Change and Urban Growth in England and the USA.* New York: Berg, 2003.

Clark, Clifford, Jr. *The American Family Home.* Chapel Hill: University of North Carolina Press, 1986.

———. "Ranch House Suburbia: Ideals and Realities." In *Recasting America,* edited by Larry May, 171–91. Chicago: University of Chicago Press, 1989.

Clarke, Alison J. "Tupperware: Suburbia, Sociality and Mass Consumption." In *Visions of Suburbia,* edited by Roger Silverstone, 132–60. London: Taylor & Francis, 1997.

Cochran, Thomas N. "Offerings in the Offing: Centex Construction in Products." *Barron's,* March 28, 1994, 50.

Cohen, Jean-Louis. *Architecture in Uniform: Designing and Building for the Second World War.* Montreal: Canadian Centre for Architecture, 2010.

Cohen, Lizabeth A. *A Consumers' Republic: The Politics of Mass Consumption in Postwar America.* New York: Knopf, 2003.

———. "Embellishing a Life of Labor: An Interpretation of the Material Culture of American Working-Class Homes, 1885–1915." *Journal of American Culture* 4 (1980): 752–74.

———. *Making a New Deal: Industrial Workers in Chicago, 1919–1939.* Cambridge: Cambridge University Press, 1990.

Colby, Nancy, and Kelly Behnke. *Images of America: Elk Grove Village.* Charleston, SC: Arcadia, 2008.

Colker, David. "Building a Future in 1948: A Riddle and a Single House Launched 'American Way of Life' in Panorama City." *Los Angeles Times,* September 4, 1999, 1.

Colomina, Beatriz. *Domesticity at War.* Cambridge, MA: MIT Press, 2007.

———. "The Exhibitionist House." In *At the End of the Century: One Hundred Years of Architecture,* edited by Richard Koshalek and Elizabeth A. T. Smith, 126–65. Los Angeles: Museum of Contemporary Art and Harry N. Abrams, 1998.

———, ed. *Sexuality and Space.* New York: Princeton Architectural Press, 1992.

Committee on Banking and Currency. *Housing Constructed under VA and FHA Programs: Hearings before the Subcommittee on Housing of the Committee on Banking and Currency, Parts 2–4.* Washington, DC: House of Representatives, 1952.

"Community Shopping Center Is Planned for Green Valley." *Chicago Daily Tribune,* December 15, 1946.

Connally, Ernest Allen. "The Cape Cod House: An Introductory Study." *Journal of the Society of Architectural Historians* 19, no. 2 (1960): 47–56.

Contosta, David R. *Suburb in the City: Chestnut Hill, Philadelphia 1850–1990.* Columbus: Ohio State University Press, 1992.

Cooper-Marcus, Clare. *House as a Mirror of Self: Exploring the Deeper Meaning of Home.* Berkeley, CA: Conari Press, 1995.

Corcoran, Mary P., Jane Gray, and Michel Peillon. *Suburban Affiliations: Social Relations in the Greater Dublin Area.* Syracuse, NY: Syracuse University Press, 2010.

Cortese, Ross. Sales brochures, 1952–58.

Cowan, Ruth Schwartz. *More Work for Mother: The Ironies of Household Technology from the Open Hearth to the Microwave.* New York: Basic Books, 1983.

Crawford, Margaret. "Daily Life on the Home Front: Women, Blacks, and the Struggle for Public Housing." In *World War II and the American Dream,* edited by Donald

Albrecht, 90–143. Washington, DC: National Building Museum, 1995.

Creighton, Thomas H. *Planning to Build*. Garden City, NY: Doubleday, 1946.

Creighton, Thomas H., and Katherine Ford. *Contemporary Houses, Evaluated by Their Owners*. New York: Reinhold, 1961.

Creighton, Thomas H., Frank G. Lopez, Charles Magruder, and George A. Sanderson. *Homes: Selected by the Editors of Progressive Architecture*. New York: Reinhold, 1947.

Cromley, Elizabeth Collins. *Alone Together: A History of New York's Early Apartments*. Ithaca, NY: Cornell University Press, 1990.

———. "Domestic Space Transformed, 1850–2000." In *Architectures: Modernism and After*, edited by Andrew Ballantyne, 163–201. Malden, MA: Blackwell, 2004.

———. *The Food Axis: Cooking, Eating, and the Architecture of American Homes*. Charlottesville: University of Virginia Press, 2010.

———. "A History of American Beds and Bedrooms." In *Perspectives in Vernacular Architecture, IV*, edited by Thomas Carter and Bernard L. Herman, 177–86. Columbia: University of Missouri Press, 1991.

Cronon, William. *Nature's Metropolis: Chicago and the Great West*. New York: Norton, 1991.

Csikszentmihalyi, M., and E. Rochberg-Halton. *The Meaning of Things: Domestic Symbols and the Self*. New York: Cambridge University Press, 1981.

Cuff, Dana. *The Provisional City: Los Angeles Stories of Architecture and Urbanism*. Cambridge, MA: MIT Press, 2000.

Cullen, Jim. *American Dream*. New York: Oxford, 2003.

Culver, Lawrence. *The Frontier of Leisure: Southern California and the Shaping of Modern America*. Oxford: Oxford University Press, 2010.

Cunnion, Don. "A Home That Has Everything." *Farm Journal* 81 (May 1957): 36–37.

Curtis Publishing Company. *Urban Housing Survey: The Saturday Evening Post, Ladies' Home Journal, Country Gentleman*. Philadelphia: Curtis Publishing Company, 1945.

Cutler, Irving. *Chicago: Metropolis of the Mid-Continent*. Carbondale: Southern Illinois University Press, 2006.

Daday, Eileen O. "Historical Film Strikes Chord in Schaumburg." *Arlington Heights (IL) Daily Herald*, September 9, 2006.

Dalton, Peggy Coleman. *Torrance, a City for Today: A Contemporary Portrait*. Torrance, CA: Torrance Chamber of Commerce, 1990.

Daniels, Roger. *Coming to America: A History of Immigration and Ethnicity in American Life*. Rev. ed. New York: HarperCollins, 2002.

Darley, Gillian. *Villages of Vision*. London: Granada, 1978.

Date, Shruti. "Y's Benefactor to Get First Look." *Arlington Heights (IL) Daily Herald*, June 4, 2002.

Davis, Mike. *City of Quartz: Excavating the Future in Los Angeles*. London: Verso, 1990.

Davis, Sam. *The Architecture of Affordable Housing*. Berkeley: University of California Press, 1995.

Davison, Graeme. "The Suburban Idea and Its Enemies." *Journal of Urban History* 39, no. 5 (September 2013): 829–47.

Dean, John P., and Simon Breines. *The Book of Houses: Planned for Beauty and Utility at Low Cost*. New York: Crown, 1946.

Decision Resources. *Executive Summary, 2003 Rolling Meadows Residential Study*. Chicago: Decision Resources, 2003.

DeLyser, Dydia. *Ramona Memories: Tourism and the Shaping of Southern California*. Minneapolis: University of Minnesota Press, 2005.

Deverell, William. *Whitewashed Adobe: The Rise of Los Angeles and the Remaking of Its Mexican Past*. Berkeley: University of California Press, 2004.

de Wit, Wim, and Christopher James Alexander, eds. *Overdrive: Los Angeles Constructs the Future*. Los Angeles: Getty Research Institute, 2013.

DiBacco, Thomas V. "Builder Levitt Dies at 86; Low-Cost Housing Revolutionized Suburbia in U.S." *Washington Times*, January 30, 1994, A1.

DiFilipo, Thomas J. *The History and Development of Upper Darby Township*. 2nd ed. Upper Darby, PA: Upper Darby Historical Society, 1992.

Dixon, Dean O. *Buena Park*. Mount Pleasant, SC: Arcadia, 2004.

Doan, Mason C. *American Housing Production, 1880–2000: A Concise History*. Lanham, MD: University Press of America, 1997.

Dobriner, William M. *Class in Suburbia*. Englewood Cliffs, NJ: Prentice Hall, 1963.

Dolan, Michael. *The American Porch: An Informal History of an Informal Place*. Guilford, CT: Lyons Press, 2002.

Donaldson, Scott. *The Suburban Myth*. New York: Columbia University Press, 1969.

"Don't Build a Box, There's Appeal in a Rambling Profile." *Good Housekeeping* 126 (1948): 65–71.

Doucet, Michael J., and John C. Weaver. *Housing the North American City*. Montreal: McGill-Queen's University Press, 1991.

Duany, Andres, Elizabeth Plater-Zyberk, and Jeff Speck. *Suburban Nation: The Rise of Sprawl and the Decline of the American Dream*. New York: North Point Press, 2000.

Duncan, James S., and Nancy Duncan. *Landscapes of Privilege: Aesthetics and Affluence in an American Suburb*. London: Taylor & Francis, 2004.

Dunlop, Beth. *Building a Dream: The Art of Disney Architecture*. New York: Harry N. Abrams, 1996.

Dunlop, John T., and Walter Galenson. *Labor in the Twentieth Century*. New York: Academic Press, 1978.

Earley, Tony. "The Hallway." In *Somehow Form a Family*, 19–49. Chapel Hill, NC: Algonquin Books, 2001.

Ebner, Michael H. *Creating Chicago's North Shore: A Suburban History*. Chicago: University of Chicago Press, 1988.

———. "The Result of Honest Hard Work: Creating a Suburban Ethos for Evanston (Summer 1984)." In *A Wild Kind of Boldness: The Chicago History Reader*, edited by Rosemary K. Adams, 176–89. Chicago: Chicago Historical Society, 1998.

Edel, Matthew, Elliot D. Sclar, and Daniel Luria. *Shaky Palaces: Homeownership and Social Mobility in Boston's Suburbanization*. New York: Columbia University Press, 1984.

Ehrenreich, Barbara. *Fear of Falling: The Inner Life of the Middle Class*. New York: Harper, 1990.

Ehrenreich, Barbara, and Deirdre English. "The Manufacture of Housework." *Socialist Revolution* 5, no. 4 (October–December 1975): 5–40.

Eichler, Ned. *The Merchant Builders*. Cambridge, MA: MIT Press, 1982.

"Eight Houses for Modern Living." *Life*, September 26, 1938, 45–67.

"800 Houses—3 ½ Months." *American Builder*, July 1943, 36–37.

Eisinger, Larry, ed. *Low Cost Homes*. New York: Arco, 1958.

Elk Grove Village. "Elk Grove Village Model Home Plans." Sales brochure. Ca. 1960.

Ellis, Russell, and Dana Cuff, eds. *Architects' People*. Oxford: Oxford University Press, 1989.

Elsaesser, Thomas. "Tales of Sound and Fury: Observations on the Family Melodrama." In Nichols, *Movies and Methods*, 2:165–89.

"The Emerging American Style. . . ." *House Beautiful* 92 (May 1950).

Espie, Jason, Megan Findley, and Ebony Walden. "Pennsylvania Suburbs Population Projection and Forecast." Unpublished manuscript, April 14, 2005.

Evans-Daly, Laurie, and David C. Gordon. *Framingham*. Mount Pleasant, SC: Arcadia, 1997.

"Every 9 Minutes a New Prefab House." *Changing Times*, December 1959, 33–36.

Ewen, Elizabeth, and Stuart Ewen. *Channels of Desire: Mass Images and the Shaping of American Consciousness*. Minneapolis: University of Minnesota Press, 1992.

Faragher, John Mack. "Bungalow and Ranch House: The Architectural Backwash of California." *Western Historical Quarterly* 3, no. 2 (Summer 2001): 148–73.

Farber, Evan Ira. "General Periodicals." *Library Trends* 10, no. 3 (Winter 1962): 318. https://www.ideals.illinois.edu/handle/2142/5244/browse?value=Farber%2C+Evan+Ira&type=author.

Fausch, Deborah. "Ugly and Ordinary: The Representation of the Everyday." In Harris and Berke, *Architecture of the Everyday*, 75–106.

Federal Housing Administration. *Land Planning Bulletin, No. 1: Successful Subdivisions: Planned as Neighborhoods for Profitable Investment and Appeal to Home Owners*. Washington, DC: Federal Housing Administration, March 1941.

———. *Land Planning Bulletin, No. 3: Neighborhood Standards*. Washington, DC: Federal Housing Administration, January 1947.

———. *Land Planning Bulletin, No. 3–5B: Neighborhood Standards*. Los Angeles: Federal Housing Administration, May 1953.

———. *Principles of Planning Small Houses*. Washington, DC: Federal Housing Administration, July 1, 1940.

———. *Principles of Planning Small Houses*. Washington, DC: Federal Housing Administration, June 1, 1946.

———. *Technical Bulletin No. 2: Modern Design*. Washington DC: Federal Housing Administration, March 1, 1941.

———. *Technical Bulletin No. 5: Planning Neighborhoods for Small Houses*. Washington DC: Federal Housing Administration, July 1, 1936.

———. *Technical Bulletin No. 5: Planning Neighborhoods for Small Houses*. Washington, DC: Federal Housing Administration, July 1, 1938.

———. *Typical Subdivision Requirements*. Washington, DC: Land Planning Division, Federal Housing

Administration, 1940–49.

Ferrer, Margaret L., and Tova Navarra. *Levittown: The First 50 Years*. Mount Pleasant, SC: Arcadia, 1997.

———. *Levittown*. Vol. 2. Mount Pleasant, SC: Arcadia, 1999.

"15,000 'Trade Secrets' House." *Life*, January 5, 1953, 8–15.

Findlay, John M. *Magic Lands: Western Cityscapes and American Culture after 1940*. Berkeley: University of California, Berkeley, 1992.

"The First Postwar House, Built in Los Angeles by F. Burns for Demonstration and Experimentation." *House Beautiful* 88 (May 1946): 82–123.

Fischel, William A. "An Economic History of Zoning and a Cure for Its Exclusionary Effects." Hanover, NH: Dartmouth College, December 18, 2001.

———. *The Economics of Zoning Laws: A Property Rights Approach to American Land Use Controls*. Baltimore: Johns Hopkins University Press, 1985.

———. *The Homevoter Hypothesis: How Home Values Influence Local Government Taxation, School Finance, and Land-Use Policies*. Cambridge, MA: Harvard University Press, 2001.

Fishman, Robert. *Bourgeois Utopias: The Rise and Fall of Suburbia*. New York: Basic Books, 1989.

———. *Urban Utopias of the Twentieth Century: Ebenezer Howard, Frank Lloyd Wright, and Le Corbusier*. New York: Basic Books, 1977.

"Five Prize Houses, Eleventh Annual Small House Competition." *House Beautiful* 81 (January 1939): 25–33.

Flagg, Ernest. *Small Houses, Their Economic Design and Construction: Essays on the Fundamental Principles of Design and Descriptive Articles on Construction*. New York: Scribner, 1922.

Fogelson, Robert M. *Bourgeois Nightmares: Suburbia, 1870–1930*. New Haven, CT: Yale University Press, 2005.

Ford, James, and Katherine Morrow Ford. *Design of Modern Interiors*. New York: Architectural Book Publishing, 1942.

———. *The Modern House in America*. New York: Architectural Book Publishing, 1940.

Ford, Katherine Morrow, and Thomas H. Creighton. *The American House Today: 85 Notable Examples*. New York: Reinhold, 1951.

———. *Designs for Living: 175 Examples of Quality Home Interiors*. New York: Reinhold, 1955.

———. *Quality Budget Homes: A Treasury of 100 Architect-Designed Houses from $5,000 to $20,000*. New York: Reinhold, 1954.

Forty, Adrian. *Objects of Desire: Design and Society 1750–1980*. New York: Pantheon, 1986.

The Forum Study of the House Market. New York: Architectural Forum, 1945.

Foster, Mark S. *Henry J. Kaiser: Builder in the Modern American West*. Austin: University of Texas Press, 1989.

Foy, Jessica H., and Thomas J. Schlereth, eds. *American Home Life, 1880–1930: A Social History of Spaces and Services*. Knoxville: University of Tennessee Press, 1992.

Freeman, Dawni. "Home and Work: The Use of Space in a Nebraska Farmhouse." In Lane, *Housing and Dwelling*, 231–32.

Friedan, Betty. *The Feminine Mystique*. New York: Norton, 1963.

Friedman, Avi. *The Adaptable House: Designing Homes for Change*. New York: McGraw-Hill, 2002.

———. "Design for Flexibility and Affordability: Learning from the Post-War Home." *Journal of Architectural and Planning Research* 14, no. 2 (Summer 1997): 150–70.

———. "The Evolution of Design Characteristics during the Post-Second World War Housing Boom: The US Experience." *Journal of Design History* 8, no. 2 (1995): 131–46.

———. "Prefabrication versus Conventional Construction in Single Family Wood-Frame Housing." *Building Research and Information: The International Journal of Research, Development and Demonstration* 20, no. 4 (1992): 226–28.

Friedman, Diana. *Sitcom Style*. New York: Clarkson Potter, 2005.

"Fritz Burns." *Life* 26, no. 5 (January 31, 1949): 82–85.

"Fritz Burns' 500 New Homes." *Architectural Forum*, November 1949, 84–85.

"From Old Mexico." *House and Garden*, April 1941, 40–41.

Frykman, Jonas, and Orvar Löfgren. *Culture Builders: A Historical Anthropology of Middle-Class Life*. Translated by Alan Crozier. New Brunswick, NJ: Rutgers University Press, 1987.

Galinou, Mireille. *Cottages and Villas: The Birth of the Garden Suburb*. New Haven, CT: Yale University Press, 2010.

Gallegos, Laura. "Cliff May and the California Ranch House." Unpublished manuscript.

Gans, Herbert J. *The Levittowners: Ways of Life and Politics in a New Suburban Community*. New York: Vintage, 1967.

———. "Park Forest: Birth of a Jewish Community." *Commentary* 2 (May 1951).

———. "Progress of a Suburban Jewish Community: Park Forest Revisited." *Commentary* 22 (February 1957).

———. *The Urban Villagers: Group and Class in the Life of Italian Americans.* New York: Collier Macmillan, 1982.

Garlinghouse. *All American Homes.* Topeka, KS: Garlinghouse, 1940.

———. *America's Best Low-Cost Homes.* Topeka, KS: Garlinghouse, 1940s.

———. *Bungalow Homes.* Topeka, KS: Garlinghouse, 1920.

———. *Low Budget Homes.* Topeka, KS: Garlinghouse, 1940s.

———. *New American Homes.* Topeka, KS: Garlinghouse, 1937.

———. *New American House.* Topeka, KS: Garlinghouse, 1940.

———. *New Brick Homes.* Topeka, KS: Garlinghouse, 1945.

———. *New Small Homes.* Topeka, KS: Garlinghouse, 1940s.

———. *Our Future Home.* Topeka, KS: Garlinghouse, 1940s.

———. *Ranch and Suburban Homes.* Topeka, KS: Garlinghouse, 1948.

———. *Ranch and Suburban Homes.* Topeka, KS: Garlinghouse, 1951.

———. *Split Level Homes.* Topeka, KS: Garlinghouse, 1950s.

Garreau, Joel. *Edge City.* New York: Doubleday, 1991.

Gebhard, David, ed. *Los Angeles in the Thirties: 1931–1941.* Los Angeles: Hennessey and Ingalls, 1989.

Gebhard, David, and Robert Winter. *A Guide to Architecture in Southern California.* Los Angeles: Los Angeles County Museum of Art, 1965.

Gerstle, Gary. *American Crucible: Race and Nation in the Twentieth Century.* Princeton, NJ: Princeton University Press, 2001.

Ghirardo, Diane, ed. *Architecture After Modernism.* New York: Thames and Hudson, 1996.

———. *Out of Site: A Social Criticism of Architecture.* Seattle: Bay Press, 1991.

Gibbs, Jocelyn, et al., eds. *Carefree California: Cliff May and the Romance of the Ranch House.* Santa Barbara, CA: Design & Architecture Museum, University of California, Santa Barbara, 2012.

Gillette, Jane Brown. "Garden District: Landscape and Urban Design in Anaheim and Disneyland Resorts." *Land Forum* 12 (2002): 46–65.

Glaser, Edward L., and Matthew E. Kahn. *Decentralized Employment and the Transformation of the American City.* NBER working paper, 2001.

Glassie, Henry H. *Folk Housing in Middle Virginia.* Knoxville: University of Tennessee Press, 1975.

———. *Material Culture.* Bloomington: Indiana University Press, 1999.

———. *Vernacular Architecture.* Bloomington: Indiana University Press, 2000.

Gledhill, Christine, ed. *Home Is Where the Heart Is: Studies in Melodrama and the Woman's Film.* London: BFI, 1987.

Glickman, Lawrence B., ed. *Consumer Society in American History: A Reader.* Ithaca, NY: Cornell University Press, 1999.

Goldstein, Carolyn M. *Do It Yourself: Home Improvement in 20th-century America.* Washington, DC: National Building Museum, 1998.

———. "Home Economics: Mediators." In *Gender & Technology: A Reader*, edited by Nina E. Lerman, Ruth Oldenziel, and Arwen P. Mohun, 359–91. Baltimore: Johns Hopkins University Press, 2003.

Gonzales, Jerry. "'A Place in the Sun': Mexican Americans, Race, and the Suburbanization of Los Angeles, 1940–1980." PhD dissertation, University of Southern California, 2009.

Gottman, Jean. *Megalopolis: The Urbanized Northeastern Seaboard of the United States.* New York: Twentieth Century Fund, 1961.

Gowans, Alan. *The Comfortable House: North American Suburban Architecture, 1890–1930.* Cambridge, MA: MIT Press, 1986.

"The Greatest House-Building Show on Earth." *Architectural Forum*, March 1947, 105–13.

Grebler, Leo. *Large Scale Housing and Real Estate Firms: Analysis of a New Business Enterprise.* New York: Praeger, 1973.

Gregory, Daniel P. *Cliff May and the Modern Ranch House.* New York: Rizzoli, 2008.

Gross, Irma M. "Governor Francis Farms: A Planned Residential Community." Unpublished manuscript, Warwick Historical Society, January 20, 1982.

Groth, Paul. "Les minimal bungalows, ou l'inscription des valeurs de progrès de la classe moyenne dans la construction de l'habitatat ouvrier (1900–1930)." In *Refaire l'Amérique: imaginaire et histoire des États-Unis*, edited by Didier Aubert and Hélène Quanquin, 75–96. Paris: Presses Sorbonne Nouvelle, 2011.

———. "Workers'-Cottage and Minimal-Bungalow Districts in Oakland and Berkeley, California, 1970–1945." *Urban Morphology* 8, no. 1 (2004): 13–25.

Grow, Lawrence. *Old House Plans—Two Centuries of American Domestic Architecture.* New York: Universe Books, 1978.

Gutheim, Frederick. *One Hundred Years of Architecture in America, 1857–1957: Celebrating the Centennial of the American Institute of Architects.* New York: Reinhold, 1957.

Gutman, Marta, and Ning de Coninck-Smith, eds. *Designing Modern Childhoods: History, Space, and the Material Culture of Children.* New Brunswick, NJ: Rutgers University Press, 2008.

Gutman, Robert. *The Design of American Housing: A Reappraisal of the Architect's Role.* New York: Publishing Center for Cultural Resources, 1985.

Halle, David. *America's Working Man: Work, Home, and Politics among Blue-Collar Property Owners.* Chicago: University of Chicago Press, 1984.

Halsey, Elizabeth T. *Ladies' Home Journal Book of Interior Decoration.* Philadelphia: Curtis, 1954.

Halttunen, Karen. "From Parlor to Living Room: Domestic Space, Interior Decoration and the Culture of Personality." In *Consuming Visions: Accumulation and Display of Goods in America, 1880–1920,* edited by Simon J. Bronner, 157–89. New York: Norton, 1989.

Handbook of Kitchen Design: A Report of an Investigation in Space Use Conducted by the University of Illinois Small Homes Council and Agricultural Experiment Station. Champaign: Small Homes Council, University of Illinois, 1950.

Handel, Gerald, and Lee Rainwater. "Persistence and Change in Working-Class Life Style." In *Blue-Collar World: Studies of the American Worker,* edited by Arthur B. Shostak and William Gomberg, 36–41. Englewood Cliffs, NJ: Prentice Hall, 1964.

Haralovich, Mary Beth. "Sit-coms and Suburbs: Positioning the 1950s Homemaker." In *Critiquing the Sitcom: A Reader,* edited by Joanne Morreale, 69–85. Syracuse, NY: Syracuse University Press, 2003.

Harmon, Lindsey R., and Herbert Soldz, eds. *Doctorate Production in United States Universities 1920–1962.* National Research Council Publication 1142. Washington, DC: National Academy of Sciences, 1963.

Harris, Dianne. *Little White Houses: How the Postwar Home Constructed Race in America.* Minneapolis: University of Minnesota Press, 2013.

———. "Making Your Private World: Modern Landscape Architecture and *House Beautiful,* 1945–1965." In *The Architecture of Landscape, 1940–1960,* edited by Mark Trieb, 180–205. Philadelphia: University of Pennsylvania Press, 2002.

———. "Race, Class, and Privacy in the Ordinary Post-war House, 1945–1960." In *Landscape and Race in the United States,* edited by Richard H. Schein, 127–56. London: Taylor & Francis, 2006.

———, ed. *Second Suburb: Levittown, Pennsylvania.* Pittsburgh: University of Pittsburgh Press, 2010.

Harris, Dianne, and J. Fairchild Ruggles, eds. *Sites Unseen.* University Park: Penn State University Press, 2007.

Harris, Richard. *Building a Market: The Rise of the Home Improvement Industry 1914–1960.* Chicago: University of Chicago Press, 2012.

———. *Changing Suburbs: Foundation, Form and Function.* London: Spon Press, 1999.

———. "Chicago's Other Suburbs." *Geographical Review* 84, no. 4 (October 1994): 394.

———. "Reading Sanborns for the Spoor of the Owner-Builder, 1890s–1950s." In *Exploring Everyday Landscapes,* edited by Annemarie Adams and Sally McMurry, 251–67. Knoxville: University of Tennessee Press, 1997.

———. "Self-Building and the Social Geography of Toronto, 1902–1913: A Challenge for Urban Theory." *Transactions of the Institute of British Geographers,* New Series 15, no. 4 (1990): 387–402.

———. "The Talk of the Town: Kit Manufacturers Negotiate the Building Industry, 1905–1929." *Journal of Urban History* 36, no. 6 (2010): 868–96.

———. *Unplanned Suburbs: Toronto's American Tragedy, 1900–1950.* Baltimore: Johns Hopkins University Press, 1996.

Harris, Steven, and Deborah Berke, eds. *Architecture of the Everyday.* New York: Princeton Architectural Press, 1997.

Hayden, Dolores. *Building Suburbia: Green Fields and Urban Growth.* New York: Pantheon, 2003.

———. *A Field Guide to Sprawl.* New York: Norton, 2004.

———. *The Grand Domestic Revolution: A History of Feminist Designs for American Homes, Neighborhoods, and Cities.* Cambridge, MA: MIT Press, 1981.

———. *Redesigning the American Dream: The Future of Housing, Work, and Family Life.* New York: Norton, 2002.

———. *Seven American Utopias: The Architecture of Communitarian Socialism, 1790–1975.* Cambridge, MA: MIT Press, 1976.

Hayward, Mary Ellen. *Baltimore's Alley Houses: Homes for Working People since the 1780s.* Baltimore: Johns Hopkins University Press, 2008.

Hazel, Michael V. *Dallas: A History of "Big D."* Austin: Texas State Historical Association, 1997.

Heath, Kingston Wm. *The Patina of Place: The Cultural*

Weathering of a New England Industrial Landscape.
Knoxville: University of Tennessee Press, 2001.

Hedges, James. *The Browns of Providence Plantations.*
Providence: Brown University Press, 1968.

Helbock, Richard W. "New Towns in the United States."
Professional Geographer 20, no. 4 (1968): 242–46.

Henthorn, Cynthia Lee. *From Submarines to Suburbs: Selling
a Better America, 1939–1959.* Athens: Ohio University
Press, 2006.

"Here's the New Trend in Houses; Levitt Houses." *Good
Housekeeping* 130 (January 1950): 65–72.

Hess, Alan. *The Ranch House.* New York: Harry N. Abrams,
2004.

Hill, Kimball. "'I Built 20 Model Houses to See What
People Wanted!'" *Practical Builder*, June 1959, 108–13.

Hinchcliffe, Tanis. "Review Essay: Elusive Suburbs,
Endless Variation." *Journal of Urban History* 31, no. 6
(September 2005): 899–906.

Hine, Thomas. *Populuxe.* New York: Knopf, 1987.

———. "The Search for the Postwar House." In *Blueprints
for Modern Living: History and Legacy of the Case Study
Houses,* edited by Elizabeth A. T. Smith, 167–81. Los
Angeles: Museum of Contemporary Art, 1989.

Hise, Greg. "The Airplane and the Garden City: Regional
Transformations during World War II." In *World War II
and the American Dream,* edited by Donald Albrecht, 144–
83. Washington, DC: National Building Museum, 1995.

———. "Home Building and Industrial Decentralization in
Los Angeles: The Roots of the Postwar Urban Region."
Journal of Urban History 19 (1993): 95–125.

———. "Homebuilding and Industrial Decentralization in
Los Angeles: The Roots of the Post–World War II Urban
Region." In *Planning the Twentieth-Century American
City,* edited by Mary Corbin Sies and Christopher Silver,
95–123. Baltimore: Johns Hopkins University Press, 1996.

———. *Magnetic Los Angeles: Planning the Twentieth-
Century Metropolis.* Baltimore: Johns Hopkins University
Press, 1997.

Historical Statistics of the United States. Millennial
ed., edited by Richard Sutch and Susan B. Carter.
Cambridge: Cambridge University Press, 2006. http://
hsus.cambridge.org/HSUSWeb/index.do.

"History of the National Association of Home Builders
of the United States (through 1943)." Unpublished
manuscript, Archives of the NAHB.

Hitchcock, Henry Russell. *Frank Lloyd Wright.* New York:
Museum of Modern Art, 1932.

———. *In the Nature of Materials: The Buildings of Frank
Lloyd Wright 1887–1941.* New York: Duell, Sloan and
Pearce, 1942.

Hodgell, Murlin Ray. *Farmhouse Flexi-Plans: A New Idea
in Farmhouse Planning.* Urbana: University of Illinois,
College of Agriculture, Extension Service in Agriculture
and Home Economics, 1953.

Hodgins, Eric. "Mr. Blandings Builds His Castle." *Fortune,*
April 1946, 138–43.

"The Home of Tomorrow." *Architectural Digest* 13, no. 1
(1951): 105–12.

Home Owners Service Institute. *The Book of a Thousand
Homes: Volume 1 Containing 500 Plans of Moderate Cost.*
New York, 1923. Reprinted as *500 Small Houses of the
Twenties.* Vol. 1. New York: Dover, 1990.

"Honeywell Advertisement (Featuring Ralph Bodek
Home)." *Life,* September 6, 1954, 42–43.

Hornstein, Jeffrey M. "The Rise of the Realtor: Profession-
alism, Gender, and Middle-Class Identity, 1908–1950." In
Bledstein and Johnston, *Middling Sorts,* 217–33.

"House Beautiful's Twelfth Annual Small House
Competition." *House Beautiful* 82 (January 1940): 14–22.

"A House Can Be Modern and Not Look It." *House Beautiful*
87 (October 1945): 108–15.

"House in Massachusetts; Architect: Barry Wills." *Architect
and Building News* 176 (October 22, 1943): 60.

"A House Is Just a Couple of Truckloads." *Business Week,*
October 6, 1956, 114–20.

House-of-the-Month Book of Small Houses, Garden City. New
York: Garden City Publishing, 1946.

*The House of the Week's Selection of 24 Popular Ranch Homes
Designed by Outstanding Small Home Architects.* New
York: Associated Press, 1967.

"House with Split-Level Plan: V.J. Hamar Home Near
Portland." *Architectural Record* 87 (April 1940): 64–65.

Hovinen, Gary. "Suburbanization in Greater Philadelphia,
1880–1941." *Journal of Historical Geography* 11, no. 2 (April
1985): 174–95.

"How a Texas Outfit Builds a Good Cheap House." *Fortune,*
April 1976, 164.

"How William Levitt Helped to Fulfill the American
Dream." *New York Times,* February 6, 1994, 19.

Hubka, Thomas C. "The American Ranch House:
Traditional Design Method in Modern Popular Culture."
Traditional Dwellings and Settlements Review 7 (1995):
33–39.

———. *Big House, Little House, Back House, Barn: The*

Connected Farm Buildings of New England. Lebanon, NH: University Press of New England, 2004.

——. "From Working-Class to Middle-Class: The Transformation of American Housing, 1880–1940." Lecture at Bryn Mawr College, October 7, 2013.

——. *Houses without Names: Architectural Nomenclature and the Classification of America's Common Houses*. Knoxville: University of Tennessee Press, 2013.

Hubka, Thomas C., and Judith T. Kenny. "The Workers' Cottage in Milwaukee's Polish Community: Housing and the Process of Americanization, 1870–1920." In *People, Power, Places: Perspectives in Vernacular Architecture, VIII*, edited by Sally McMurry and Annmarie Adams, 33–52. Knoxville: University of Tennessee Press, 2000.

Hunt, D. Bradford. *Blueprint for Disaster: The Unraveling of Chicago Public Housing*. Chicago: University of Chicago Press, 2009.

Hunter, Christine. *Ranches, Rowhouses, and Railroad Flats: American Homes: How They Shape Our Landscapes and Neighborhoods*. New York: Norton, 1999.

Hunter, Paul Robinson, and Walter L. Reichardt. *Mediterranean to Modern: Residential Architecture in Southern California, 1939*. Santa Monica, CA: Hennessey & Ingalls, 1998.

Hutchison, Janet. "Building for Babbitt: The State and the Suburban Home Ideal." *Journal of Policy History* 9, no. 2 (1997): 184–210.

Isenstadt, Sandy. "Four Views, Three of Them through Glass." In Harris and Ruggles, *Sites Unseen*, 213–40.

——. *The Modern American House: Spaciousness and Middle-Class Identity, 1850–1950*. Cambridge: Cambridge University Press, 2006.

——. "The Rise and Fall of the Picture Window." *Harvard Design Magazine*, Fall 1998, 27–33.

——. "Visions of Plenty: Refrigerators in America around 1950." *Journal of Design History* 11, no. 4 (1998): 311–21.

Ishizuka, Karen L., and Patricia R. Zimmerman, eds. *Mining the Home Movie: Excavations in Histories and Memories*. Berkeley: University of California Press, 2007.

"Is Ranch House the Name for It?" *Sunset* 92, no. 5 (May 1944): 10–13.

Jackson, John Brinckerhoff. *Discovering the Vernacular Landscape*. New Haven, CT: Yale University Press, 1984.

——. *The Interpretation of Ordinary Landscapes: Geographical Essays*. Edited by D. W. Meinig. New York: Oxford University Press, 1979.

——. *A Sense of Place, a Sense of Time*. New Haven, CT: Yale University Press, 1994.

——. "The Westward Moving House." *Landscape* 2, no. 3 (1953): 8–21.

Jackson, Kenneth T. *The Crabgrass Frontier: The Suburbanization of the United States*. Oxford: Oxford University Press, 1985.

Jacobs, James A. *Detached America: Building Houses in Postwar Suburbia*. Charlottesville: University of Virginia Press, 2015.

Jakle, John A., Robert W. Bastian, and Douglas K. Meyer. *Common Houses in America's Small Towns: The Atlantic Seaboard to the Mississippi Valley*. Athens: University of Georgia Press, 1989.

Jenkins, Virginia Scott. *The Lawn: A History of an American Obsession*. Washington, DC: Smithsonian, 1994.

Johansen, H. O. "Split-Level Designed to Cut Costs." *Popular Science* 166 (April 1955): 104–6.

Johnson, Charles W., and Charles O. Jackson. *City Behind a Fence: Oak Ridge, Tennessee 1942–1946*. Knoxville: University of Tennessee Press, 1981.

Jones, Robert Taylor, ed. *Authentic Small Houses of the Twenties: Illustrations and Floor Plans of 254 Characteristic Homes*. New York: Harper, 1929. Reprint, New York, Dover, 1987.

——, ed. *Small Homes of Architectural Distinction: A Book of Suggested Plans Designed by the Architects' Small House Service Bureau, Inc*. New York: Harper, 1929.

Kaiser, Henry J. *Panorama City Shopping Center: The Center of the San Fernando Valley in Los Angeles, California*. Los Angeles: Kaiser Aluminum, 1959.

Kaplan, Wendy, ed. *Living in a Modern Way: California Design 1930–1965*. Cambridge, MA: MIT Press, 2011.

Karlak, Pat. "Ground Broken on Campanelli YMCA." *Arlington Heights (IL) Daily Herald*, September 17, 2000.

Kaufman, Michael T. "Tough Times for Mr. Levittown." *New York Times*, September 24, 1989.

Keach, Leon. "The Architect and the House: Royal Barry Wills, Small Home Specialist." *Pencil Points*, February 1937, 66–80.

Keane, James Thomas. *Fritz B. Burns and the Development of Los Angeles: The Biography of a Community Developer and Philanthropist*. Los Angeles: Historical Society of Southern California, 2001.

Keating, Ann Durkin. *Building Chicago: Suburban Developers and the Creation of a Divided Metropolis*. Columbus: Ohio State University Press, 1988.

Keats, John. *The Crack in the Picture Window*. Boston: Houghton Mifflin, 1956.

Keil, Rob. *Little Boxes: The Architecture of a Classic midcentury Suburb*. Daly City, CA: Advection Media, 2006.

Kelley, H. Roy. "A House in the California Style." *Good Housekeeping* 99 (July 1934): 68–69.

Kelly, Barbara M. *Expanding the American Dream: Building and Rebuilding Levittown*. Albany: State University of New York Press, 1993.

Kennedy, David M. *Freedom from Fear: The American People in Depression and War, 1929–1945*. New York: Oxford, 1999.

Kennedy, Robert Woods. *The House and the Art of Its Design*. New York: Reinhold, 1953.

Kerr, Robert. *The Gentleman's House (Or, How to Plan English Residences)*. London: J. Murray, 1864, 1871.

King, Anthony D. *Buildings and Society: Essays on the Social Development of the Built Environment*. London: Routledge and Kegan Paul, 1980.

———. *The Bungalow: The Production of a Global Culture*. London: Routledge and Kegan Paul, 1984.

"King of the Builders." *Time*, October 11, 1954, 106–10.

Kneebone, Elizabeth, and Alan Berube. *Confronting Suburban Poverty in America*. Washington, DC: Brookings Institution, 2013.

Korecki, Natasha. "Schaumburg Housing Mogul Campanelli Dies." *Arlington Heights (IL) Daily Herald*, April 11, 2003.

Koues, Helen. *Encyclopedia of Decorating*. Chicago: Consolidated, 1948.

Kovacic, Kristin. "Proud to Work for the University." In *What We Hold in Common: An Introduction to Working-Class Studies*, edited by Janet Zandy, 12–16. New York: Feminist Press at the City University of New York, 2001.

Krulikowski, Anne E. "'A Workingman's Paradise': The Evolution of an Unplanned Suburban Landscape." *Winterthur Portfolio* 42, no. 4 (2008): 243–85.

Kruse, Kevin M., and Thomas J. Sugrue, eds. *The New Suburban History*. Chicago: University of Chicago Press, 2006.

Kurtti, Jeff. *The Art of Disneyland*. New York: Disney Editions, 2006.

Lancaster, Clay. *The American Bungalow, 1880–1930*. New York: Abbeville Press, 1985.

Lane, Barbara Miller. *Architecture and Politics in Germany 1918–1945*. Cambridge, MA: Harvard University Press, 1985.

———. *National Romanticism and Modern Architecture in Germany and the Scandinavian Countries*. New York and Cambridge, England: Cambridge University Press, 2000.

———, ed. *Housing and Dwelling: Perspectives on Modern Domestic Architecture*. London: Taylor & Francis, 2007.

Larrabee, Eric. "The Six Thousand Houses That Levitt Built." *Harper's Magazine* 197 (September 1948): 79–88.

Lasch, Robert. "Houses from the Assembly Line." *Nation* 162 (March 30, 1946): 372–73.

Lasner, Matthew. *High Life: Condo Living in the Suburban Century*. New Haven, CT: Yale University Press, 2012.

Le Bien, Mark. "Bold Builders Created Suburbs." *Arlington Heights (IL) Daily Herald*, November 2, 1995.

Leigh, Nancy Green, and Sugie Lee. "Philadelphia's Space in Between: Inner-Ring Suburb Evolution." *Opolis* 1, no. 1 (2005): 16.

Levitt, William J. "A House Is Not Enough: The Story of America's First Community Builder." In *Business Decisions That Changed Our Lives*, edited by Sidney Furst and Milton Sherman, 57–71. New York: Random House, 1964.

Levittown, NJ, sales brochure. 1958. http://levittownbeyond.com/LevittownNJ.html. Accessed May 12, 2009.

"Life Houses." *Life*, July 1, 1940, 76–92.

Lifshey, Earl. *The Housewares Story: A History of the American Housewares Industry*. Chicago: National Housewares Manufacturers, 1973.

"Like an Early Ranch House." *House Beautiful*, March 1936, 86–87.

Lindstrom, Matthew J., and Hugh Bartlin, eds. *Suburban Sprawl: Culture, Theory and Politics*. Lanham, MD: Rowan & Littlefield, 2003.

Little, Anne. "Northwest Corridor Suburbs Fashion a Boomtown U.S.A." *Chicago Tribune*, September 14, 1988, Sports sec., 3.

Little, Margaret Ruth. "Getting the American Dream for Themselves: Postwar Modern Subdivisions for African Americans in Raleigh, North Carolina." *Buildings and Landscapes* 19, no. 2 (Spring 2012): 73–86.

"Lively's the Name." *Newsweek*, March 26, 1956, 84–86.

Livingston, M. "Judges' Report (Parents' Magazine's Eighth/Ninth Annual Builders Competitions)." *Parents' Magazine and Family Home Guide* 33 (February 1958): 61–68.

———. "Judges' Report (Parents' Magazine's Fourth/Fifth Annual Builders Competitions)." *Parents' Magazine and*

Family Home Guide 29 (February 1954): 63.

"Lockweld Home News." *Chicago Construction News*, December 30, 1948.

Loeb, Carolyn S. *Entrepreneurial Vernacular: Developers' Subdivisions in the 1920s.* Baltimore: Johns Hopkins University Press, 2001.

Logan, Thad. *The Victorian Parlour: A Cultural Study.* Cambridge: Cambridge University Press, 2001.

Longstreth, Richard W. *City Center to Regional Mall: Architecture, the Automobile, and Retailing in Los Angeles, 1920–1950.* Cambridge, MA: MIT Press, 1997.

———. "Levitts, Mass-Produced Houses, and Community Planning in the United States during the Mid Twentieth Century." In Harris, *Second Suburb*, 123–74.

Los Alamitos History Project, Rossmoor, timeline. http://www.localsports.biz/history/timeline1950s. Accessed May 12, 2010.

Lotchin, Roger W. *The Martial Metropolis: US Cities in War and Peace.* New York: Praeger, 1984.

"Low Cost Housing." NAHB *Correlator* 6 (1952): 14–29.

Lüdtke, Alf. *The History of Everyday Life.* Princeton, NJ: Princeton University Press, 1995.

Lupton, Ellen, and J. Abbott Miller. *The Bathroom, the Kitchen, and the Aesthetics of Waste: A Process of Elimination.* Cambridge, MA: MIT Press, 1992.

Mack, Arien, ed. *Home: A Place in the World.* New York: New York University Press, 1993.

Mah, Theresa. "The Limits of Democracy in the Suburbs: Constructing the Middle Class through Residential Exclusion." In Bledstein and Johnston, *Middling Sorts*, 256–66.

Maisel, Sherman J. *Housebuilding in Transition, Based on Studies in the San Francisco Bay Area.* Berkeley: University of California Press, 1953.

Marling, Karal Ann. *As Seen on TV: The Visual Culture of Everyday Life in the 1950s.* Cambridge, MA: Harvard University Press, 1994.

———. "Disneyland, 1955: Just Take the Santa Ana Freeway to the American Dream." *American Art* 5, nos. 1–2 (Winter/Spring 1991): 169–207.

———. " 'Don't Fence Me In.' " In Gibbs et al., *Carefree California*, 116–29.

Marsh, Margaret. *Suburban Lives.* New Brunswick, NJ: Rutgers University Press, 1990.

Martin, Brenda, and Penny Sparke, eds. *Women's Places: Architecture and Design 1860–1960.* London: Taylor & Francis, 2003.

Martin, Christopher. "Tract-House Modern: A Study of Housing Design and Consumption in the Washington Suburbs, 1946–1960." PhD dissertation, George Washington University, 2000.

Martinson, Tom. *American Dreamscape: The Pursuit of Happiness in Postwar Suburbia.* New York: Carroll & Graf, 2000.

Mason, Joseph B. *History of Housing in the US, 1930–1980.* Houston: Gulf, 1982.

———. "Levitt and Sons of Virginia Set New Standards in Title VI War Homes." *American Builder and Building Age*, June 1942, 48–53, 84–85.

Masotti, Louis, ed. *Suburbia in Transition.* New York: New Viewpoints, 1974.

Mathis, Mike. *Marple and Newtown Townships.* Mount Pleasant, SC: Arcadia, 1998.

Matarrese, Lynne. *The History of Levittown, New York.* Levittown, NY: Levittown Historical Society, 1997.

Mattie, Erik. *World's Fairs.* New York: Princeton Architectural Press, 1998.

May, Cliff. *Sunset Western Ranch Houses.* San Francisco: Lane, 1946. Reprint, Santa Monica, CA: Hennessey & Ingalls, 1999.

———. *Western Ranch Houses.* Santa Monica, CA: Sunset Books, 1958. Facsimile reprint, Santa Monica, CA: Hennessey & Ingalls, 1997.

May, Elaine Tyler. *Homeward Bound: American Families in the Cold War Era.* New York: Basic Books, 1988.

McCarthy, Mary. *Elk Grove: The Peony Village.* Elk Grove Village, IL: Elk Grove Village Public Library, 1981.

McCoy, Esther, and Evelyn Hitchcock. "The Ranch House." In Moore, Smith, and Becker, *Home Sweet Home*, 84–89.

McLeod, Mary. "Everyday and 'Other' Spaces." In *Architecture and Feminism*, edited by Debra Coleman, Elizabeth Danze, and Carol Henderson, 1–37. New York: Princeton Architectural Press, 1996.

McManis, Douglas R. *The Initial Evaluation and Utilization of the Illinois Prairies 1815–1840.* Chicago: University of Chicago Press, 1964.

McManus, Ruth, and Philip J. Ethington. "Suburbs in Transition: New Approaches to Suburban History." *Urban History* 34, no. 2 (2007): 316–37.

McMurry, Sally. "City Parlor, Country Sitting Room: Rural Vernacular Design and the American Parlor, 1840–1900." *Winterthur Portfolio* 20, no. 4 (1985): 261–80.

Mennel, Timothy. " 'Miracle House Hoop-La': Corporate Rhetoric and the Construction of the Postwar American

House." *Journal of the Society of Architectural Historians* 64, no. 3 (September 2005): 340–61.

Miles, Arlene. "Weathersfield Has Range of Ranches." *Arlington Heights (IL) Daily Herald*, September 16, 2005.

Miller, Daniel, ed. *Home Possessions: Material Culture Behind Closed Doors*. Oxford: Berg, 2001.

Miner, Curtis. "Picture Window Paradise." *Pennsylvania Heritage* 28, no. 2 (Spring 2002): 12–21.

Mock, Elizabeth B. *If You Want to Build a House*. New York: MOMA, 1946.

——, ed. "Tomorrow's Small House: Models and Plans." *Bulletin of the Museum of Modern Art* 12, no. 5 (1945).

"Model 'Home of Tomorrow.'" *Architectural Record*, July 1951, 32.6—32.8.

Modern American Dwellings with Constructive Details by Numerous Architects: Practical Designs for Builders. New York: D. Williams, 1897. Reprint, Rockville Center, NY: Antiquity Reprints, 1982.

"Modern in Ranch House Manner." *House and Garden*, April 1940, 48–49.

"Modern Ranch Homes in the Old Tradition." *Sunset*, April 1938, 48–49.

"A Modern Ranch House." *Good Housekeeping* 100 (March 1935): 72–73.

Monthly Small House Club. *The Best 42 House-of-the-Month Homes: By Outstanding Architects*. Edited by Kenneth Duncan. New York: Monthly Small House Club, 1953.

Moore, Charles W., Kathryn Smith, and Peter Becker, eds. *Home Sweet Home: American Domestic Vernacular Architecture*. Los Angeles: Craft and Folk Art Museum, 1983.

Morley, James W. *Hometown Natick 1945–2000*. Natick, MA: Natick Historical Society, 2010.

Mott, Seward H. *Better Subdivisions Mean Better Homes*. Washington, DC: Land Planning Division, Federal Housing Administration, 1941.

Motz, Marilyn Ferris, and Pat Browne, eds. *Making the American Home: Middle-Class Women and Domestic Material Culture, 1840–1940*. Bowling Green, OH: Bowling Green State University Popular Press, 1988.

"Mt. Vernon, NY: Split-Level Eliminates Waste Space." *Architectural Record* 86 (July 1939): 45.

Mulvey, Laura. *Visual and Other Pleasures*. Bloomington: Indiana University Press, 1989.

Mumford, Eric. "National Defense Migration and the Transformations of American Urbanism, 1940–1942." *Journal of Architectural Education* 61, no. 3 (2008): 25–34.

Mumford, Lewis. "Reflections on Modern Architecture." *Twice a Year*, no. 2 (Spring–Summer 1939).

Nash, Gerald D. *The American West Transformed: The Impact of the Second World War*. Bloomington: Indiana University Press, 1990.

——. *World War II and the West: Reshaping the Economy*. Lincoln: University of Nebraska Press, 1990.

National Association of Home Builders. *The Correlator: The Journal of Home Building*. Washington, DC: National Association of Home Builders of the United States. 1947–57. Continues as NAHB *Journal of Home Building*, 1957–72.

National Research Council. *A Survey of Housing Research in the United States*. Washington, DC: Housing and Home Finance Agency, 1952.

Needham, Andrew, and Allen Dietrich-Ward. "Beyond the Metropolis: Metropolitan Growth and Regional Transformation in Postwar America." *Journal of Urban History* 35, no. 7 (2009): 943–69.

"New Homes Accelerate Sales." *American Builder*, March 1949, 79–81.

"The New Look in Builder Houses." *Architectural Forum*, July 1949, 90–91.

"A New Method of Merchant Building." *Architectural Forum* (September 1949): 75–77.

"New Operating Chief Is Selected at Centex." *New York Times*, January 8, 1990, D3.

Nichols, Bill, ed. *Movies and Methods*. 2 vols. Berkeley: University of California Press, 1985.

Nicolaides, Becky M. *My Blue Heaven: Life and Politics in the Working-Class Suburbs of Los Angeles, 1920–1965*. Chicago: University of Chicago Press, 2002.

Nicolaides, Becky M., and Andrew Wiese, eds. "Exploring Social and Civic Engagement in Postwar Los Angeles." Chicago Urban History Seminar, May 10, 2012.

——. "Exploring Social and Civic Transformations in Suburban Los Angeles since 1945: Surveying the Landscape of Los Angeles Suburbia." Autry Western History Workshop & LA History Group, January 26, 2010.

——. "Suburban Landscapes of Los Angeles." In de Wit and Alexander, *Overdrive*, 126–35.

——. "Suburbia and Community: Untangling a Historical Conundrum." *UCLA Center for the Study of Women Newsletter*, 2008.

——. *The Suburb Reader*. London: Taylor & Francis, 2006.

——. "Where the Working Man Is Welcomed: Working-Class Suburbs in Los Angeles, 1900–1940." In *Looking for*

Los Angeles, edited by Charles G. Salas and Michael S. Roth, 57–96. Los Angeles: Getty Research Institute, 2001.

The 1938 Book of Small Houses by the Editors of the Architectural Forum. New York: Simon & Schuster, 1937.

"$9,990 Levitt Houses Boast 70 Lots." *Architectural Forum* 95, no. 4 (October 1951): 217–219.

Nye, David. *Electrifying America: Social Meanings of a New Technology 1880–1940.* Cambridge, MA: MIT Press, 1990.

Official Street Guide, City of Buena Park, Orange County, Calif. Buena Park: City of Buena Park, 1967.

"On the Level, 3 Ways! Split-Level House." *American Home* 48 (October 1952): 50–53.

Once upon a Time: Walt Disney, the Sources of Inspiration for the Disney Studios. New York: Prestel, 2007.

"100 Years, 100 Builders." *Builder,* January 1999: 109–50.

Ore, Janet. *The Seattle Bungalow: People and Houses, 1900–1940.* Seattle: University of Washington Press, 2007.

"Original Kimball Hill Laid Foundation for Rolling Meadows." *Chicago Daily Herald,* June 1983.

Orvell, Miles. *The Death and Life of Main Street: Small Towns in American Memory, Space, and Community.* Chapel Hill: University of North Carolina Press, 2012.

Ovnick, Merry. *Los Angeles: The End of the Rainbow.* Los Angeles: Balcony Press, 1994.

Packard, Vance. *The Status Seekers: An Explanation of Class Behavior in America, and the Hidden Barriers That Affect You, Your Community, Your Future.* New York: Pocket Books, 1959.

Pacyga, Dominic A., and Charles Shanabruch, eds. *The Chicago Bungalow.* Chicago: Chicago Architecture Foundation, 2003.

Papineau, Katherine Kaford. "The Carefree Californian: Cliff May Homes, 1952–1958." In Gibbs et al., *Carefree California,* 181–91.

"Park Forest, Illinois: Proving Ground for Community Planning Techniques." *Architectural Record,* May 1951, 95–110.

Parr, Joy. *Domestic Goods: The Material, the Moral and the Economic in the Postwar Years.* Toronto: University of Toronto Press, 1999.

Patterson, James T. *Grand Expectations: The United States 1945–1974.* New York: Oxford University Press, 1996.

Paul, Samuel. *The Giant Book of House Plans: Homes for Living.* New York: Simmons-Boardman, 1952.

Paxton, Edward Thurber. *What People Want when They Buy a House: A Guide for Architects and Builders Based Principally on a Survey by the Survey Research Center,* *Institute for Social Research, University of Michigan, and a Study by the Small Homes Council, University of Illinois.* Washington, DC: US Department of Commerce, 1955.

Penick, Monica Michelle. "The Pace Setter Houses: Livable Modernism in Postwar America." PhD dissertation, University of Texas at Austin, 2007.

Perica, Esther. *They Took the Challenge: The Story of Rolling Meadows.* Rolling Meadows, IL: Rolling Meadows Library, 1979.

Perry, Clarence Arthur. *Housing for the Machine Age.* New York: Russell Sage Foundation, 1939.

Peterson, Eric. "Past, Present, Future. Documentary Explores Schaumburg's First 50 Years as Village Residents Guide Viewers to Attractions of Today." *Arlington Heights (IL) Daily Herald,* September 7, 2006.

Peterson, Gary G. "Home Off the Range: The Origins and Evolution of Ranch Style Architecture in the United States." *Design Methods and Theories* 23, no. 3 (1989): 1040–59.

Philadelphia Architects and Buildings Database. Part of the American Architects and Buildings Database. William Penn Foundation, 2015. http://www.americanbuildings .org/pab/.

Philadelphia Tri-State District, Regional Planning Federation. *The Regional Plan of the Philadelphia Tri-State District.* Philadelphia: W. F. Fell, 1932. http://library .temple.edu/collections/urbana/rpf-330.jsp;jsessionid =DE62CCBB1F1582818B33B5511BC61EA2?bhcp=1.

Phillips, Michael. *White Metropolis: Race, Ethnicity, and Religion in Dallas, 1841–2001.* Austin: University of Texas Press, 2006.

Popenoe, David. *The Suburban Environment: Sweden and the United States.* Chicago: University of Chicago Press, 1977.

"Popular Split-Level Design Produces a House and a Half." *Good Housekeeping* 139 (October 1954): 80–86.

Postal, Matthew A. " 'Toward a Democratic Esthetic?' The Modern House in America 1932–1955." PhD dissertation, City University of New York, 1998.

President's Conference on Home Building and Home Ownership, John M. Gries, and James Ford, eds. *Farm and Village Housing.* Vol. 7. Washington, DC: National Capital Press, 1932.

———, eds. *House Design, Construction and Equipment.* Vol. 5. Washington, DC: National Capital Press, 1932.

———, eds. *Negro Housing: Physical Aspects, Social and Economic Factors, Home Ownership and Financing.* Vol. 6. Washington, DC: National Capital Press, 1932.

Press, Andrea L. *Women Watching Television: Gender, Class, and Generation in the American Television Experience.* Philadelphia: University of Pennsylvania Press, 1991.

Price, Marjorie, and Jason Hytes. *Trick or Treat and Split Level Sin.* New York: Midwood-Tower, 1964.

Prosser, Daniel J. "Chicago and the Bungalow Boom of the 1920s." *Chicago History* 10 (1981): 86–95.

"Racial Discrimination in Housing." *University of Pennsylvania Law Review* 107, no. 4 (February 1959): 515–50.

Rafferty, Kevin, and Bruce Gordon. *Walt Disney Imagineering: A Behind the Dreams Look at Making the Magic Real.* New York: Disney, 1996.

Rainwater, Lee. "Fear and the House-as-Haven in the Lower Class." *Journal of the American Institute of Planners* 32, no. 1 (January 1966): 123–31.

Rainwater, Lee, Richard P. Coleman, and Gerald Handel. *Workingman's Wife: Her Personality, World and Life Style.* New York, Oceana, 1959.

"A Rambling Ranch House." *House Beautiful*, March 1936, 66–67.

"Ranch House: For the (Once) Wild West." *Architectural Record*, March 1953, 162–64.

"A Ranch House in California." *House Beautiful*, January 1931, 32–35.

"Ranch House in the City." *Sunset*, February 1946, 48–49.

"Ranch House in the Northwest." *Sunset*, April 1946, 20–21.

"A Ranch on Spurling Mesa." *House and Garden*, November 1941, 32–33.

Randall, Gregory C. *America's Original GI Town: Park Forest, Illinois.* Baltimore: Johns Hopkins University Press, 2000.

Ranlett, William H. *Early Victorian House Designs.* 1847. Reprint, New York: Dover, 2006.

Rasmussen, Celia. "He Turned a Dream into Reality." *Los Angeles Times*, December 16, 2001, B4.

———. "Western Building Empire Spawned Kaiser HMO." *Los Angeles Times*, October 5, 2003, B4.

Rebori, Stephen J. *The Influence of Disney Entertainment Parks on Architecture and Development.* Chicago: Council of Planning Librarians, 1995.

Reed, Mort. "Home, Home Off the Range." *Better Homes and Gardens*, March 1947, 40–41.

———. "Why Not a Split-Level Plan?" *Better Homes and Gardens* 29 (May 1951): 70–71.

Reiff, Daniel Drake. *Houses from Books: Treatises, Pattern Books, and Catalogs in American Architecture, 1738–1950:*

A History and Guide. University Park: Pennsylvania State University Press, 2000.

Reynolds, Christopher. "LA's Invisible Builder; Long Overlooked Welton Becket Is Getting His Due." *Los Angeles Times*, March 6, 2003, E36.

Rifkind, Donna. "L.A. Story—A Rising Star of West Coast Lit Shines Dimly." *New Republic*, November 20, 2012.

Robinson, Arthur Neal. *Interiors and Decorating.* Boston: Architectural Forum, 1926.

Roderick, Kevin. *The San Fernando Valley: America's Suburb.* Los Angeles: Los Angeles Times Books, 2001.

Rodney, Marguerite C. "Oakdale Farms: Levitt's Prototype for Postwar Suburban Housing." Unpublished paper, George Washington University, April 30, 1993.

Rogers, Kate Ellen. *The Modern House, USA: Its Design and Decoration.* New York: Harper, 1962.

Rogers, Tyler Stewart. *Plan Your House to Suit Yourself.* New York: Charles Scribner's Sons, 1950.

Rome, Adam. *The Bulldozer in the Countryside: Suburban Sprawl and the Rise of American Environmentalism.* New York: Cambridge University Press, 2001.

Rooney, Andy. *My War.* New York: Random House, 2000.

Rosenman, Dorothy Reuben. *A Million Homes a Year.* New York: Harcourt, Brace, 1945.

Ross, Susan M., ed. *American Families Past and Present.* New Brunswick, NJ: Rutgers University Press, 2006.

Rouillard, Dominique. *Building the Slope: California Hillside Houses, 1920–1960.* Santa Monica, CA: Hennessey & Ingalls, 1999.

Ruff, Joshua. "Levittown: The Archetype for Suburban Development." *American History* 42, no. 5 (December 2007): 49–52.

Ruggles, Steven. "Living Arrangements and Well-Being of Older Persons in the Past." Paper presented to the UN Technical Meeting on Population. http://www.un.org/esa/population/publications/bulletin42_43/ruggles.pdf. Accessed February 3, 2014.

———. "Multigenerational Families in Nineteenth-Century America." In Ross, *American Families Past and Present*, 101–16.

"Rurban Homes Project Near El Monte Now Nearing Completion." *Southwest Builder and Contractor* 86, no. 6 (August 9, 1935): 12–13.

Rybczynski, Witold. *Home: A Short History.* New York: Viking, 1986.

———. *Last Harvest: How a Cornfield Became New Daleville: Real Estate Development in America from George*

Washington to the Builders of the Twenty-First Century, and Why We Live in Houses Anyway. New York: Scribner, 2007.

Samon, Katherine Ann. *Ranch House Style.* New York: Clarkson Potter, 2003.

Saylor, Henry S. *Bungalows: Their Design, Construction and Furnishing, with Suggestions Also for Camps, Summer Homes and Cottages of Similar Character; Illustrated by Photographs and Plans.* New York: R.M. McBride, 1926.

Schindler, Sarah B. "Of Backyard Chickens and Front Yard Gardens: The Conflict between Local Governments and Locavores." *Tulane Law Review* 87 (2012): 2–72.

Schlegel, Marvin W. *Conscripted City: Norfolk in World War II.* Norfolk, VA: Norfolk War History Commission, 1951.

Schmocker, Erdmann, and Robert Eyrich. "Schaumburg 1956, Robert Acher [sic] and Alfred Campanelli." In *Planned Cities in America.* Course packet. Chicago: Illinois Institute of Technology.

Schnay, Jerry. *Park Forest: Dreams and Challenges.* Mount Pleasant, SC: Arcadia, 2002.

Schnore, Leo F. "City-Suburban Income Differentials in Metropolitan Areas." *American Sociological Review* 27 (April 1962): 252–55.

Schoenauer, Norbert. *6,000 Years of Housing.* New York: Norton, 2000.

Schrenk, Lisa. *Building a Century of Progress: The Architecture of Chicago's 1933–34 World's Fair.* Minneapolis: University of Minnesota Press, 2007.

———. "The Impact of the Architects' Small House Service Bureau on Early Twentieth Century Domestic Architecture." MA thesis, University of Virginia, School of Architecture, 1988.

———. "The Small House Bureau." *Architecture Minnesota* 12 (May–June 1988): 50–55.

Schroeder, Ashley. *Rolling Meadows.* Mount Pleasant, SC: Arcadia, 2012.

Schroeder, Fred E. H. *Front Yard America: The Evolution and Meanings of a Vernacular Domestic Landscape.* Bowling Green OH: Bowling Green State University Popular Press, 1993.

Schultz, Robert. "The Levittown Look." In Harris and Berke, *Architecture of the Everyday,* 182–90.

Schwartz, Alex F. *Housing Policy in the United States.* London: Taylor & Francis, 2010.

———. *Housing Policy in the United States: An Introduction.* London: Taylor & Francis, 2006.

Schweitzer, Robert, and Michael W. R. Davis. *America's Favorite Homes: Mail Order Catalogues as a Guide to Popular Early 20th-Century Houses.* Detroit, MI: Wayne State University Press, 1990.

Schwieterman, Joseph P., and Dana M. Caspall. *The Politics of Place: A History of Zoning in Chicago.* Chicago: Lake Claremont Press, 2006.

Scully, Vincent J., Jr. *The Shingle Style.* New Haven, CT: Yale University Press, 1955.

Sears Roebuck Modern Homes. New York: Sears Roebuck, 1908.

Seney, N. "Split-Level That Makes Sense." *Better Homes and Gardens* 38 (May 1960): 56–57.

"$75,000 Showcase." *Architectural Forum,* March 1946, 98–104.

Severgnini, Beppe. *An Italian in America.* New York: Rizzoli, 2001.

Sexton, R. W. "The Small House in Warm Climates." *Small Home* 11 (October 1931): 8–10.

Shanken, Andrew M. *194X: Architecture, Planning, and Consumer Culture on the American Home Front.* Minneapolis: University of Minnesota Press, 2009.

Shiller, Robert J. *Understanding Recent Trends in House Prices and Home Ownership.* NBER working paper, 2007.

Shnay, Jerry. *Park Forest: Dreams and Challenges.* Mount Pleasant SC: Arcadia, 2002.

"Show Place Like Home." *Architectural Record,* April 1946, 90–93.

Sibbet, David. "Mayor Atcher Looms Larger Than Life." *Chicago Tribune,* September 22, 1968.

———. "Schaumburg Fights to Keep 'Way of Life on the Land.'" *Chicago Tribune,* September 8, 1968.

———. "Schaumburg's Development—Dream Coming True." *Chicago Tribune,* September 15, 1968.

———. "Suburbia, Farms Mingle in Schaumburg." *Chicago Tribune,* September 1, 1968.

Sides, Josh. *L.A. City Limits: African American Los Angeles from the Great Depression to the Present.* Berkeley: University of California Press, 2003.

Sies, Mary Corbin. "North American Suburbs, 1880–1950: Cultural and Social Reconsiderations." *Journal of Urban History* 27 (March 2001): 313–46.

———. "Toward a Performance Theory of the Suburban Ideal, 1877–1917." *Perspectives in Vernacular Architecture* 2 (1986): 197–207.

Silver, Christopher. "Neighborhood Planning in Historical Perspective." *Journal of the American Planning Association* 51 (1985): 161–74.

Silver, Marc L. *Under Construction: Work and Alienation in the Building Trades.* Albany: State University of New York Press, 1986.

Silverstone, Roger, ed. *Visions of Suburbia.* London: Taylor & Francis, 1997.

"6 Ranch Houses for Modern Living." *Architectural Record,* April 1947, 82–87.

Sloane, David C., ed. *Planning Los Angeles.* Washington, DC: American Planning Association Planners Press, 2012.

Small House Planning Bureau. *Master House Plan Book: A Volume of Nationally Recognized Small House Planning Bureau's Outstanding Plan Books.* St. Cloud, MN: Small House Planning Bureau, 1966.

Smiley, David J. "Making the Modified Modern." *Perspecta* 32 (2001): 38–54. Excerpted in Lane, *Housing and Dwelling,* 285–96.

———, ed. *Sprawl and Public Space: Redressing the Mall.* Washington, DC: National Endowment for the Arts, 2002.

Smith, Carlton L. "What Ever Happened to Mr. Blandings' Dream House?" *Yankee,* November 1975, 271–72.

"Sold: 100 Houses a Month." *Architectural Forum* 95, no. 4 (October 1951): 214–16.

Sonoc, Scott. "Defining the Chicago Bungalow." In Pacyga and Shanabruch, *Chicago Bungalow,* 9–30.

Souers, M. "Split-Level Plan." *Better Homes and Gardens* 31 (March 1953): 32.

Souter, Gerry, ed. *Chronicle of a Prairie Town: Arlington Heights, Illinois: Its People and Progress.* Arlington Heights, IL: Arlington Heights Historical Society, 1997.

Souter, Gerry, and Janet Souter. *Arlington Heights Illinois: A Brief History.* Charleston, SC: History Press, 2009.

Spears, Beverly. *American Adobes: Rural Houses of Northern New Mexico.* Albuquerque: University of New Mexico Press, 1986.

Spigel, Lynn. *Make Room for TV: Television and the Family Ideal in Postwar America.* Chicago: University of Chicago Press, 1992.

———. *Welcome to the Dreamhouse: Popular Media and Post-war Suburbs.* Durham, NC: Duke University Press, 2001.

Spigel, Lynn, and Denise Mann, eds. *Private Screenings: Television and the Female Consumer.* Minneapolis: University of Minnesota Press, 1992.

"Split-Level House for Cincinnati." *Architectural Record* 111 (February 1952): 142–45.

"Split-Level House with Plans You Can Buy." *House and Garden* 107 (March 1955): 112–13.

"Split-Level or Regular, These Units Build It." *Business Week,* July 28, 1962, 72–74.

Springer, J. L. "Split-Level Houses Are Best-Sellers Nowadays." *Popular Science* 166 (April 1955): 102–3.

Starr, Kevin. *Golden Dreams: California in an Age of Abundance 1950–1963.* New York: Oxford University Press, 2009.

State Museum of Pennsylvania. *Levittown, PA: Building the Suburban Dream: May 4, 2002–January 5, 2003.* Exhibition. Harrisburg: State Museum of Pennsylvania, 2002.

Steinbeck, John. *The Grapes of Wrath.* New York: Viking, 1939.

Stern, Robert, David Fishman, and Jacob Tilove. *Paradise Planned: The Garden Suburb and the Modern City.* New York: Monacelli Press, 2013.

Stewart, Janet Ann. *Arizona Ranch Houses: Southern Territorial Styles, 1867–1900.* Edited by John Bret Harte, 1974. Reprint, Tucson: University of Arizona Press, Arizona Historical Society, 1987.

Stilgoe, John R. *Borderland: Origins of the American Suburb, 1820–1939.* New Haven, CT: Yale University Press, 1988.

Stoltzner Builders. *Arlington Estates in Beautiful Arlington Heights.* Sales brochure, ca. 1963.

———. *Fine Homes as Designed and Constructed by Stoltzner Building Company (Builders of over 3000 Homes in 28 Years).* Sales brochure, ca. 1946.

———. *Homes by Stoltzner (Stoltzner Building Co.).* Sales brochure, ca. 1950.

———. *Stoltzner Construction Co. Presents Arlington Estates in Arlington Heights (Builders of over 10,000 Quality Homes).* Sales brochure, ca. 1962.

Story, Robert C. *Earned Degrees Conferred by Higher Educational Institutions, 1948–49.* Circular no. 262A. Washington, DC: Federal Security Agency, Office of Education, 1949.

———. *Earned Degrees Conferred by Higher Educational Institutions, 1949–50.* Circular no. 282. Washington, DC: Federal Security Agency, Office of Education, 1950.

Stowe, Eric, and John Rehfuss. "Federal New Towns Policy: 'Muddling Through' at the Local Level." *Public Administration Review* 35, no. 3 (May–June 1975): 222–28.

Strasser, Susan. *Never Done: A History of American Housework.* New York: Pantheon, 1982.

———. *Satisfaction Guaranteed: The Making of the American Mass Market.* New York: Pantheon, 1989.

Strasser, Susan, Charles McGovern, and Matthias Judt,

eds. *Getting and Spending: European and American Consumer Societies in the Twentieth Century.* Washington, DC: German Historical Institute, 1998.

Strawther, Larry. *A Brief History of Los Alamitos and Rossmoor.* Charleston, SC: The History Press, 2012.

"Streamlining the Ranch House: Cliff May." *House and Garden*, November 1941, sec. 2, 20–21.

"Subsistence Homesteads Are Planned for Economy and Comfort." *Southwest Builder and Contractor* 84, no. 19 (November 19, 1934): 26–28.

Sugrue, Thomas J. "Jim Crow's Last Stand: The Struggle to Integrate Levittown." In Harris, *Second Suburb*, 175–99.

Sullivan, Thomas D. "A Country Transformed by Wartime Construction." *Washington Times*, November 13, 1994, Arts sec., D1.

Sunset. San Francisco: Southern Pacific, 1898–.

Swain, C. H. "You Save Steps with a Split-Level Plan [J. Marlow Home, Denver]." *Better Homes and Gardens* 30 (February 1952): 120–21.

Talen, Emily. *City Rules: How Regulations Affect Urban Form.* Washington, DC: Island Press, 2012.

Tall, Deborah. "Dwelling: Making Peace with Space and Place." In *Rooted in the Land: Essays on Community and Place*, edited by Wes Jackson and William Vitek, 104–12. New Haven, CT: Yale University Press, 1996. Excerpted in Lane, *Housing and Dwelling*, 408–39.

Taylor, Angela. "25 Years Ago, Levittown Was a Joke, but Today It's Thriving." *New York Times*, April 18, 1972, 52.

Taylor, Lisa, ed. *Housing: Structure, Symbol, Site.* New York: Cooper–Hewitt Museum, 1990.

Teaford, Jon C. *The American Suburb: The Basics.* London: Taylor & Francis, 2008.

———. *The Metropolitan Revolution: The Rise of Post-Urban America.* New York: Columbia University Press, 2006.

Teyssot, Georges, ed. *The American Lawn.* New York: Princeton Architectural Press, 1999.

"They Ranch for Fun, Not Profit." *House and Garden*, November 1941, 44–45.

Tolliver, Wayne E., and Henry H. Armsby. *Engineering Enrollments and Degrees 1959.* Washington, DC: Government Printing Office, 1960.

Toomey, Shamus. "Campanelli First Joined a 'Y' at 15." *Arlington Heights (IL) Daily Herald*, March 28, 2000.

———. "Twinbrook YMCA Gets $3.85 Million Gift: Officials Plan to Rename Facility for Schaumburg Builder." *Arlington Heights (IL) Daily Herald*, March 28, 2000.

Treib, Marc, ed. *An Everyday Modernism: The Houses of William Wurster.* Berkeley: University of California Press, 1995.

Trillin, Calvin. "A Reporter at Large: Wake up and Live." *New Yorker*, April 4, 1964, 120–77.

Tuan, Yi-Fu. *Space and Place: The Perspective of Experience.* Minneapolis: University of Minnesota Press, 1977.

"Two Levels." *Sunset*, February 1944, 16–17.

"Two Room Economy House." *Architectural Forum*, September 1949, 80.

University of Illinois Small Homes Council-Building Research Council. *Basementless House Construction.* Urbana: Small Homes Council-Building Research Council, University of Illinois, 1950.

———. *Handbook of Kitchen Design.* Urbana: Small Homes Council-Building Research Council, University of Illinois, 1950.

———. *New House Designs for Wall-Panel Construction: Designs for 1-Story, Split-Level and 2-Story Houses.* Urbana: Small Homes Council-Building Research Council, University of Illinois, 1955.

"Up from the Potato Fields." *Time* 56 (July 3, 1950): 67–72.

Upton, Dell. *Architecture in the United States.* Oxford: Oxford University Press, 1998.

Urban Land Institute. *The Community Builders Handbook.* Washington, DC: Urban Land Institute, 1968.

US Bureau of Agricultural Engineering and President's Conference on Home Building and Home Ownership, Committee on Farm and Village Housing. *Representative Plans for Farm Houses: An Extract from a Report Submitted to the President's Conference on Home Building and Home Ownership by the Committee on Farm and Village Housing.* Vol. 8. Washington, DC: US Department of Agriculture, Bureau of Agricultural Engineering, 1932.

US Bureau of the Census. *Housing Construction Statistics 1889 to 1964.* Washington, DC: US Government Printing Office, 1966.

US Department of Health, Education, and Welfare. *Biennial Survey of Education in the United States.* Washington, DC: Government Printing Office, 1955–62.

US Office of Education. *Biennial Survey of Education in the United States: Statistics of Higher Education.* Washington, DC: Government Printing Office, 1945–52.

Vanderweel, Nanci L. *The History of Elk Grove Township 1850 to 2000.* Elk Grove Village, IL: Elk Grove Village Township, 2000.

Vandruff, Jean Valjean. Cinderella Estates sales brochure. Ca. 1956.

VanHorn, Susan Householder. *Women, Work, and Fertility, 1900–1986.* New York: New York University Press, 1988.

Venturi, Robert, and John Rauch. *Signs of Life: Symbols in the American City, Exhibition at the Renwick Gallery of the National Collections of Fine Arts, Smithsonian Institution, from February 26 through September 30, 1976.* Washington, DC: Aperture, 1976.

Village of Schaumburg. *Zoning Map.* March 15, 2010.

Voith, Richard P., and Susan M. Wachter. "Urban Growth and Housing Affordability: The Conflict." *Annals of the American Academy of Political and Social Science* 626 (November 2009): 112–31.

Waldie, D. J. "Falling in Love with Where You Are." *New Geography,* October 10, 2013. http://www.newgeography .com/content/003763–falling-in-love-with-where-you-are. Accessed October 5, 2013.

———. *Holy Land—A Suburban Memoir.* New York: Norton, 1996.

———. *Where We Are Now: Notes from Los Angeles.* Los Angeles: Angel City Press, 2004.

Walker, Nancy A. *Shaping Our Mothers' World: American Women's Magazines.* Jackson: University Press of Mississippi, 2000.

———, ed. *Women's Magazines, 1940–1960: Gender Roles and the Popular Press.* Boston: Bedford/St. Martin's, 1998.

Wallis, Allan D. *Wheel Estate: The Rise and Decline of Mobile Homes.* Oxford: Oxford University Press, 1991.

Warner, Sam Bass, Jr. *Greater Boston: Adapting Regional Traditions to the Present.* Philadelphia: University of Pennsylvania Press, 2001.

———. *The Private City: Philadelphia in Three Periods of Its Growth.* Philadelphia: University of Pennsylvania, 1987.

———. "The Public Invasion of Private Space and the Private Engrossment of Public Space." In *Growth and Transformation of the Modern City,* edited by Ingrid Hammarström and Patrik Reuterswärd, 171–77. Stockholm: Swedish Council for Building Research, 1979.

Watkins, Arthur Martin. *How to Judge a House before You Build or Buy.* Piermont, NY: All About Houses, 1960.

Watts, Jennifer, and Claudia Bohn-Spector, eds. *This Side of Paradise: Body and Landscape in Los Angeles Photographs.* New York: Merrell, 2008.

Weems, Robert E., Jr. *Desegregating the Dollar: African American Consumerism in the Twentieth Century.* New York: New York University Press, 1998.

Weingarten, David, and Lucia Howard, eds. *Ranch Houses: Living the California Dream.* New York: Rizzoli, 2009.

Weintraub, Jeff, and Krishnan Kumar, eds. *Public and Private in Thought and Practice: Perspectives on a Grand Dichotomy.* Chicago: University of Chicago Press, 1997.

Weiss, Marc A. "Developing and Financing the 'Garden Metropolis': Urban Planning and Housing Policy in Twentieth-Century America." *Planning Perspectives* 5 (1990): 307–19.

———. *The Rise of the Community Builders: The American Real Estate Industry and Urban Land Planning.* New York: Columbia University Press, 1987.

Wendt, Paul F. *Housing Policy—The Search for Solutions: A Comparison of the United Kingdom, Sweden, West Germany, and the United States since World War II.* Berkeley: University of California Press, 1962.

Wertheimer, Barbara. *We Were There: The Story of Working Women in America.* New York: Pantheon, 1977.

Wetherell, W. D. *The Man Who Loved Levittown.* Pittsburgh: University of Pittsburgh Press, 1985.

"What Builders Plan for 1952." *Architectural Forum* 95, no. 4 (October 1951): 206–8.

"What Is a Ranch House?" *Sunset,* November 1946, 26–27.

"What Is a Western Ranch House?" *Sunset,* February 1944, 12–13.

"What's Been Happening to That Easy-going Western Favorite the 'Ranch House'?" *Sunset* 120, no. 2 (February 1958): 54–59.

"What's the Future of the Ranch House?" *Sunset* 92, no. 5 (June 1944): 10–13.

White, Roger B. *Home on the Road: The Motor Home in America.* Washington, DC: Smithsonian Institution Press, 2000.

Whitehand, J. W. R., and C. M. H. Carr. *Twentieth-Century Suburbs: A Morphological Approach.* London: Taylor & Francis, 2001.

Whyte, William H., Jr. *The Organization Man.* New York: Simon & Schuster, 1956.

Wiese, Andrew. *Places of Their Own: African American Suburbanization in the Twentieth Century.* Chicago: University of Chicago Press, 2004.

Wilkie, Richard W., and Jack Tager. *Historical Atlas of Massachusetts.* Amherst: University of Massachusetts Press, 1991.

"William J. Levitt, Pioneer of Postwar Suburbia, Dies." *Washington Post,* January 30, 1994, Metro sec., B6.

Williams, Raymond. *The Country and the City.* Oxford: Oxford University Press, 1973.

Williamson, June. "New Visions of Suburban Life." *Places*

17, no. 2 (Summer 2005): 84–85.

———. "Revisiting Levittown." *Places* 17, no. 2 (Summer 2005): 46–51.

Wills, Royal Barry. "The Approach to Practice: With an Eye to Making It Businesslike." *Pencil Points*, April 1939, 199–202.

———. *Better Houses for Budgeteers: Sketches and Plans* (New York, NY: Architectural Book Publishing, 1946.

———. "Confessions of a Cape Codder." *Architectural Record*, April 1949, 132–33.

———. "Flexibility for the Small House." *Architectural Record*, May 1945, 76–84.

———. *Houses for Good Living.* New York: Architectural Book Publishing, 1946.

———. *Houses for Homemakers.* New York: F. Watts, 1945.

———. *Living on the Level: One-Story Houses by Royal Barry Wills.* Cambridge, MA: Riverside Press, 1954.

———. "Model House." *Life*, December 26, 1938, and January 2, 1939.

Wilson, Sloan. *The Man in the Gray Flannel Suit.* New York: Perseus, 1955.

Winter, Robert. *The California Bungalow.* Los Angeles: Hennessey & Ingalls, 1980.

———, ed. *Toward a Simpler Way of Life: The Arts & Crafts Architects of California.* Berkeley: University of California Press, 1997.

Wolfe, Jane. *The Murchisons: The Rise and Fall of a Texas Dynasty.* New York: St. Martin's Press, 1989.

Wolff, Janet L. *What Makes Women Buy: A Guide to Understanding and Influencing the New Woman of Today.* New York: McGraw-Hill, 1958.

Wright, Frank Lloyd. *An Autobiography.* New York: Longman's, 1932.

———. "Broadacre City: An Architect's Vision." *New York Times Magazine*, March 20, 1932, 8–9.

———. *Broadacre City: A New Community Plan.* New York, 1935.

———. *Modern Architecture: The Kahn Lectures for 1930.* Princeton: Princeton University Press, 1931.

———. *An Organic Architecture: The Architecture of Democracy.* Lectures at the RIBA, London, 1939. London: Lund Humphries, 1939.

———. *The Taliesin Fellowship.* Madison: Wisconsin Alumnae Association, 1934.

———. *When Democracy Builds.* Chicago: University of Chicago Press, 1945.

Wright, Gwendolyn. *Building the Dream: A Social History of Housing in America.* New York: Pantheon, 1981.

———. *Moralism and the Model Home: Domestic Architecture and Cultural Conflict in Chicago 1873–1913.* Chicago: University of Chicago Press, 1985.

Wright, Richardson Little, ed. *House & Garden's Complete Guide to Interior Decoration.* New York: Simon & Schuster, 1942.

———. *House & Garden's Second Book of Houses, Which Contains over Five Hundred Illustrations of the Exteriors, Decoration and Landscaping of Four Ideal Smaller Houses, Forty-Eight Pages Showing How a House Is Built and a Portfolio of over Sixty Small and Large Houses with Plans, Summer Camps and Garages.* 1887–1961 ed. New York: Condé Nast, 1925.

Wright, Richardson Little, and Margaret McElroy, eds. *House & Garden's Second Book of Interiors.* New York: Condé Nast, 1926.

Yost, L. M. "Split-Level, a Trend in House Design." *Parents' Magazine* 21 (January 1946): 36–37.

Zukin, Sharon. *Landscapes of Power: From Detroit to Disney World.* Berkeley: University of California Press, 1991.

Video Recordings

The Best of I Love Lucy. Vol. 1. CBS, 2001.

Father Knows Best. Schiller Park, IL, 1999.

Gilmore, H. James, Laurence Jaquith, and Neil D. Novello. *Chronicle of an American Suburb.* Berkeley: University of California Extension Center for Media and Independent Learning, 2002.

It's a Wonderful Town. Video series. Lakewood, CA, 2004.

Lakewood Stories. Video series. Lakewood, CA, 2004.

The Lakewood Story. Video series. Lakewood, CA, 2004.

Leave it to Beaver. http://www.retroweb.com/universal _leave_it_to_beaver.html.

Schaumburg: An Oral History; Village of Schaumburg: 50th Anniversary 2006; Images of Schaumburg. DVD/ video series. Schaumburg, IL: Village of Schaumburg, Schaumburg Prairie Center for the Arts, 2006.

Sudsy Television no. 426 (1953). Four live kinescopes of early TV's soap operas, complete with commercials. Shokus Video, 1985.

Urban Land Institute. *Density by Design: Concepts, Concerns and Challenges.* Washington, DC: Urban Land Institute, 1990.

ILLUSTRATION CREDITS

*Note: When no source is named, illustrations either
are in the public domain or come from the author's collections*

Abbot, *Tenements of Chicago*, 206

American Builder, Simmons-Boardman, Chicago 1942, 62

Better Homes and Gardens magazine, originally published in
October 1949, 70, 71

Tara Stoltzner Blum, 145, 151, 152, 159

Courtesy *Boston Herald*, 140

Mark Bourne, 146

Diane Brannon, 119, 121, 122

Fritz Burns Collection CSLA-4, series 3, box 100, Department
of Archives and Special Collections, William H. Hannon
Library, Loyola Marymount University, 53

Jon Campanelli, 117, 127, 133, 134, 135, 142, 143

Courtesy of the Clarke Historical Library, Central Michigan
University, 33, 218

Cornell University Archives, redrawn by Gregory C. Randall
from the original plan by Elbert Peets, 40

Heidi Cortese, 82, 90

Damon & Foster Engineers, 114

Dover Publications, *Authentic Small Houses of the Twenties*, 203,
207

English Heritage, National Monuments Record, 4

Marianne Ezell, 215, 216

Mrs. FC, 15, 34, 37, 200, 205, 222

Courtesy of General Electric Company, 128

The J. Paul Getty Museum, Los Angeles, William A. Garnett,
"Finished Housing, Lakewood, California," 1950, Gelatin
Silver Print, 18.7 × 24 cm, 39

Paul Groth, 207, 208

Pedro E. Guererro Archives © 2015, 66

Christine Hunter, *Ranches, Rowhouses, and Railroad Flats*,
Copyright © 1999 by Christine Hunter, used by permission
of W.W. Norton & Company, Inc., 209, 210, 211

Courtesy of the Huntington Library, San Marino, CA, 72;
Maynard Parker Photographer, 47, 48, 81, 83, 84, 86, 88;
"Dick" Whittington Studio, 54

Mrs. KD, 107

City of Lakewood, 1, 10, 22, 30

Copyright the Dorothea Lange Collection, the Oakland Museum
of California, City of Oakland, Gift of Paul S. Taylor, 221

Library of Congress, Prints & Photographs Division, FSA/OWI
Collection, 223 (LC-USF34-063706-D)

Library of Congress, Prints & Photographs Division,
Gottscho-Schleisner Collection: 12 (LC-G613-T-64801),
31 (LC-G613-T-64801), 45 (LC-G612-T-35261), 46
(LC-G612-T-35262)

Ken Liss, 110

Mr. LT, 10, 28

Cliff May, *Sunset Western Ranch Houses*, 1946, 67, 68, 69

Cliff May Papers, Architecture and Design Collection. Art,
Design & Architecture Museum, University of California,
Santa Barbara, 91, 92

From the Collection of the Mercer Museum Library of the
Bucks County Historical Society, photo by Fairchild Aerial
Surveys, 38

Courtesy of The MIT Press from *The Comfortable House: North
American Suburban Architecture, 1890–1930*, by Alan Gowans,
213

Modern American Dwellings, 2, 3

Ralph Morse/LIFE Picture Collection/Getty Images, 220

Nassau County Dept. of Parks, Recreation & Museums, Photo
Archives Center, 18, 19

Courtesy National Archives, 11 (photo no. 306-PS-56-16564)

Leonard Dove/The New Yorker Collection/The Cartoon Bank, 35

Pencil Points, 1937, 65

Used with permission of *Philadelphia Inquirer* © 2014, all rights
reserved, 105

Courtesy of State University of New York Press from *Expanding the American Dream* by Barbara M. Kelly, 20

Special Collections Research Center, Temple University
Libraries, Philadelphia, 32

William W. Wurster/Wurster, Bernardi & Emmons Collection,
Environmental Design Archives, University of California,
Berkeley, 64

Library Special Collections, Charles E. Young Research
Library, University of California, Los Angeles, "A Collection
of Material Relating to Prefabricated Housing Studies in
Europe and the United States" (Collection 1582), 165, 166

University of Southern California Libraries, Special Collections, 56

Marissa Vigneault, 212

INDEX

Page numbers in boldface refer to figures

Engineering Service Corporation, Los Angeles, 60, 249n39

engineers (civil), 34, 44, 50–51, 59–60, 109–12, 126, **130**, 131–32, 141, 167, 177, 194, 240, 246n47, 249n39, 253n129, 259n115; and curvilinear street patterns, 14, 37; in design of street and lot layout, 13; and master plans, 38. *See also* Damon and Foster; De Botton, Claude; Jordan, Thomas A.; Marlow, Fred; Newville, J. R.; Saivetz, Bradford

entertaining neighbors, 6, 202, **203**, 207

Equi, Frank, 260n136

Erikson, Erik, 263n40

estates in Philadelphia area, 94–95

exhibitions. *See* MoMA; World's Fairs

extended family. *See* family size

Facciolo, Frank, 96–103, **96–102**; and California, 95–97, 99; in conflicts with local officials, 101, 103; education of, and early career in building, 96; family background of, 96; and Frank Lloyd Wright, 98, 99; on housing for low-income people, 103; own house, 100; Rose Tree Woods, 96–101; Waynewoods, 101

Fairless steel works, Bucks County, PA, 30

family photographs, **26**, 27

family room, 21, 78–79, 84–85, 108, 184, 202–3, 245n20; and kitchen, continuous, 181–82, 186, 253n122, 258n91, 268n160. *See also* den; recreation room

family size: among those interviewed, 196–97; extended, 198–99, 211; nuclear, 5, 46, 196–97

Farina kitchens, 258n92

farmhouses, 212–13, **214**, 271n62

farms, nostalgia for life on, 199, 221, 271n61. *See also* agriculture

Father and Son Construction Co., Tucson, AZ, 166, 176, 266n107. *See also* Hoffman Estates

Father Knows Best (TV sitcom), 269–70n37

Federal-Aid Highway Acts, 244n6

Federal Highway Acts, 244n6

Federal Housing Administration. *See* FHA

fences, absence of, 9, 11, 145, 203, 269nn28 and 29. *See also* hedges

Feroli, Gregory, 244n5, 258n99

FHA: definitions of "functional" design, 36; guidelines for builders and lenders, 35, **36**, **37**, 38, 39, 257n65; minimum house, **36**; mortgages, 5, 37, 45, 50, 167, 201

Findlay, John M., 246n38

finishing materials. *See* construction

fireplace, 21, 69, 182, 189, 221, 223, 266n114; in Campanelli houses, 120, 135; in Cinderella

homes, 79–80, 85; in Elk Grove Village 173; in Kimball Hill houses, 163; in Rose Tree Woods houses, 98–100, **100**

Fischel, William A., 228, 271n9

Five Fields, 128, 258n102

Fletcher Engineering, 158

Ford, Henry, 39

foremen, use of, 105, 108–9, 136–38, 147, 149, 154, 223, 263n43

Forest Hills Garden, 36

Framingham, MA, 116, **117**, **123**, 123–24, **126–27**, 133–36, 258nn91 and 96, 259nn104 and 127

Francis, John Brown, governor of RI, 119

Fred Bixby Ranch Company, 254n137

Frematic Homes, Inc., Anaheim, CA, 85, **90**, 91, 253nn125 and 134, 254n140, 258n95; and award from NAHB, 90. *See also* Choate, Chris; Cortese, Ross; Jones, Erie; May, Cliff

Friedan, Betty, 246n36

front-to-back split-level house, **19**, **26**, **150**, **152**, **153**

front yard plantings, 203, 269n29

frontier, imagery of, 216, 271n63

Furness, Betty. *See* appliances; kitchens

furniture, **10**, **21**, **22**, **58**, **69**, **70**, **87**, **106**, **124**, **125**, **129**

Gans, Herbert J., 107

garage: absence of, 6, 65, 104, 145, 150, 167; attached, 17, 18, 41, 63, 72, 74, 78, 85, 98, 106–8, 120, 152, 174, 179, 189, 248n17, 250n63, 255n39, 256n39, 259n104; carport instead of, 67, 161, 171

Garden City ideas, 14, 33; Garden City movement in Europe, 225; Garden City movement in the United States, 33, 36, 38, 225–26, 246n56

gardens, 11, 71, 130, 228. *See also* zoning ordinances

Garlinghouse, Lewis F., 246n53

Garlinghouse Company, 35, 66, 69, 107, 153, 215, 245n17, 246n53; calendar advertising Stoltzners, 263n52

Garnett, William A., aerial view Lakewood (1950), **31**

Gaspee Builders (Campanellis at Governor Francis Farms), 119, 257n82

General Electric, 39, 44, 124, 179, 257n82, 260n128

Gentleman's House, 215

Gershenfeld, Lee, 254nn8–9, 255n37

Gerstle, Gary, 201

Gherin-Ghelli, Dominic, 260n136

GI Bill, 198, 235–37

Gibbs, Jocelyn, 251n80

Giovaniello, Amalio, 258n104

Glassie, Henry, 224, 270n58

Goetten, Armor, 254n142

"Golden Corridor," Chicago, 45, 138–85; defined, 142, 208, 226

Golden Estates at Rossmoor, 84; and design award from NAHB, 253n119

Gordon, Richard and Katherine, 27

Gottman, Jean, *Megalopolis*, 248n1

government, federal: and contracts for war housing, 48, 53; and defense research laboratories, 115; and highway system, 4, 5, 115, 142, 224, 244; and housing research, 38; and NAHB, 48–49; and redlining, 269; and regional planning, 111–12; and town planning, 226. *See also* FHA; GI Bill; mortgages; Natick Industrial Park; new towns movement

government, local, 13, 37, 185, 224, 227

Governor Francis Farms, Warwick, RI, **18**, **120**, **121**, 128, 182, 235, 257nn66, 77, and 82, 258n99; and restrictive covenants, 119–20, 268n14; site and terrain, 118–21, 223

Granacki Historic Consultants, Chicago, 165, 265n101

"grand expectations," 220, 230, 271n80

Grapes of Wrath (novel, movie), 205, 270n42

grass strips, 9–10, 12, 51, 149, 185, 248n22

Greater Chicago Home Show, 165

greenbelt, 14–15, 225; "Greenbelt" settlements, 36

Greene and Greene, 250n61

Greenview Estates, Arlington Heights, IL, 149–54; design of houses in, 153–54, 262n36, 263nn40, 43, 44, 49, 51, and 52; house prices in, 152; house types at, **12**, **19**, **26**, **149–53**; street layout in, **148**. *See also* Appendix 2; Stoltzner Builders

Greenwich, Framingham, MA, 123

Grey, Zane, 216

grid plans, 13–14, **31**, 59–60, 76, **77**, 141, 177, 246n47

Gropius, Walter, 39, 128, 247n61

Groth, Paul, 208, **209**

Gulla, Dominic (Mego), 260n140

Haesler, Otto, 247n66

Hanover Mall, Hanover, MA, 259n111

Harlow, England, 225

Harnischfeger. *See* Pawling & Harnischfeger

Harris, Dianne, 31, 256n46

Harris, Richard, 247n76, 269n31

Harris Brothers, 246n53

Hauser, Gottlieb, 264n77

Hayden, Dolores, 246n38, 269n35

hedges, 6, 9, 11, 199, 203, 269n29. *See also* fences

Hemel Hempstead, England, 225
Hersey, Sumner, 257n65
highway system. *See* Federal-Aid Highway Acts
highways, 5, 48, 94–95, 115, 142, 147, 229
Hill, David, 155
Hill, Kimball, 154, **155–57, 160–62**, 163–66, 264nn62, 63, 64, and 66–79, 265nn80–100, 265–66nn103 and 104; and architects, 156, 164–66; and California, 163–64, **164–65**; career of, 155–59; family background of, 154, 156; market research of, 162–64; and prefabrication, 156–58. *See also* Rolling Meadows, IL
Hingham, MA, 116, **117**, 123, **124**
Hise, Greg, 29, 59, 246n38, 249n31
Hispanic Americans. *See* Mexican Americans
historians: of architecture, 27, 29, 43, 48, 63, 67, 140, 206, 212; local, 2, 159, 187; of urbanization 28
Hodlmair, Charles, 168–69
Hoffman, Jack, 266n107
Hoffman Estates, 166, 176, 194, 241–42, 266n107. *See also* Father and Son Construction Co.
Holbrook, MA, 121, **125, 136**
Hollywood, 58, 254n142; Campanellis and, 260; romance of, 65, 74. *See also* Cinderella Homes; Rossmoor
Home Builders associations, 41, 101, 125, 133, 155, 165, 265n100
Home Modernizing Bureau, 66
home shows, 41, 72, 78, 128, 165, 247n74, 252n107
homeowners' associations, 159, 227
homeownership, 3, 66, 189, 191, 200, 244n1, 246n40
Homestead Acts, 271n70
homesteading, 216
Honeymooners, The (TV sitcom), 269n36
Hoover, Herbert, president, and "Own Your Own Home" campaign, 66
Horndasch, Mickey, 261n18
Hotpoint, 124
house as an investment, 189, 192, 200, 220, 227–28, 240
House Beautiful, 64, 69, 72, 247n72, 251n86
house designs. *See* design of houses
"house of the future," 41, 42, 247n63
"house of tomorrow," 39, 41, 247nn63 and 67; at Disneyland, 91
Housing and Home Finance Agency, 38, 188
housing development. *See specific subdivisions*; subdivision, defined
housing reformers, 141, 213, 215, 230, 270–71n60
housing research, 38, 188. *See also* Housing

Research Laboratory; market research
Housing Research Laboratory, Rolling Meadows, Kimball Hill, 41, 163, 166, 247n59, 265n90
housing shortage, 4, 132, 167
How and Why People Buy Houses, 113
Howard, Ebeneezer, 225
Hubka, Thomas C., 269n32
Hudson, MA, **117**, 123, 258n96
Hughes aircraft, 54, 248n21
Hunnewell property, 259m122
Huntington Library, 251n86

I Love Lucy (TV sitcom), 269n36
Illinois political divisions, 262n35
Illinois Small Homes Council, 162–63, 188, 263n46, 265n90, 95
immigration, 200; in Boston, 115; in Chicago, 140; in Dallas 167
incorporation, of subdivision as political entity, 32, 158–59, 175–76, 227, 264
"indoor-outdoor living," 18, 71, 74. *See also* light and windows
industrial parks. *See specific subdivisions*
industries, technological and service, migration of, 115, 142
industry, included in new subdivisions, 14, 134. *See also* Garden City ideas; *individual subdivisions*
infill development, 226, 227
innovation, process of, in design of houses, 66–67, 128, 223–24. *See also* Glassie, Henry
instant settlements, 220
International Style of modernism, 38, 39, 41, 64, 203, 221
interpretations of the history of tract houses, 27–33. *See also* critics of tract houses; research and methods in studying the history of tract houses
interviews with original buyers, 1, 35, 45, 113, 187, 188, 196–97, 219. *See also* Voices from the Fifties; Appendix 3
Ipswich, MA, **117**, 123, 135
Irvine Company, Irvine, CA, 90, 226, 254n137
Isenstadt, Sandy, 29, 245nn27, 31, and 33, 246n40, 271n1. *See also* Levittown, NY
Island Trees, 30. *See also* Levittown, NY
It's a Wonderful Life (movie), 205, **206**

Jackson, Helen Hunt (*Ramona*), 73, 252n94
Jackson, Kenneth T., 27, 29
Jacobs, James A., 246n42
Jacobs, Jane, 24
jobs, migration of, 224–26
Johnson, Glenn Q., 156
Johnson, Philip, 38
Jones, Erie, 163, 265nn95 and 96

Jones, Robert G., 254n140, 271n67
Jordan, Thomas A., civil engineer, 59–60
"journey to work," 5, 113, 189, 197, 238, 247n59. *See also* commuting

Kaiser, Henry J., 54–56, **56, 58–60**, 248nn25 and 26. *See also* Burns, Fritz B.; Kaiser Community Homes (KCH)
Kaiser Community Homes (KCH), 50, 54, 248n10, 249n29
Kaltenbach, Earl G., Jr., 91
Kaufman and Broad, 30, 175, 259n113
KCH. *See* Kaiser Community Homes (KCH)
Keagle, Beverley, 265n79
Keane, James, 29, 59, 249n31, 250n55, 252n96
Keats, John, 24, 27, 245n27, 246n36
Kelly, Barbara M., 31, 245n13
Kent, Atwater, 96, 255n13
Kerr, Robert, 215, 271n285
Kingston House, Worcester, MA, **6**
kit builders, 35, 66, 246n53, 261n8
"kitchen debate" between Khrushchev and Nixon, 260n145
kitchens, **22**, 41–43, 85, **87**, 124, 200, 202, 204, 205, 221–22, 247n59, 255n121, 271n73; Betty Furness and, in Rossmoor, 253nn122 and 125, 256n63; Campanellis and, **129**, 181; Centex and, 175; Cliff May and, **71**; color in, 22, 25, 79, 152, 193, 240; "eat-in" kitchens, **9**, **53**, 67, 152, **161**, 166, 181, 186, 189, 215; Hill and, 158, **161–62**; and "house of the future," 204; manufacturers and, 24; Moscow Kitchen, **10**; research on, 38. *See also* appliances; *individual builders*; *individual subdivisions*
Klafter, Josef, **144**, 262n22
Klutznick, Philip M., 33
Knott's Berry Farm, 76
Koch, Carl, 128, 258n100
Koch, Richard, Ramsey House, *Life* house of 1938, 250n63
Kodak Brownie camera, 27, 245n34

labor unions, 264n66, 265–66n103, 268n166
laborer's cottages, 208, **209**, 215
Ladies Home Journal, 250n74
Lakewood, CA, **5, 10–11, 13, 16–17, 22**; incorporation of, 32; planners and engineers of, 31; population of, in 1957, 31; street and lot layout of, **31–32**
Lakewood Rancho Estates, **89**, 89–90, 253n128. *See also* Choate, Chris; Cortese, Ross; May, Cliff
land hunger, 199, 220
land prices, 226, 229–30
Landefeld & Hatch, architects, Pittsburgh Plate Glass Company, house 4, World's

influence of, 43–44, 188, 204–5, 253n125, 270n38; marketing in, 85; sets, ownership of by buyers, 202, 229, 236
"ten wide" trailer, 218–19
tenement dwellings, 44, 141, 208, **209**, 214, 270n53
ticky-tacky (from Reynolds, *Little Boxes*), 27
Tigerman, Stanley, 165, 265n102
Toll Brothers, 175, 267n138
tollways, in Chicago, 142, 158–59, 168, 261n12
Toluca Wood, Los Angeles, CA, 50–51, 53, **54**, 62–63, 248nn8–9, and 14, 250n55
Tomorrow Town (1939–40), 41
tools, 23–24, 42, 203
Torrance, CA, **13**, **25**, **26**, 195, **203**, 207, 268n9, 272n1
town planning. *See* planning legislation in Massachusetts
tract maps, 59, **60**, **78**, **178**; defined, 249n36
tracts, defined, 3–4
trailers, 218–19, 222, 271n73
Trent Construction Co., 254n11
triple-decker apartment buildings, **211**
trolleys, 93, 96, 104, 192. *See also* streetcars
two-flat, Chicago, IL, 241

United Homes, 132–33, 136, 259n121
University of Illinois Small Homes Council, 38, 162, 163, 188, 263n46, 265n90
University of Michigan Institute for Social Research, 188
Urbano, Don, 254n8, 255n27
US Department of Agriculture, 213, **214**

VA. *See* Veterans' Administration
Vällingby, Sweden, 225
Van Tine, Gordon, 246n53
Vandruff, Jean Valjean, **75–81**, 76–81. *See also* Cinderella Homes
Vanport, Oregon, 55, 218
veneers, 24, 157, 161, 171, 182, 262
Veterans' Administration (VA), 5, 43
veterans' housing, 4, 33–34, 46, 147, 156, 189, 218–19, 264n66
visitors to model houses, Lakewood, CA, **1**
visual impact of postwar developments upon American landscape, 230
visual sophistication of buyers, 202
Voices from the Fifties, 190–97
Voith, Richard P., 9

Waldie, Donald J., 32, 200
wall-mounted refrigerator. *See* refrigerator
wallpaper, 21, 193, 237, 245n21
war. *See* World War II
war housing, 36, 48–49, 53, 55, 57, **66**–67, 70, 147, 154, **216–19**, 262n32, 272n1

war industry. *See* war work
war service, 50, 77, 88, 103, 118, 128, 147, 156, 217, 220, 267. *See also* armed services, *individual builders*, Appendix 3
war work, 4, 77, 118, 147, 218–20
Warner, Sam Bass, 254n6, 272n15
Warwick, RI, 116–22, **117**, 124, 179, 235
Wayland, MA, 123, 179
Waynewoods, Wayne, PA, 101–2, **104**
Weathersfield, Schaumburg, IL, 175–86, 258n90; and Bradford Saivetz, 177; changes in social composition in, 185; community facilities in, 178, 185, 267n154; community identity, loss of, 185–86; construction of, 178, 181, 184; design of houses in, **180–84**, 186, 265–66nn103; incorporation of, 176; land acquisition for, 176–77; multifamily units in, 267n165; New England themes in advertising, street naming, and names of model houses, **179**, 245n22; population of, 185; street and lot layout in, **177–78**, **185**. *See also* Atcher, Bob; Campanelli, Alfred; Campanelli Brothers in Chicago; Celia, Ray; Del Bianco, A. J.; Schaumburg, IL
Weber, Arthur, 249n31
Weingart, Ben, 16, 29, 31
Weiss, Marc A., 225
Wellesley-at-Natick, 259n122
Welwyn Garden City, England, 225
West Palm Beach, FL, 135–36, 267n139
Westchester, Los Angeles, CA, **14**, 50–54, **55**, 57, **57**, 61
"Western" movies, 65, 205
Western themes, popular enthusiasms for, 65, 186
Westfield, Natick, MA, 15, 122–23, **122**, **133**, 135, **138**, 257n85, 260nn129 and 134
Westford, MA, 123
Westinghouse, 44, 85–86, 253n125
Westside Village, Los Angeles, CA, 50–51, **53**, 62, 248nn16–17, 249n53, 250n55
Wetherell, W. D., *The Man Who Loved Levittown*, 228
Wethersfield, Natick, MA, 123, **131**, 176, 257n85, 258n90
Wethersfield, spelling of, 258n90
White City, 141
white flight, 201
Whyte, William H., Jr., 245–46n36
Wiese, Andrew, 201
Wilder, Mary Ingalls, 216
Will, Phillip Jr., 264n65
Williams, Ralph I., **107**, 128, 255n39, 256n39, 258n104
Williamsburg model, two story house at Rossmoor, 253
Wills, Royal Barry, 67–68, 128, 203, 250n72,

255n39, 257n65; one-story house (ca. 1937), **68**
Wilson, Sloan, 246n36
window types, 22, **24**, 46, 79, 82, 121, 146, 150–51, 161, **162**, 173, 182. *See also* picture window
Windsor Hills, Los Angeles, CA, **50**, **51**
women: active in church, community organizations, and schools, 199; changing roles of, 195–96; expectations of, 230; new occupations of, 195–96, 268n12; stereotypes, 27; in war work, 53, 218, 248n21
Woodfield, Framingham, MA, 123
Woodfield Mall, Schaumburg, 185
work ethic, 200
working class, 25, 55, 95–96, 114, 140, 141, 191, 208, 211–12, 221, 224, 227, 207n60, 265n79, 269n32; in Boston metropolitan area, 115; Burns and, 91; and buyers' childhood dwellings, 195, **205–14**, 214–16; in Chicago, 140–41; Kaiser and, 55; new prosperity for, 6; in Philadelphia metropolitan area, 25, 96, 114
working drawings, 98, 105, **109**, 128, 153, 165, 223
World War II: effect on Boston industries and building, 115; impact on popular ideas and attitudes, 45, 224, 228; new building materials in, 218, new methods of construction in, 218. *See also* armed services; war housing; war work
World's Fairs, and other exhibitions, 39–44, 247n67; 1939–40, Flushing Meadows, NY, **22**, **40**
Wright, Frank Lloyd, 38, 39, 64, 98, 140, 222, 250n74, 255n38; Ardmore, PA, 99, 255n24; Broadacre City houses, 99, 250n55; Falling Water, Bear Run, PA, 99; Jacobs House (1937), **66**; Suntop Homes, 99; Usonian houses, **68**, 203
Wrightwood bungalows, Chicago, IL, **144–45**, 261n18, 262n22
Wurdeman and Becket (Burns research house), 41, **42**, 249n45. *See also* Becket, Welton
Wurster, William, 64, 67, 71, 128, **203**, 222, 251n80, 251n84, 258n101; Butler House, Gregory Farm House, Pope House, Voss House, 250n71; Miller House, Carmel, CA, **67**. *See also* May, Cliff

yards: against front yard gardens, 272n10; restrictions on the use of, in 1970s, 228

zoning ordinances, 12, 95, 158, 169, 176, 227, 264; of the 1970s, 228, 255n28. *See also individual subdivisions*